D1528634

Interpretations of the Name Israel
in Ancient Judaism
and Some Early Christian Writings

Interpretations of the Name Israel in Ancient Judaism and Some Early Christian Writings

From Victorious Athlete to Heavenly Champion

C. T. R. HAYWARD

OXFORD
UNIVERSITY PRESS

Great Clarendon Street, Oxford OX2 6DP

Oxford University Press is a department of the University of Oxford.
It furthers the University's objective of excellence in research, scholarship,
and education by publishing worldwide in

Oxford New York

Auckland Cape Town Dar es Salaam Hong Kong Karachi
Kuala Lumpur Madrid Melbourne Mexico City Nairobi
New Delhi Shanghai Taipei Toronto

With offices in

Argentina Austria Brazil Chile Czech Republic France Greece
Guatemala Hungary Italy Japan Poland Portugal Singapore
South Korea Switzerland Thailand Turkey Ukraine Vietnam

Oxford is a registered trade mark of Oxford University Press
in the UK and in certain other countries

Published in the United States
by Oxford University Press Inc., New York

British Library Cataloguing in Publication Data

Data available

Library of Congress Cataloging in Publication Data

Data available

ISBN 0-19-924237-2
EAN 978-0-19-924237-5

1 3 5 7 9 10 8 6 4 2

Typeset by RefineCatch Limited, Bungay, Suffolk
Printed in Great Britain by
Biddles Ltd., King's Lynn

Acknowledgements

So many conversations, formal and informal, with friends and colleagues over the last few years have contributed to the final form of this book that it is not possible to list them all here, let alone do justice to them. My near neighbours in Abbey House, however, Loren Stuckenbruck and Walter Moberly, have always been so generous with their time and their comments that they must be the first to be thanked for their valuable observations and criticisms, sought and offered at every stage of this book's composition. To other Durham colleagues, also, I owe important insights and ideas, especially to Jimmy Dunn, Stuart Weeks, Stephen Barton, David Brown, and Ann Loades. Tony Gelston, now flourishing in 'early retirement', was, as always, unstinting in his help, advice, and kindness. Another 'retired' colleague, Sheridan Gilley, has helped to improve the book's literary style. To these, and many others in Durham, this book owes much: its imperfections and mistakes, however, are most certainly not their responsibility!

Outside Durham, too, I have benefited immensely from discussions with colleagues working in the area of Jewish Studies. My thanks are due particularly to George Brooke for his comments on the Ben Sira material; to Geza Vermes, Martin Goodman, and Tessa Rajak for their suggestions on the chapters dealing with Philo's works; and to Joanna Weinberg and Piet van Boxel for their observations on the discussion of Josephus and his writing. To the Cambridge Old Testament Seminar and its chairman, Robert Gordon, I owe a number of valuable remarks about the Septuagint version's account of Jacob's change of name; and Philip Alexander has helped me with some of the puzzles which the *Book of Jubilees* so expansively sets before us. Linda Munk, formerly of the University of Toronto, has supported this project from the outset; and her clear-sightedness and penetrating comments have never failed to lead me to deeper understanding of what this or that text was saying. To all these friends and colleagues, I am at last able to express my gratitude in public, with the proviso that any mistakes the reader may find here are not theirs, but mine.

To the hard-pressed staff of the Palace Green section of Durham University Library I offer not only thanks, but congratulations on their ability and willingness to provide high-quality library service in often trying circumstances. Their cheerfulness, helpfulness, and professionalism have not been unappreciated, and it is only right that it should be known more widely. Finally, to the Abbey House secretaries, Anne Parker, Margaret Parkinson, and Ellen Middleton, I owe more than I can say for their patience, help, and practical advice during the regular, systematic 'break-downs' which my old university computer maliciously enjoyed (it showed a particular aversion both to the Septuagint and to Philo, and at one stage managed to consume all the *Jubilees* material it could find). Their timely help more than once salvaged desperate situations.

Robert Hayward
Abbey House, Palace Green,
Durham

Contents

Abbreviations

Bible and Versions

For the text of the Hebrew Bible and its versions, the following editions have been used. Translations, unless otherwise indicated, are mine.

Field	*Origenis Hexaplorum Quae Supersunt*, ed. F. Field, 2 vols. (Clarendon Press: Oxford, 1875), for citations of Aquila, Symmachus, Theodotion, and other 'minor' Greek versions
FTP, FTV	The Fragment Targums preserved respectively in MS Paris, Bibliothèque nationale Hébreu 110, and MS Vatican Ebr. 440, *The Fragment-Targums of the Pentateuch*, ed. M. L. Klein, 2 vols., Analecta Biblica 76 (Biblical Institute Press: Rome, 1980)
GM	*Genizah Manuscripts of Palestinian Targum to the Pentateuch*, ed. M. L. Klein, 2 vols. (Hebrew Union College Press: Cincinnati, 1986)
LXX	The Septuagint: *Septuaginta, Vetus Testamentum Graecum*, ed. J. Ziegler (Auctoritate Academiae Scientiarum Gottingensis editum: Göttingen, 1931–)
MT	The Masoretic Text of the Hebrew Bible: ed. K. Elliger and W. Rudolph, *Biblia Hebraica Stuttgartensia* (Deutsche Bibelstiftung: Stuttgart, 1967–77)
Ngl	Marginal and interlinear glosses of TN
NT	The New Testament: *Novum Testamentum Graece*, ed. E. Nestle and K. Aland, 4th revised edn. (Deutsche Bibelstiftung: Stuttgart, 1981)
PJ	*Targum Pseudo-Jonathan of the Pentateuch*, ed. E. G. Clarke, W. E. Aufrecht, J. C. Hurd, and F. Spitzer (Ktav: Hoboken, 1984)
Syriac	*The Peshitta Version* (United Bible Societies: London, 1979)

Targ.	Targum, followed by name of biblical book, cited from *The Bible in Aramaic*, ed. A. Sperber, vols. II and III (Brill: Leiden, 1959, 1962)
TN	Targum *Ms. Neophyti 1*, 5 vols., ed. A. Díez Macho (Consejo Superior de Investigaciones Científicas: Madrid–Barcelona, 1968–78)
TO	Targum Onqelos, ed. A. Sperber, *The Bible in Aramaic, I: The Pentateuch According To Targum Onkelos* (Brill: Leiden, 1959)
Vg	Vulgate: *Biblia Sacra iuxta Vulgatam Versionem* (Deutsche Bibelgesellschaft: Stuttgart, 1994)
VL	Vetus Latina: *Vetus Latina: Die Reste der alt-Lateinischen Bibel, Genesis*, ed. B. Fischer (Herder: Freiburg, 1951–4)

Non-biblical Primary Sources

The following editions have been used. (Abbreviations of the tractates of the Mishnah, Tosefta, and Talmuds will be found in the following section of abbreviations.)

ARN	*Aboth de Rabbi Nathan*, ed. S. Schechter (Vienna, 1887)
b.	Babylonian Talmud: *Der Babylonische Talmud*, ed. L. Goldschmidt, 9 vols. (Martinus Nijhoff: The Hague, 1933–5), followed by name of tractate
Ben Sira	P. C. Beentjes, *The Book of Ben Sira in Hebrew: A Text Edition of All Extant Hebrew Manuscripts and a Synopsis of All Parallel Hebrew Ben Sira Texts* (Brill: Leiden, 1997)
Genesis Rabbah	*Bereschit Rabba mit kritischem Apparat und Kommentar*, ed. J. Theodor and Ch. Albeck (Akademie für die Wissenschaft des Judentums: Berlin, 1912–29)
Josephus	*Josephus I–IX*, Loeb Classical Library, Greek text with translations, notes, appendices, and bibliographies by H. St. J. Thackeray, R. Marcus, and L. H. Feldman (Harvard University Press: Cambridge, Mass., 1926–69)
Jubilees	As translated by Ch. Rabin in H. F. D. Sparks (ed.), *The Apocryphal Old Testament* (Clarendon Press: Oxford, 1984), 1–193. Also consulted: J. C. VanderKam, *The Book of*

	Jubilees, 2 vols., CSCO 510–511 (Peeters: Leuven, 1989)
LAB	Pseudo-Philo's *Liber Antiquitatum Biblicarum*, text as in H. Jacobson, *A Commentary on Pseudo-Philo's* Liber Antiquitatum Biblicarum, vol. 1 (Brill: Leiden, 1996)
m.	Mishnah: *Shisha Sidre Mishnah*, ed. H. Albeck and H. Yalon (Dvir: Jerusalem, 1958)
Mekhilta of R. Ishmael	*Mekhilta de Rabbi Ishmael*, ed. J. Z. Lauterbach, 3 vols. (Jewish Publication Society of America: Philadelphia, repr. 1961)
Mekhilta of R. Simeon b. Yoḥai	*Mekhilta de R. Simeon bar Yoḥai* ed. J. N. Epstein and E. Z. Melamed (Hillel Press: Jerusalem, 1955)
Midrash Rabbah	With the exception of *Genesis Rabbah*, noted above, cited from *Midrash Rabba 'al Ḥamisha Ḥumshe Torah veḤamesh Megillot* (Vilna, 1884–7)
Philo	*Philo I–X*, Loeb Classical Library, Greek text with translations, notes, and appendices by F. H. Colson and G. H. Whitaker (Harvard University Press: Cambridge, Mass., 1929–62)
PR	*Pesiqta Rabbati*, ed. M. Friedmann (Vienna, 1880)
PRE	*Pirqe de Rabbi Eliezer* (Vilna, 1837)
PRK	*Pesiqta de Rab Kahana*, 2 vols., ed. B. Mandelbaum (New York, 1962)
Qumran Texts	*Discoveries in the Judaean Desert* (Clarendon Press: Oxford, 1955–)
Sifra	I. H. Weiss, *Sifra De Be Rab* (Vienna, 1862; repr. Om Publishing Company: New York, 1946)
Sifre Deuteronomy	L. Finkelstein, *Sifre on Deuteronomy* (The Jewish Theological Seminary of America: New York, 1969)
Sifre Numbers	H. S. Horovitz, *Sifre de Be Rab* (Sifre Wahrman: Jerusalem, 1966)
tos.	Tosefta: S. Lieberman, *The Tosefta According to Codex Vienna* (Jewish Theological Seminary of America: New York, 1955–67)
yer.	Jerusalem Talmud, *Talmud Yerushalmi*, Pietrokov and Wilna editions, repr. in 7 vols. (Otzar Ha-Sepharim: New York, 1959)

Other Abbreviations: Philo's Work; Tractates of Mishnah, Tosefta, and Talmud; Standard Reference Works; Dictionaries; and Journals

ABD	*The Anchor Bible Dictionary*, 6 vols. (ed.) D. N. Freedman (Doubleday: New York, 1992)
Ant.	Josephus, *Jewish Antiquities*
BASOR	*Bulletin of the American School of Oriental Research*
BDB	F. Brown, S. R. Driver, and C. A. Briggs, *Hebrew and English Lexicon of the Old Testament* (repr. Clarendon Press: Oxford, 1968)
Bek.	*Bekhorot*
Ber.	*Berakhot*
CBQ	*Catholic Biblical Quarterly*
CBQMS	Catholic Biblical Quarterly Monograph Series
CRINT	*Compendium Rerum Iudaicarum ad Novum Testamentum*
CSCO	Corpus Scriptorum Christianorum Orientalium
De Abr.	*De Abrahamo*
De Cher.	*De Cherubim*
De Conf. Ling.	*De Confusione Linguarum*
De Cong.	*De Congressu*
De Dec.	*De Decalogo*
De Ebr.	*De Ebrietate*
De Gig.	*De Gigantibus*
De Mig.	*De Migratione Abraham*
De Mut. Nom.	*De Mutatione Nominum*
De Op. Mun.	*De Opificio Mundi*
De Plant.	*De Plantatione*
De Post.	*De Posteritate*
De Praem.	*De Praemiis*
De Sac.	*De Sacrificiis*
De Sob.	*De Sobrietate*
De Som.	*De Somniis*
De Spec. Leg.	*De Specialibus Legibus*
De Virt.	*De Virtutibus*
De Vita Cont.	*De Vita Contemplativa*
De Vit. Mos.	*De Vita Mosis*
DJD	*Discoveries in The Judaean Desert* (Clarendon Press: Oxford, 1951–)
DSD	*Dead Sea Discoveries*
Eccles. Rab.	*Ecclesiastes Rabbah*
Exod. Rab.	*Exodus Rabbah*

Frag. Targ. P	Fragment Targum Paris Ms 110
Frag. Targ. V	Fragment Targum Vatican Ms 440
Gen. Rab.	*Genesis Rabbah*
Ḥag.	*Ḥagigah*
Hist. Ecc.	Eusebius, *Historia Ecclesiastica*
HTR	*Harvard Theological Review*
HUCA	*Hebrew Union College Annual*
Ḥull.	*Ḥullin*
JAB	*Journal for the Aramaic Bible*
Jastrow	M. Jastrow, *A Dictionary of the Targumim, The Talmud Babli and Yerushalmi, and the Midrashic Literature* (New York: Pardes, 1950)
JE	*The Jewish Encyclopedia*, ed. I. Singer, 12 vols. (Funk & Wagnall: New York, 1901–6)
JJS	*Journal of Jewish Studies*
JQR	*Jewish Quarterly Review*
JSNT	*Journal for the Study of the New Testament*
JSOT Supp.	*Journal for the Study of the Old Testament*, Supplement Series
JSS	*Journal of Semitic Studies*
JTS	*Journal of Theological Studies*: followed by n.s. denotes new series
Jub.	*The Book of Jubilees*
KB	L. Koehler and W. Baumgartner, *The Hebrew and Aramaic Lexicon of the Old Testament*, revised by W. Baumgartner and J. J. Stamm, 5 vols. (Brill: Leiden, 1994–9).
Lam. Rab.	*Lamentations Rabbah*
Leg. All.	*Legum Allegoria*
Leg. ad Gaium	*Legatio ad Gaium*
Lev. Rab.	*Leviticus Rabbah*
Liddell and Scott	*A Greek-English Lexicon*, compiled by H. G. Liddell and R. Scott, with a revised Supplement (Clarendon Press: Oxford, 1996)
m.	*Mishnah*, followed by name of tractate
Meg.	*Megillah*
MGWJ	*Monatsschrift für Geschichte und Wissenschaft des Judentums*
MHG	*Midrash Ha-Gadol*
Mid. Pss.	*Midrash Psalms*
MT	Masoretic Text
Ned.	*Nedarim*
NTS	*New Testament Studies*
Num. Rab.	*Numbers Rabbah*

Paid.	Clement of Alexandria, *Paidagogos*
PG	*Patrologia Graeca*, ed. J. P. Migne (1857–66)
PJ	Targum Pseudo-Jonathan
PL	*Patrologia Latina*, ed. J. P. Migne (1844–64)
Pes.	*Pesaḥim*
Praep. Evan.	Eusebius, *Praeparatio Evangelica*
PRE	*Pirqe de Rabbi Eliezer*
QE	Philo's *Quaestiones in Exodum*, trans. R. Marcus, *Philo Supplement II*, Loeb Classical Library (Harvard University Press: Cambridge, Mass., 1953)
Quod Det.	*Quod Deterius Insidiari Solet*
RQ	*Revue de Qumrân*
San.	*Sanhedrin*
SBT	Studies in Biblical Theology
SCS	Septuagint and Cognate Studies
Sheb.	*Shebi'it*
Sokoloff	M. Sokoloff, *A Dictionary of Jewish Palestinian Aramaic of the Byzantine Period* (Bar-Ilan University Press: Ramat-Gan, 1990)
Song Rab.	*Song of Songs Rabbah*
Soṭ.	*Soṭah*
Sukk.	*Sukkah*
Ta'an.	*Ta'anit*
Tanḥuma	*Midrash Tanḥuma*, ed. H. Zandel (Eshkol: Jerusalem, 1966)
Targ.	Targum
TDNT	*Theological Dictionary of the New Testament*, ed. G. Kittel (Eerdmans: Grand Rapids, Mich., 1964–)
TDOT	*Theological Dictionary of the Old Testament*, ed. G. J. Botterweck and H. H. Ringgren, trans. D. E. Green (Eerdmans: Grand Rapids, Mich., 1970–)
Test.	*Testament*
tos.	*Tosefta*, followed by name of tractate
TN	Targum Neofiti 1
TO	Targum Onqelos
VT	*Vetus Testamentum*
VTSupp	*Supplements to Vetus Testamentum*
WUNT	Wissenschaftliche Untersuchungen zum Neuen Testament
yer.	*Jerusalem Talmud*, followed by name of tractate

Introduction

The ten chapters which compose this book explore the diverse and manifold ways in which the name Israel was interpreted and understood, in the days after the Law of Moses had been formally adopted as the standard by which Jewish life should be regulated. The Hebrew Bible records how a great assembly of Jews, in the presence of Ezra the scribe and Nehemiah the governor, heard that Law publicly proclaimed, and bound themselves by solemn covenant to abide by its commandments and to accept the obligations thus placed upon them (Neh. 8–9). This great assembly was also called 'the people of Israel' (Neh. 9: 1), so named after their ancestor Jacob who, according to that same Law which they had sworn to honour, had received the title Israel, which thereafter was to be borne by his descendants. The first eight chapters set out to explore Jewish understandings of that title: they examine some of the most significant Jewish writings from Second Temple times down to the end of the Talmudic period, or thereabouts, which addressed themselves to questions of what Israel might signify, and what it might mean for Jewish self-understanding. The two final chapters offer some observations on Christian perceptions of what Israel might mean. The appropriation of this title by the early Church is well known and has been much studied: here, we observe how some early Christians, in seeking to understand the meaning of the term, necessarily had recourse to Jewish sources, although their use of those sources often led to surprising results.

In the course of our explorations, I shall necessarily have to pay careful attention to details, some of them small, most of them complex and involved. I shall be concerned with the intricacies of Jewish and early Christian Scriptural interpretation and exegesis; with the techniques and conventions brought to bear on Scripture by different groups of people in different times and places, in their efforts to make the Bible yield its hidden secrets; and with the implications of those interpretations so painstakingly achieved and handed on. With this in mind, it seemed sensible that the Introduction to this volume should set out as plainly as possible, without the notes and supporting evidence which will be found in sufficient quantity, I trust, elsewhere in the book, the general outlines of what Israel signified to the authors of the sources at our disposal. Some of those authors lived in the Land of Israel: Jesus Ben Sira and the author of the *Book of Jubilees*, whose writings are discussed in Chapters 3 and 4 respectively, certainly lived in the Jewish homeland, and their expositions of the name Israel were undoubtedly affected by this fact. But not all Jews were at home. Many lived abroad, in the Diaspora, as it came to be called, in Jewish communities confronted with challenges and difficulties arising directly from their sojourn among the Gentiles: this, too, has left its mark on their sense of what Israel might in reality mean.

The celebrated biblical lament of Jews exiled in Babylon demands how they may sing the Lord's song in a foreign land (Psalm 137: 4). Throughout the period covered by the writings investigated in this book, that is, from around 300 BCE up to the beginning of the sixth century CE or thereabouts, Jews were certainly to be found settled in foreign lands far and wide. This was particularly so after the twin disasters of the First and Second Revolts against Rome (66–73 CE and 132–5 CE respectively), which made life in the Jewish homeland impossible for many. Indeed, the foreign lands afforded homes for Jews, and even environments where Jewish life and culture might prosper, in an exile from the Land of Israel which was to prove longer and often enough harsher than that first exile hymned by the Psalmist. Egypt and Babylonia, in particular, were hosts to large Jewish communities. The former had been seen as a refuge from disasters in the land of Judah as early as the time of the prophet Jeremiah (see Jer. 42: 19–44: 30) and, with the advent of Alexander the Great and the founding of that great cosmopolitan settlement of Alexandria, had eventually come to provide a relatively stable, and more or less secure, dwelling place for expatriate Jews.

These same Jews generally adopted the Greek language as their medium of communication: their knowledge of Hebrew after around 300 BCE, it would seem, went into a sharp decline. But they remained intensely loyal to their ancestral traditions; and it was for them that the five Books of Moses were eventually translated into Greek, probably around 250 BCE. This scholarly enterprise was followed not so long afterwards by a translation into Greek of the writings of the Hebrew Prophets, and then of the rest of the writings which make up today's Hebrew Bible, along with some other Jewish compositions, like the books of the Maccabees, of Tobit, of Sirach, and of Judith, which Rabbinic Judaism does not accept as Scripture. This 'Greek Bible' is commonly called the Septuagint (LXX), although, strictly speaking, that name should be granted only to the Greek version of the Books of Moses, the Torah, for according to the famous account of its origins set forth in the *Epistle of Aristeas*, the version was produced by seventy translators working independently of each other. The Greek version of the Torah was regarded as sacred and divinely inspired by the Greek-speaking Jews of Egypt; for the Jewish scholar, exegete, and philosopher Philo, writing at the end of the first century BCE and the beginning of the first century CE, it had the status of holy writ, and he took pains to make this clear in his *Vita Mosis* II. 37–44. The Greek translation of the Books of Moses is one of the earliest interpretations of the Pentateuch known to us. Its importance can hardly be exaggerated, and it will receive due attention in what follows.

Unlike Egypt, whither Jews had fled for safety, Babylonia was a place to which Jews had been taken by force as exiles (see 2 Kings 24: 10–16; 25: 8–12); and it was Babylon which had earned the Psalmist's wrath as he prayed for her overthrow (Ps. 137: 8–9). Yet Babylonia, too, was destined to become a haven for Jews. By the end of the second century CE Rabbinic activity had been well established there, particularly in Nisibis; and the academies of Sura and Nehardea, which came into their own in the following century, were destined to be famed throughout Jewry. The Talmud compiled in Babylonia, one of the more recent texts discussed in this book, would come to speak of the head of the Jewish community in Babylon as a figure already foretold in Scripture. Evidently, by the time that the Rabbinic academies began to flourish, the Jews had found a means of singing the Lord's song in a foreign land whose first impact on their lives, if the Psalmist is to be believed, had been largely negative.

Such acceptance of life in a foreign land depended, however, on the ability of the Jews to preserve their identity. This much should be plain from almost every page of what follows. Jews in exile showed a determination to preserve the unique character of their nation, and constantly referred to their homeland and its people, past and present, to guide their understanding. The scholars, exegetes, commentators, and jurists whose words are the subject of this study were profoundly aware of their responsibility to communicate to the Jews of their own days a proper sense of what it meant to be 'the children of Israel'; for 'Israel' was no mere human appellation. They understood that the Patriarch Jacob, ancestor of all Jews, had been privileged to receive the title Israel as a supernatural gift, first announced to him by a mysterious, otherwordly being (Gen. 32: 22–33), and then confirmed by God Himself (Gen. 35: 9–15). The Bible itself had offered, at Gen. 32: 29, an explanation of what the title 'Israel' might signify; yet this exposition of the name was anything but simple or straightforward. As we shall see, the unvocalized Hebrew of this verse held out an invitation to students of Torah to expound the name from all manner of different Hebrew verb stems. Thus we shall encounter understandings of the name which associate it with the Hebrew words *śārāh*, 'exert oneself'; *śārar*, 'be a prince, gain superiority'; *śārar*, 'be hard, firm'; *šûr*, 'behold'; *yāšār*, 'upright'; and *šîr*, 'sing'. This does not exhaust the catalogue; and different expounders of the Bible could use one or more of these root-words to explain to their contemporaries just what Israel might signify, and thus what the children of Israel might themselves represent both in this world and in the world to come. Indeed, one of the most striking features of ancient interpretation of this name is its 'future reference', the sense that Israel as a this-worldly reality is only part of a larger canvas.

It was, of course, inevitable that the ancient commentators on Scripture would be influenced by the political, religious, and social needs of their times, and this much, I trust, will be apparent as we journey through their writings. One matter, however, must be signalled from the outset, and leaves little room for doubt. The very fact that the title 'Israel', borne through history by the descendants of Jacob, could be taken as signifying so many different aspects of the Patriarch's character proved to be a source of immense strength to Jews as they coped with the changes and chances of this world. The word 'strength' is entirely appropriate here, since one of the oldest meanings of the name Israel recorded outside the Hebrew Bible is one set forth by LXX, expressed precisely in the language of being strong, gaining strength. For those translators, as we shall see, Israel was a name confirming Jacob as one now having sufficient strength to inherit the land promised by God, and to bring to fruition in this world God's promises for his descendants in the future. From the point of view of the commentators, therefore, Israel may point to the past, as a title once bestowed on Jacob; may constitute a present reality, as indicating the descendants of that Jacob who received the name Israel and their character; and may allude to a future Israel as inheriting a land and as a source of peoples and kings, as promised by God according to Gen. 35: 11–12.

The sense that Israel is a name pointing to the future comes to the fore in different ways in the different kinds of literature we have to deal with, but two particular examples may be anticipated briefly here. The *Book of Jubilees* (*c*.150 BCE), intensely concerned to define exactly the nature and status of the Israel of its own days, does so always with an eye to the future: Israel is to be a divinely ordered society consisting of kings, priests, and a holy people as defined by the author(s) of that book, in such a way that God may finally be able to renew the whole of His creation, and establish for ever His sanctuary on Mount Zion in a world re-created in peace, harmony, and righteousness and justice. For the compilers of *Genesis Rabbah* (late fifth–early sixth century CE), Israel is Jeshurun, something of a play on words in Hebrew: Jeshurun is taken to be one who is 'like God' in that, through the agency of the most noble in Israel like Elijah and Elisha, God has already anticipated in this world the mighty deeds of the world to come, including the resurrection of the dead. This insight, which opens the section of the midrash treating of Jacob's change of name, informs all the exegesis which follows, and intimates that whatever opposition Jews have to face in a present dominated by the might of Rome, the future is an assured one. Jacob's change of name to Israel signified his victory over opposing forces, over the angelic representative of Rome. This angel, says the midrash, is one of many who every day are changed by God; these angels are impermanent. But Israel as Jeshurun will endure, unlike the Roman power and its celestial counterpart which will pass away, never to be re-created.

These two examples of concern for the Jewish future (and there are many more) demonstrate that the ancient exegetes were not involved in some sort of antiquarian or archaeological enterprise. They were determined to ensure that the texts spoke directly to Jewish concerns for Jewish identity in a world which could often be hostile and threatening. The Hebrew Bible was their great resource, and it proved inexhaustible. For it offered them certain facts, principally two short accounts of Jacob's acquisition of the name Israel (Gen. 32: 22–33; 35: 9–15) and an even briefer

prophetic allusion to this (Hosea 12: 3–6). Although these biblical
texts in Hebrew are short in compass, they turn out to be extra-
ordinarily complex in language, structure, and content. In the
hands of a skilled interpreter their very complexity offers a never-
failing source of material for reflection on what Israel might
mean, and what it might mean to be Israel's descendants. The first
chapter of this book, therefore, sets out to describe this complexity
within the Hebrew texts, and to indicate some of the challenges
and opportunities it afforded for ancient exegetical endeavour. A
brief account of some modern approaches to the texts is included,
and is now compared, now contrasted, with ancient interpretative
techniques. Within this first chapter a special place is given to a
Hebrew manuscript from Qumran (4Q158), which reproduced the
biblical text of parts of Gen. 32 with remarkable modifications
(some would say annotations) which both illustrate the complexities of that biblical text, and point to the interpreter's overriding
concerns—in this case, to show that Jacob was truly blessed (the
words used to bless him are supplied), and to ensure proper
implementation of the law forbidding Israelites to eat the sinew of
the thigh of slaughtered animals. These are the concerns of what
remains of 4Q158, for whom the Israel of the Hebrew Bible stands
revealed as a truly blessed people, duly and rightly observing the
commandments of the Torah in accordance with an authoritative
standard of interpretation. They are not the concerns of every
interpreter. For example, we shall find that *Jubilees* has nothing to
say about the law of the sinew of the thigh, and that Josephus was
silent about the blessing of Jacob; by way of contrast, the Mishnah
will certainly refer to Gen. 32 in discussion of the sinew of the
thigh and the correct interpretation of the law concerning it, and
Ben Sira will have a good deal to say about the blessed status of
Jacob. The ancient interpreters were selective; and their selection
of matters for comment often depended on their circumstances,
and the exigencies of the times.

The insights of the LXX translators form the subject matter of
Chapter 2. A good deal of space has been allocated to this version,
which in many respects adumbrates later interpretative strategies,
and singles out particular themes for elaboration which would be
taken up and developed by later exegetes. The translators of this
version were the first Jews known to us who perceived an organic
connection between Jacob's first visit to Bethel (Gen. 28: 10–22),
where he dreamed of a ladder with angels linking earth and

heaven, and the change of Jacob's name to Israel recorded in Gen. 32: 22–33 and 35: 9–15. This connection was later to play an important part in Philo's definition of the name Israel; earlier, it had provided the author of *Jubilees* with essential elements for his rearranging of biblical texts to support his view that the name Israel was bound up with the proper worship of God and the eventual construction of the true sanctuary. Most striking, however, is LXX's presentation of the story of Jacob's life from the days of his sojourn with Laban up to the time of his second visit to Bethel which, whatever their own intentions, allows the reader to see in this part of Jacob's life a kind of anti-type of events in the life of the later people Israel, from their slavery in Egypt (corresponding to Jacob's servitude with Laban) up to their settlement in the promised land (corresponding to Jacob's dwelling in the same land after his second visit to Bethel and the second account of his acquisition of the name Israel). Throughout the story Esau had lurked in the background, constantly posing a potential threat to Jacob; LXX were aware of this, and explicitly interpreted the name Israel in Gen. 32: 29 with reference to it, by expounding that name in terms of the *strength* which Jacob required to overcome Esau and to claim the promised land as his rightful inheritance.

The translators, however, appear to have been equally aware that Israel is a name redolent of sight, vision, and seeing; for during the first account of his reception of the name Israel, Jacob was to declare that he had seen God face to face, and his life had been preserved (Gen. 32: 31). The chapter also examines how this theme of sight is brought into play; in particular, it plays a major part in the LXX presentation of the covenant at Sinai, and would be introduced by the translators into their version of Jacob's covenant with Laban in Gilead. The first divine commandment given at Sinai spoke of the Lord who had brought Israel out of Egypt; the second required that Israel worship no other gods except the Lord. These two commandments the LXX translators appear to have related to the two accounts of Jacob's change of name, the first relating to his flight from and covenant with Laban and the announcement of his new name (Gen. 31: 1–33, the Lord having brought him out from Laban's power to a point where covenant can be made), the second to his putting away foreign deities (Gen. 35: 2), to prepare for his second visit to Bethel and the second revelation of the name Israel (Gen. 35: 9–15) with its accompanying blessing.

A further important element in the LXX presentation of Jacob's new name is angelic in character. I have already noted how the translators chose a word having to do with *strength* in their definition of the name Israel at Gen. 32: 29. The word they chose is not common: its occurrences are discussed, and its use by the LXX translators at Deut. 32: 43 is singled out for special attention. They offered their own, very distinctive form of this verse, which differs markedly from the Masoretic Hebrew, and speaks of angels *strengthening themselves* in God: the verb used at this point is the same as that used by the translators earlier to explain the name Israel. The implications of this are spelled out, particularly in respect of other references to angels in the biblical narrative. The significance of this becomes apparent when the translators, turning to the second account of Jacob's change of name, speak of God's *epiphany* to him in order to confirm the name Israel. Such language of epiphany is extremely rare in LXX Pentateuch; and where it occurs again, at LXX Deut. 33: 2, it is accompanied by a reference to angels. On his first visit to Bethel Jacob had seen angels in a dream-vision; and LXX appear to have chosen their vocabulary very carefully so as to point to an angelic dimension to the new name Israel which the Patriarch has received. This aspect of Israel's name was to receive much more thorough and systematic treatment in later literature; but the evidence of LXX suggests strongly that the association of Israel with the angelic world went back far into Second Temple times.

Hebrew manuscripts of Ben Sira's Wisdom book speak of an Israel whose existence is to be for days without number, a matter addressed in Chapter 3: here the rare biblical title Jeshurun as a descriptor of Israel makes one of its few appearances in post-biblical literature. On the one hand, Ben Sira took up the sense of Israel as indicative of strength, relating this sense of the name to notions of strength and length of days spoken of in Deut. 33: 25 as understood within the Judaism of his day; on the other hand, the LXX understanding of Jeshurun as beloved or first-born son allowed the sage to accord to Jacob-Israel that status of first-born sonship granted to him by the Hebrew Bible (Exod. 4: 22). The textual witnesses to Ben Sira's work display an interest in wordplay between the first-born status, Hebrew *bᵉkōrāh*, and blessing, Hebrew *bᵉrākāh*, allotted to Jacob-Israel, allusions to first-born sonship carrying with them overtones of kingly status. The occurrence of the rare term Jeshurun in relation to promised length of days for Israel points to the future; indeed, Ben Sira seems to have envisaged Israel as God's appointed royal representative on earth, enjoying *ad multos annos* the blessings associated in biblical times with Solomon, son of David, who, as king, was both builder of the Temple and heir to first-born status by virtue of his kingship.

Chapter 4 addresses the drastic rewriting of the biblical accounts of Jacob's change of name found in the *Book of Jubilees*, an influential text which assumed its final form around 150 BCE. The author had experience of the 'Hellenistic Crisis', and was determined to remind Jews of their true status and purpose in the universe. Axiomatic for the author is the notion that Israel obedient to Torah on earth shares the same privileges as, and acts in consort with, the two highest orders of heavenly angels who serve God directly, the Angels of the Presence and the Angels of Sanctification; like them alone out of all the angels, Israel alone out of all the nations keeps the Sabbaths and the festivals, observes the divine commandments, is marked with the sign of the covenant, and permits no defilement in its midst. Given this, the biblical story of Jacob's engagement with a supernatural being which resulted in his being named Israel (Gen. 32: 22–33) was something of an embarrassment for the author of *Jubilees*, who deemed it inappropriate and eliminated the episode entirely.

Central to the author's understanding of Israel is Exod. 19: 6, a divine command issued to the house of Jacob and the sons of Israel that they be a kingdom, priests, and a holy nation. *Jubilees* carefully charted the steps which Jacob had to take to become Israel. This involved the author in serious rearrangement of biblical texts, omission of whole sections of biblical narrative, and the introduction of non-biblical traditions into his completed work. Most important of the latter is an extended account of Jacob's visit to his aged father Isaac, along with his sons Levi and Judah; this the author regarded as proof that Jacob had returned 'to his father's house'—no small detail, but evidence that he was now obligated to pay the tithe he had promised on his first visit to Bethel (Gen. 28: 20–1). I note in passing the importance granted yet again to Gen. 28 in the process of Jacob's becoming Israel. Isaac blessed in prophetic fashion Levi as head of the priestly family, and Judah, as head of the royal tribe, and reminded Jacob of his obligation to pay the promised tithe.

Jubilees then turned its attention to a thorough reconstruction of Gen. 35: 9–15, the events of which the book located at the feast of Sukkoth. Of key importance here is the reference to Jacob's wife, now pregnant with Benjamin: that is to say, the 'house of Jacob' is now complete in number. Jacob proceeded to carry out his promise to tithe: he tithed his sons, Levi emerging as the allotted portion, now duly appointed or elevated to the priesthood by his father. Judah, it will be recalled, had already been blessed as a royal figure; and earlier, *Jubilees* had taken care to rewrite Gen. 34 in such a way as to leave no doubt that 'Israel' is home to nothing impure or defiled. By these means, described in great detail by the author, there came into the world a 'house of Jacob' with kings (represented by Judah) and priests (represented by Levi) all characterized by purity and holiness. At this point Israel is prepared, and can come into being in the world. In the night following the last day of the feast of Sukkoth God reveals to Jacob that he is indeed Israel; and an extra festival day (the feast known today as *Shemini 'Atseret*) is instituted. The association of this feast with the name Israel is peculiar to *Jubilees*, and I explore its significance at some length. Here I may observe that this extra festival seems to represent both the celebration of something now brought to successful conclusion (that is, the steps by which Jacob became Israel), and the inauguration in the world of a sacral order intended by God for the well-being of the universe (that is, the due observance on earth of the service of God as it is in heaven). *Jubilees* was written to ensure that this inaugurated harmony between earth and heaven was appreciated in all its fullness, and that it was maintained and fostered by the Israel to whom the book was addressed.

Jubilees is not commonly spoken of in tandem with the writings of Philo, although discussion of the latter in Chapter 6 will reveal them as not worlds apart. To Philo belongs one of the best-known interpretations of the name Israel, as 'one who sees God', an explanation which the exegete-philosopher never proves from Scripture and which, I suggest, in agreement with other students of his work, he may have derived from a non-biblical tradition. Philo took the name Jacob to mean a 'practiser', one who by hard labour and discipline strove to acquire the virtues; and he emphasized in particular the element of physical struggle which LXX Gen. 32: 22–33 describe in their version of Jacob's wrestling with his mysterious opponent. The opponent, according to Philo, was an angel, but no ordinary angel: it was the most senior angel of all, whom Philo identified with the Logos. Philo pictured the

Logos as trainer of the athlete Jacob: through hard, disciplined, sustained effort, and with the help of the Logos, Jacob the practiser was able to overcome the passions, and to win the prize awarded to the succesful wrestler. This is the prize of a new name, Israel, one who sees God, and it brings with it a real change of character, a 'reminting' of the personality into new coinage, to use Philo's metaphor.

This Israel, Philo tells us, is a boundary figure, set 'on the cusp', as it were, between the heavenly and the earthly realms. In this he resembles his mentor, the Logos, one of whose principal functions is the effecting and maintaining of harmony between the upper and lower worlds: both Israel and the Logos have dealings with earth and with heaven, conversing now with angels, now with men, turned now to contemplation of the heavenly realities, now to ensuring the right order of things on earth. What Israel sees, Philo explains, is the fact that God is the One who Is. Human beings may, indeed should, strive like Jacob to train with the Logos so that they may become Israel, and thus advance from subduing the passions to the vision of God. Philo may envisage this change of character as something which can be achieved by non-Jews, as well as by his own people; certainly, he speaks generally of the 'sensible man' as one who can attain to such privileges, and can refer to 'the class which is capable of seeing' without further qualification.

On the other hand, Philo's constant definition of Israel as 'one who sees God' may lead in another direction. According to LXX, which for Philo was inspired Scripture, God had ordered Moses to construct the sanctuary, the prototype of the Jerusalem Temple, as a place where He might be seen, the chapter notes other LXX references to the sanctuary, both as a place where God might appear, and also as a place where He may be known; and it goes on to consider some of the implications of these LXX interpretations of the original Hebrew. When these Scriptural references are set alongside Philo's presentation of Judaism as the supreme 'mystery religion', whose hierophant is Moses, Philo's emphasis on Israel as one who sees acquires an added dimension; for the climax of the Eleusinian mysteries, the most renowned of all the ancient mystery cults, consisted in a vision of brilliant light, this 'seeing', on the part of the initiates being the culmination of an arduous preparation. Certainly, Philo's ideal type of the religious philosopher was represented by the Therapeutae, whose devotion to contemplation had made them, he tells us, citizens of the two worlds of earth and heaven.

Philo's descriptions of the heavenly characteristics of Israel as 'one who sees God' show some uncanny resemblances to the vocabulary of an obscure apocryphal text known as the *Prayer of Joseph*, preserved chiefly in the writings of the third century CE Christian writer Origen. Chapter 6 is devoted to detailed analysis of this mysterious fragmentary document; the results of that analysis suggest that the *Prayer* is likely to have been a Jewish composition, owing nothing to Christianity or to Gnosticism. It defines Israel as 'a man who sees God', and this name is the heavenly designation which corresponds to the earthly character known as Jacob. The analysis undertaken here also suggests that the *Prayer* was intended, among other things, to resolve difficulties inherent in the biblical texts about Jacob-Israel, his parentage, his titles, and his status. While much of what it has to say is foreign to Philo's cast of mind, students of the *Prayer* have pointed to curious similarities between Philo's writings and some aspects of the *Prayer*; and an argument is developed here that both the *Prayer* and Philo's writings depend on earlier, traditional material, supported to some degree by evidence already adduced in discussion of the *Book of Jubilees* and Qumran texts. The *Prayer of Joseph* is especially important in a study of the name Israel, however, not simply because of its possible affinities with Philo's writings. This text brings to the fore the theme of angelic rivalry, in that it tells how Jacob-Israel was opposed by the initiative of the archangel Uriel, who sought to counter Jacob-Israel's right to be chief, first, and principal minister of God. Angelic hostility to Israel will feature prominently in some of the Rabbinic traditions discussed in Chapter 8; indeed, it is possible that it plays a part in what Josephus had to say about Israel, which is the subject of Chapter 7.

In his *Jewish Antiquities* (Book I), Josephus asserted his understanding of the name Israel by a drastic remodelling of Gen. 32: 22–33. He made virtually no use of Gen. 35: 9–15. His account of Jacob's change of name is terse, but highly ambiguous; indeed, he seems to have contrived matters so that an educated, devout Jew could have understood his account of things in a way quite different from an educated non-Jew without knowledge of the Bible. He defined Israel in terms of opposition to an angelic being, who had begun a fight with the Patriarch (shades of the *Prayer of Joseph*); and he seems to have implied with some care that this opposition on Jacob's part was restricted to his encounter with a supernatural being on this one occasion in his life. Writing his *Antiquities* for

Gentiles after the end of the first Jewish war against Rome, he was careful to avoid associating the name Israel with opposition to earthly forces, or with a particular territory granted by God to the Jewish Patriarchs; furthermore, he eliminated from his version of events any sense that Israel had anything to do with 'seeing God'. Rather, the strongly delineated 'visual' aspects of the biblical narrative he replaced with a report of a kind of prophetic oracle delivered by Jacob's opponent, whom Josephus refers to as a *phantasm*. The oracle itself may be understood in different ways, although it certainly holds out the promise that Jacob's nation would never cease. In all this, however, an educated Jew might discern in particular words and phrases which Josephus chose to adopt, a rather more traditional picture of Israel lurking beneath the surface of his text, though quite what impression his words might have made on his contemporaries is open to debate.

The Rabbinic texts surveyed in Chapter 8 exhibit four main areas of interest in their approach to Jacob's change of name. First, there are those texts whose main concern lies in discussion of the law of the 'sinew of the thigh'; the first biblical account of Jacob's acquisition of the name Israel ends (Gen. 32: 33) with a note that he was lame in his thigh following his engagement with a super-natural being, and that as a result of this his descendants do not eat the sinew of the thigh up to this day. Those sections of the Mishnah, Tosefta, Talmud, and Midrashim which debate this issue point to an Israel properly constituted by correct understanding and observance of the halakhah (religious law), a holy people determined to do God's will in this world in order to inherit the blessings promised in the next. Rigorous discussion of the halakhah itself is also a characteristic mark of the Israel emerging from these texts; and 4Q158 provides evidence for the antiquity of such discussion. The precise relationship between present-day Israel's observance of this commandment, and the incident in the life of the Patriarch which it in some sense commemorates, was a matter on which not all authorities were agreed, although the accepted halakhah favours a particular stance which reserves the use of 'Israel' as a designation for the whole Jewish people only from the time of the giving of the Torah on Sinai onwards. Such a stance implicitly invalidates the kind of thinking displayed in earlier writings such as *Jubilees*.

A second group of texts, including the Tosefta, *Mekhilta de R. Ishmael*, *Genesis Rabbah*, and the Babylonian Talmud, noting that

Scripture continues to address Israel as Jacob after he has received
his new name, enquire what precisely might be the relationship
between the two names. The general answer to this question is that
one is an essential, fundamental name, the other an addition to it;
once again, the authorities are not agreed on which name is which.
What makes this debate particularly important is its involvement
with hopes for the future redemption of the Jewish people; the
famous prophecy of Jeremiah, that in the final days they will not
mention the Exodus from Egypt, is discussed in connection with
which of the Patriarch's names might be the fundamental name,
and which the addition. The resolution of the debate lies in acceptance that, just as the Exodus from Egypt will be mentioned in the
final days as an 'addition' added to mention of the final great
redemptive act, so the 'additional' name of the Patriarch (whichever it be!) will still be spoken.

For *Genesis Rabbah* in particular, and for some other later midrashim which most likely depend upon it, the name Israel is understood most clearly against the background of a powerful and, at
times, brutal Roman power symbolically represented by Esau. The
uncommon title Jeshurun once more makes its appearance to
introduce the topic of 'Israel', bearing with it intimations of future
deliverance from the Roman tyranny. *Genesis Rabbah* leaves the
reader in no doubt that the being who opposed Jacob was none
other than the celestial representative of Esau, who stands for
Rome. Jacob overcame this angel, who, according to some authorities, was nothing less than a sorcerer; the angel's defeat at Jacob's
hand signifies not only the inevitable end of Roman power, but
also the futility of demonic attacks on Israel, whose possession
of the merits of the Fathers is sufficient to protect them against all
the enemy's tricks. Israel is thus a name indicating victory over the
angel; and not unnaturally this leads to a complex discussion in
Genesis Rabbah concerning the nature of angels. The majority of
the Rabbis cited in this section of the midrash assert that angels,
apart from the chief angels Michael and Gabriel, are transient
beings: their names, and thus their natures, are changed every day.
This discussion is conducted in terms of a larger contrast between
matters permanent and matters ephemeral. Israel stands revealed
as permanent over against the ever-changing angels because, the
midrash declares, Israel's likeness is depicted on the Throne of
God. The implication that the impermanent angels might be
jealous of this privilege of Israel is not explicitly stated; but it is

present as a subtext, and will be developed in other Rabbinic discussions, as we shall see. The greatest change of all will be the resurrection of the dead, granting the righteous in Israel permanent status before God; once more, this ultimate permanence is contrasted with the fleeting power of Rome, seemingly so solid, yet in reality already defeated long ago.

A fourth major Rabbinic concern comes to light in the Babylonian Talmud and the Aramaic Targumim, where the angels once again occupy centre-stage. The main Talmudic passage discussing the events recorded in Gen. 32: 22–33 is to be found in Tractate *Ḥullin* 91a–92a, and it is concerned, amongst other things, to portray Jacob as a dutiful scholar and as a man of prayer. Jacob was opposed by an angel; but Jacob was made prince over the angel: Israel is a name which indicates the Patriarch's superiority to the angels as a group. This is the Talmud's verdict, after a discussion laying bare the angels' hostility towards Jacob, their jealousy of his privileges, and their inability to do anything about the situation. And Jacob-Israel's privileges are greater than theirs; for the Talmud demonstrates with some panache that Israel's service of God on earth takes precedence over the angelic service in heaven, and that the Divine Name itself may be uttered by Israel after only two preliminary words, whereas the highest angels must proclaim the word 'holy' three times before daring to utter the Name. The beginnings of this highly developed understanding of Israel's relationship with the angelic world may be discerned already in LXX, gathering pace in the *Book of Jubilees*, being further refined in writings like the *Prayer of Joseph*, and achieving its classic expression in the Talmud.

The Aramaic Targumim, like the Talmud, understood the name Israel to be bound up with the angelic world: it signifies for them one who is a prince, or angel, and the Palestinian Targumim in particular emphasize the liturgical character of this Israel, who acquired the title following his victory over the angel in charge of the heavenly praise of God. By this means his descendants, the people of Israel in worship on earth, have acquired the right to chant the praises of God, and they know that their worship takes precedence over that of the heavenly choirs. The strongly marked liturgical character of Israel revealed by the Targumim is not surprising if, as seems certain, some at least of the tradition which found its way into the final form of the Targumic texts had a place, at some time in its transmission, within the synagogue service. But the Targumic attitude to the name Israel does not depend on any specific linkage between the Targum and the synagogue service. Indeed, Targum Pseudo-Jonathan, in some of the material it has preserved, shows an astonishing affinity with the *Book of Jubilees*, a text which would not have been welcome in the synagogue in the Rabbinic period. This observation provides a convenient end-point for this part of my introduction, since it illustrates what should become more and more clear as the book proceeds: that the various writings surveyed here draw upon and develop in their own ways, for their own particular purposes, ideas and understandings of what is meant by Israel, most of which can be traced back to Second Temple times. The LXX translators themselves seem to have been aware of that link between Israel and the angels which comes to occupy such a place in Talmudic and Targumic interpretation; Ben Sira's insights into the implications of the title Jeshurun for Israel resurface in *Genesis Rabbah*, though whether there is any direct link between these texts we cannot tell; the highly contrived presentation of Israel by Josephus echoes earlier understandings of the name, for those with the knowledge to perceive it; and Philo's musings on the 'one who sees God', while calling the reader to philosophical contemplation, can also evoke real awareness of an actual Temple service offered in unison with the highest angels, itself an ideal expressed in different words in the *Book of Jubilees*. I have attempted, however, to let each text speak for itself, rather than labouring to point out links which the 'sensible person' spoken of by Philo might perceive easily enough for herself or himself.

The last two chapters of the book briefly examine some Christian material. The New Testament offers no explicit definition of the name Israel, although in the first part of Chapter 9 I suggest that the opening chapter of St John's Gospel yields up one or two matters of interest to students of Judaism if it be set alongside the comments which Philo, Josephus, and *Jubilees* in particular have made about the meaning of Israel. The second part of the chapter is devoted to Luke 22: 43–44. These verses make up a notorious *crux interpretum*, and I suggest that they are original to the Gospel. Since they portrayed Jacob-Israel as a type of Christ, they fell foul of anti-Jewish Marcionites on the one hand and modalist Monarchians on the other. Careful analysis of their wording reveals close affinities with LXX and other Jewish texts examined in this book. Chapter 10 looks at ways in which some Church

Fathers understood Israel. While most, following Philo and Origen (who adopted his etymology), took the name to mean 'one who sees God', some still display a lingering familiarity with the rich Jewish exegesis surrounding the name: they include Clement of Rome, Justin Martyr, and, of course, St Jerome, who listed a number of interpretations, himself opting for a meaning of the name Israel as one who is prince with God, the interpretation we find to this day in the Babylonian Talmud and the Aramaic Targumim.

I

The Hebrew Bible and Jacob's Change of Name

Three particular sections of the Hebrew Bible will occupy our attention in what follows. For the sake of convenience, an English translation of each of these passages according to the traditional Masoretic text is given here, with a brief account of their literary settings.[1] The first of the sections (Gen. 32: 23–33), describing Jacob's nocturnal fight with a mysterious being, is also the best-known, as well as the most complex. It appears at a crucial point in the Bible's account of Jacob, and the narrative background to it is especially important for our purposes. It will be presented, therefore, in some detail.

1. JACOB'S NAMING

1.1 *Jacob Meets an Opponent and Receives a New Name—Genesis 32: 23–33*

This episode begins with Jacob's flight from the wrath of his brother Esau, whose paternal blessing he has acquired by cunning with the help of his mother Rebeccah: she consequently advises him to seek refuge with his uncle, Laban the Aramaean (Gen. 27: 1–45). His journey to Laban takes him to Bethel, where he spends the night and dreams of a ladder set up between earth and heaven, with angels going up and down; the Lord stands there, and promises that Jacob's descendants shall inherit the land where Jacob lies. On awaking, Jacob acknowledges that the Lord is in this place, and declares it to be the house of God, the gate of heaven, and names it Bethel. He furthermore vows that if God preserve him on his journey, so that he return safely to his father's house,

---

[1] All quotations from the Masoretic Text (MT) of the Hebrew Bible are from K. Elliger and W. Rudolph (eds.) *Biblia Hebraica Stuttgartensia* (Deutsche Bibelstiftung: Stuttgart, 1967–77). Translations, except where indicated, are mine.

then he will grant to God a tithe of all that is given to him (Gen. 28: 10–22). Jacob reaches Laban's household, and begins a period of service with his kinsman to obtain Laban's daughters Leah and Rachel as wives; this service is a strained affair, revealing tensions between Jacob and Laban which will develop into mutual distrust (Gen. 29: 1–30). Nonetheless, Jacob remained with Laban, and fathered eleven sons and a daughter, Dinah (Gen. 30: 1–24); he then sought to return home, only to become embroiled in an acrimonious dispute with Laban about his wages, which leaves him far richer than before (Gen. 30: 25–43). This provokes the ire of Laban's family, so that Jacob and his wives determine to leave Laban, Rachel taking her father's teraphim (most probably statuettes of household deities) with her in secret (Gen. 31: 1–24). Laban pursues and overtakes Jacob in Gilead, where the two parties settle their differences, make a covenant, and part on good terms (Gen. 31: 25–55).

As Jacob continues his journey, angels of God meet him at a place he names Mahanaim, or 'Two Camps'. He proposes to inform his brother Esau of his return, only to be told by his messengers that Esau is coming with 400 men to meet him, apparently with hostile intent (Gen. 32: 1–8). Jacob therefore prepares for the worst, prays for deliverance from his brother, and provides for suitable 'presents' to be given to Esau to mollify him (Gen. 32: 9–22). Then we read:

(23) And he arose in that night, and took his two wives and his two handmaids and his eleven children, and crossed over the ford Jabbok. (24) And he took them, and brought them across the wadi, and brought across what belonged to him. (25) And Jacob was left alone; and a man engaged with him until the dawn came up. (26) And he saw that he did not have power over him, and he touched the hollow of his thigh; and the hollow of Jacob's thigh was dislocated as he engaged with him. (27) And he said: Send me away, because the dawn has come up. And he said: I shall not send you away, unless you bless me. (28) And he said to him: What is your name? And he said: Jacob. (29) And he said: Your name shall no longer be said as Jacob, but Israel; for you have persisted with God and with men and have prevailed. (30) And Jacob asked and said: Declare your name, I pray! And he said: Why is it that you ask my name? And he blessed him there. (31) And Jacob called the name of the place Peni'el: for I have seen God face to face, and my life has been preserved. (32) And the sun arose for him when he crossed over Penu'el; and he was limping upon his thigh. (33) Therefore the sons of Israel do not eat the sinew of the nerve which is upon the hollow of the thigh until this day: for he touched the hollow of Jacob's thigh on the sinew of the nerve.

Subsequently, Jacob and Esau meet in friendly reunion, embrace, and kiss (Gen. 33: 1–4); and Jacob remarks to his brother that he has seen his face as one sees the face of God (Gen. 33: 10).

1.2. *God Grants to Jacob the Name Israel—Genesis 35: 9–15*

After the brothers' friendly meeting, Esau returned to Se 'ir, while Jacob journeyed to the vicinity of Shechem (Gen. 33: 14–20). Here the Bible recounts the story of Dinah, her seduction by Shechem, son of Hamor, and the overtures of the Shechemites to Jacob as they seek intermarriage with Israel after undergoing circumcision. Jacob's two sons Simeon and Levi take vengeance on the Shechemites, kill them, and plunder their city; their father Jacob is left in some fear that the surrounding peoples will seek reprisals for this action (Gen. 34). At this point, Jacob receives a divine command to return to Bethel, and he begins the purification of his household preparatory to that pilgrimage (Gen. 35: 1–8). Jacob's second visit to Bethel issues in a second divine revelation to him (Gen. 35 9–15).

(9) And God appeared to Jacob again when he came from Paddan-Aram, and he blessed him. (10) And God said to Him: Your name is Jacob. Your name shall no longer be called Jacob, but Israel shall be your name; and he called his name Israel. (11) And God said to him: I am 'El Shaddai. Be fruitful and increase. A nation, and a congregation of nations, shall issue from you, and kings shall go forth from your loins. (12) And the land which I gave to Abraham and to Isaac, to you I shall give it; and to your descendants after you I shall give the land. (13) And God went up from him in the place where he had spoken with him. (14) And Jacob set up a pillar in the place where he had spoken with him, a pillar of stone; and he poured out a libation over it, and poured oil upon it. (15) And Jacob called the name of the place where God had spoken with him Bethel.

After these things, the Bible records that Rachel gave birth to Jacob's twelfth son, Benjamin; she died after he was born, and was buried on the road to Ephrath, Jacob setting up a pillar to mark her grave. Thereafter, Israel went and pitched his tents beyond Migdal Eder (Gen. 35: 16–21).

1.3 *The Prophet Hosea's Note on Jacob's Life—Hosea 12: 3–6*

This prophetic oracle is found towards the end of Hosea's book, and is part of an indictment of Israel (Hosea 12: 13) preceding a final proclamation of God's love for His people (Hosea 14), and His determination to restore them to favour.

(3) And the Lord has a law-suit with Judah, even to punish Jacob according to his ways: according to his actions he will recompense him. (4) In the womb he took his brother by the heel, and in his strength he strove with God. (5) And he strove with an angel and prevailed: he wept and made supplication of him. He found him at Bethel, and there he speaks with us, (6) even the Lord, the God of Hosts: the Lord is his memorial.

Evidently verses 5 and 6 refer to the events spoken of in the Genesis verses I have set out above; and it should be clear that Hosea was aware of the traditions reported by both passages, the tale of struggle being related in Gen. 32: 22–33, the place Bethel and the record of divine speech with Jacob being noted particularly in Gen. 35: 9–15. The prophet adds details not found in the Genesis narrative: Jacob weeps, utters supplications, and has speech with the Lord of Hosts. The attentive reader will note that Hosea might be implying here that Jacob's struggle with the 'angel' took place at Bethel: the ford of Jabbok is not named.

Even in English translation, these Scriptural texts confront the reader with many difficulties. For the ancient interpreters, as we shall see, the difficulties were no less complex than they are for us; and this book will try to explore and elucidate the efforts of those ancient exegetes as they worked to reveal the inner meanings of the sometimes confusing information the Bible presents, and to relate their deliberations to the often turbulent religious and political circumstances in which they wrote. Modern scholars, likewise, have often been fascinated by these texts, and much has been written about them; but it is not my purpose here to rehearse, or even to survey, what has been discussed at length elsewhere.[2] Two particular aspects of the Masoretic tradition which will concern us directly have nonetheless been debated by modern scholars, and they will need to be considered here. They are, first, the exact nature of the difficulties presented by the texts; and secondly, the relationship of the Masoretic Hebrew to other Hebrew forms of

[2] For scholarly treatments of these passages, see the convenient bibliographies in G. Wenham, *Genesis 16–50*, Word Biblical Commentary, 2 (Word Books: Dallas, 1994), 292–3, 319, and H. W. Wolff, *A Commentary on the Book of the Prophet Hosea*, Hermeneia, trans. G. Stansell (Fortress Press: Philadelphia, 1974), 205, along with the commentary of A. A. Macintosh, *Hosea*, International Critical Commentary (Clark: Edinburgh, 1997), 481–91. The most recent analysis of the Genesis material by K. A Walton, *Thou Traveller Unknown* (Paternoster: London, 2003), offers further useful bibliography: see esp. pp. 66–96.

the texts attested among the Samaritans and the manuscripts found at Qumran.

2. QUESTIONS PRESENTED BY THE MASORETIC TEXT

The three different records of events accompanying Jacob's reception of a new name lead us to ask how and why these accounts have arisen. Hosea's version *might* be explained as the prophet's idiosyncratic re-presentation, for his own very particular homiletic purposes, of a story well known to him;[3] but the two little stories in Genesis differ so extensively that they cannot adequately be explained as variants either of each other, or of a putative lost common source. 'Source analysis', indeed, is one of the first tools employed by modern biblical scholars in situations of this kind; but the idea of formal and systematic use of such an instrument was unknown to the ancient commentators, who had perforce to offer other solutions of problems in the biblical text. Thus they had no recourse to explanations deriving Gen. 35: 9–15 from a hypothetical Priestly document, while supposing that Gen. 32: 23–33 belonged originally to entirely different sources. Unlike many modern commentators, they could not attempt to resolve perceived difficulties in the latter text by further hypothesizing that it was itself composed of the two sources, J and E, or concocted out of various discrete elements thought to constitute those same sources.[4]

---

[3] Assuming, that is, the conventional view that the older sources of the Pentateuch pre-date the prophet, who is understood to have been active from *c.* 750–720 BCE: see Macintosh, *Hosea*, p. lxxxiii; cf. *ibid.* 481–2. The possibility that Hosea is a source of the Genesis material, however, must be entertained if the latter was formed out of traditions crystallizing in the last days of the Judaean monarchy and later: see J. van Seters, *Prologue to History: The Yahwist as Historian in Genesis* (Westminster/John Knox Press: Louisville, 1992).

[4] Students who adhere to the documentary hypothesis of the Pentateuch often ascribe Gen. 35: 9–15 to the Priestly document, with the exception of verse 14, which is assigned to the Elohist source: see O. Eissfeldt, *The Old Testament: An Introduction*, trans. P. R. Ackroyd (Blackwell: Oxford, 1966), 189; G. Fohrer, *Introduction to the Old Testament*, trans. D. Green (SPCK: London, 1970), 179. The well-known tendency for this hypothesis to produce discordant findings, however, is apparent in the discussion of this passage by C. Westermann, *Genesis 12–36*, trans. J. J. Scullion (SPCK: London, 1986), 553, where verse 15 is denied to the Priestly document. Genesis 32: 23–33, by contrast, is said to be made up of material from the sources J, E, and, according to Eissfeldt and Fohrer, from earlier traditions out of which those two sources were allegedly composed: see Eissfeldt, *Old Testament*, 195, 201, and Fohrer, *Introduction*, 147, 161. For a succinct account and critique of

Nor were they at all concerned with the relative dating of such putative sources. Where the modern investigator might expend considerable effort attempting to determine the 'original' form of a narrative in what might be considered the oldest source,[5] carefully distinguishing it from secondary additions and elaborations in later sources, the ancients were content, for the most part, to take the narratives as they found them. That said, both ancient and modern students of the texts which concern us often concur in their sense of what requires explanation and clarification.

To illustrate this last point we may refer to an essay of R. Martin-Achard, which enumerates difficulties confronting the modern reader of Jacob's experience at the Jabbok which Gen. 32: 22–33 recorded.[6] He notes how verse 23 states that Jacob had crossed the Jabbok, while verse 24 may be taken to mean that he had not done so. He points to the undefined subject 'he' of the verbs in verses 26–8 obscuring the identity of who prevailed over whom, a matter not clearly resolved until verse 29. Even then, if Jacob were the victor, as verse 29 suggests, why does verse 31 suggest that he had come close to death? How, precisely, was Jacob's thigh dislocated? Did it happen in the course of a fight, or by some magical or supernatural means? Why are there two references to blessing (verses 27 and 30)? In what did the blessing eventually granted consist: the name Israel, perhaps? Why do we hear three times of daybreak (verses 25, 27, and 32)? Why is the place name Peni'el given also as Penu'el?

Except for the last, all the questions posed by Martin-Achard were addressed by one ancient commentator or another. It will be observed that many of them arise from *repetitions* of words and

source criticism, and of the historical-critical method generally, see J. Barton, *Reading the Old Testament: Method in Biblical Study*, 2nd edn. (Darton, Longman, & Todd: London, 1996), 20–9.

[5] Form criticism (*Gattungsgeschichte*) is the discipline most often employed with written sources to this end: on its methods and limitations, see Barton, *Reading the Old Testament*, 30–43. Tradition-history or Tradition criticism (*Überlieferungsgeschichte*) attempts to search out the oldest oral form of a given narrative, and to trace its typical development in the course of oral transmission until it is fixed in writing: for a convenient survey of its application and results, see W. E. Rast, *Tradition History and the Old Testament* (Fortress Press: Philadelphia, 1972), and D. A. Knight, article 'Tradition History', *ABD*, vi. 633–8.

[6] See R. Martin-Achard, 'Un exégète devant Genèse 32: 23–33', in R. Barthes, F. Bovon, *et al.*, (eds.) *Analyse structurale et exégèse biblique* (Delachaux et Niestlé: Neuchâtel, 1971), 41–62, esp. 47–8.

phrases in the remarkably few verses which make up the story of Jacob at the Jabbok: the verbs עבר, 'cross over' (vv. 22, 23, 24, 32); שלח, 'send away' (v. 27 twice); ברך, 'bless' (vv. 27, 30); נגע, 'touch' (vv. 26,33); and some form of עלה, 'go up' followed by שחר, 'dawn' (vv. 25, 27). Like their modern counterparts, the ancients carefully noted such repetitions; but whereas the former might see in some of them evidence of narrative doublets, sources, or redactional activity on the part of editors, the latter viewed them as significant invitations to the reader to perceive additional meanings in or beneath the surface of the text. The repetitions might also lead the ancient exegete to other parts of Scripture: it did not pass unnoticed, for example, that the repeated verb ברך, 'bless', is found also at Gen. 35: 9, a verse which also contains the verb ראה, 'see', itself found twice in Gen. 32 at verses 26 and 31. Similarly, the verb יכל, 'prevail', appears not only in Gen. 32: 26, 29, but also in Hosea 12:5. This state of affairs suggested to the ancients that these texts could, and should, be used to cast light on one another, the repetitions indicating that they are part of the same organic whole. Thus where one of the narratives appeared lacking in information or incomplete in sense, the defects could be remedied by recourse to the other two biblical accounts.[7]

Of all the repeated words in these passages, the most common is שם, 'name'. It is used in Gen. 32: 28, 29, 30 (twice), 31, and four times in Gen. 35: 10. Specifically, it refers to the names Jacob and Israel (Gen. 32: 28, 29; Gen. 35: 10), to his opponent (Gen. 32: 30), and to the place Peni'el (Gen. 32: 31). The message conveyed by this to the ancient exegetes was clear: 'name' is a central concern of these texts, and the name Israel is the most important concern of all. The true significance of that name may, indeed, be multi-faceted; and we shall see presently the ancient interpreters offering many differing attempts to derive its sense from several different Hebrew roots. Modern critics, however, especially those influenced by the traditio-historical method, view this concern with name as

---

[7] Ancient Jewish exegetes viewed individual repeated words as particularly significant, believing that no word of Scripture could be redundant: everything written therein is word of God, and the exegete's duty is to lay open the extra layer of meaning implied by the repetition: cf. the famous saying (in Aramaic) of Ben Bag Bag in *m. Aboth* 5: 25. For the hermeneutic significance attributed to repeated words and phrases in Rabbinic exegesis of both Scripture and Mishnah, see A. Samely, *Rabbinic Interpretation of Scripture in the Mishnah* (Oxford University Press: Oxford, 2002), 5, 8, 53–4, 328–58.

evidence for the aetiological character of the narratives. Indeed, this method uncovers no fewer than four aetiologies in Gen. 32: 23–33, relating to the place-name Peni'el/Penu'el; the name Israel; the names Jacob and Jabbok; and the law forbidding consumption of the sinew of the thigh nerve. Ancient readers accepted this rich series of explanations, rejoiced in it, and sought to understand further why so much should be explained in so few verses. Moderns, by contrast, tend to suggest that only one of the aetiologies can be central to the oldest layers of the narrative, viewing the others as secondary elaborations or accretions.[8]

This last point highlights another major difference between ancient exegetes and many exponents of the historical-critical or traditio-critical methods. The latter, by one means or the other, seek to establish an original form of the narrative which almost invariably turns out to be different from the text of the narrative as we know it. In the case of Gen. 32: 23–33, practitioners of these methods are more or less agreed that the original narrative consisted of a folk-tale which told how the ancestor of the Jewish people fought against a river spirit (or perhaps a river demon, or supernatural entity safeguarding a boundary, or demonic aspect of God), sustained an injury (through physical combat, supernatural agency, or magical artifice), subdued his opponent, and received a blessing (as reward for his victory, or by using his superior strength to extort it) consisting of a new name. This original folk-tale, we are assured, is very old.[9] But such an approach to the narrative raises in acute form the question where the meaning of the text so analysed is to be found. Is it to be discerned in the 'original folk-tale'; in one or other or all of the 'secondary' additions; or in some scholarly construction, an 'ideal text', as it were, assembled out of component parts of the biblical narrative reordered and disposed according to the judgement of an individual critic?

[8] For a convenient summary of traditio-historical approaches to Gen. 32: 22–33 in particular, and discussion of the aetiologies, see Walton, *Traveller Unknown*, 67–72, and Wenham, *Genesis 16–50*, 294–304. Application of the traditio-historical method by different scholars can produce quite divergent results: contrast e.g. the theologically integrated exposition of G. von Rad, *Genesis: A Commentary*, trans. J. H. Marks (SCM: London, 1970), 314–21, 333–4, with Westermann's insistence on the search for meaning both in 'the narrative without additions' and in the individual additions themselves, *Genesis 12–36*, 520.

[9] See e.g. Westermann, *Genesis 12–36*, 514–15. For the variety of attempts to discern historical elements in the narrative, see H.-J. Zobel, article 'ישׂראל *yiśrā'ēl*', *TDOT*, vi. 410–12, and literature there cited.

Such questions are difficult, and perhaps impossible, to answer convincingly. Indeed, their intractability may have contributed to a world where more recent developments in biblical criticism have tended to eschew such fragmenting of the text. Structuralist analyses, canon criticism, and the various scholarly attempts to read the biblical documents as literature tend to deal with the biblical text as we now possess it, and in this have an affinity with the ancient interpreters.[10] Whatever their differences, all these methods of reading the biblical text insist that the interpreter has a duty to give an account of the final form of the text, rather than the individual elements which may have gone into its production.[11] So read, the repetitions, which are characteristic of many kinds of biblical narrative, present themselves as a means of deepening the narrative structure, expressing emphasis, and nuancing dialogue: they are seen not as evidence of narrative doublets or secondary additions, but are viewed as a regular and, indeed, essential aspect of biblical discourse.[12] Against them stand out rare words, unusual expressions, and items which break the apparently regular pattern of the narrative. These consequently stand revealed as of especial interest to the modern critic, just as they were to the

[10] For comprehensive discussion and evaluation of these approaches to the text, see J. Barton, *Reading the Old Testament*, 77–236. Gen. 32: 22–33 has elicited what is now regarded as a 'classical' example of structuralist criticism of a biblical text: see R. Barthes, 'La Lutte avec l'ange: analyse textuelle de Genèse 32.23–33', in R. Barthes, F. Bovon, *et al.* (eds.), *Analyse structurale*, 27–40. For Barton's generally sympathetic comments on this essay, see *Reading*, 116–19. Barthes provides a poststructuralist 'update' of this analysis in his 'Wrestling with the Angel: Textual Analysis of Genesis 32: 23–33', in his *The Semiotic Challenge* (New York, 1988), 246–60, analysed in Barton, *Reading*, 223–4.

[11] Their approaches differ entirely from redaction criticism, however, which is concerned (*inter alia*) with the strategies adopted by the ancient arrangers of their sources to produce the final form of the text and its resulting *Tendenz*: see Barton, *Reading*, 45–60. Canon criticism is associated particularly with the name of B. S. Childs, whose approach to Genesis is represented in his *Introduction to the Old Testament as Scripture* (SCM: London, 1979), 136–60. Both Barton, *Reading*, 77–103, 153–4, and J. Barr, *The Concept of Biblical Theology* (SCM: London, 1999), 378–438, offer extensive criticisms of Childs's work. For a defence of canon criticism, see R. W. L. Moberly, *The Bible, Theology, and Faith: A Study of Abraham and Jesus* (Cambridge University Press: Cambridge, 2000).

[12] See esp. R. Alter, *The World of Biblical Literature* (SPCK: London, 1992), 35–40, 71–8, and Barton's comments in *Reading*, 205–8. Note especially also what Barton has to say about 'rhetorical criticism', *ibid.* 199–205, in respect of structuring of biblical narrative in the case of LXX Gen 31: 44–50 discussed below, pp. 44–9.

ancient interpreters, who lavished attention on them. In the texts treated here we may note the rare forms מעבר, 'ford' (Gen. 32: 23, only twice elsewhere in MT); the verbs אבק, 'intertwine', often translated 'wrestle' (only Gen. 32: 25, 26) and שרה, 'persist' (only Gen. 32: 29; Hosea 12: 4, 5); and the phrase גיד הנשה, 'the sinew of the nerve' (only Gen. 32: 33). Given their rarity, these words and expressions prompt questions about their precise meaning and interpretation: why should they be used here, particularly, in these few verses? What is their function? Does their appearance somehow define the character of these brief texts? To them we should add common words, whose meaning is not in doubt, but which are found here in rare combinations. At Gen. 35: 11, God's revelation of Himself as אני אל שדי, 'I am 'El Shaddai', occurs again only when He so addresses Abraham in Gen. 17: 1. In the same verse, God's command to Israel in the second person singular, פרה ורבה, 'be fruitful and increase', is found in the whole MT only at Gen. 35: 11 (although it recalls the plural version of the same command, פרו ורבו, given to Adam at Gen. 1: 28). Uncommon also is the phrase קהל גוים, 'a congregation of nations', used in the same verse: its only other use is at Jer. 50: 9. The appearance of three rare phrases in one verse evidently signals that verse as carrying a weight to which any interpreter must pay due attention.

The meaning of the name Israel itself has considerably exercised modern interpreters, because the form of the name suggests to most that it should be understood as ' 'El (God, the Mighty One) persists/rules/shines forth/contends', whereas Gen. 32: 29 explains it with reference to Jacob as meaning 'for you have struggled/persisted with God'. H.-J. Zobel lists one after another the many and varied modern attempts to explain the name, himself opting for the sense ' 'El rules, is exalted'.[13] The biblical explanation he categorizes as 'clearly a fiction of the etymology', like the Bible's own understanding of the verb, שרה in Gen. 32: 29 and Hos. 12: 4 as 'strive', when it most probably means 'rule'.[14] From rather different standpoints, the ancient exegetes also discerned in the Bible's explanation of the name Israel a number of possible different meanings. Interestingly, Zobel includes in his list of modern explanations of the name a suggestion of Albright and

[13] See H. -J. Zobel, article 'ישראל *yiśrā'ēl*', 399–401.
[14] Ibid. 399, 400.

others that Israel be derived from the Hebrew root יָשַׁר, 'upright', an etymology we shall presently encounter in Rabbinic and Patristic sources; but two of the most significant explanations of the name among the ancients, as referring to 'singing' (via Hebrew root שִׁיר) or 'seeing God' (via Hebrew רָאָה, or possibly שׁוּר, both meaning 'see'), do not feature there.[15] It should not come as a surprise to find the ancient interpreters offering a multiplicity of meanings for any name, since for them a name possesses mysterious qualities which may help to define its bearer. Here again, the desire of some modern authorities to find a single sense for the name contrasts sharply with an older interpretative tradition which revels in endeavours to derive as many meanings as possible from a text.

The three portions of the Masoretic text which treat of Jacob's change of name to Israel, although anything but lengthy, confront the interpreter with questions to be answered, problems to be resolved, and mysteries to be contemplated. Into this last category falls the name Israel itself, in form so reminiscent of the names of the great angels Michael, Gabriel, Raphael, and Uriel. Is this resemblance accidental? Or is Jacob's engagement with the mysterious 'man' at the ford of the Jabbok indicative of some special status, such that the Almighty may later (Exod. 4: 22) refer to Israel as 'My son, My first-born'? We have seen that many of the questions posed by the ancient interpreters remain to be addressed by their modern counterparts; ancient engagement with the text, however, often has surprises of its own, and we shall meet them in due course. Meanwhile, we must briefly consider Hebrew texts other than the Masoretic which tell of Jacob's change of name.

3. OTHER ANCIENT HEBREW TEXTS AND THE NAME ISRAEL

The Samaritans have neither preserved nor recognized as authoritative the prophetic writings. In consequence, I consider here only the Samaritan version of Gen. 32: 23–33; 35: 9–15; and there is little to report. In Gen. 32: 23, the unusual Hebrew doing duty for 'on that night', בלילה הוא, represents one of only four appearances of this phrase for the expected בלילה ההוא, which last the Samaritan Pentateuch actually reads at this point, in agreement with the

[15] Ibid. 400, n. 14, referring to W. F. Albright, *JBL* 46 (1927), 151–85.

Jewish *Sᵉbirin*, or scribal 'suggestions'.[16] In the same verse, the Samaritan text speaks of 'the Jabbok', rather than simply 'Jabbok', making the phrase 'the ford of the Jabbok' quite definite, stressing the place, perhaps, as being of great significance; such concern with the place is a feature of some ancient comments on this verse, a matter which the Samaritan text may reflect.[17]

The Masoretic text of Gen. 32: 24 states that Jacob took across the Jabbok 'what belonged to him'; the Samaritan specifies 'all that belonged to him', as do the LXX, Vulgate, and Peshitta. This reading creates problems for a Rabbinic interpretation of the verse (*b. Hullin* 91a) to the effect that Jacob had left behind some small vessels, an interpretation which requires the reading of MT.[18] Finally, we may note that the Samaritan, along with Symmachus, the Vulgate, and the Peshitta, harmonizes the text of Gen. 32: 31 with that of the following verse, such that the place of Jacob's struggle is named Penu'el in both verses.

The Hebrew of these chapters found in sometimes very fragmentary manuscripts from Wadi Muraba'ât and the Qumran caves offers little which does not agree for the most part with the consonantal text of MT.[19] The Qumran document 4Q158, however, exhibits a number of peculiarities which merit exploration. Its *editio princeps* was the work of John Allegro, who entitled it 'Biblical paraphrase: Genesis, Exodus'.[20] The first fragment of this work, labelled by Allegro 1–2, apparently contains parts of Gen. 32: 25–32 along with Exod. 2: 27–8, while a fragment labelled 3 is further defined as Gen. 32: 31(?). In his notes to these fragments, Allegro records several instances where the biblical verses quoted by the manuscripts differ from the consonantal text of MT.[21]

[16] On the *sᵉbirin*, see E. Tov, *Textual Criticism of the Hebrew Bible* (Fortress Press: Minneapolis, 1992), 64; and for the Masorah on Gen. 32: 23, see B. Ognibeni, *La Seconda Parte del* Sefer 'Oklah We'oklah (Instituti de Filología del CSIC: Madrid-Fribourg, 1995), 365. For discussion of the characteristics of the Samaritan Pentateuch, see Tov, *Textual Criticism*, 80–100.

[17] Samaritan thus has מעבר היבק for MT's מעבר יבק, as also at Deut. 2: 37 and 3: 16.

[18] See below, p. 273.

[19] The manuscripts concerned are MurGen 32: 30, 33; SdeirGen 35: 6–10; and 4Q82 (4QXII^g). For translations, see M. Abegg, Jr., P. Flint, and E. Ulrich, *The Dead Sea Scrolls Bible: The Oldest Known Bible Translated For the First Time into English* (Harper-Collins: New York, 1999), 11, 13, 425.

[20] See J. M. Allegro, with the collaboration of A. A. Anderson, *DJD. V Qumrân Cave 4 I (4Q158–4Q186)* (Clarendon Press: Oxford, 1968), 1–6.

[21] Ibid. 1–2.

Further research on these fragments reveals that they possibly belong to the same work as 4Q364–367, which Emanuel Tov names 4QReworked Pentateuch[b–e], the five manuscripts having much in common.[22] 4Q364 frg. 5b col. ii, in particular, includes elements of Gen. 32: 26–30 which we shall need to note. Tov sees them as part of the same composition, containing a running Pentateuchal text: 'The greater part of the preserved fragments follows the biblical text closely, but many small exegetical elements are added, while other elements are omitted, or, in other cases, their sequence altered.'[23] Whatever the nature of this text, it evidently sets itself an agenda, seeking to answer real or implied questions perceived in the original Scriptural narratives. So much is clear from a translation of fragments 1–2, lines 1–14, as edited by John Allegro, given here without additional material usually supplied by translators on the basis of the biblical text.[24]

[22] See E. Tov in H. Attridge *et al.*, *DJD. XIII Qumran Cave 4. VIII Parabiblical Texts Part 1* (Clarendon Press: Oxford, 1994), 189–91; and brief notes in J. Maier, *Die Qumran-Essener: Die Texte vom Toten Meer. Band II Die Texte der Höhle 4* (Reinhardt: München, 1995), 58. On the name of this text, which appears to have been one of the longest at Qumran, see E. Tov, '4QReworked Pentateuch: A Synopsis of Its Contents', *RQ* 16/64 (1995), 647, and n. 2 on that page.

[23] So Tov, *DJD. XIII*, 191; see also his observations in '4QReworked Pentateuch', 647–53. The precise nature of this text, its purpose, and its objectives are matters of current debate: see M. Segal, '4QReworked Pentateuch or 4QPentateuch?', in L. H. Schiffman, E. Tov, and J. C. VanderKam (eds.), *The Dead Sea Scrolls: Fifty Years After their Discovery 1947–1997. Proceedings of the Jerusalem Congress July 20–25, 1997* (Israel Exploration Society and Shrine of the Book: Jerusalem, 2000), 391–9; 4Q158 is discussed on pp. 395–7, Segal concluding that it has much in common with 're-written Bible' compositions like *Jubilees*. Important matters of principle and method in naming such documents are addressed by M. Bernstein, 'Contours of Genesis Interpretation at Qumran: Contents, Contexts and Nomenclature', in J. Kugel (ed.), *Studies in Ancient Midrash* (Harvard University Press: Cambridge, Mass., 2001), 57–85. Furthermore, Tov's insights into the relationship between 4Q158 and 4Q364–367 must be qualified in the light of the thorough analysis undertaken by G. J. Brooke, 'Reworked Pentateuch[a] or Reworked Pentateuch A?', *DSD* 8 (2001), 219–41, which demonstrates important disagreements between the several manuscripts, even in overlapping passages, and concludes that 4Q158 did not contain the same composition as 4Q364–367, even though 'in terms of overall textual affinity, date, and especially genre, all five manuscripts clearly deserve to be associated with one another' (p. 241).

[24] The translation is mine, and is restricted to intelligible words. For other renderings, which supply biblical text to give continuity to the material, see G. Vermes, *The Complete Dead Sea Scrolls in English* (Penguin Books: Harmondsworth, 1997), 442–3; F. García Martínez and E. J. C. Tigchelaar, *The Dead Sea Scrolls Study Edition*, 2 vols. (Brill: Leiden, 1997, 1998), i. 305; and J. Maier, *Die*

(1) . . . so that . . . (2) . . . you have persisted and . . . (3) . . . and [J]ac[ob] was [left a]lone there, and [. . .] engaged . . . (4) . . . when he engaged with him [and] he seized him, and sai[d] to [him] . . . (5) . . . me. And he said to him: What is your name? [And he declared] to him . . . (6) . . . men and you have prevailed. And J[a]cob asked [and] sai[d]: [Decla]re now to me wh[at] . . . (7) [and he bless]ed him there, and said to him: May the Lo[rd] make you fruitful [and ble]ss you . . . (8) kno]wledge and understanding; and may He deliver you from all violence and . . . (9) unto this day and unto everlasting generation[s . . .] (10) And he went on his way when he had blessed him there. And . . . (11) for him the sun when he crossed over Penu'e[l . . . (12) on that day, and he said: Do not ea[t] . . . (13) upon the two hollows of the thigh unto th[is day . . .

Although many of the Hebrew words in this fragment are identical with material contained in Genesis 32: 25–33, some are certainly not; and the biblical text, where it is recognizable, is not always quoted in its biblical order. Thus, in line 1 we find the final consonant of one Hebrew word, and another complete word, which do not appear in the biblical verses; and in line 2 the complete word 'you have persisted' is followed by 'and'. Certainly 'you have persisted' occurs exactly as in Gen. 32: 29; but in that verse it is followed by 'with', not 'and'. Line 3 of the fragment then deals with Jacob's being left on his own, which the Bible had mentioned four verses earlier, at Gen. 32: 25; but the fragment treats it out of biblical order, and includes a word not found in MT. The word is 'there', שמה, referring to the place where Jacob was alone. Although the context is fragmentary, this tiny addition may suggest that 4Q158 attaches importance to the precise location of these events; that possibility is something I have already noted in respect of the Samaritan text of Gen. 32: 23, and will feature again when Targum Pseudo-Jonathan is considered. Although certainty is impossible in this matter, the repetition of 'there' in line 10 of this fragment, informing us that 'he went on his way when he had blessed him *there*', suggests that the geographical location of this event mattered for the compiler of 4Q158.

Line 4 of the fragment faithfully represents words found at the end of MT Gen. 32: 26, adding '[and] he seized him'. This addition, which represents a unique reading, ensures that the reader understands the biblical בהאבקו, 'when he engaged with

Qumran-Essener, 59. The third fragment, which probably treated of Gen. 32: 31, according to Allegro preserves only the words: 'And Jacob called . . . in this land . . . my fathers to come to.'

him', as a physical action on the part of Jacob's companion.[25] As we have already seen, the biblical term is very rare, and its precise significance was of interest to the ancient interpreters. 4Q158, it seems, took the word to imply struggle, in much the same way as the LXX translators had done; was this precision felt necessary because the composer was aware of texts like *Jubilees*, which had eliminated the element of struggle altogether from the episode? At the end of this line part of another word not represented in MT is signalled, and restored (almost certainly correctly) by Allegro as אליו, 'to him'. This word follows the initial 'and he said' of Gen 32: 27, and concurs with LXX, Vulgate, and Peshitta, which have the same reading.[26]

Line 5 opens with a word which may be incomplete: it is אלי and, if it is deemed to be complete, it means 'to me'. Nothing in MT corresponds to it; and, although it may have featured in 4Q364 at this point, there is no evidence to show that it did so.[27] Its presence suggests further explanatory material in 4Q158 which has been lost. Line 5 then reproduces part of Gen. 32: 28. Here the companion asks Jacob's name, and is told it; but two of the words in this short sentence do not correspond with MT; the lacuna is filled by Allegro quite conjecturally with 'and he declared'; and there is a further 'to him' at the end of the line which has no place in MT.[28] The beginning of line 6 is lost: the first legible words are identical with the last two words of MT of Gen. 32: 29, 'men and you have

[25] See Tov's comments, *DJD. XIII*, 190, 213, noting that 4Q158 at this point differs from 4Q364 frg. 5b, col. ii, line 8, which agrees with MT, Samaritan, and LXX in reading simply 'with him' after בהאבקן. For other texts found at Qumran citing biblical verses longer than those of MT and not preserved elsewhere, see Tov, '4QReworked Pentateuch', 649, n. 9. Segal, '4QReworked Pentateuch', 393–5, 398, suggests that 4Q364 should be regarded as a biblical text similar in nature to the Samaritan Pentateuch.

[26] This evidence is too narrow to conclude that 4Q158's biblical texts was of a non-Masoretic type; indeed, the fragment and all the ancient versions may have seen fit to add 'to him' to the verse in an attempt to identify the speaker and the one addressed, a matter of some ambiguity in MT. 4Q364 frg. 5b, col. ii, line 9 represents three words of Gen. 32:27, לוא אשלחכהכי, 'I shall not send you away unl[ess]', which appear in MT as כי אשלחך לא; see further Tov, *DJD. XIII*, 213.

[27] Ibid. 213.

[28] The MS has ויאמר לו מה שמכה [ ] לו, 'and he said to him what is your name? . . . to him'. The corresponding section of MT has ויאמר מה שמך אליו ויאמר. The Hebrew of Gen. 32: 28 set forth in 4Q364 frg. 5b, col. ii, line 10, also differs from MT, having the form מ[ש]מכה and the word לו, 'to him' after the final 'and he said': see ibid. 213.

prevailed'. The photographic plate of the fragment supplied by Allegro makes it clear that the amount of space available could not possibly have accommodated the whole of Gen. 32: 29 up to these last words; the fact that line 2 of the fragment includes a word from this verse suggests that part of the verse, at least, may have been treated out of sequence.[29] Naturally, such a possibility remains only a suspicion; but it is of interest, given that later Josephus would expound these verses in a way which similarly rearranges the order of the biblical text. It is just possible that 4Q158 is something of a precursor of his method.[30]

The rest of line 6 seems to give us Gen 32: 30 more or less in accordance with MT, except that the last two words of the line are not found in MT, although one of them certainly, and the other possibly, are represented in the ancient versions.[31] Line 7 records the last three words of this Scriptural verse, 'and he blessed him there'.[32] The text of the blessing follows, in what is the first of two substantial additions to the biblical story by the author of 4Q158. What can certainly be read of the Hebrew presents this blessing as granting to Jacob progeny, knowledge, understanding, and rescue from violence (lines 7 and 8); if the text of it continues into line 9, as seems probable, the blessing is to have effect from the moment it is uttered and to everlasting generations.

To the best of my knowledge, no other Jewish sources treat Gen. 32: 30 in quite this way. Indeed, we shall see that Targum

---

[29] For the photograph, see Allegro, *DJD. V*, pl. 1. The fact that line 6 could not possibly have contained the whole of Gen. 32: 29 might need to be taken into account in suggested restorations of the lacuna in line 5. By contrast, it is fairly clear that 4Q364 did contain much of the biblical verse: see Tov, *DJD. XIII*, 213, where frg. 5b, col. ii, line 11 preserves [א עם שריתה כי ישראל[י, '[I]srael, for you have persisted with G[od]'. That 4QReworked Pentateuch did rearrange Pentateuchal verses is shown by Tov, '4QReworked Pentateuch', 648.

[30] On Josephus, see below, pp. 220–40.

[31] Thus MT has נא הגידה ויאמר יעקב וישאל, 'and Jacob asked and said, Declare now . . .', which either appears, or can reasonably be restored, in 4Q158, the only differences being that in the Qumran fragment Jacob is spelled *plene* as [י]קוב, and the emphatic imperative הגידה is given as a simple imperative, the final *daleth* alone remaining legible. The line has clearly been subject to scribal correction, the *aleph* of ישאל being written superlinearly, as is the particle נא. The line ends with the words 'to me wh[at', which appear also in 4Q346, there followed by שמכה, '(is) your name', the rest of the verse in the latter text having been lost. 'To me' is read also by LXX, Vulgate, and Peshitta.

[32] Allegro restores ויברך, 'and he blessed', at the beginning of the line; only the final letter is legible, but the restoration seems reasonable.

Pseudo-Jonathan of this verse seems to reject the idea that Jacob's companion blessed him at all. Likewise, Josephus too eliminated from his version of this episode all references to blessing; it is not found in the *Prayer of Joseph*; and it plays very little part in the classical midrashim.[33] It is also clear that the blessing does not consist in Jacob's new name of Israel, an interpretation favoured by some modern scholars.[34] Rather, the blessing consists of a mixture of biblical material with what may well be particular aspirations of the Qumran *yaḥad*. Thus the plea that God make Jacob fruitful (יפרכה) ultimately derives from the divine command פרה ורבה of Gen. 35: 11, a verse whose importance we noted earlier; while the petition that he be delivered from all violence recalls Gen. 32: 12, 31, where the verb 'deliver' (stem נצל) is used specifically of Jacob.[35] The request for knowledge and understanding, however, powerfully recalls the great interest displayed in these qualities by the Qumran *yaḥad*, whose members prayed specifically for the gift of knowledge (דעת) in their version of the Priestly Blessing each time they renewed the covenant. There is an everlasting or eternal quality attaching to these gifts, for which the *yaḥad* prayed; the same seems to be implied by line 9 of the fragment, expressing the hope that the blessing be effective 'unto everlasting generations'.[36] Despite the brevity of the preserved text, it is not exceeding the evidence to suggest that the blessing granted to Jacob was seen by the compiler of 4Q158 as in some way central to the whole proceedings, since line 10 underlines the departure of Jacob's companion 'when he had blessed him there', words not found in the Bible. As we have seen, this contrasts sharply with some other interpretations of Gen. 32: 30.

Line 11 presents words of Gen. 32: 32 which are exactly the

---

[33] See below, pp. 265–6. *Pesiqta de Rab Kahana* supp. 1: 11 enumerates five blessings received by Jacob, of which this is one; but its content is not specified.

[34] See H. Gunkel, *Genesis*, trans. M. E. Biddle (Mercer University Press: Macon, Ga., 1997), 350–1; and discussion in Walton, *Traveller Unknown*, 81–4.

[35] See above, pp. 19–20; and note also Jacob's first visit to Bethel, where God promises him descendants (Gen. 28: 14) and he begs protection from God (Gen. 28: 20–2).

[36] The version of the Priestly Blessing recorded in 1 QS 2: 3 begs that God 'favour you with everlasting knowledge' (ויחונכה בדעת עולמים), and in 1 QS 4: 3 'understanding' (בינה) is a prerequisite for true righteousness. On the introduction of knowledge and understanding into blessing texts at Qumran, see further B. Nitzan, *Qumran Prayer and Religious Poetry* (Brill: Leiden, 1994), 145–71, esp. 148–50, 161–5.

same as MT of that verse; but the last two lines of the fragment,
dealing with the last verse of the chapter, sharply diverge from MT
of Gen. 32: 33. Thus line 12 opens with 'on that day; and he said',
words featuring not at all in either MT or the ancient versions.
What follows is an immediate prohibition, אל תואנכל, 'do not
ea[t]': Allegro's restoration of the Hebrew is firmly based and not
disputed. These two words do not agree at all with MT of Gen. 32:
33, which reports that 'the sons of Israel do not eat (לא יאכלו) the
sinew of the nerve which is on the hollow of the thigh'; this may
also quite legitimately be translated as meaning that the sons of
Israel 'shall/may not eat the sinew of the nerve'.[37] Enough survives
of 4Q158 line 12, however, to indicate that here a single individual,
Jacob, is presented by another individual ('and he said') with a
negative command to be observed long before the giving of the
Torah to Moses at Sinai. Similarly, enough survives of the end of
line 13 to authorize with some confidence restoration of 'unto this
day' on the basis of Gen. 32: 33, which suggests that, once given,
this commandment continued to be observed. Furthermore, line
13 unambiguously requires that the prohibition be applied to 'the
two hollows of the thigh': the Bible speaks only of 'the hollow of
the thigh'.[38]

The importance of these lines can properly be appreciated only
when set alongside Rabbinic discussion of גיד הנשה in *m. Hullin*
7:1,6; *tos. Hullin* 7:1, *b. Hullin* 91ab; and *Gen. Rab.* 78: 6. These
sources will be examined in detail below; but in the meantime it
will be useful to point out that these texts present differences of
opinion between 'the Rabbis' and R. Judah.[39] The latter, according
to *m. Hullin* 7: 6, argued that the single commandment about the
sinew of the thigh was given to Jacob and observed by his descendants before the revelation at Sinai; this seems also to be the position
adopted by 4Q158. The Rabbis disagree, stating that the commandment was actually given and made binding only at Sinai, but
was recorded by the Bible 'out of place', as it were, in the story of
Jacob. Then there is debate whether the commandment refers to
one or to both thighs of an animal. The halakhah enunciated in

[37] That is to say, the Hebrew of MT may be understood *either* as a statement of
what Israelites do in general (and this is how TO, PJ, and TN understood it); or as a
commandment not to eat this portion addressed to all Jacob's descendants (so a
marginal note in TN).

[38] As noted by Allegro, *DJD. V*, 2.

[39] See below, Ch. 7, sec. 1.

the opinion of 'the Rabbis' states that both thighs are involved: this is the view of 4Q158, which thus incidentally and effectively demonstrates the antiquity of the ruling. R. Judah, however, believes only one thigh is meant. The terms in which 4Q158 is couched demonstrate that differences of opinion about the precise status and manner of application of the law of Gen. 32: 33 go back well into the Second Temple period; and it is of some interest to note that later Rabbinic law agrees with the Qumran fragment on one matter, while disagreeing on another.

4Q158 is written in an early Herodian hand, and thus probably dates to the second half of the first century BCE.[40] It is not possible to deduce how much older than the Herodian period the material it contains might be, but its significance for the history of interpretation of Jacob's meeting with his mysterious companion is out of all proportion to its length. The fragment seems concerned with the place of this meeting, and to ensure that the events are regarded as a struggle: Jacob's companion, it will be recalled, is said to have seized hold of him. It is apparently willing to alter the order of the biblical narrative, although its reasons for doing so cannot now be discerned clearly. That said, there seems little doubt that the meaning of the name Israel implied by the fragment cannot be separated from notions of struggle and, perhaps, a fight. 4Q158 evidently regards the blessing of Jacob by his companion as a central element in the narrative, and goes so far as to provide the words of that blessing. Finally, it offers a clear, distinctive wording and interpretation of the law of גיד הנשה, thereby indirectly proving that later Rabbinic debates about this commandment continue discussions of Second Temple times. In this matter, however, 4Q158 displays no qualms about presenting the biblical injunction to support its own view of the law, in wording quite different from MT, any of the extant ancient versions, or any Rabbinic text. The description 'reworked Pentateuch' is certainly appropriate here.

Already I have indicated some of the similarities and dissimilarities between 4Q158 and other interpretations of events at the Jabbok; more will be said about these in the relevant chapters which follow. It is fitting that this text conclude a chapter which began by setting out some of the many interpretative questions which these brief biblical sections provoke; for 4Q158 brings forcibly to our attention a method almost constantly in use among

---

[40] See Vermes, *The Complete Dead Sea Scrolls in English*, 442.

ancient commentators. That method is selectivity, the isolation by the commentator of particular elements within the given biblical material which are deemed central or essential to the real meaning of the text. Short as 4Q158 might be, it has no difficulty in promoting blessing and a very definite understanding of a biblical food law to prime positions; these, for the author, are what ought to concern us most of all when we read the story of Jacob's change of name. What other Jews made of that same story we must now investigate.

2

Jacob's Change of Name as Represented by the Septuagint Translators

Outside the Hebrew Bible itself, the oldest Jewish understanding of the name Israel, its interpretation, and the circumstances in which it was granted to Jacob are preserved in the Greek version of the Pentateuch commonly called the Septuagint. This translation was made in Egypt sometime in the third century BCE. The Greek version of the Hebrew Prophets, which includes Hosea's rather hostile description of Jacob's behaviour when his name was changed, may be dated to the early second century BCE or slightly earlier. In preparing their versions, the translators not only took account of the Egyptian-Greek world inhabited by those who would read the results of their efforts, but also sought to incorporate Jewish exegesis of Scripture familiar to them, and regarded as traditional in their days. What they produced, in the words of John W. Wevers, was 'a humanistic document of great value for its own sake' representing what Alexandrian Jews of the third century BCE thought their Hebrew Bible meant; it is, Wevers continues, 'the earliest exegetical source that we have for understanding the Pentateuch', and as such should be 'the first document to which one turns when trying to understand the Torah'.[1] In the case of the

---

[1] See John W. Wevers, *Notes on the Greek Text of Genesis*, Septuagint and Cognate Studies, 35 (Scholars Press: Atlanta, 1993), pp. xiv–xv. For the dates of the Greek versions of the Pentateuch and the Prophets, see E. Tov, *Textual Criticism of the Hebrew Bible* (Van Gorcum: Assen, 1992), 136–7, E. Schürer, *The History of the Jewish People in the Age of Jesus Christ*, vol. III. 1, rev. and ed. G. Vermes, F. Millar, and M. Goodman (Clark: Edinburgh, 1986), 474–93; and particularly M. Harl, G. Dorival, and O. Munnich, *La Bible Grecque des Septante. Du Judaïsme Hellénistique au Christianisme ancien* (Cerf: Paris, 1988), 83–111. On the characteristics of LXX's translation and exegesis of Genesis, and for select bibliography on this subject, see esp. M. Harl, *La Bible d'Alexandrie, 1: La Genèse* (Cerf: Paris, 1986), 15–82. A brief discussion of selected verses of LXX Gen. 32: 23–33 may be found in W. T. Miller,

Jacob stories, the translators were careful to observe the precise wording of the Hebrew text before them, bringing the narratives into association with other matters discussed in the Pentateuch, interpreting Scripture by means of Scripture. In so doing, they left behind a connected, sustained exegesis which, whatever their own intentions, invited a particular understanding of how Jacob became Israel, and why. The first part of this chapter will therefore be devoted to showing how their translation may be understood in this way, and the consequences for the reader of their explanation of Jacob's encounter with the 'man' who announced that his name would henceforth be Israel. That encounter will form the subject-matter of the second part of the chapter, while the third will examine the effects of Jacob's name-change as LXX developed the story up to the end of Gen. 35.

1. JACOB AND LABAN, ISRAEL'S SLAVERY IN EGYPT, AND HER REDEMPTION

The starting-point for LXX's understanding of the name Israel is the well-known story of the Patriarch's first visit to Bethel, where he dreamed of a ladder joining heaven and earth, angels going up and down, and the presence of the Lord, awaking to name the place Bethel and to bind himself with a vow (Gen. 28: 11–22). Time and again throughout the chapters immediately following this event, LXX make direct or indirect allusion to it. This first of Jacob's two visits to Bethel is the preliminary stage of a longer journey undertaken to seek refuge from his brother Esau's anger, which ends eventually in the territory of Paddan-Aram. There Jacob was to dwell with his uncle, Laban the Aramaean, at whose insistence he undertook servile work to acquire as wives his uncle's daughters, Leah and Rachel (Gen. 29). The Hebrew term used to describe Jacob's work to obtain these wives is עָבַד, 'to work, serve'.[2] It may indicate merely that Jacob undertook work for a wage; indeed, Jacob's agreement with Laban that he work for Rachel to be given to him, recorded in Gen. 29: 18, suggests a contract between the two men which Jacob freely entered into. On the other hand, this same Hebrew root often refers to slavery and

---

Mysterious Encounters at Mamre and Jabbok, Brown Judaic Studies 50 (Scholars Press: Chico, 1984), 153.

[2] This root is found six times in Gen. 29: 15, 18, 20, 25, 27, 30.

the subjection of one person or group to another: it is used in the sense of Israel's enslavement in Egypt by the Pharaoh and his task-masters (Exod. 1: 14), who impose עבודה קשה, 'harsh servitude' on the people (Exod. 1: 14; 6: 9). In their interpretation of Gen. 31, narrating Jacob's plan to escape with his wives from Laban's clutches, the LXX interpreters give us to understand that his sub-servience to Laban was analogous to Israel's future slavery to the Pharaoh, and that his escape from his uncle in some manner anticipates Israel's exodus from Egypt.

In a variety of ways, the Hebrew text of Gen. 31 invites the discerning reader to see in its story a prefiguring of Israel's des-tiny; and it seems that LXX responded to that invitation by translating the chapter so that affinities with events in Israel's forthcoming Egyptian experiences would be made plain. Already in the Hebrew text before them, the translators found Jacob com-plaining of the עני, 'misery', which Laban had inflicted on him (Gen. 31: 42); this word is not common in the Pentateuch, and can be used to express Israel's misery under Pharaoh's taskmasters (Exod. 3: 7, 17; 4: 31; Deut. 26: 7; cf. Deut. 16: 3), such use sug-gesting an association of Jacob's experiences with the Egyptian enslavement of the Jews.[3] Jacob, with divine help, 'despoils' Laban of his property (Gen. 31: 9, 16): the Hebrew verb נצל describes this action, just as it tells of Israel later 'despoiling' the Egyptians (Exod. 3: 22; 12: 36). Yet this same verbal root may signify deliver-ance and rescue from hostile powers, as Jacob prays to be delivered from his brother (Gen. 32: 12), and Israel is to be delivered from

---

[3] In the Pentateuch, עני is found at Gen. 16: 11; 29: 32; 31: 42; 41: 52; Exod. 3: 7, 17; 4: 31; Deut. 16: 3; 26: 7; and outside Genesis refers to Israel's Egyptian servitude. Yet even in Gen. 41: 52, Joseph uses the word to describe Egypt as 'the land of my misery'; and Hagar is in Shur, on the very border of Egypt, when she declares (Gen. 16: 11) that God has heard her 'misery'. Gen. 29: 32 is a declaration by Leah that the Lord has looked upon her misery, and may not be unnaturally linked to Jacob's misery spoken of in 31: 42, since both are under Laban's author-ity at the time. LXX use ταπείνωσις, 'humiliation, abasement', throughout Gen. and at Deut. 26: 7 to render the word: in the last cited verse, the Egyptian enslavement is in mind. Wevers, *Notes*, 520, understands Gen. 31: 42 as speaking of abasement rather than oppression; even so, the Egyptian element in these verses is suggestive. At Exod. 3: 7, 17; Deut. 16: 3, they translate עני as κάκωσις, 'ill-treatment', and as θλῖψις, 'tribulation', at Exod. 4: 31. For the first of these renderings, made possibly under the influence of Exod. 1: 11; 5: 22, 23, see A. Le Boulluec and P. Sandevoir, *La Bible d'Alexandrie, 2: L'Exode* (Cerf: Paris, 1989), 93, and C. Dogniez and M. Harl, *La Bible d'Alexandrie, 5: Le Deutéronome* (Cerf: Paris, 1992), 215–16.

the Egyptians (Exod. 3: 8; 6: 6).[4] Jacob suspects that, had he not taken property belonging to him, Laban would have sent him away רֵיקָם, 'empty-handed' (Gen. 31: 42); God, indeed, promises Israel later on (Exod. 3: 21) that they shall not leave Egyptian slavery in that very state.[5] The Bible itself, therefore, set the stage for LXX's further interpretation of the Jacob and Laban episode in the light of Israel's later experiences in Egypt.

In the opinion of LXX, Jacob's time of service with Laban amounts to enslavement. Marguerite Harl has already noted their choice of πέπρακεν γὰρ ἡμᾶς to translate Hebrew מְכָרָנוּ ('he has sold us') at Gen. 31: 15, remarking on the use of these verbs in Hebrew and Greek respectively at Deut. 15: 12 to refer to the sale of slaves. Similarly, she comments on Gen. 31: 20, where the translators render Hebrew בֹּרֵחַ הוּא with the verb ἀποδιδράσκει to describe Jacob's hurried departure from Laban, that the Greek word describes the flight of a slave or deserter.[6] Already at 31: 15 Rachel and Leah have noticed that their father is treating them like foreigners, an observation which LXX underline.[7] We may go further, and note how LXX have seemingly modelled their account of an angel's appearance to Jacob in a dream (Gen. 31: 11–13) on other incidents of a similar kind, including Moses's experience at the burning bush. The angel calls Jacob by name, and he answers הִנֵּנִי, 'here I am'. LXX translate this reply as Τί ἐστιν, 'what is it?', just as they translated Moses's identical response to God at the burning bush in Exod. 3: 4. Some witnesses to LXX of Gen. 31: 11 even make the angel say, 'Jacob, Jacob', just as the angel calls, 'Moses, Moses' (Exod. 3: 4) at the burning bush.[8] LXX conclude the angel's speech to Jacob (Gen.

---

[4] The verb means 'despoil' in *pi'el*, as at Exod. 3: 22; 12: 36; it may bear this same sense in *hiph'il*, as at Gen. 3: 19; but its more usual sense in that conjugation is 'deliver, rescue'.

[5] The word is particularly associated with slaves and their status through the law of Deut. 15: 13–14, whose bearings on this episode in Jacob's life are discussed by S. Kogut, 'Midrashic Derivations Regarding the Transformation of the Names Jacob and Israel According to Traditional Jewish Exegesis: Semantic and Syntactic Aspects', in M. Cogan, B. L. Eichler, and J. H. Tigay (eds.), *Tehillah le-Moshe: Biblical and Judaic Studies in Honor of Moshe Greenberg* (Eisenbrauns: Winona Lake, 1997), 226* [in Hebrew].

[6] See M. Harl, *La Bible*, 235, 236, and on 31: 20 Wevers, *Notes*, 506.

[7] They are considered ὡς αἱ ἀλλότριαι, on which see Wevers, *Notes*, 503.

[8] See J. W. Wevers, *Septuaginta. Vetus Testamentum Graecum I Genesis* (Vandenhoeck and Ruprecht: Göttingen, 1974), 296. Witnesses to this repeated

31: 13) with the words καὶ ἔσομαι μετὰ σοῦ, 'and I shall be with you', a sentence unrepresented in the Hebrew, but recalling God's words to Moses according to LXX of Exod. 3: 12, as well as his words to Isaac at Gen. 26: 3.

Likewise, LXX paraphrase that same angel's words of self-identification (Gen. 31: 13), which in Hebrew read אנכי האל בית אל ('I am the God of Bethel'), with ἐγώ εἰμι ὁ θεὸς ὁ ὀφθείς σοι ἐν τόπῳ θεοῦ, 'I am the God who appeared to you in the place of God'. As the rest of this verse makes clear, LXX have not removed the Hebrew text's reference to Jacob's dream at Bethel (Gen. 28: 1–22). Indeed, they go on to interpret the angel's reminder to Jacob that he had vowed a vow in that place, אשר נדרת לי שם נדר, as meaning that he had prayed a prayer there (καὶ ηὔξω μοι ἐκεῖ εὐχήν), which recalls exactly their interpretation of what Jacob had done at Bethel according to Gen. 28: 20, namely, that 'Jacob prayed a prayer there'. But their translation of the angel's words of self-identification introduces elements which are not found in the original Hebrew, and which serve to recall their version of events at the burning bush. Thus the clause 'the God who appeared to you' would remind the attentive reader that an angel of the Lord had appeared (ὤφθη) to Moses in the bush (Exod. 3: 2), and that Moses had said (Exod. 3: 3): 'I shall see this great vision' (ὄψομαι τὸ ὅραμα τὸ μέγα τοῦτο); whereas the LXX account of Jacob's dream at Bethel had said nothing at all of Jacob *seeing*, or of his experiencing a *vision* or *appearance* of God. In view of the emphasis which the LXX translators are about to place on vision and sight in respect of divine mysteries, which we shall presently encounter, these words of the angel's self-revelation are invested with a particular force.

Again, LXX make the angel say that he appeared 'in the place of God', which in this verse constitutes their rendering of the Hebrew name Bethel. This, too, will turn out to be of tremendous significance. The word 'place' (Hebrew מקום, LXX τόπος) occurs no fewer than six times in the short account of Jacob's first visit to Bethel, and it is this element of the story which LXX want to draw to the reader's attention in this verse. God's *being seen* at a place, not articulated by LXX in their version of Gen. 28: 10–22, may

---

address of Jacob include Codex Alexandrinus and other significant manuscripts. For Hebrew 'here am I' translated as 'what is it?', see also Gen. 22: 7, 46: 2; and Wevers, *Notes*, 501. In the first of these instances, Isaac calls Abraham; but in the second, God calls Israel in night visions and says 'Jacob, Jacob', eliciting the reply 'what is it?'

also be intended to lead the reader to consider that place which is holy ground, where God *appeared* to Moses (Exod. 3: 5). Once more, however, the stated biblical link with Jacob's dream at Bethel is not broken; for there Jacob had declared that 'this *place*' was terrible and the Lord was there, even though he did not know it; and he called it 'house of God' and 'gate of heaven' (Gen. 28: 16–17).[9]

LXX understood the angel's appearance to Jacob, then, as somehow prefiguring Moses's experience at the burning bush; and they doubtless felt justified in understanding the one episode in the light of the other because both narratives indicated that God has seen what is happening, and that his agent in both instances should leave his present abode. Thus at LXX Gen. 31: 12 the angel says to Jacob: 'For I have seen what Laban is doing to you', and at LXX Exod. 3: 7 God says to Moses: 'I have certainly seen the ill-treatment of my people who are in Egypt.' Jacob is ordered to 'go out from this land' (LXX Gen. 31: 13), and God tells Moses: 'So go now, and I will send you away to Pharaoh' (Ex. 3: 10). Both men are to set in train a movement which will bring freedom from slavery to their people.[10] This, as we have already seen, will for both men involve the 'despoiling' of the oppressors.

In the event, not only does Jacob reclaim all that is rightly his (Gen. 31: 17–18), but his wife Rachel also steals Laban's household deities, the תְּרָפִים, which all witnesses to LXX in Gen. 31: 19, 34, 35 translated as τὰ εἴδωλα.[11] There are references to these objects elsewhere in the Hebrew Bible; but only here did LXX understand them as εἴδωλα. At Gen. 31: 19 Symmachus transliterated the Hebrew into Greek θεραφειν or θεραφειμ, while Aquila put μορφώματα, 'shapes, figures'.[12] In other words, LXX were not

---

[9] See Wevers, *Notes*, 502, remarking that LXX Gen. 28: 19 call Bethel 'house of God', which designation might have been expected here. The emphasis on God's place in LXX Gen. 31: 13 coupled with his appearing may also be intended to recall later events at Sinai, on which see below, pp. 81–7.

[10] Thus in 31: 13 LXX use ἀπέρχομαι to render Hebrew שׁוּב, as also in Exod. 4: 19. In both verses, God orders Jacob and Moses respectively to return to the place *they have come from* (see Wevers, *Notes*, 502), to effect the liberation of their people.

[11] For LXX's rendering of this word in other parts of the Bible, see Harl, Dorival, and Munnich, *La Bible Grecque*, 156, 207, 262. Sometimes (Judg. 17: 5; 1 Reigns 15: 23) it is transliterated; at other times, it becomes κενοτάφιον (1 Reigns 19: 13, 16) or γλυπτά (Ezek. 21: 26).

[12] Aquila's understanding of the word reflects that of the Aramaic Targumim, which mostly translated it as 'images': see B. Grossfeld, *The Targum Onqelos to Genesis*, The Aramaic Bible, 6 (Clark: Edinburgh, 1988), 112. Targum of Judges rendered it as 'figures': see W. F. Smelik, *The Targum of Judges* (Brill: Leiden, 1995), 594–5.

compelled to translate here as they did; and it is entirely possible
that their choice of word to represent the Hebrew 'teraphim' here
was influenced by a wish to provide an 'audible contrast' of
Laban's false idols, εἴδωλα, with the εἶδος θεοῦ, the 'Form of God',
which Jacob would encounter in his vision of the true God, when
he learned that his name would be no longer Jacob, but Israel
(Gen. 32: 28–31).

So Jacob and his family escaped like fugitive slaves, crossing
over the river to Mount Gilead, only to be pursued after three days
by Laban and his brothers (31: 21–3). Even in the Hebrew Bible,
Jacob's flight and pursuit by enemies is reminiscent of Israel's
later escape from Egypt. LXX leave the reader in no doubt that
Jacob has escaped downright slavery under Laban, when they
make Jacob accuse the latter of seeking to deprive him not only of
his wives, but of everything belonging to him (31: 31) and of falsi-
fying (παρελογίσω, 31: 41) his wages.[13] In both episodes the flight
leads to a mountain where a covenant is to be made. In Jacob's
case, Mount Gilead proves to be the venue for a covenant with his
enemy Laban, who has been divinely ordered not to harm his son-
in-law (31: 24); and the LXX translators have left us clear signs
that they discerned some correspondence, at least, between that
covenant and the one which would later be mediated between God
and Israel through the agency of Moses.

1.1. *Covenants at Gilead and Sinai*

A most striking indication that LXX perceived an affinity between
the covenants on Mounts Gilead and Sinai is found in Gen. 31: 46,
54. In these two verses, the Hebrew Bible records that Jacob and
Laban ate (verse 46) or ate bread and lodged the night (verse 54)
on the mountain. In both verses LXX insert an additional note
that they ate *and drank* there: this recalls the covenant made
at Mount Sinai, when we are told of Moses and his companions
וַיֶּחֱזוּ אֶת הָאֱלֹהִים וַיֹּאכְלוּ וַיִּשְׁתּוּ, 'they saw God and ate and drank'
(Exod. 24: 11) after offering sacrifice (Exod. 24: 5); Jacob and
Laban, likewise, had offered sacrifice according to Gen. 31: 54.
LXX also heavily emphasize that God is present when Jacob and
Laban make their covenant; whether they, like Moses, Aaron, and

---

[13] At 31: 31, LXX 'and everything belonging to me' is an addition to the
Hebrew, and at 31: 41 'you have falsified it' is LXX rendering for Hebrew וַתַּחֲלֵף,
'and you have changed': see Wevers, *Notes*, 512, 519.

the elders, indeed see Him remains something of an open question, to be considered presently. For the moment, however, it should be observed that when Laban first invited Jacob to make a covenant, LXX embellish his words, adding material to the Hebrew of Gen. 31: 44. What Laban proposes, according to their version, is that he and Jacob make a covenant to act as a witness between them, adding:

Behold, no one is with us: see, God is witness between me and you. (Gen. 31: 44)

LXX have taken these words from the second part of the Hebrew of Gen. 31: 50, and have transferred them here to the very beginning of the covenant-making, thus setting the tone for LXX's understanding of it. In so doing, they have also prepared the way for a rewriting of verses 46 and 48, where they assert somewhat laboriously that the heap of stones and the pillar which the two men set up constitute a witness between them.[14] When they finally reach Gen. 31: 50 itself, LXX again translate the Hebrew clause 'no one is with us', but omit the rest of the Hebrew verse, which speaks of God as witness to the covenant. The effect of this rewriting is to create a little *inclusio*, consisting now of LXX Gen. 31: 44–50, such that the repeated words, 'Behold, no one is with us', form a boundary enclosing all talk of the stones and pillar as witness. *No human being is present* when Jacob and Laban express their understanding of their covenant in the presence of God; at Sinai, Moses would be completely alone with God. It falls to Laban to expound the meaning of the heap of stones. According to the Hebrew text, he says:

And Laban said: This heap (of stones) is a witness between you and me today. Therefore he called its name Gal'ed, and Mizpah (המצפה); for he

[14] LXX Gen. 31: 44–50 may be translated as follows: 'So come now, let us make a covenant, I and you; and it shall be for a witness between me and you. And he said: *See, no one is with us.* Behold, God is witness between me and you. So Jacob took a stone, and set it up as a stele. And Jacob said to his brothers: Collect stones. So they collected stones and made a heap, and ate and drank there upon the heap. And Laban said to him: This heap witnesses between me and you today. And Laban called it 'Heap of Witness'; but Jacob called it 'Heap is Witness'. And Laban said to Jacob: Behold this heap, and the stele which I have set up between me and you: this heap witnesses and this stele witnesses. Therefore its name was called Heap Witnesses, and The Vision, inasmuch as he said: May God look upon me and you because we are going to depart the one from the other. If you humiliate my daughters, if you take wives in addition to my daughters: *See, no one is with us.*' For the relationship of this to the Hebrew, see further Wevers, *Notes*, 521–3.

said: May the Lord watch (יִצֶף יְהוָה) between me and you when we are
absent one from another. (Gen. 31: 48–9)

LXX, within the *inclusio* formed by the note that no human being
is present with Jacob and Laban, interpret these words as follows:

And Laban said to Jacob: Behold, this heap, and the pillar which I have set
up between me and you, this heap is a witness and this pillar is a witness.
Therefore its name was called 'The heap is a witness' and 'The Vision' ('*H*
ὅρασις), since he said: May God look upon me and you ('*Ἐπίδοι ὁ θεὸς ἀνὰ*
μέσον ἐμοῦ καὶ σοῦ), because we are going to depart the one from the other.

According to the Hebrew, Jacob had set up a pillar (31: 45) whose
significance is explained in 31: 51–2. LXX have so rearranged the
text that these latter verses are now treated earlier as at 31: 48,
within the little *inclusio*.[15] Mention of this pillar cannot fail to
remind the reader of another pillar which Jacob set up at Bethel
when he was alone (MT and LXX Gen. 28: 18, 22). Yet, as we have
had occasion to note, no verb of seeing, or noun associated with
vision, is found in MT or LXX of that story. Here, however, sight
and seeing form the keynotes of LXX's interpretation, and it
would seem that they have gone to some considerable lengths
to arrange the text in such a way that the reader is not allowed to
escape the prominence of this sight and seeing. Both are used to
sum up the meaning of the covenant which Jacob and Laban have
concluded, the place-name Mizpah, occurring only here in the
Pentateuch, being understood as 'vision'. The Hebrew text had
used the root צָפָה, 'look out, spy, keep watch', to explain the name
Mizpah; this, too, is the only occurrence of the verb in the entire
Pentateuch. LXX's renderings of both words, therefore, deserve
careful scrutiny.

1.2. *Covenant and Vision*

Their choice of ὅρασις to translate Mizpah, more naturally rendered by the Aramaic Targumim as 'lookout' or 'watchpost',[16] is
distinctive, not least because the noun occurs in LXX Pentateuch
only eight times (including Gen. 31: 49). Just two of these

---

[15] The *inclusio* draws attention to the loneliness of Jacob on this occasion, which,
from a literary and exegetical point of view is of some import: Jacob was alone when
he had his dream at Bethel, and will be alone when he encounters the mysterious
'man' who will herald his change of name to Israel (Gen. 32: 25).

[16] See R. le Déaut, *Targum du Pentateuque*, vol. 1, *Genèse* (Cerf: Paris, 1978),
300–1.

occurrences describe ordinary human vision. In Gen. 2: 9 εἰς ὅρασιν translates Hebrew למראה in the phrase 'desirable to look upon', qualifying the trees which God created in the Garden of Eden; and in Lev. 13: 12 ὅρασις, translating מראה once more, refers to the priest's inspection of a victim of skin disease. The word's other appearances, however, are invested with clearly supernatural significance. In Gen. 24: 62; 25: 11 it figures in translation of the Hebrew place-name באר לחי ראי (Be'er Lahai Ro'i) as τὸ φρέαρ τῆς ὁράσεως, 'The Well of the Vision', the place where God had appeared to Abraham's wife Hagar according to Gen. 16: 13–14. The precise nature of Hagar's vision of God will be investigated in more detail shortly. In Gen. 40: 5 the translators appear to have used ὅρασις to represent the Hebrew פתרון, 'interpretation', in a phrase 'according to the interpretation of his dream', referring to the dreams of Pharaoh's butler and baker: LXX speak of each of these men as having experienced in one night 'the vision of his dream' in which secrets were supernaturally revealed to them. Likewise, but more strikingly, the word is twice used in Balaam's oracles at Num. 24: 4, 16, where it renders an original Hebrew מחזה, 'vision', the object of which is God under His title of 'El Shaddai. In rendering Mizpah with this word, LXX suggest that Jacob's covenant with the non-Jew Laban involved a supernatural revelation of the sort accorded to Pharaoh's (non-Jewish) servants and to the Gentile seer Balaam, and an encounter with the divine like that experienced by Hagar, ancestress of the Ishmaelites.

It was evidently this latter event, however, which was uppermost in the translators' minds when they came to put into Greek the story of Jacob and Laban, since they elected to take up again the word ὅρασις, and also to introduce the verb ἐπιδεῖν, which had played such an important role in their version of Hagar's story. In Gen. 16: 13–14 we read how Hagar, having been rescued from death at a well of water by divine intervention, gave names both to the God who had rescued her and to the place where she was saved:

And she called the Name of the Lord who had spoken to her אתה אל ראי, since she said, 'Have I also here looked (ראיתי) after the One who sees me (אחרי ראי)? Therefore the well was called Be'er Lahai Ro'i. (Gen. 16: 13–14)

LXX offered the following interpretation of the Hebrew:

And Agar called the Name of the Lord who spoke to her: You are the God who looks upon me (Σὺ ὁ θεὸς ὁ ἐπιδών με) since she said, 'For indeed I have seen openly the One who appeared to me (ὀφθέντα μοι). For this reason she called the well: Well of the One whom I have seen openly (Φρέαρ οὗ ἐνώπιον εἶδον).

Here, God's looking upon Hagar is expounded in terms of His having openly appeared to her. When these verses from LXX's story of Hagar are set alongside the explanation of the covenant between Laban and Jacob reported in LXX Gen. 31: 48–9, it is at once apparent that the translators understood that covenant as having included a revelation of God, which should properly be expressed with the language of vision and sight. These two narratives alone in the whole of the Greek Pentateuch have the words ὅρασις and ἐπιδεῖν appearing in tandem: as we have seen, the former occurs only eight times in all, the latter, only four.[17] LXX's choice of vocabulary in Gen. 31: 48–9 can therefore hardly be accidental; and its effect is to insinuate into their version of the covenant made between Jacob and Laban a *vision* of God, which is entirely absent from the original Hebrew form of the story, but which recalls in particular God's appearing in a similar vision to Hagar. In such a manner the translators once more suggest an affinity between this event and the covenant made on Mount Sinai, where, as LXX have it, Moses, Aaron, Nadab, Abihu, and the seventy elders of Israel both 'saw the place where the God of Israel stood' (Exod. 24: 10), and 'appeared in the place of God and ate and drank' (Exod. 24: 11). In both narratives, sight of the supernatural realities is restricted to named individuals; but LXX's reformulation of the Hebrew account of Jacob and Laban has a further, dramatic effect, in that it heightens the privilege accorded to these two men. Their vision at the moment of covenant is relayed to the reader within an *inclusio*, a literary device which is used here to emphasize that no other person was with the two main characters in the narrative. Anticipating a little evidence to be brought forward in the next section, we may say that, by means of this *inclusio*, LXX are paving the way for the moment when God will be seen by Jacob alone, an

---

[17] The two remaining occurrences of the verb in LXX Pentateuch are also instructive. At Exod. 2: 25 it represents Hebrew רָאָה, 'see', in the note that God *saw* the Israelites as they were enslaved by the Egyptians; and at Gen. 4: 4 it translates the verb וַיִּשַׁע, indicating God's favourable acceptance of Abel's sacrifice. In both instances the notion of divine providence is very much to the fore; and such is not surprising, since in classical Greek ἐφορᾶν, which does duty for the present tense forms of ἐπιδεῖν, frequently expresses the gods' oversight of and care for the world and human beings.

event with which not even the momentous happenings at Sinai can compare.[18]

By the end of Gen. 31, when Laban takes his leave of Jacob, the LXX translators seem to have made clear the fundamental pattern adopted as their means of expounding the Patriarch's activities at this point in the narrative. The conditions which he and his wives endured under Laban were a form of slavery analogous to that servitude his descendants would later experience in Egypt. From that slavery escape was a necessity, urged upon him by a dream which the translators expressed in words strongly redolent of Moses's later experience at the burning bush. Escape means crossing water, the River Euphrates, just as Israel would need one day to cross the Red Sea to flee from Pharaoh. Jacob and his wives despoiled Laban, just as later Israel would despoil the Egyptians. The enemies overtook Jacob, just as later they would overtake Israel; but all is well. God leads them to a mountain, where a covenant is made, the participants eating and drinking together. Indeed, the translators seem to go out of their way to show how the future covenant at Sinai is, in some mysterious manner, in part prefigured in the agreement between Jacob and Laban on a mountain with no one else present, but where God is experienced in vision and in His seeing what shall take place. With the beginning of chapter 32, LXX do not slacken their pace: as we shall see, they have perceived a relationship between this chapter, where Jacob prepares for and experiences an encounter with his hitherto alienated brother Esau, and the story of later Israel's journey to and successful acquisition of the Land, the place which God had sworn to their ancestors.

---

[18] Even at the end of ch. 31, LXX are falling over themselves to draw attention away from Laban and to concentrate on Jacob: see Wevers, *Notes*, 526, commenting on LXX 31: 54, where the translators have included the second half of the Hebrew of 31: 53. This change of versification, he suggests, is intended to indicate that the narrative is essentially about Jacob, not Laban, intimating what Jacob did in respect of this covenant. Note also below (p. 50) how LXX make Jacob depart from Laban 'on his own way' (32: 1 [2]), the contrast with Laban's departure being emphasized (see also Wevers, *Notes*, 529).

2. JACOB, ESAU, AND THE CHANGE OF JACOB'S NAME TO ISRAEL

2.1. *Jacob and the Angels*

Once Laban had left to return home, the Hebrew Bible notes simply that Jacob 'went on his way; and angels of God met him' (Gen. 32: 2). LXX, however, included in their translation of this simple note material not found in the Hebrew and indicated here by italics:

And Jacob departed on his own way (εἰς τὴν ἑαυτοῦ ὁδόν); *and he looked up and saw a camp of God encamped* (παρεμβολὴν θεοῦ παρεμβεβληκυῖαν), and the angels of God met (συνήντησαν) him. (LXX Gen. 32: 2)

Marguerite Harl suggests that the material inserted by the translators may be intended to make us understand that the 'camp of God', which Jacob will speak of in the following verse, is composed of angels: there LXX tell us that Jacob said, when he saw the angels, 'This is a camp of God', and he called the name of that place 'Camps'; and she notes how Psalm 33: 8 speaks of the angel of the Lord camping around those who fear Him.[19] We should also be aware, however, that the Hebrew of the following verse (Gen. 32: 3) records the first occurrence in Scripture of the noun 'camp', Hebrew מחנה, which LXX regularly translated as παρεμβολή and whose first occurrence in the text they have effectively pre-empted with their rendering of Gen. 32: 2. From the moment Israel are delivered from slavery in Egypt, the Hebrew Bible will regularly refer to them as a 'camp'. This word is first so used of the whole nation in Exod. 14: 19, and frequently thereafter; and it signifies not only a society organized as a military force (e.g. Num. 2: 32), but also as a holy assembly, formally ordered for the service of God who is present in its midst (e.g. Exod. 19: 6; Deut. 23: 15). In biblical texts referring to the period *before* the Exodus from Egypt, however, the word 'camp' is restricted (with one exception) to the story of Jacob's meeting with Esau described in this and the following chapter.[20]

The LXX translators have already discerned in the story of Jacob and Laban a 'foreshadowing' of later events, culminating in a covenant which they present as a kind of precursor of what will

---

[19] See M. Harl, *La Bible*, 239.
[20] The one exception is Gen. 50: 9. The word מחנה otherwise occurs in Gen. 32: 3, 8, 9, 11, 22; 33: 8.

later take place at Mount Sinai, where Israel assemble as a 'camp' (Exod. 19: 16–17). The appearance of מחנה in the story of Jacob after Laban's departure fits well with their scheme: they seemingly go on to read the story of Jacob's encounter with Esau in the light of later Israel's experiences as a 'camp' after the covenant at Mount Sinai. The camp has military connotations: just as Israel was to face opposition from hostile nations in her desert wanderings and in her conquest of her Land, so Jacob her ancestor faced the opposition of his powerful brother Esau. But the camp is also part of a supernatural reality: angels encounter Jacob, just as later Israel's camp would be preceded on its journeys by an angel in whom is God's Name (Exod. 23: 20–4; 32: 34; 33: 2). The theme of angelic presence, so dramatically announced and emphasized at the beginning of this chapter, will continue to exercise a powerful effect on the LXX translators, making its influence felt directly or indirectly until Jacob's second visit to Bethel is completed.

In what follows, LXX draw out what is implicit in the Hebrew and faithfully represent it: Jacob sends messengers ('angels') of his own to Esau (32: 4), who in turn reports through those same messengers that he is coming to meet (εἰς συνάντησίν) Jacob with 400 companions (32: 7). The translators' choice of Greek words is able neatly and unmistakeably to represent the parallel between Jacob's meeting with the angels on the one hand (32: 2, συνήντησαν) and Esau's coming to meet (32: 7, εἰς συνάντησίν) his brother with 400 men on the other; and the thoughtful reader is thus invited to ask what relationship there might be between these angels which LXX have virtually identified as the camp of God, the camp of Jacob, and Esau and his retinue? Later interpreters would state without hesitation that the 'messengers' which Jacob sent to Esau were in reality some of the angels who met him at the camp of God.[21] The question is intensified by Jacob's actions: following the Hebrew, LXX report that he divided his people into two camps (32: 8), supposing that, should Esau destroy the first, the second would be saved (32: 9). As we shall see very soon, LXX may have thought of these as 'angels' which serve to protect Jacob. Even in this prudent scheming, however, Jacob discerns God's blessing: he had

---

[21] See *Gen. Rab.* 75:3, and Rashi's commentary on Gen. 32: 3(4) in M. Rosenbaum and A. M. Silbermann, *Pentateuch with Targum Onkelos, Haphtaroth and Rashi's Commentary*, vol. 1, *Genesis* (Hebrew Publishing Co.: New York, 1946), 155.

originally crossed the Jordan to go to Laban with only his staff for company, while now he has become two camps (32: 11). He prays for deliverance from Esau, recalling God's promise made to him at Bethel (Gen. 28: 13–15) that He would do good to Jacob, and make his descendants like the sand such that they could not be numbered for multitude (32: 13).

LXX report Jacob's immediate preparations for meeting Esau in agreement with the Hebrew, apart from one small but telling alteration. Jacob assembles various livestock as gifts for his brother, divides them into three groups, and instructs his servants what to say should they meet Esau. These servants are to 'cross over', עברו, before Jacob (MT 32: 17), a command which LXX, however, interpret as 'walk on in front of, precede'. In the LXX version, these gifts for Esau never 'cross over'. They go in front of Jacob: the verb προπορεύω is used, and the translators go out of their way to emphasize this. Indeed, it should be observed particularly here that the translators will go on to use this very verb at Exod. 14: 19 in respect of the angel who went on in front of the camp of Israel as they fled from Egypt.[22] Thus, when in Gen. 32: 18 Jacob imagines Esau asking one group of his servants: 'To whom do these things before you belong?', LXX translated: 'And to whom belong these things which are walking in front (προπορευόμενα) ahead of you?' The same verb represents the neutral Hebrew ההלכים describing the movements of the livestock at 32: 20 and again at 32: 21, which explains why the translators were so keen to make the point that the animals go on ahead, in front. The servants are to say to Esau:

Behold, your servant Jacob is coming behind us. For he was saying: I shall propitiate his face with the gifts which are going on ahead to him, and after this I shall see his face, for perhaps he will receive my face.[23]

---

[22] Exod. 14: 19 speaks of מלאך האלהים ההלך לפני מחנה ישראל, which LXX translated as ὁ ἄγγελος τοῦ θεοῦ ὁ προπορευόμενος τῆς παρεμβολῆς τῶν υἱῶν Ἰσραήλ. Apart from a single appearance in some witnesses only of LXX Gen. 2: 14 (see Wevers, *Septuaginta*, 85–6), the translators use this verb only in Gen. 32 before taking it up again for Exod. 14: 19 to speak of Israel's angelic guide. Its other uses in Exodus are instructive. Whereas in 17: 5; 33: 1, 14 it is used of Moses, in 32: 1, 23 it is put on the lips of the people in their blasphemous demand for idol 'gods' to 'go on in front of' them: once the sin of the calf is expiated, God makes plain that it is his angel who will in reality 'go on in front of' Israel (32: 34). The same verb is used of the Ark (Num. 10: 33).

[23] On the unique use of προσδέχομαι to translate Hebrew נשא פנים here, see Wevers, *Notes*, 539.

Where the Hebrew of 32: 22 records that the gift crossed over (ותעבר) before Jacob, LXX again take this to mean that the gifts went past (παρεπορεύετο), and he slept that night in the camp.[24] It will help if we anticipate here one all-important detail. As we have seen, LXX insist that the gifts for Esau 'precede' Jacob. In this, they are like the angels who will go before Israel on their journey to the Land; but they never, at any point, 'cross over'. It is only Jacob who, later in the narrative, will 'cross over' (32: 23); and when he does, the face that he will see initially will not be the expected face of Esau, but God's (32: 31). Only after seeing God's face will he see the face of Esau; and then he will declare that it is as if he were seeing the face of God (33: 10).

2.2. *Jacob Crosses the Jabbok*

The LXX translators once more seem to be interpreting the Genesis story with an eye to the note in Exodus, that on their way to 'cross over' into the land of Israel the descendants of Jacob would be led by an angel who would guard them and bring them to God's appointed place. Should Israel obey the angel, then God would be an enemy to their enemies, and an adversary to their adversaries (Exod. 23: 20–2). But LXX introduce a certain ambiguity into their version of the Genesis narrative. The angels which Jacob sees are called 'camp of God'; yet his own people are also a camp or camps. He lifts up his eyes and sees the camp of God (32: 2), an additional piece of information not found in the Hebrew text which the reader is sure to connect with the next occasion on which Jacob will 'lift up his eyes'; and that will be when he lifts his eyes and sees Esau and his retinue approaching (33: 1). Through-out their version of Gen. 32: 1–22, LXX seem to be intent on hinting at mysterious associations between the angels, the camps, and Esau and his followers, while preparing the reader for Jacob's momentous 'crossing over', a crossing prepared by gifts sent on in advance. In certain respects, LXX recall the concerns of later Jewish exegetes regarding the identity of the angels; and it is pos-sible that they therefore attest the antiquity of exegetical activity in relation to these verses.[25] For their part, however, LXX seem to be

---

[24] Some witnesses again read προεπορεύετο, 'went on ahead': see Wevers, *Septuaginta*, 313.

[25] See esp. Targ. Neof., Ps.-J., and Frag. Targ. P and V of Gen. 32: 3 and discussion in *Tanhuma* וישלח 3; *Gen. Rab.* 74: 4; *Exod. Rab.* 29:2.

pointing their readers in a particular direction: Jacob's preparations for dealing with a hostile Esau, who must be mollified with
gifts before his face can be seen and before Jacob can safely 'cross
over' and inherit what is rightly his, conceal the makings of a
supernatural drama involving angels. Once again, the midrashim
would later spell out what might well be implicit in LXX's account,
that the figure with whom Jacob was to wrestle in the night was
none other than Esau's heavenly representative or angel.[26]

With Gen. 32: 22, the events leading directly to Jacob's change
of name begin. The Hebrew text notes that he got up that night,
took his wives, maidservants, and sons, 'and crossed (ויעבר) over the
ford of Jabbok'. The last phrase only need concern us, for here, at
last, LXX declare that he *crossed over* or *passed over* (διέβη). LXX
of the Pentateuch use this verb outside Genesis (twenty-nine
times) and in the Book of Joshua (nineteen times) almost invariably
as a translation of Hebrew עבר when it speaks of Israel's crossing
over into the land of Israel, often via the Jordan river. They restrict
its use in Genesis (where Hebrew עבר is found some twenty-three
times) to five occasions, all of them in chapters 31 and 32 where, as
we have seen, they are interpreting Jacob's crossing of various
rivers in the light of later Israel's passing through the Red Sea and
the Jordan to gain access to the Land.[27] Evidently they are set on
interpreting what will next happen to Jacob in the light of later
Israel's experiences in taking possession of her land, because the
River Jabbok itself is an important boundary. Indeed, it was the
earliest boundary of the Land which she secured in her first
attempts at conquest, according to Num. 21: 24 and Deut. 3: 16.

As if to insist that Jacob's activities must properly be interpreted
in the light of Israel's taking possession of the Land, LXX adopt a
particular reading of Gen. 32: 23, which tells of Jacob and his
household and remarks:

And he took them and made them cross over (ויעברם) the wadi, and he
made to cross over (ויעבר) what belonged to him.

In the MT, both verbs given above in Hebrew are vocalized as *hiph–
'il*. LXX seem to have read the first of these as *qal*, removing from
it the attached third person masculine plural suffix, to read:

---

[26] See e.g. *Gen. Rab.* 77: 2 (R. Hama bar Hanina, citing Gen. 33: 31 as proof).
[27] Gen. 31: 21, 52; 32: 10 (11), 22 (23), 23 (24). For the motif of 'crossing over' in
the Hebrew text here, see A. Butterweck, *Jakobs Ringkampf am Jabbok*, Judentum
und Umwelt, 3 (Peter Lang: Frankfurt-am-Main, 1981), 8–9, 16–17, 24–5.

And he took them, and he crossed over (διέβη) the torrent; and he brought across (διεβίβασεν) all his possessions.

The effect of this is once more to stress that Jacob himself crossed over the wadi, and may be intended to underline what is made clear in the following verse (32: 24), that he was alone; later Rabbinic exegetes also found it necessary to explain how Jacob could be alone if, as this verse states, he was accompanying people across the river (Rashi *ad loc.*, following *b. Ḥull.* 91a). That he was indeed alone seems to be a matter which LXX wished to emphasize, for reasons which will soon be apparent. As for the note that he brought across his possessions, this too furnishes important proof that the translators had juxtaposed in their minds Jacob's crossing of this wadi and the conquest of the Land of Israel. So much is clear from their use of the verb διαβιβάζειν here, a rare form found only twice elsewhere in LXX Pentateuch and on six further occasions in the version. In the latter, the verb is used with reference to crossing the Jordan (LXX Josh. 7: 7; 2 Reigns 19: 15, 18, 41) and the Red Sea (Wisd. 10: 18). The two Pentateuchal occurrences speak of Israel crossing the Jordan, and are of some interest.

According to Num. 32: 5, the tribes of Reuben and Gad requested Moses not to compel them to cross over Jordan to settle in the Land of Israel: LXX present their request with the words μὴ διαβιβάσῃς ἡμᾶς τὸν Ἰορδάνην, 'do not make us cross over the Jordan'. Moses agrees to their request on condition that they take part in the general military conquest of the Land, and thereafter return to their possessions in Transjordan. Should they fail to comply with this condition, says Moses, their inheritance shall be in the land of Canaan with the other tribes: so insists Num. 32: 30. LXX greatly expand this verse with material not found in the Hebrew text, and represented in italics in the following translation.

But if they will not pass over with you armed *to the war before the Lord, then you shall make to cross over* (διαβιβάσετε) *their possessions and their wives and their cattle before you into the land of Canaan*; and they shall inherit along with you in the land of Canaan.[28]

---

[28] For the possibility of a *Vorlage* different from MT underlying LXX here, see G. Dorival, *La Bible d'Alexandrie, 4: Les Nombres* (Cerf: Paris, 1994), 540, who correctly notes the rarity of the verb διαβιβάζειν and the fact that the phrase 'before you' in this addition cannot simply be a harmonizing note intended to bring the verse into line with 32: 17.

The similarities between the situation described here and that of Jacob and his family in Gen. 32: 24 are so striking that the mind of the translators stands revealed beyond doubt. Jacob crosses the Jabbok, and thereby as it were prefigures the crossing over into the Land of Israel which one day his descendants will undertake. At the same time, LXX invite readers to interpret what is happening to Jacob with their minds directed towards that future crossing, which will be achieved only with God's help against always powerful and sometimes terrifying enemies. That Esau may prefigure those enemies is not surprising, since the Bible itself relates his marriages to Canaanite women (Gen. 36: 1–5), whose descendants would pose a threat to Israel. The power which Jacob will encounter as he prefigures his descendants' conquest of the Land, however, is altogether more disturbing: it is a force which is able to announce that his own name, his very character and essence, will be changed.

2.3. *Jacob Becomes Israel*

With Gen. 32: 25 the narrative at once becomes mysterious and foreboding. The Hebrew reports what is happening in the night. Gen. 32: 23 has already established the time of activities; indeed, this chapter seems particularly concerned with such things, as is clear from an earlier note of time in Gen. 32: 14. So it is in the course of the night that the next incident takes place.

And Jacob was left alone; and a man wrestled with him until the dawn came up (ויאבק איש עמו עד עלות השחר).

The LXX translation of this verse is remarkable on a number of accounts. At first blush it appears to be more or less literal, but closer inspection betrays items of the greatest interest. The first clause in Greek, ὑπελείφθη δὲ Ιακὼβ μόνος, faithfully reproduces the Hebrew note that Jacob was left on his own. In translating the verb 'wrestled', however, LXX will have observed that the Hebrew root אבק is used only here and in the following verse in the whole of the Pentateuch; they elected to translate with παλαίειν, 'to wrestle', a verb whose use in the Pentateuch they themselves restricted to this and the following verse. The meaning of the Hebrew verb is in fact unclear; but there exists a noun אבק meaning 'dust' (e.g. at Exod. 9: 9; Deut. 28: 24; Isa. 5: 24; 29: 5), which allowed ancient commentators to explain the verb as a reference to fighting men rolling in the dust.[29] Thus Aquila, according to some witnesses, translated the Hebrew as ἐκονίετο, no doubt linking it with the noun אָבָק which LXX themselves translated as κονιορτός, 'dust', at Exod. 9: 9; Deut. 28: 24; Isa. 5: 24; 29: 5; Ezek. 26: 10; Nah. 1: 3, that is, in each one of those places in the Bible where the noun אָבָק is found.[30] Their choice of παλαίω to translate the verb אָבַק in these verses is therefore somewhat unexpected, and in need of explanation.

A pagan Greek reading LXX's account of Jacob's exchange with the mysterious 'man' might easily imagine the two as engaged in a wrestling bout of a kind commonplace in his own society. Not only was wrestling an essential part of the educational curriculum offered to young men in the gymnasium; it also featured prominently in the various, regularly occurring games so beloved of the Greek cities. The latter were mostly held in honour of some god or hero, sometimes commemorating an event celebrated in myth, always bringing great honour to the victor, who might be crowned with a laurel wreath or granted some other mark of esteem. Such wrestling in athletic contests often had sacral associations which could not be divorced from the cult of the god in whose honour particular games were celebrated, and the victor was thus inevitably bound up in some measure with the god as his special votary or favourite.[31] The translators, therefore, imply that Jacob's fight at the Jabbok had both an educational and a sacred significance. At the same time, however, they manage to distance his wrestling bout from the Greek athletic contests in two important respects. While he wrestled, Jacob and his opponent were alone: there were

[29] See Wevers, *Notes*, 540–1, who remarks that the meaning of the Hebrew root is quite uncertain, comparing LXX's rendering of it as 'wrestle' with Rashi's explanation of the word through its Aramaic cognate meaning 'to entwine'. Although he dismisses the explanation, Rashi nonetheless records Menahem ben Seruk's association of the verb with the corresponding noun אָבָק, 'dust', imagining the fighters raising the dust with their feet (Rosenbaum and Silbermann, *Pentateuch with . . . Rashi's Commentary*, 159). See also Butterweck, *Jakobs Ringkampf*, 9.

[30] For Aquila's reading, see Wevers, *Septuaginta*, 314, also noting another rendering ascribed to Aquila and Symmachus ἐκυλίετο, 'rolled'; and cf. Miller, *Mysterious Encounters*, 153. See also *LAB* XVIII. 6 speaking of Jacob, *qui cum luctaretur in pulvere cum angelo*, and the remarks of H. Jacobson, *A Commentary on Pseudo-Philo's* Liber Antiquitatum Biblicarum, 2 vols. (Brill: Leiden, 1996), i. 587, who draws attention to *Gen. Rab.* 77: 3 as making use of the same etymology.

[31] See V. Tcherikover, *Hellenistic Civilization and the Jews* (Atheneum Books: New York, 1974), 26–36, on the significance of games and athletic contests for the Hellenistic *polis*, and M. Hengel, *Judaism and Hellenism*, 2 vols., trans. J. Bowden (SCM: London, 1974), i. 65–78.

therefore no spectators of the sort commonly found in gymnasia and at the games. Furthermore, the contest took place at night, whereas Greek wrestling matches normally took place during the day. We may add a further difference: Jacob, as victor, will not receive a laurel crown or some such ephemeral trophy, but a new name in perpetuity. As LXX present it, therefore, his victory in such a wrestling contest implies that he has successfully completed his education, and that he has been specially favoured by his God, with whom he has some kind of personal relationship.[32]

As for the subject of the verb which they translated as 'wrestled', the majority of LXX witnesses represented the Hebrew word 'man' as Greek ἄνθρωπος, without further definition. The Hebrew expression 'until the dawn came up', however, they rendered simply as ἕως πρωί, 'until early morning', even though they were to translate much more precisely the very similar words of verse 27, 'for the dawn has come up', as ἀνέβη γὰρ ὁ ὄρθρος. The effect of their decision to translate in this way is to defer until later in the narrative a more precise description of who was involved in the wrestling bout and when it took place; rather, they have contrived to draw attention to the fight itself and to the implications of that fight earlier considered. Although some later witnesses to the text of LXX identify the 'man' as an angel, an identification well established in Jewish exegetical tradition, it is clear that the oldest and most reliable Greek manuscripts eschew the option at this point, even though the parallel account of this incident in Hosea 12: 5 might well suggest that the opponent was, indeed, an angel.[33] In the first instance, LXX wish the reader to envisage Jacob engaged in a wrestling bout with an unnamed opponent until the morning; and the fight is of a kind which a Greek reader would know well.

---

[32] In this respect, Philo merely makes explicit what is already implicit in LXX's interpretation of the wrestling incident: see *De Som.* I. 129–32, where he employs the imagery of gymnastic training and exercise to the full in his exposition of Gen. 32: 25–33.

[33] For the evidence, see Wevers, *Septuaginta*, 314. Only one uncial reads 'angel', but this interpretation of the Hebrew, if not the reading itself, is certainly ancient, being represented in the work of Demetrius the Chronographer (writing *c.*220–204 BCE) *apud* Eusebius, *Praep. Evan.* IX. 21. 7, πορευομένῳ δ' αὐτῷ εἰς Χαναάν ἄγγελον τοῦ παλαῖσαι (text cited from E. H. Gifford, *Eusebii Pamphili Evangelicae Praeparationis Libri XV* (Oxford: Clarendon Press, 1903), i. 533). Evidently Origen was aware of it: see discussion of M. Harl, *La Bible*, 243. But the identification is certainly as old as Philo's time: see (e.g.) *De Som.* I. 87. In *Gen. Rab.* 77: 3; *Song Rab.* 3: 3 the angel is identified as Esau's guardian: see further Miller, *Mysterious Encounters*, 102.

Describing the progress of the wrestling bout, LXX remain close to the Hebrew of 32: 26, and translate:

And he saw that he did not prevail against him (οὐ δύναται πρὸς αὐτόν), and he touched the broad part of his thigh; and the broad part of Jacob's thigh became numb while he was wrestling with him.

The Hebrew speaks rather of the 'hollow' of Jacob's thigh which was 'put out of joint', וַתֵּקַע; otherwise, the absence of explicit subjects of the verbs in this verse leaves the LXX as ambiguous as the Hebrew original. Marguerite Harl, however, is right to point out that Jacob's opponent must be the subject of the first three verbs if this verse is not flatly to contradict 32: 28–9, where the opponent announces Jacob's change of name. She also signals another ambiguity, apparent both in the Hebrew and the Greek: Jacob's opponent wrestles *with him*, Hebrew עִמּוֹ, Greek μετ᾽ αὐτοῦ (32: 25,26). This could be understood to mean that the man wrestled in company with Jacob, that is, fighting alongside him against an otherwise unnamed and unknown opponent. The customary interpretation, that the man wrestled *against* Jacob, fits more easily with the Hebrew original than with the Greek version, the preposition μετά most often representing 'in company with' rather than 'against'. Even so, the translators may have seen the possibility of understanding the preposition in an antagonistic sense.[34] LXX make no effort, however, to remove this ambiguity, which adds to the air of mystery surrounding the whole event. By now, it is becoming clear that the translators are setting before their readers no ordinary conflict, and the expectation must be that no ordinary prize will befit the victor.

2.4. *The Meaning of 'Israel' According to LXX*

That the 'man' opposing Jacob is indeed taken by LXX as the subject of the first three verbs of 32: 26 is possibly confirmed by a small detail in their translation of 32: 27. The Hebrew introduces the verse simply with: 'And he said', to which LXX add 'to him', which is most likely an indication of their desire to explain that the man spoke to Jacob. His words faithfully represent the Hebrew:

Send me off; for the dawn has come up. And he said: I shall not send you off, unless you bless me.

[34] See Harl, *La Bible*, 243, 77; and on the subject of the verbs see Wevers, *Notes*, 541.

Having passed over the coming up of the dawn in their translation of 32: 25, LXX now allow the expression to stand. Their translation thus links Jacob's *dismissal* of the man, rather than his wrestling, with the coming up of the dawn. The struggle is confined to the darkness, when Jacob is unable to see his opponent. The dawn allows Jacob to see and to make requests of his adversary, and it is in the full light of day that his new name will be announced. Although not explicitly drawn to the readers' attention, Jacob's change of name is naturally to be associated with the light of the rising sun and his own ability to see the one with whom he has wrestled. In short, light and vision are in some manner essential requirements for the conferring of the name Israel. The next verse in LXX again exactly represents the Hebrew:

And he said to him: What is your name? And he said: Jacob.

The identification of a subject here helps to clarify the identity of the speakers in the preceding verses,[35] and with 32: 29 the clarification is final: the 'man' is addressing Jacob, and offers an interpretation of Jacob's new name, which he announces is Israel. A commonly accepted translation of the Hebrew reads as follows:

And he said, 'Thy name shall be called no more Jacob, but Israel: for thou hast contended (כי שרית) with God and with men, and hast prevailed (ותוכל).[36]

LXX made several alterations and additions to the Hebrew, represented below in italics: these changes alter the internal rhythm and formal structure of the verse, and clearly represent a definite attempt on the part of the translators to give the meaning of the verse as they understood it:

And he said *to him*: 'Your name shall not still be called Jacob, but Israel *shall be your name*: because you have *been strong* (ὅτι ἐνίσχυσας) with God, and with men (you are) *powerful* (δυνατός).

Although this single verse is undoubtedly central to LXX's understanding of the name Israel, it must not be forgotten that the

---

[35] See Wevers, *Notes*, 542.

[36] Translated by M. Rosenbaum and A. M. Silbermann, *Pentateuch with . . . Rashi's Commentary*, vol. 1, *Genesis*, 159–60. For a recent study of this verse, and its interpretation in the Midrashim, see S. Kogut, 'Midrashic Derivations', 219*–233* [in Hebrew]. On the use of the term 'Israel' in the Hebrew Bible, see now G. Harvey, *The True Israel: Uses of the Names Jew, Hebrew, and Israel in Ancient Jewish and Early Christian Literature* (Brill: Leiden, 1996), 148–88.

translation they adopted here is the result of their broader perceptions of Jacob, as in some manner prefiguring the history of his
descendants in their deliverance from Egyptian servitude and their
eventual acquisition of the Land promised to them by divine
decree. Presently we shall see in some detail how this verse relates
to that larger picture imagined by the translators. For the moment,
however, the significance of individual details in their rendering
must command attention. First, they again add 'to him', suggesting a concern to make more precise the subject and the one
addressed: the man is speaking to Jacob. Second, and more important, is the addition of words indicating that Israel 'shall be your
name', ἔσται τὸ ὄνομά σου. This same clause is found in the second
account of Jacob's change of name at Gen. 35: 10, translating
Hebrew יִשְׂרָאֵל יִהְיֶה שְׁמֶךָ. By introducing these words here, LXX
indicate their concern to interpret the words of the unnamed subject of the verb to Jacob in the light of events at Bethel described
later in the book, where the speaker is not 'the man', but God. The
translators may have had a further reason for adding these words.
The original Hebrew of this verse leaves some doubt whether the
old name of Jacob is henceforth to be abandoned in favour of an
exclusive use of the new name Israel, or whether the new name is
to be regarded as an additional designation of Jacob. Indeed,
Scripture continues to refer to Jacob by that name throughout the
rest of Genesis, occasionally calling him Israel; perhaps, then,
Gen. 32: 28 might mean that he is no more to be called simply
Jacob, but also Israel. LXX have an equally ambiguous translation,
allowing the reader to understand that from now on the Patriarch's
name is not simply Jacob, but also Israel.[37]

The second half of the verse the translators substantially
change. By omitting the conjunction 'and' prefixed to the Hebrew
וַתּוּכָל, and by changing this verbal form ('and thou hast prevailed')
into an adjective, they are able to apply one quality of Jacob's
actions to his relationship with God, another to men. Thus with
God he has been strong, and in respect of men he is powerful or
mighty: such should be clear from the translation given above. Yet
it should be noted that many witnesses to the text of LXX add
to the verse ἔσῃ, to give the sense: 'and with men you shall be

[37] See Kogut, 'Midrashic Derivations', pp. 222*–223*, for discussion of such an
understanding of the verse in Rabbinic texts, especially *Gen. Rab.* 78: 3; *Mekhilta de
R. Ishmael Pisha* 16: 79–81; and cf. Miller, *Mysterious Encounters*, 104.

powerful', possibly suggesting a successful outcome of his forthcoming meeting with Esau.[38] These witnesses presumably envisage
Jacob as having been strong with God during the wrestling bout
just described, and as now receiving a promise of future power
over men. That he has been strong with God during the fight
might be deduced from LXX's explicit association of the episode
with forthcoming events at Bethel described in 35: 9–15 which,
as we have seen, the translators have seen fit to make in this
verse.

The Hebrew text of 32: 29 expounds the proper name Israel
with reference to שָׂרִיתָ, the second person masculine singular perfect *qal* of root שׂרה, meaning 'you have persisted, exerted yourself,
contended'. LXX translated this word with 'ἐνισχύειν, whose meaning in classical Greek is 'to confirm, strengthen; prevail in or
among', and in later Greek 'to gain strength; recover from illness;
strengthen; urge'.[39] In so doing, they seem to have perceived in the
Hebrew שָׂרִיתָ a verb deriving from the root שׂרר, 'be firm, be strong,
be hard'.[40] Their translation seems to signify that Jacob has been
strong or, perhaps, has strengthened (*sc.* himself) with God, inasmuch as he has prevailed in the wrestling bout. Here two aspects of
LXX's translation, already remarked upon more than once, make a
reappearance. First, we are faced with *ambiguity*. Has Jacob been
strong with God in the sense of prevailing over him; or has he
strengthened himself with the help of God and, as a result, gained
power over men? In short, the ambiguity of LXX at Gen. 32: 25,
26, in using the preposition μετά is once more apparent.[41]

Secondly, in using ἐνισχύειν, the translators made use of a word

---

[38] For the variant, see Wevers, *Septuaginta*, 315, who doubts (see *Notes*, 543)
whether the translators understood the words to mean that Jacob was powerful in
respect of Laban and Esau, as Rashi did: see Rosenbaum and Silbermann, *The
Pentateuch ... with Rashi's Commentary*, i. 160. See also Miller, *Mysterious
Encounters*, 153. For the later view that the 'man' was Esau's guardian angel, see
above, n. 33.

[39] The following meanings of the verb are listed by J. Lust, E. Eynikel, and K.
Hauspie, *A Greek-English Lexicon of the Septuagint*, 2 parts (Deutsche Bibelgesellschaft: Stuttgart, 1992, 1996), part 1, p. 153: strengthen, confirm; prevail on, among;
be strong.

[40] LXX's understanding of שָׂרִיתָ as deriving from this root is shared by the Vulgate's *fortis fuisti* and the Peshitta's *d'ʾštrrt*. The root they have invoked is common
in Aramaic, but attested in Biblical Hebrew only, it would seem, in nominal forms
deriving from it: see BDB, 1057; old KB 1012; Sokoloff (also for MH).

[41] See above, p. 59, and Marguerite Harl's comment in *La Bible*, 243, where she
also notes that, from the time of Aristotle, this verb had the sense of *mesurer sa force*.

which they do not commonly use in their Pentateuch: compare their use of παλαίειν in Gen. 32: 24–5. Outside this verse they use it only eight times. Its precise significance here may be clarified on appraisal of its use elsewhere in the Pentateuch. We shall meet it again in Gen. 33: 14, where it will be discussed in the course of my examination of that chapter. Of the remaining seven occurrences, four find it used to render the Hebrew root כבד (Gen. 12: 10; 43: 1; 47: 4, 13), in verses speaking of famine as being 'heavy', such that it compels people to act in extraordinary ways. The sense conveyed is that the famine has mastery and prevails over its victims. Twice it represents forms of the verb חזק, 'be strong, strengthen', in Gen. 48: 2 and Deut. 3: 28; and in both these instances its use is highly revealing.

Gen. 48: 2 tells how Jacob, now old and sick, is visited by Joseph and his two sons Manasseh and Ephraim. On being informed of their arrival, we hear that *Israel* strengthened himself, ויתחזק ישראל, and sat upon the bed. In view of what follows, it should be observed particularly that the name Israel is used here. LXX translated ויתחזק as καὶ ἐνισχύσας, indicating a resurgence of Israel's strength to recall the divine assurance he had received at Luz in the land of Canaan. There, God had blessed him, and had promised that he would become a populous nation and that his descendants would inherit the land (Gen. 48: 3–4). Israel thus reminds Joseph of the events spoken of in Gen. 35: 9–15, the second account of his receiving the name Israel. The discerning reader could not fail to recall the interpretation of the name Israel given earlier, in LXX of Gen. 32: 29.

According to Deut. 3: 28, God told Moses that he should issue command to Joshua and strengthen him (וחזקהו) and make him firm, since he is to cross over (יעבר) before the people, and he will make them inherit the Land of Israel. Codex Alexandrinus and other witnesses to LXX translated these verbs as ἐνίσχυσον and διαβήσεται respectively, thus associating the uncommon verb ἐνισχύειν with Israel's crossing over the Jordan, led by Joshua, to take possession of the promised land.[42] The way in which LXX have handled Jacob's crossing over the Jabbok, discussed above at some length, should now be recalled: there seems little doubt that the translators have sought to represent his change of name to Israel as being inextricably linked to his descendants' crossing over

---

[42] Other witnesses read κατίσχυσον: see Zeigler, *ad loc.*

the Jordan to take possession of the Land. Given all this, they interpreted the name Israel as expressing the strength necessary to achieve the goal of inheriting that Land. In his struggle with the mysterious 'man', Jacob becomes Israel, one who is sufficiently strong to endow his descendants with the power and the strength to fulfil their divinely appointed destiny.

The single remaining use of ἐνισχύειν by LXX of the Pentateuch is of very great interest, and the appearance of this verb in their expanded version of Deut. 32: 43 may help to deepen our appreciation of the translators' choice of this particular verb when they came to expound the name Israel specifically in relation to God, ὅτι ἐνίσχυσας μετὰ θεοῦ. The verse in question forms the climax and conclusion of the lengthy Song of Moses, and a translation of it as represented by MT might run as follows:

O nations, make His people cry aloud, for the blood of His servants He will avenge: and vengeance He shall render to His adversaries, and make atonement for His land, His people.[43]

LXX offer a quite distinctive rendering, divergences from the Hebrew of MT being represented by italics in the translation given below:

Rejoice, O heavens, along with Him; and may all sons of God prostrate themselves to Him.

Rejoice, O nations, *with* His people, *and may all angels of God be strong with (or: in) Him* (ἐνισχυσάτωσαν αὐτῷ).

For the blood of His *sons is* avenged; and *He shall take* vengeance *and* repay *punishment* to His enemies;

And He shall requite those who hate Him, and *the Lord* shall purify *the* land *of* His people.[44]

It would be of the greatest interest and importance to know the exact Hebrew *Vorlage* which LXX had before them in translating this verse; and the discovery at Qumran of a fragmentary manuscript of Deuteronomy which includes this verse (4Q44 = 4QDeut[q]) demonstrates beyond doubt the existence in antiquity of a Hebrew text differing from MT and leaning in some respects

---

[43] The unpointed Hebrew of the first clause may also be taken to mean: 'Shout aloud, O nations, with Him.'

[44] For another translation, see Dogniez and Harl, *La Bible . . . Le Deutéronome*, 340–1, where they also note that LXX's divergences from MT indicate a Jewish milieu for the translation.

towards LXX.[45] It may, indeed, now be possible to reconstruct the Hebrew underlying LXX, and to offer explanations as to how such a Hebrew text and Greek version of it may have evolved.[46] But such an exercise remains speculative. Whatever its ultimate origins, the preserved text of LXX Deut. 32: 43 uses the verb ἐνισχύειν in a plea to all God's angels. Recalling the meanings of this verb given earlier,[47] we may observe that the translation of LXX suggested here, 'may all the angels of God be strong with Him', is only one of a number of possibilities, all of which reflect the difficulty of the Greek. Taking the verb in its classical sense of 'confirm, strengthen', we might translate: 'let all the angels of God strengthen (*sc.* themselves) by/in/with Him'. In the classical language, the verb when followed by ἔν may mean 'prevail'; but this circumstance is not in view here. If we invoke the semantic range of the word in post-classical Greek, we may translate: 'may all the angels of God gain strength by/in/with Him'. The most likely translation would seem to be one which expressed a hope that the angels acquire strength through God's assistance.

This last use of the verb is of undoubted interest when we return to the story of Jacob, and LXX's explanation of his new name Israel as meaning 'because you have been strong with God', ὅτι ἐνίσχυσας μετὰ θεοῦ. Here Marguerite Harl's important observation on the meaning of the preposition must be emphasized: while it is possible that, in the story of Jacob's wrestling bout, the meaning of the word might have been extended to include the sense of 'against' ('with' in a hostile sense), the primary meaning of the word followed by the genitive remains 'with' meaning 'in the company of, alongside'. The ambiguity of LXX Gen. 32: 29 is therefore heightened, not diminished, by what we find in LXX Deut. 32: 43. This latter verse allows us to perceive Jacob, now named

[45] See P. W. Skehan, 'A Fragment of the "Song of Moses" (Deut. 32) from Qumran', *BASOR* 136 (1954), 12–15; id. 'Qumran Manuscripts and Textual Criticism', Congress Volume Strasbourg, *VTSupp.* 4 (Brill: Leiden, 1957), 150. The MS agrees with LXX in invoking the 'heavens' rather than the 'nations' at the beginning of the verse; in including after the first command an order to *'elohim* to prostrate themselves to Him; and in reading 'His sons' rather than 'His servants'.

[46] See e.g. P. M. Bogaert, 'Les Trois Rédactions conservés et la forme originale de l'envoi du Cantique de Moïse (Dt 32, 43)', in *Das Deuteronomium: Entstehung, Gestalt, und Botschaft*, ed. F. Lohfink (University Press: Louvain, 1985), 329–40; J. H. Tigay, *The JPS Torah Commentary, Deuteronomy* (The Jewish Publication Society: Philadelphia, 1996), pp. 516–18.

[47] See above, p. 62.

Israel, strengthening himself or gaining strength along with God in the manner of the angels, who are exhorted to do that very thing according to LXX Deut. 32: 43. Thus on one level the LXX invite the reader to imagine Jacob as having been victorious over a super- natural antagonist and powerful with men, a victory encapsulated in his new name Israel. On another, and equally valid, understanding, his victory and the new name Israel consequent upon it are achieved by his strengthening himself along with God, like an angel, to over- come his opponent (whoever it might be) and to be strong with men. This angelic dimension of the name will occupy us again, and very soon. In sum, what this brief study of the verb ἐνισχύειν as used in LXX Pentateuch brings to light is the sophistication of the trans- lators' method in dealing with a verse so vital to Jewish self- understanding as Gen. 32: 29. In the carefully considered version set forth by LXX, the name Israel is bound up with the crossing over into the Land granted by God, overcoming all human ob- stacles; and it may signify both one who prevails over supernatural forces, and at the same time one who, like the angelic beings them- selves, gains strength along with God. All this will have important repercussions as the translators treat the following verses.

2.5. *Israel and the Vision of God*

The LXX version of 32: 30 as given by Wevers represents a close translation of the Hebrew:

And Jacob asked and said: Tell me your name. And he said: Why do you ask my name? And he blessed him there.

Many witnesses, however, including an uncial manuscript of the fifth–sixth century, following the words 'why do you ask my name?' add: 'and it is to be wondered at', καὶ αὐτό (τοῦτο) ἐστι θαυμαστόν[48]. Since this reading is so well attested, it deserves some explanation, not least since it represents an attempt to identify the speaker, the mysterious 'man' who has wrestled with Jacob, as an angel: the words are those put on the lips of the angel who appeared to

---

[48] See Wevers, *Septuaginta*, 315 and id., *Notes*, 544. Given the identification of the 'man' as an angel by Demetrius the Chronographer (see above, n. 33), this gloss might be old, and intended in some way to associate the name Israel with the kind of near miraculous victories achieved by Samson. See, however, Miller, *Mysterious Encounters*, 205, 206, n. 44, for Rabbinic discussion of Judg. 13: 18 as indicating that God frequently changed angels' names, so that they were unaware of their identity from one moment to the next; and further on this below, pp. 259–66.

Manoah, the father of Samson, according to LXX Judg. 13: 18. We should not, however, overlook the fact that the adjective θαυμαστός is used by LXX Deut. 28: 58 to qualify the Name of God in the phrase τὸ ὄνομα τὸ ἔντιμον καὶ τὸ θαυμαστὸν τοῦτο, translating the Hebrew השם הנכבד והנורא הזה. At Exod. 15: 11 God is described as 'fearful in praises', which LXX turned into θαυμαστὸς ἐν δόξαις. The two remaining occurrences of the word in LXX Pentateuch (Exod. 34: 10; Deut. 28: 59) tell us nothing of its possible significance in Gen. 32: 30. In all probability, the witnesses which have added these words toyed with the notion that Jacob had wrestled with a (supernatural) being *almost* like God, who had announced the birth of Samson, one of Israel's mightiest victors, and one whose name is 'to be wondered at', but not in truth 'honoured and wonderful' or 'wonderful in glories'. This is hardly surprising, given the import of the preceding verse and, perhaps more dramatically, LXX's rendering of what comes next (32: 31), which in Hebrew reads:

And Jacob called the name of the place Peni'el, because 'I have seen God face to face (ראיתי אלהים פנים אל פנים), and my life has been preserved (ותנצל נפשי).

This astonishing verse, which appears to contradict a general biblical principle that no human being may see God's face and live (see Exod. 33: 20; Judg. 13: 22; Isa. 6: 5), is interpreted by LXX in no uncertain terms:

And Jacob called the name of that place Form of God (Εἶδος θεοῦ), 'for I have seen God face to face, and my life has been saved'.

The word εἶδος has the sense of 'visible form, appearance, shape, figure', and on one level may be understood as part of an etymologizing explanation of the place-name Peni'el. Marguerite Harl, however, notes an important consequence of the translation: it allows an etymological link to be forged with the verb εἶδον which follows, 'I have seen'.[49] It also invites the reader to recall Gen. 31: 48–9, where the covenant between Laban and Jacob, itself in a manner figuring the later covenant at Sinai, is expounded in terms of 'vision' and of God's 'looking upon' the participants (ἐπίδοι). It would seem that Jacob's renaming as Israel is to be regarded as in some sense a realization of the essence of that covenant, in a setting

---

[49] See Harl, *La Bible*, 244.

where Israel meets God face to face and his life is preserved. Indeed, in translating the account of the Sinai covenant, LXX twice make use of this same word εἶδος, first to describe the brick-work of sapphire beneath the Lord's feet, which was 'like the visible form of the firmament of heaven' (Exod. 24: 10, καὶ ὥσπερ εἶδος στερεώματος τοῦ οὐρανοῦ, representing Hebrew וּכְעֶצֶם הַשָּׁמַיִם), and then to speak of the *sight* or *vision* of the Lord's glory (Exod. 24: 17, τὸ δὲ εἶδος τῆς δόξης τοῦ Κυρίου, representing Hebrew וּמַרְאֵה כְּבוֹד יְהוָה). Yet it is also evident that this verse looks forward to a more immediate event. Once more, Marguerite Harl has noted the salient point: LXX here speak of Israel's having seen God 'face to face', πρόσωπον πρὸς πρόσωπον; in 33: 10 they will make Jacob say on encountering Esau: 'I have seen your face πρόσωπον as one might see the face πρόσωπον of God.'[50] Throughout the episode of Jacob's change of name, the reader's attention is drawn not only to the supernatural realities which lie behind it and its implications for the future of Israel as God's people, but also to the reality which Jacob-Israel himself has to confront, a meeting with a potentially hostile brother.

But this is not all. If indeed the newly named Israel has seen God's face, the question arises how he has been able to do so and to survive, to his own evident surprise. The place-name Εἶδος θεοῦ, with its overtones of the covenant made with Moses at Sinai, offers the clue. For it is precisely while he is on Sinai that Moses receives divine assurance that God's 'face' (פָּנִים) will go before him as he and the people journey to the Land of Israel, a journey Moses will not undertake without such reassurance (Exod. 33: 15–16). Even so, God warns Moses (Exod. 33: 20):

You shall not be able to see My face (לֹא תוּכַל לִרְאֹת אֶת פָּנָי), because a man shall not see My face and live.

This LXX translated as:

You shall not be able to see My face (Οὐ δυνήσῃ ἰδεῖν μου τὸ πρόσωπον), for a man shall not see My face and live (οὐ γὰρ μὴ ἴδῃ ἄνθρωπος τὸ πρόσωπόν μου καὶ ζήσεται).

Jacob, however, is not Moses. Following his victory in the wrestling bout, he is 'powerful with men', μετὰ ἀνθρώπων δυνατός, and has been strong with God, according to the LXX of Gen. 32: 29.

---

[50] Ibid.

While it is true that a mere ἄνθρωπος cannot see (οὐ δυνήσῃ ἰδεῖν) the face of God, one who is himself δυνατός with men might well see it, especially if he has also 'strengthened himself with God', like the angels. Now LXX have explained the name Israel precisely as meaning one who is strong with God and powerful with men; and in so doing they have at the very least implied that the same name has something to do with an ability to see God's face, since they echo the phraseology of God's words to Moses in Exod. 33: 15–16. In their explanation of the name Israel, therefore, we might properly discern a Scriptural foundation for Philo's reiterated understanding of that name as 'one who sees God'. This understanding must surely be based on something more profound than a simple etymological derivation of the term 'Israel' from (say) the Hebrew root שׁוּר, 'to regard, behold, gaze', if only because Exod. 33: 15–16 denies *tout court* the sight of God's face to human beings. Rather, the name Israel itself must embody the special characteristics which allow Jacob as Israel to become the exception to the general rule; and the LXX seem to have been aware of this, and to have made provision for it in their exegesis of the name.[51]

LXX repeat their translation of the place-name in the next verse (32: 32), even though the Hebrew form is no longer Peni'el, but Penu'el: we read that the sun arose for Jacob when he passed by the Εἶδος θεοῦ, and that he was lame in his thigh. Apart from the rendering of the place-name, LXX represent the Hebrew virtually without alteration. One small detail, however, should be noted. Where the Hebrew remarks that the sun rose for him (ויזרח לו השׁמשׁ) when he passed, or crossed over (עבר) Penu'el, LXX declare that the sun arose for him when he παρῆλθεν the Visible-Form-of-God. The verb παρῆλθεν in classical Greek is patient of

---

[51] Philo's explanation of 'Israel' as meaning 'one who sees God' is commonplace in his writing: see e.g. *De Mut. Nom.* 81; *De Praem.* 27; *De Som.* I. 171; *De Ebr.* 82; *De Conf. Ling.* 72; *Leg. All.* II. 34; III. 15, 172; *De Cong.* 51; and below, Ch. 6. He may have arrived at this interpretation etymologically by deriving the name from שׁוּר II, 'to regard, behold, gaze', or by understanding it as אִישׁ ראה אל, 'a man seeing God': see L. L. Grabbe, *Etymology in Early Jewish Interpretation: The Hebrew Names in Philo*, Brown Judaic Studies, 115 (Scholars Press: Atlanta, 1988), 172–3; Kogut, 'Midrashic Derivations', 219* and Hebrew literature cited there. It is possible that Philo's etymologies of Hebrew names derive ultimately from traditions native to the Land of Israel: see G. J. Brooke, *Exegesis at Qumran. 4QFlorilegium in its Jewish Context*, JSOT Supp. Series, 29 (JSOT Press: Sheffield, 1985), 17–25. Grabbe, *Etymology*, 102–3, suggests that he may have used an already existing onomasticon.

several meanings, the most straightforward of which is 'passed by'; but it may also signify 'when he had the advantage of the Visible-Form-of-God', or even 'when he outwitted the Visible-Form-of-God'. Even though the last two possible meanings of this verb seem not to be attested in LXX usage generally, their presence in the classical language is revealing, and their influence at this point on the LXX translators, or indeed on the readers of LXX, cannot be entirely ruled out.[52] In this way LXX may wish to convey the notion that Israel had indeed wrestled with a supernatural being, and that his capacity to outwit others remains as potent as ever it did.[53]

LXX conclude the episode (32: 33) by indicating that the damage done to Jacob's thigh forms the basis of a law binding on all his descendants:

Because of this, the sons of Israel *may* not eat (οὐ μὴ φάγωσιν) the sinew *which was numbed*, which is on the *broad part* of the thigh, up to this day; because he touched the *broad part* of Jacob's thigh, the sinew *which was numbed*.

What is achieved here is the transformation of a verse which, in the original Hebrew, may be read as a statement of fact (Israelites do not eat the sinew) into a prohibition specifically related to that part of the thigh which was numbed, an idea not explicit in the Hebrew of the verse. If anything, LXX seek to root a well-established custom somewhat more firmly in the account of Jacob's wrestling bout than the Hebrew text itself.[54]

2.6. *Israel, Strong in Supernatural and Human Realms*

This legal ruling, however, is merely a brief parenthesis in the continuing drama of Jacob-Israel as it is worked out on both the supernatural and earthly planes. The attentive reader of LXX will

---

[52] These classical meanings for the verb are not listed by Lust, Eynikel, and Hauspie, *A Greek-English Lexicon*, part II, p. 358. That the verb should be carefully scrutinized for other meanings is suggested also by another peculiar circumstance. Here in Gen. 32: 31 (32) Jacob 'passed over', παρῆλθεν, and limped, ἐπέσκαζεν. Later, describing the Passover of Egypt, LXX Exod. 12: 23 tells how the Lord would 'pass over to smite' (παρελεύσεται κύριος πατάξαι) the Egyptians so as to protect (ἐσκέπασεν) Israel (Exod. 12: 27). Are the translators here resorting to puns, and hinting again at some typological significance for Jacob-Israel's conflict with the 'man'? For LXX's interpretation of Pesaḥ, see le Boulluec and Sandevoir, *La Bible . . . 2: L 'Exode*, 48–51.

[53] If this should prove to be the case, it would indicate that LXX perhaps saw Israel as a name additional to Jacob, not as a replacement for it: see above, n. 37.

[54] For the prohibition, see Harl, *La Bible*, 244, and Wevers, *Notes*, 545; above, pp. 35–6 and below, pp. 242–8.

recall that the translators had added to 32: 2 material not found in the Hebrew, that Jacob looked up (ἀναβλέψας) and saw God's camp, which consisted of angels;[55] now, in their version of 33: 1, they again have Jacob 'looking up' (ἀναβλέψας), which they offer as their inter-pretation of the common Hebrew expression that he 'lifted up his eyes'. On this occasion of 'looking up', Jacob sees, not the angelic camp of God, but Esau and 400 men. Just as in the preceding chap-ter Jacob had divided his household and possessions as a precaution against a possible attack by Esau, so again he divides his immediate entourage into two parts (33: 2). And again, just as earlier he had made gifts 'go on in front' of him to Esau, so now he himself (not gifts on this occasion) 'went on in front' (προῆλθεν) of his household (33: 3). The Hebrew had said that he 'crossed over' (עבר) before them; but LXX continue to avoid the term 'cross over', reserving it, as we have seen and shall see again, for Jacob-Israel's crossing over into the Land of Israel. The translators have apparently understood chapter 32 as setting forth a kind of programme for Jacob's activ-ities, discerning in chapter 33 the event towards which that pro-gramme is directed. What is planned in the first chapter, with its talk of camps and gifts for a potential enemy, is a conflict with Esau. In the event, Jacob's meeting with Esau is entirely amicable: the latter, 'looking up' (ἀναβλέψας) when he meets Jacob, asks to whom the assembled people and livestock belong (33: 5), the very question which Jacob had so dreaded and had so carefully instructed his ser-vants to answer (32: 18–19). But it is now Esau's turn to ask what are all these camps that he has met (LXX 33: 8), and, learning their purpose, to insist that Jacob keep them as his own (33: 8–9). From all this, it is evident that the only conflict which Jacob will have to face is now in the past; his wrestling bout with the 'man' is not going to be replicated in a battle with his brother. That brother should receive Jacob's gifts, now pressed upon him: the Hebrew of 33: 10 expresses all this with some feeling, following Esau's refusal of the present:

And Jacob said: No, I pray you. If I have found favour in your sight, then take my gift (or: offering) from my hand; because therefore I have seen your face as one sees the face of God (כראת פני אלהים) and you have accepted me (ותרצני).

In the programme, Jacob has taken much trouble to prepare a gift, present, tribute, or offering (מנחה) for Esau (32: 14, 19, 21, 22), as if

---

[55] See above, pp. 50–2.

he were paying homage to or propitiating an overlord, king, or divine being; his words here are a reminder of this, but are accommodated to the different circumstances of the event. Esau is urged to take the gifts because he has accepted Jacob, who sees Esau as one sees the face of God. LXX's interpretation of Jacob's words involves subtle alterations of the Hebrew, which substantially changes the purport of the original:

And Jacob said: If I have found favour before you, receive the gifts by my hands. For this reason I have seen your face, as if anyone might see the face of God;[56] and you shall be pleased with me.

The thrust of Jacob's words to Esau is now profoundly ambiguous, and might be understood to mean: 'If you will, take the gifts, which in any event constitute the reason for my coming to see you in the first place; then you will be pleased with me. And, incidentally, meeting with you is as surprising and momentous as would be an encounter with God; so it is only proper that you should accept my gifts.' Alternatively, Jacob may be advocating Esau's acceptance of the gifts on the grounds that the meeting is as significant as an encounter with God, even supposing that such a thing might happen, and strongly implying that indeed no such thing has happened; on this understanding, Jacob would be concealing from Esau any intimation that the meeting of the two might be connected with his nocturnal struggle with the 'man'. By this means, LXX rescue *for the reader* the significant words about seeing God's face, on which so much of the preceding chapter was focused, while 'defusing' *in the narrative* words which, in the original Hebrew, could be taken *by Esau* as meaning that Jacob had indeed seen God's face. Should Esau even suspect that Jacob had 'seen God's face', he would be bound to ask Jacob when he had done so, in what circumstances, and to what purpose. This ploy is vital for the translators, since they are about to make a direct reference to Jacob's wrestling bout, and it is crucial for the narrative that Esau should not recognize the significance of what has happened in the preceding chapter.

Having accepted the gifts, Esau asks Jacob to accompany him (33: 11–12). This is the last thing Jacob wishes to do, so he must make an excuse (33: 13). And now a remarkable thing happens in

[56] Wevers, *Notes*, 550, translates 'as someone might see the face of God', and remarks that 'the potential character of seeing God's face is not present in the Hebrew infinitive': see further the comments of Marguerite Harl, *La Bible . . . 1: La Genèse*, 245.

LXX. Whereas previously Jacob had expended effort in ensuring that gifts 'went on ahead' to prepare for his meeting with Esau, now he asks Esau himself to 'go on ahead' (rather than Hebrew יעבר, 'cross over') in the following words:

Let my lord go on ahead (προελθέτω) before (his) servant; and I will be strong/strengthen myself on the road (ἐγὼ δὲ ἐνισχύσω ἐν τῇ ὁδῷ) according to the slow pace of the journey (κατὰ σχολὴν τῆς πορεύσεως) which is before me, and according to the pace (*lit.*: foot) of the little children, until I come to my lord into Seir. (LXX Gen. 33: 14)

This is significantly different from the Hebrew, which reads:

Let my lord cross over, I pray, before his servant; and I shall journey on gently (ואני אתנהלה לאטי) at the pace of the property which is before me, and according to the pace of the children, until I come to my lord to Seir.

LXX could not make the point more clearly: having 'been strong' with God, now Jacob 'is strong' with men. The programme enunciated in Jacob's nocturnal wrestling bout is now realized in the event of his dealings with Esau. Adroitly, Jacob has avoided telling Esau that he has 'seen God face to face'; but he has no qualms about declaring openly what his new name Israel truly signifies: he will *be strong* or *strengthen himself*, now on this journey away from Esau. Marguerite Harl suggests that the translators may have understood the Hebrew root נהל as 'lead to a place of rest', and thus 'to nourish, care for, strengthen', and this may be the case; but even so, their translation of that Hebrew root with Greek ἐνισχύειν inevitably drags the reader's mind back with some force to the last appearance of that uncommon verb, in the story of Jacob's wrestling bout and his acquisition of the name Israel.[57] For LXX, Esau is to go on ahead, while Jacob (renamed Israel) is strong, gains strength, or strengthens himself on a journey.

What journey might that be? This question forces itself on us, because LXX introduce yet another peculiar expression into their translation, by replacing the Hebrew לרגל המלאכה, 'at the pace of the property', with κατὰ σχολὴν τῆς πορεύσεως, 'according to the pace of the journey'. The word πόρευσις is very rare, being *hapax*

---

[57] See *La Bible . . . 1: La Genèse*, 246. Wevers, *Notes*, 552, renders ἐνισχύειν in this verse as 'retain energy, strength', referring both to the children and the cattle, understanding Hebrew אתנהלה as meaning probably 'let me lead, guide for myself'. He suggests that LXX did not understand the Hebrew, and translated with ἐνισχύειν which they had used at 32: 28, 'though in a different sense'.

legomenon in LXX.[58] Here they have used it either to replace, to paraphrase, or to translate Hebrew הַמְּלָאכָה, which in its present setting is best translated as 'property', but is more commonly found with the sense of 'work, occupation, business' of both ordinary and sacred kinds.[59] Given their understanding of Jacob's change of name and the reasons for that change, it seems reasonable to conclude that the translators have specifically interpreted the word as the work which Jacob is now strong enough to undertake—and that work is a journey, as the Bible now describes it. But it is not an ordinary journey. Once more Jacob's shrewdness manifests itself: his use of a very rare word to his brother at once superficially reveals what he is doing, at the same time concealing what is in his mind, namely, a unique journey which will bring him to take formal possession of the Land of Israel, a journey prefiguring the work of his descendants, the twelve tribes of Israel, in the conquest of the Land.

The Hebrew text now tells how Jacob journeyed to Succoth, where he built for himself a house and booths (סֻכֹּת) for his cattle, the latter construction giving the name to the place (33: 17). Then he went to Salem, a city of Shechem, where he encamped (וַיִּחַן) before the city (33: 18), thus preparing for the violent incident between his two sons Simeon and Levi and the inhabitants at Shechem which would follow (34). There, he also purchased (וַיִּקֶן) a piece of ground from Hamor, father of Shechem, and spread his tent (33: 19). In 33: 20 we read that he set up there an altar, and called it 'El-'Elohe-Israel. Thus Jacob, who is Israel, constructs a dwelling for himself, buys land to spread his tent, and sets up an altar to the God of Israel; he has not only arrived in the land promised by God to him and his descendants, but has also taken formal, if token, possession of it.

LXX's translation generally strengthens the information given by the Hebrew. Thus Jacob built for himself houses, according to

---

[58] See M. Harl, *La Bible . . . 1: La Genèse*, 246–7, who notes its equivalence to πορεία and πόρευμα and its status as a feminine singular abstract noun perhaps deliberately put here to reflect the Hebrew מְלָאכָה, 'work', understood as the convoy for which Jacob is responsible.

[59] Wevers, *Notes*, 552–3, is rightly uncertain whether the word represents a translation or paraphrase of the Hebrew, and wonders whether the translators discerned in מְלָאכָה the root הלך, 'go, journey'. Elsewhere, LXX translated the word almost invariably with terms relating to work or business of some kind: for details, see T. Muraoka, *Hebrew/Aramaic Index to the Septuagint. Keyed to the Hatch-Redpath Concordance* (Baker Books: Grand Rapids, Mich., 1998), 82.

LXX Gen. 33: 17. On this verse, Wevers comments that Jacob is presented as founding a semi-permanent settlement in the land.[60] The translators also understood Salem, Hebrew שָׁלֵם, as the name of a city ('a city of Sikima'). Other interpretations of this word were available, among them the (perhaps more obvious) reading that Jacob arrived at the city of Shechem 'safe and sound', taking Hebrew *šālēm* as an adjective qualifying the Patriarch. The translators, however, evidently wished to root Jacob in a particular locality.[61] They confirm this by using the same verb ἔστησεν for his setting up of the altar (33: 20, Hebrew וַיַּצֶּב) and his spreading of his tent (33: 19, Hebrew נָטָה), suggesting that both these things might be around for some time.[62] The name of this altar, therefore, turns out to be of some importance; indeed, LXX seem to have rendered it (deliberately?) ambiguous. The Hebrew states simply that Jacob called the altar ''El-'Elohe-Israel'; but LXX note (33: 20) that Jacob ἐπεκαλέσατο, that is, either *named* the altar 'The God of Israel', or himself *invoked* in that place the God of Israel.[63] This ambiguity serves only to underline Jacob-Israel's settlement in the land: the altar is itself called 'God of Israel', and Jacob can there call upon that very same God. So it is that Jacob, following his escape from slavery under Laban, his covenant with the latter, and his consequent crossing over the Jordan, safe from his brother, is now in possession of the Land of Israel. In all this, the changing of his name to Israel confers on him the strength to fulfil his destiny—a strength which is mysteriously related to the vision of God and the company of angels. The complete significance of his change of name, however, has not yet been made plain; this is reserved for the LXX's interpretation of the biblical story which tells of Jacob's second visit to Bethel and its concomitant second account of his change of name.

---

[60] See his *Notes*, 554.

[61] See further M. Harl, *La Bible . . . 1: Genèse*, 247; Wevers, *Notes*, 554–5; and C. T. R. Hayward, *Jerome's* Hebrew Questions on Genesis: *Translated with an Introduction and Commentary* (Clarendon Press: Oxford, 1995), 212–13. Interestingly, *Jub.* 30: 1 viewed the word both as a place-name and as an adjective qualifying Jacob.

[62] Wevers, *Notes*, 556, remarks that only here is this Greek verb used with reference to the setting up of an altar.

[63] On the ambiguity, see M. Harl, *La Bible . . . 1: Genèse*, 247. Wevers, *Notes*, 556, prefers to understand the Greek here as synecdoche for 'he invoked the name of the God of Israel'.

3. THE INCIDENT AT SHECHEM, AND JACOB'S SECOND VISIT TO BETHEL

The well-known account of Shechem, son of Hamor, his attempt to acquire Dinah as wife after he has violated her, and the vengeance exacted on him, his household, and all the men of Shechem by Jacob's two sons Simeon and Levi, appears in LXX with few differences from the Hebrew (Gen. 34). Nonetheless, three peculiarities of the LXX translation of this chapter should be observed as germane to a correct appreciation of the second account of Jacob's acquisition of his new name. First, Hamor is described (34: 2) as ἄρχων, 'ruler' of the land (for Hebrew נשיא), a hint that the conflict which follows is perhaps of wider significance than a local skirmish.[64] Secondly, Shechem's violation of Dinah provokes Jacob's sons to anger: he has committed a shameful act in Israel, ἄσχημον ἐποίησεν ἐν Ισραὴλ (34: 7), words which express their sense of a scandalous wrong directed against the nation as a whole.[65] Thirdly, LXX also make plain their anxiety about the assimilation of Jews and those of another people. Shechem wishes to marry Dinah, but 'the sons of Jacob' lay down conditions (MT 34: 13–17). LXX explicitly bring to the fore Simeon and Levi, who are not spoken of in the Hebrew of 34: 13. These two men insist on the circumcision of Shechemite males. According to the Hebrew text of 34: 15, the speakers say to Hamor and Shechem: 'in this we shall consent to you (נאות לכם): if you shall be like us in circumcising for yourselves every male person.' LXX change the Hebrew quoted here and make additions to the verse, making Simeon and Levi say that on this condition alone 'we shall be like unto you (ἐν τούτῳ ὁμοιωθησόμεθα ὑμῖν) and dwell with you, if you yourselves also become like us, in that every male of you be circumcised' (34: 15). By translating this way, and in particular by adding the note that the sons of Israel will 'dwell with' the Shechemites, LXX make plain that what Simeon and Levi apparently hold out is the prospect of 'complete cultural assimilation' on the part of the

[64] It is perhaps worth pointing out that LXX use ἄρχων to translate Hebrew מלך at Gen. 49: 20; Deut. 17: 14, 15; 28: 36.
[65] See Wevers, *Notes*, 560, for the strongly pejorative sense of ἄσχημον contrasted with the milder Hebrew נבלה 'folly, lawlessness', which it renders here. In both the Hebrew and LXX the phrase 'in Israel' is used here for the first time to categorize the totality of Jacob's descendants.

Shechemites to Jewish customs.[66] In the following verse (34: 16), however, they are careful to make Simeon and Levi say that, if the Shechemites accept these conditions and marry Israelite women, 'we shall be like one nation', ἐσόμεθα ὡς γένος ἕν, carefully modifying the Hebrew, which states baldly 'we shall become one people', והיינו לעם אחד. Hamor and Shechem persuade the men of the city to agree to this condition, pointing out that, while it is not negotiable, the stipulation carries with it benefits for the city:

Only in this will the men consent to us (יאתו לנו) to dwell with us, to be one people (להיות לעם אחד), in our circumcising for ourselves every male . . . shall not their cattle and their possessions and all their beasts be ours? Only let us consent to them (נאותה להם) and they shall dwell with us. (34: 22–3)

The translators have significantly altered the Hebrew of these verses. In LXX they read:

Only in this will the men be like unto us (ὁμοιωθήσονται) to dwell with us so as to be one people, in every male of ours being circumcised . . . and shall not their cattle, and their possessions and their beasts be ours? Only in this let us be like (ὁμοιωθῶμεν) unto them, and they shall dwell with us.

Note how Simeon and Levi's cautious 'we shall be like one nation' becomes in the mouth of Hamor and Shechem a definite proposal that they and the sons of Israel 'be one people', the very suggestion which the carefully nuanced words of the former is intended to exclude.[67] In each of these verses, LXX have taken the opportunity to speak of one group 'becoming like' the other. In the larger exegetical setting which concerns us, this ploy has an obvious goal: Jacob-Israel, having taken formal possession of the Land granted by God, will be extremely wary about allowing the indigenous inhabitants to assimilate in part to Israelite ways (34: 15, 23); the corresponding notion, that Israel might assimilate to the Shechemites, is skilfully ruled out of order (34: 22). No such possibility is even considered.

Such is the immediate prelude to the second account of Jacob's

---

[66] The phrase is in Wevers, *Notes*, 565. As he has already indicated, what is being discussed is intermarriage (in 34: 9 LXX render Hebrew התחתנו with ἐπιγαμβρεύω) between the Shechemites and the sons of Israel, giving both groups the advantages of dwelling with each other, freedom of travel, and the right to buy land: see *Notes*, 561–2. On LXX's translation of the terms discussed here, see also M. Harl, *La Bible . . . 1: Genèse*, 249.

[67] See Wevers, *Notes*, 566.

change of name to Israel, which LXX have interpreted with great
care. Their first account of the change is, as we have seen, inseparable from their understanding of Jacob as a 'type' of later Israel
enduring slavery in Egypt, crossing the Red Sea to freedom, entering into covenant with God, and crossing into the Land unharmed
by foes, natural or supernatural. The second account evidently will
be bound up with Jacob-Israel's absolute fidelity to God, and that
in a most striking and dramatic manner. LXX of Gen. 34 has
already given us an inkling of what might be involved, in the
refusal of Jacob's sons to become like the Canaanite inhabitants of
the land. This fidelity will involve the rejection of other deities, so
that the name Israel will become inseparably linked with the forth-
right removal of foreign cults from the Land.

The narrative opens (Gen. 35: 1) with God's command to Jacob
to go up to Bethel, which LXX translate as 'the place Bethel',
thereby insisting on its status as a sanctuary. This translation not
only underlines the sacred nature of the place revealed later in the
chapter (35: 7, 13, 14, 15), but also recalls to the reader's memory
two important features of earlier stories about Jacob. The first of
these is the importance of Bethel specifically as a place (τόπος),
already repeatedly signalled in the narrative of Jacob's first visit
there described in Gen. 28: 11 (three times), 16, 17, 19. The second
is Jacob's earlier encounter in a dream with the One who appeared
to him 'in the place of God' (LXX Gen. 31: 13), a particular interpretation of the Hebrew 'the God of Bethel' which has already
been discussed.[68] There he is told to build an altar to 'the God who
appeared to you when you fled from the face of Esau your brother';
this is a close translation of the Hebrew, which recalls Jacob's first
visit to Bethel described in Gen. 28: 10–22, even though those
verses, it will be recalled, say nothing directly of Jacob's having
seen God, or of God's having appeared to him.

Jacob now (35: 2) orders his household and all who are with him
to remove the 'alien gods', τοὺς θεοὺς τοὺς ἀλλοτρίους: the Hebrew
describes these as being 'in your midst' (אשר בתכבם), but LXX
refines this, by ordering the removal of the alien gods 'which are
with you from your midst'. The translators may hope to suggest
that these deities are only incidentally 'with' Israel, and do not
properly belong to her; later tradition, and possibly the LXX translators, thought of them as the *teraphim* which had once belonged to

---

[68] See above, pp. 42–3; and cf. Wevers, *Notes*, 575.

Laban and had played an incidental role in Jacob's escape from that taskmaster (31: 17–55).[69] Furthermore, they are to purify themselves and change their garments (Hebrew and LXX 35: 2), orders recalling the preparations which a later generation would be required to make before God appeared to Israel at Sinai (Exod. 19: 10). Indeed, recollection of Sinai is entirely in place here, and in keeping with Jacob's command to get rid of alien gods. This is precisely what the second of the 'Ten Words' uttered at Sinai requires: Israel is to have no other gods apart from the Lord, and the people are never to make פֶסֶל, which in LXX (Exod. 20: 4) is translated as εἴδωλον, the very word they used (Gen. 31: 19, 34, 35) to render the *teraphim* which belonged to Laban. But it will be recalled that the 'Ten Words' begin with God's self-identification as the One who brought Israel out of Egypt. This, and the succeeding command that Israel have no other gods, seem to have influenced the LXX translators in a most powerful way. They have already presented the first account of Jacob's change of name to Israel as the climax of a series of events which they have taken care to portray as a foreshadowing, or as a type, of Israel's slavery in and redemption from Egypt, to which God Himself alludes in the opening of the Decalogue. Now, in their version of the second account of the change of name, they direct us to God's very next statements in that same Decalogue, that Israel must have no other deities, and fashion no idol. Their earlier introduction of references to Sinai in their account of Jacob's covenant with Laban at Mizpah begin to bear fruit.[70]

So Jacob and his household will go up to Bethel where, says Jacob, 'we shall make' (ποιήσωμεν) an altar (35: 3); the Hebrew reserves the activity for Jacob himself. This altar is built, says Jacob, to 'the God who answered me on the day of affliction, who was with me and rescued me (καὶ διέσωσέν με) on the road which I travelled'. The translators faithfully represented the Hebrew, but added the words 'and rescued me'. The composite verb διασώζειν is not found in the story of Jacob. Nonetheless, the simple verb σώζειν makes one momentous appearance with reference to the Patriarch at Gen. 32: 31, when he declares that he has seen God face to face, and his life has been preserved, saved (ἐσώθη). Thus

---

[69] See M. Harl, *La Bible . . . 1: Genèse*, 251.
[70] Wevers, *Notes*, 575–6, also records the similarities between these verses and Exod. 20: 3; 19: 10–15.

the translators prepare the reader for another encounter of Jacob with this same God who has rescued him and changed his name to Israel.

Jacob's family then give to their father all the alien gods which were in their hands and the rings which were in their ears, according to both the Hebrew and LXX of Gen. 35: 4. The Hebrew of the verse concludes with a note that Jacob 'hid them under the terebinth which was near Shechem'. LXX expanded this to read:

. . . and Jacob hid them under the terebinth which is in Sikima, and he destroyed them (ἀπώλεσεν αὐτὰ; *or*: made them disappear) until this day.[71]

It may be that this addition of LXX to the Hebrew reflects an anti-Samaritan bias on the part of the translators, who by this means attempt to invest Shechem, the city next door to the Samaritan temple on Mount Gerizim, with a sinister reputation for concealed idols.[72] But this is far from certain, and in any event makes little difference to the main thrust of the LXX narrative. This invites the reader to perceive the complete destruction of the male population of Shechem (Gen. 34: 25–6) as a clear parallel to the destruction or disappearance of alien gods at Shechem. The same reader would no doubt recall the words of Deut. 7: 24–5, telling how God would one day deliver the Canaanite kings into Israel's hands for destruction, while Israel would destroy the graven images of their gods. A sentiment like this, lurking behind the LXX addition, may serve to heighten the importance of what is reported in LXX of the next verse (35: 5): Israel departed from Shechem, and the fear of God (φόβος θεοῦ) came on the cities round about them, so that they did not pursue the sons of Israel. Here the name *Israel* is

---

[71] For the translation 'made them disappear', see M. Harl, *La Bible . . . 1: Genèse*, 251. Wevers, *Notes*, 577, recognizes in the mention of the people's ear-rings an allusion to the incident of the calf (Exod. 32: 3–4), a further indication that the Exodus story has informed both the Hebrew original and the LXX version of this chapter. Note also LXX's translation of Hebrew צָרָתִי, referring to Jacob's distress in 35: 3, as θλᾶψις, 'affliction, tribulation': this word is rare in LXX Pentateuch (used nine times only, including this verse), and describes specifically the sufferings of Israel in Egypt at Exod. 4: 31.

[72] Wevers, *Notes*, 578, is rightly cautious about attempts to view LXX here as part of an anti-Samaritan polemic, a notion supported by H. G. Kippenberg, *Garizim und Synagoge* (Berlin, 1971), 250–1, quoted with approval by M. Harl, *La Bible . . . 1: Genèse*, 251. The object of the verse, however, is surely (as Wevers declares) to insist that these idols were put out of commission and never again saw the light of day.

deliberately brought to the fore; it does not feature in the Hebrew of the verse, which reports merely that 'they' journeyed, and that God's terror (חתת אלהים) came on the cities, which did not pursue the sons of *Jacob*. LXX make clear that what happens here is the work of *Israel*, acting in accordance with God's plan for his people once they have come out of Egypt in years to come. Then he shall send the *fear* (LXX Exod. 23: 27 φόβον for Hebrew אימתי) before Israel as leader to disconcert the Canaanites.[73] Now safely established in the Land, Jacob and his sons represent the community of Israel, and are immune from threats of attack by the native inhabitants: the translators seem intent on representing the successes of *this* Israel as an ideal picture of what later Israel should be, when it comes across Jordan to take the land in perpetuity.

So they arrive in Luz, which is Bethel (Hebrew and LXX 35: 6). In the following verse, the LXX offer a distinctive translation of the Hebrew, which states:

And he built there an altar, and called the place 'El-Bethel (אל בית אל), because there God had been revealed (נגלו) to him when he had fled from before his brother. (Gen. 35: 7)

In LXX this becomes:

And he built there an altar, and called the name of the place Bethel; for there God had manifested himself (ἐπεφάνη) to him when he had fled from the face of Esau his brother.

The change of place-name may have been dictated by the translators' concern to ensure once again that readers would be left in no doubt about the exact location of Jacob's original experience: it was to Bethel (28: 19) that he had fled from Esau, and what happened to Jacob there, and not in some other place, is what the LXX

---

[73] See Le Boulluec and Sandevoir, *La Bible . . . 2: L'Exode*, 240–1, and observe how mention of the 'fear of God' in Exod. 23: 27 is preceded both by a promise that God's angel will go before Israel into the Land, and by a command to Israel not to worship the idols of the indigenous inhabitants (Exod. 23: 23–4). In view of what has been said to date, comment is unnecessary. The φόβος of God is spoken of only twice elsewhere in LXX Pentateuch (Exod. 15: 16; 20: 20), the first of these verses recording God's terror coming upon Edom, Moab, and Canaan at the Exodus. The second gives Moses's words to the people after they have received the 'Ten Words': God has come to test Israel, so that 'the fear of Him' may be before Israel's eyes so that they do not sin. For LXX Gen. 35: 5 as having a 'midrashic sense' applying to later Israel's effect on the nations, see Wevers, *Notes*, 578.

wish to highlight.[74] And this they do, by insisting that God had there 'manifested himself' to Jacob. Marguerite Harl comments that this is the only verse in the whole of Genesis where LXX use the verb ἐπιφαίνειν, 'to shine forth, appear, come suddenly into view, manifest'.[75] The importance of this observation should not be underestimated: LXX have interpreted Jacob's dream at Bethel as a divine *epiphany*, in which God appears in awe and great majesty. The notion of such epiphany was commonplace in the Hellenistic world of the LXX translators. Amongst pagans, the epiphanies of gods in visions, manifesting their powers and their ability to offer protection to mortals, were often recorded in writing and used to promote the worship of those divinities.[76] Jacob is thus presented as returning to a place where he can be confident of God's presence, knowing that the same God had previously manifested himself in that place as Jacob's protector and provider (28: 20–22). We are, perhaps, led to expect that God will once more be manifest in that same place, on this occasion giving his imprimatur to Jacob's change of name to Israel.

So much might a non-Jewish reader deduce from the specialized language of epiphany used here. Jewish readers, however, might derive much more information from close observation of this verb ἐπιφαίνειν, which the translators of LXX Pentateuch used again on only two occasions. The first of these is concerned with blessing, the second with angels; and both help to account for the presence of the verb in LXX Gen. 35: 7. Most striking is the verb's use at LXX Num. 6: 25, in the second petition of the Priestly Blessing. This Blessing, it will be recalled, consists of three verses, the first of which (Num. 6: 24) begs God to 'bless' and 'keep' Israel. LXX's allusion to the Priestly Blessing here is entirely appropriate: God has already *blessed* Jacob-Israel in the wrestling bout (Gen. 32: 30),

---

[74] LXX may wish also to sidestep giving a divine name to a place: both the Peshitta and Vulgate also omit אל here. See Wevers, *Notes*, 579.

[75] See M. Harl, *La Bible . . . 1: Genèse*, 252.

[76] As Wevers, *Notes*, 579–80 remarks, the verb ἐπιφαίνειν was already well established in the days of Herodotus as referring to divine self-revelation: only here in LXX it renders Hebrew נגלו (treating the verb as a singular form, like the Samaritan Pentateuch, Vulgate, Peshitta, TN, and TO). For non-Jewish understanding of epiphanies of gods, the forms they were believed to take, and their effects on shrines and votaries alike, see R. Lane Fox, *Pagans and Christians in the Mediterranean World from the Second Century AD to the Conversion of Constantine* (Penguin Books: Harmondsworth, 1986), 102–67, esp. 102–23 discussing epiphanies in the pre-Christian period.

having made a solemn promise at Bethel to *keep* him (Gen. 28: 15; cf. 28: 20). It also seems that, at that same time, the petition of the Blessing's second verse was realized at Bethel. The Hebrew text of this second verse (Num. 6: 25) prays: 'May the Lord make light (יָאֵר) his countenance towards you and be gracious to you (וִיחֻנֶּךָּ)'; but LXX transformed this to read: 'May the Lord make manifest (ἐπιφάναι) his countenance upon you and be merciful (ἐλεήσαι) to you.' Now, as he sets off on his second visit to Bethel, LXX suggest that Jacob was plainly made aware of a momentous fact which hitherto may not have been made known to him: that on his first visit to the 'place' Bethel he had been blessed with a divine epiphany, of the sort which his priestly descendants would beg God to send on the whole people Israel. As for God's graciousness or mercy which the Blessing's second petition also brings, Jacob has already acknowledged to his brother Esau that God has indeed favoured him with these gifts (Gen. 33: 5, 11): the Hebrew verb used here is חָנַן, as in the Priestly Blessing (Num. 6: 25), translated by LXX on all these occasions with the verb ἐλεεῖν. What, then, of the Blessing's third prayer (Num. 6: 26), that God 'lift up his countenance' (יִשָּׂא יְהוָה פָּנָיו) and 'grant peace' to the petitioner? The first of these requests has already been granted to Jacob-Israel who, it will be recalled, has seen God 'face to face' (Gen. 32: 31) at Peni'el. The second is about to be granted: on his first visit to Bethel Jacob had vowed that the Lord should be his God 'if I return to my father's house in peace' (Gen. 28: 21). His return to Bethel for a second visit might properly be described as a return 'in peace', now that he is at peace with Esau, and the indigenous inhabitants of the land present no threat to him.

The epiphany of the Lord takes place, according to LXX, in God's blessing of Israel. When the priests utter the formula of Blessing, they put God's Name upon the people Israel (Num. 6: 23, 27; LXX Num. 6: 23). For the Pentateuch translators, therefore, divine epiphany is defined with reference to God's Name in his blessing of his people. Struggling with the 'man' at the Jabbok, Jacob had asked for a blessing (32: 27) and had demanded to know the man's name (32: 30). The man had duly blessed him and announced Jacob's name as Israel; but he carefully avoided revealing his own name (32: 30), even though, it will be recalled, Jacob could afterwards assert that he had seen God face to face (32: 31). Things are to be the same at Bethel, where God had manifested himself in epiphany before: Jacob's name will be re-confirmed as

Israel, but on this occasion the Name of the One offering that
confirmation will be made explicit (35: 11). This can properly
happen now, LXX suggest, because by the time of his second visit
to Bethel, Jacob-Israel will have been the recipient of the Priestly
Blessing.[77] Its privileges will have been fully granted to the man
whose name is changed to Israel by divine decree.

   Language of epiphany is found again, and most significantly so,
in the LXX Pentateuch at Deut. 33: 2. The Hebrew of this verse is
not easy to understand, and has long presented difficulties to
interpreters. It forms the introduction of a *blessing* explicitly so
titled in Deut. 33: 1 (again, this fact should be noted carefully),
with which Moses blessed the sons of Israel. He begins by telling
how:

. . . the Lord came up from Sinai, and rose (וזרח) from Seir unto them; He
beamed forth from Mount Paran, and came from the ten thousands of
holiness (קדש): from his right hand (went) a fiery flame (אשדת) unto them.

LXX translated as follows:

The Lord came from Sinai, and was manifest (ἐπέφανεν) from Seir to us;
and he hastened from Mount Pharan with ten thousands of Kadesh; from
his right hand were angels with him.

In this version, the Lord's rising (וזרח) for them from Seir is
interpreted as an epiphany (ἐπέφανεν) for us from Seir,[78] as an
introduction to a blessing of the whole of Israel. LXX go on to
speak of this epiphany as involving the myriads of Kadesh: thus
they have vocalized the Hebrew קדש, as the name of a place well
known in the story of the Exodus (Num. 13: 26; 20: 1), doubtless
under the influence of the other place-names in the verse. When
they arrive at the strange and unique word אשדת, however, they
interpret it to mean 'angels', who are consequently placed at God's
right hand.[79] It would seem, then, that an epiphany of the God of

---

[77] For LXX's presentation of the Priestly Blessing, the textual problems
involved, and its relationship to the Hebrew Bible and Aramaic Targums, see discussion in G. Dorival, *La Bible d'Alexandrie, 4: Les Nombres* (Cerf: Paris, 1994),
250–3.

[78] The verb זרח meaning 'rise, come forth' is used of the rising of the sun, as
noted at Gen. 32: 21, where the sun rose for Jacob as he passed by Penu'el.

[79] For a clear account of the difficulties in the Hebrew of this verse, with a
convenient summary of ancient and modern proposed solutions, including the
interpretation of אשדת as 'lightning', see J. H. Tigay, *The JPS Torah Commentary:
Deuteronomy* (The Jewish Publication Society: Philadelphia, 1996), 319–20. The

Israel is already associated in the mind of the LXX translators
with the presence of angels; and angels were likewise a prominent
feature of Jacob's dream when he first visited Bethel (Gen. 28: 12),
thus emphasizing its character of an epiphany. LXX Gen. 35: 7,
therefore, with its language of epiphany, brings us once again face
to face with the angels, whose presence throughout this story of
Jacob's change of name has been conspicuous, and whose new
name Israel the LXX even explain with a verb of which the angels
themselves are subjects.[80]

The scene is thus set for Jacob's second visit to Bethel, and for
the second account of his change of name to Israel. The verse
introducing this episode (35: 9) in any event links what is about to
happen to Jacob's immediate past servitude to Laban. LXX have:

And God appeared to Jacob again in Louza when he came out from
Mesopotamia of Syria; and God blessed him.

Apart from their usual interpretation of Paddan-Aram as Mesopotamia, the translators make two further changes to the Hebrew, in
adding the words 'in Louza', and in providing 'God' as subject of
the final verb 'blessed'. There is to be no doubt that it was God, no
less, who blessed Jacob, and that the place where this happened was
the place of the former epiphany, as LXX 35: 7 had described the
appearing of God on Jacob's first visit to Bethel. It is in this place,
and in no other, that Jacob's new name Israel is now confirmed
according to 35: 10, which in the Hebrew declares:

And God said to him: Your name (is) Jacob. Your name shall no longer be
called Jacob, but Israel shall be your name. And he called his name Israel.

The LXX transform this divine decision to read:

And God said to him: Your name (is) Jacob. It shall no longer be called
Jacob, but Israel shall be your name.

While the translators added material to 35: 10 to drive home their
message, here they have omitted words from the Hebrew, and this

---

meaning of אשׁדת is uncertain. The Rabbis commonly understood it as a compound
of two words, אשׁ 'fire' and דת 'law', and referred it to the giving of the Torah at Sinai
accompanied by fire and smoke: see TO and PJ of Deut. 33: 2; *Sifre Deut.* 343;
Mekhilta de R. Ishmael Beshallaḥ 7:55–7; and cf. the renderings of the Vulgate
(*ignea lex*), Aquila (πῦρ δόγμα), and Symmachus (πυρινὸς νόμος) discussed by A.
Salvesen, *Symmachus in the Pentateuch* (Victoria Press: Manchester, 1991), 171.

[80] See above, pp. 60–6.

is to ensure that they use exactly the same words, ἀλλ'Ἰσραὴλ ἔσται τὸ
ὄνομά σου, 'but Israel shall be your name', as they had put into the
mouth of the man who wrestled with Jacob (32: 29). The Greek
may even be rendered to yield: 'your name Jacob shall no longer be
called Jacob, but Israel shall be your name.' The suppression of the
final part of the verse in Hebrew only serves to underscore this,
and to hint that God's words here are the ratification of a state of
affairs which already obtains. Like other ancient interpreters,
LXX have attempted to answer the question why the change of
name should be reported twice: as we have seen, they have taken
this second account as having a direct association with Israel's
deliberate removal of foreign gods in obedience to the second of
the 'Ten Words', an action which they now link with a ratification
of Jacob's change of name to Israel. And unlike the first account of
this change, the second explicitly states who has conferred the new
name: it is God Himself. On this occasion, Jacob has no need to ask
who might be the author of this momentous decision. As LXX 35:
11 inform us:

And God said to him, I am your God. Increase and multiply. Nations and
assemblies of nations shall come from you; and kings shall go forth from
your loins.

According to the Hebrew, God had identified himself as אל שדי.
LXX have turned this divine title into 'your God'.[81] Having just
renamed Jacob as Israel, God might rightly be perceived by LXX
in this particular setting as the 'God of Israel', who promises to
Israel multitudinous descendants, whereas the Hebrew had spoken
of 'a nation and an assembly of nations' to arise from Jacob-Israel.
This, however, is only part of the divine promise, since LXX of
Gen. 35: 12 continue:

And the land which I gave to Abraham and to Isaac, to you I shall give it.
Yours it shall be; and to your descendants after you I shall give this land.

If Israel is to be father of assemblies of nations, he and they are to
possess the land where this promise is made. LXX once again
heavily emphasize the important elements of the promise, in this
instance the divine gift of the land, by adding words not found in

---

[81] On the renderings of Hebrew שדי by LXX, see S. Olofsson, *God is My Rock: A
Study of Translation Technique and Theological Exegesis in the Septuagint*, Coniectanea Biblica OT Series, 31 (Almqvist and Wiksell International: Stockholm, 1990),
111–16, esp. 112 for LXX Pentateuch.

the Hebrew, 'yours it shall be', and by changing the final words of the Hebrew, 'I shall give the land', to the emphatic 'I shall give *this* land'. The episode is then brought swiftly to a close, LXX making only slight alterations to the Hebrew, noted in the translation below as they occur:

And God went up from him *from* (Hebrew has 'in') the place where He spoke with him. And Jacob set up a pillar in the place where He spoke with him, a stone pillar; and he offered upon it a libation, and poured out oil upon it. And Jacob called the name of the place in which God had spoken with him Bethel. (35: 13–15)

Thus the second visit to Bethel concludes in almost exactly the same manner as the first (28: 18–19).

4. SUMMARY AND CONCLUSIONS

This study has shown beyond doubt the astonishing complexity of the Septuagint's understanding of what Jacob's change of name to Israel, and that name itself, might signify. That complexity was evidently suggested to the translators by the Hebrew Bible itself. They seem to have been impressed by four aspects of the Hebrew parent text in particular. First, there was the given fact of not one, but two biblical accounts of Jacob's being renamed Israel: the one located at the ford of Jabbok, the other at the 'place' Bethel. Next, they noted that the second account of Jacob's being named Israel was associated with a *second* visit by the Patriarch to the 'place' Bethel, and accordingly referred back to his first visit to that 'place' recorded in Gen. 28 for a fuller appreciation of the change of name which forms the conclusion of Jacob's second visit to Bethel. Third, they perceived that the story of Jacob's life, from the time of his sojourn with Laban until his second visit to Bethel, in some manner prefigured or foreshadowed the future events that would overtake his descendants from the time of their slavery in Egypt until they gained possession of the Land of Israel, which God had promised to them.[82] Finally, they observed the part played by Esau in the Hebrew Bible's account of Jacob's being renamed as Israel, and noted how angels were involved in the story, in an imprecise yet suggestive manner.

---

[82] For the use of typology by the Biblical writers, see now M. Z. Brettler, *The Creation of History in Ancient Israel* (Routledge: London, 1998), 34–41, 48–61.

With these four fundamental observations in view, the translators succeeded in expounding the Hebrew text with amazing insight and adroitness. The result, as we have seen, is an almost bewilderingly intricate picture, taking up and integrating into the story direct and indirect references to other biblical texts, and making use of rare words and allusive phraseology to engage the reader in the essentially mysterious and supernatural realities which the name Israel will evoke. Thus the two accounts of the name-change are co-related with the first two utterances of the Ten Words, namely 'I am the Lord your God, who brought you out of the land of Egypt', and 'You shall have no other gods before Me'. LXX present Jacob's fight at the Jabbok and the first account of his change of name as the culmination of a series of events (the servitude under Laban, the escape therefrom, and the covenant on Mount Gilead) corresponding typologically to later Israel's slavery in and exodus from Egypt, and the covenant between God and Israel at Mount Sinai, where the Lord revealed Himself as the one who had brought Israel out of Egypt. Furthermore, LXX introduced into their carefully crafted version of the covenant between Jacob and Laban at Gilead a number of words and expressions derived from their translation of the story of the Sinai covenant. Most significantly, they manage to convey the idea that at Gilead Jacob and Laban were alone when the covenant was made; and that there was a *vision* of God (as there was to be at Sinai, where for forty days Moses was alone), who would exercise his providence in looking after Jacob. The second account of Jacob's name-change follows the putting away of foreign deities, and LXX's account of the Shechem incident, which is so interpreted as to rule out any hint that Israel might assimilate herself to foreign customs or cult.

The many references to *seeing* and the *vision* of God allowed LXX to link these chapters about Jacob to the account of his first visit to Bethel, to the story of Hagar, and to the narrative of the burning bush. Most telling, however, is the network of allusions which they establish with the story of what happened at Mount Sinai, where God told Moses that His *face* could not be seen by mortal man. Once Jacob's name has been changed to Israel, however, he can say that he has indeed seen God *face to face*. LXX made no effort to alter this astonishing remark. They allowed it to stand, because they had already interpreted the name Israel as meaning that Jacob was strong or had strengthened himself either *along with* or *against* God. In other words, LXX suggest that the name Israel be understood in terms of the strengthening of Jacob so that he might be able to withstand vision of the divine.

At the same time, Israel might be explained as one who is strong against an opponent, designated by LXX as θεός, and as strong over other human beings. Indeed, Jacob-Israel goes on to confront his hostile brother Esau, a confrontation which turns out to be a peaceful meeting in the course of which LXX are able to allude indirectly to Jacob's new name, first making the Patriarch say that he has seen Esau's face 'as if anyone might see the face of God', and then having him declare that he will 'be strong on the road' until he joins Esau in Seir. The name Israel is here directly related to Jacob's meeting with Esau, implying that this new name has given him the equipment to cope with his brother's possibly hostile intentions.

Within the larger perspective of LXX's typological understanding of the narrative, however, Jacob-Israel's successful negotiation of the meeting with Esau prefigures the coming day when Israel, under Joshua's leadership, will take possession of the Land. Thus Jacob's struggle with the 'man' and his renaming as Israel must also be understood as God's equipping Jacob, and through him his descendants, with the necessary *strength* to overcome opposition in the fight to obtain their inheritance. For LXX, it is Jacob, and Jacob alone, who *crosses over* into the land of Israel, and that only when he has been renamed as Israel and has seen God 'face to face'.

Once in that Land of Israel, Jacob builds an altar to the God of Israel, and commands his family to get rid of such idols as they may have incidentally acquired. Any notion of assimilation to non-Israelites then occupying the Land is ruled out. Israel shall have no deity but the Lord. All this established, a second visit to Bethel confirms Jacob as Israel, the translators carefully indicating that what happens now is a direct confirmation of what happened at the wrestling bout beside the Jabbok. But here LXX introduce another important theme: they insist that, on the occasion of his first visit to Bethel, Jacob had experienced a divine 'epiphany'. Only very rarely elsewhere in the Pentateuch have they used such language. It is found in their version of the Priestly Blessing, with its petitions for divine blessing, protection, and peace, all of them featuring prominently in the chapters here surveyed. Thus LXX bring the name Israel into direct association with the Priestly Blessing, as its petitions are realized in the person of Jacob-Israel. They speak of 'epiphany' also in Deut. 33: 2, where the phenomenon is associated with angels. Thus, at the end of the story these celestial beings are recalled once more: they had been present when Jacob first visited Bethel, as well as during his stay with Laban and his preparations to meet Esau—just as an angel would be present in the burning bush, and in the pillar of cloud and fire, to lead Israel across the Jordan into the Promised Land.

The angels who appeared on the occasion of Jacob's first visit to Bethel had alerted him to the presence of the Lord in that 'place' (Hebrew מָקוֹם), which turns out to be none other than the house of God and the gate of heaven (Gen. 28: 17). The description of Bethel which we find at this point in the Hebrew Bible is strongly redolent of language which it will use in other places to speak of God's presence in the Temple; the LXX reflect the same, offering a translation which remains very close to the Hebrew.[83] On his second visit to that 'place', Jacob's name is again changed to Israel, a firm connection thus being established between the name Israel and the 'place' which is house of God and gate of heaven. To attentive and discerning readers of LXX, this connection can only be heightened and clarified by the interpretation which the translators placed on the events leading up to Gen. 35: 9–15, and which I have attempted to elucidate here.

---

[83] מָקוֹם occurs frequently in Deuteronomy with reference to the single sanctuary, more fully designated as the place in which the Lord has chosen to make His Name tabernacle: see e.g. Deut. 12: 5; 14: 23; 16: 2, 6, and, with reference to the Temple in Jerusalem, 1 Kings 8: 29; 9: 3. For the expression 'house of God' as designating the Temple, see e.g. Ps. 42:5; 1 Chron. 6: 33; 22: 2, 11. For discussion of the LXX rendering of Gen. 28: 10–22, see Wevers, *Notes*, 448–55.

3
Days Without Number: Jacob, Israel, and Jesus ben Sira

There is something approaching general agreement among students of Jesus ben Sira's wisdom book that the sage had more than a passing acquaintance with Greek literature.[1] In a book published in 1973, Middendorp summarized evidence collected from earlier scholarly writings which, he was inclined to believe, indicated the very considerable extent to which Ben Sira had alluded to poets such as Theognis, Hesiod, and Euripides, and to prose writers like Xenophon.[2] Middendorp may have exaggerated Ben Sira's fondness for Greek literature; indeed, some ten years later he was taken to task on this very matter by J. T. Sanders, who demonstrated that Ben Sira had 'borrowed' from Greek literature less than Middendorp supposed, and had used these borrowings only when their content could be reconciled with Judaism.[3] Sanders himself, while admitting Ben Sira's dependence on the poetry of Theognis, seemed more sympathetic to the idea that Ben Sira had known, and in various subtle ways had used, Egyptian wisdom texts, particularly the wisdom writing ascribed to one Phibis and preserved in Papyrus Insinger.[4] Further evaluation of Ben Sira's use of foreign writings led Alexander di Lella to write, nearly a decade

---

[1] Quotations from the Hebrew text of Ben Sira are given from the edition of P. C. Beentjes, *The Book of Ben Sira in Hebrew: A Text Edition of All Extant Hebrew Manuscripts and a Synopsis of all Parallel Ben Sira Texts* (Brill: Leiden, 1997); the Greek of Sirach is quoted from the edition of J. Ziegler, *Septuaginta Vetus Testamentum Graecum auctoritate Academiae Scientiarum Gottingensis editum* (Vandenhoeck and Ruprecht: Göttingen, 1965); and the Latin and Syriac versions from the edition of F. Vattioni, *Ecclesiastico. Testo ebraico con apparato critico e versioni Greca, latina e siriaca* (Seminario Semitistica: Naples, 1968). Translations are mine.
[2] See T. Middendorp, *Die Stellung Jesus ben Siras zwischen Judentum und Hellenismus* (Brill: Leiden, 1973), 8–24.
[3] See J. T. Sanders, *Ben Sira and Demotic Wisdom*, Society of Biblical Literature Monograph Series, 28 (Scholars Press: Chico, 1983), esp. 25–59.
[4] See ibid. 61–91.

after Sanders had published his monograph, that 'Ben Sira's dependence on several gentile sources seems beyond question'.[5]

The Wisdom of Jesus ben Sira, however, is a profoundly Jewish book. All the scholars referred to above would endorse such a statement, and could point to other distinguished commentators on the Wisdom book to support them. Such would include Victor Tcherikover, who so brilliantly perceived in Ben Sira's writings indications of the gathering storm which would come to be known as the 'Hellenistic Crisis'. Ben Sira, in Tcherikover's analysis, stands firmly in favour of traditional Judaism, and seeks to strengthen it in difficult times.[6] In similar vein, Martin Hengel, commenting on similarities between some of Ben Sira's ideas and Stoic philosophy, observes Ben Sira's faithfulness to biblical models: for the sage, he remarks, Wisdom remains 'God's property', and does not become some impersonal immanent 'world-reason' over which human beings can exert no influence. Most strikingly, he goes on to say: 'Nor did Ben Sira surrender the special election of Israel in favour of an ideal of world citizenship, although he knew of the incomparable "glory of Adam".'[7] Indeed, the central role played by the Jewish people is strengthened, not diminished, by Ben Sira's explicit identification of Wisdom with the Torah of Moses (Sirach 24: 23), and his clear understanding that this Wisdom is located in Israel (Sirach 24: 8).

Hengel's remarks are clearly of very great weight; and, in the final form of the texts as they have been transmitted to us, there are two verses of Ben Sira's book which seem particularly to support what he has to say about the status of Israel and her unique place in the world. The first is Sirach 17: 17, contrasting Israel as the Lord's allotted portion with the Gentiles, who are placed under the authority of other powers. The second is Sirach 37: 25, where the author contrasts the life of human kind, which is as for a few days, with that of Israel, which is for days without number. This verse presents many difficulties, some of which this paper will attempt to explain, and possibly resolve; but it is a verse which cannot be discussed in isolation from other passages where Ben

    [5] See A. A. di Lella, article 'Wisdom of Ben-Sira', in *ABD*, vi. 940.
    [6] See. V. Tcherikover, *Hellenistic Civilization and the Jews* (Atheneum Books: New York, 1974), 142–51.
    [7] See M. Hengel, *Judaism and Hellenism*, trans. J. Bowden 2 vols. (SCM Press: London, 1974), i. 131–53: quotations given here may be found on p. 149.

Sira speaks about Israel. However, when we come to consider in detail what Ben Sira has to say about the people called Israel, and about their ancestor Jacob who received the name Israel from God, we encounter a rather confused state of affairs. A brief survey of those verses which speak of Israel and Jacob will make this plain.

1. ISRAEL AND JACOB IN HEBREW BEN SIRA AND GREEK SIRACH: AN OVERVIEW

It is well known that the great heroes of Israel are celebrated in Ben Sira's poem in praise of the Fathers found in chapters 44–9 of his composition; but Greek Sirach, which is the oldest extant version of the complete text of the Wisdom book, speaks directly of Israel on only eighteen occasions, and of Jacob only eleven times. In the first half of the book (chapters 1–25), with the exception of a single reference to Israel in the Prologue to the Greek Sirach (line 3), only two mentions of Israel find a place (17: 17; 24: 8). In these same chapters the name Jacob is found just three times, at Sirach 23: 12, and 24: 8, 23. No Hebrew manuscript is extant for the equivalent of any of these verses, thereby compounding the problems which some of them appear to present on other grounds. Sirach 17: 17, already signalled as important for our task, is especially perplexing. It declares of God:

> For each nation He has established a ruler:
> But Israel is the Lord's portion.

The setting of this verse within a discussion of God's creation of a humanity equipped with wisdom, knowledge, and a law of life (Sirach 17: 1–24) seems to present problems. No less an authority than M. Z. Segal states bluntly that the sentiment is not apposite here, being plainly an addition, even though he concedes that Ben Sira most likely wrote the verse himself.[8] Likewise, the famous

---

[8] See M. Z. Segal, *Sefer Ben Sira Ha-Shalem* (Bialik: Jerusalem, 1958) [in Hebrew], 103; and cf. J. Haspecker, *Gottesfurcht bei Jesus Sirach. Ihre religiöse Struktur und ihre literarische und doktrinäre Bedeutung*, Analecta Biblica, 30 (Pontifical Biblical Institute: Rome, 1967), 149, n. 54. Note that, in commenting on this verse, Segal, *Sefer Ben Sira*, 106, compared its ideas with Targum Pseudo-Jonathan of Deut. 32: 8; *b. Niddah* 32a; and *PRE* 24. To his observations should be added those of J. Kugel, '4Q369 "Prayer of Enosh" and Ancient Biblical Interpretation', *DSD* 5 (1998), 131–4, which show the verse to be far less 'out of place' than Segal suggested. See further below, pp. 98–9.

statement of Sirach 24: 23, equating Wisdom with the Torah of Moses as an 'inheritance for the synagogues of Jacob', has a prosaic quality leading some to feel that its place in the text may be secondary.[9] Other puzzling features appear when we consider the second half of the book along with the first.

Of the extant Hebrew manuscripts of Ben Sira, only MsB has clear readings referring to Israel and Jacob. The name Israel is found some twenty-one times; but four of these occurrences are found in the poem following 51: 12, which is probably not from Ben Sira's pen.[10] Among the seventeen remaining verses where the name Israel is found, three times (45: 16, 17, 23) we hear of בני ישראל; twice of divine titles including the name Israel, as at 50: 17 (the Holy One of Israel) and 50: 22 (the Lord, the God of Israel); and twice (50: 13, 20) of the congregation of Israel, קהל ישראל. These are standard biblical expressions which, it might be thought, have no particular significance for the author beyond their usual biblical senses. However, it should be observed that all these verses relate directly to the Temple service, and carry with them the clear message that Israel is a society ordered by the One God (often designated by Ben Sira as God Most High), whose constitution and structure is divinely determined. To these, we may add 47: 23, where Jereboam ben Nebat is given his usual appellation of 'the one who made Israel to sin'; and 45: 11, describing the gemstones upon Aaron's vestments as being according to the number of the tribes of Israel (see Exod. 28: 21). Note also 47: 2, with its comparison of David's separation from Israel with the separation of the Lord's portion of fat from a sacrificial offering. Whatever else these verses tell us, they indicate that Ben Sira understood Israel as a distinctive society under the Law of God— the God of Israel—whose character may be discerned in the service offered in the Jerusalem Temple, a sanctuary famous in the Gentile world of the author's day for its lack of any image claiming to represent the deity.

---

[9] See P. W. Skehan, 'Structures in Poems on Wisdom: Proverbs 8 and Sirach 24', *CBQ* 41 (1979), 379, who describes the reference to the covenant here as 'a descent into prose'. The difficulties inherent in reconstructing the supposed Hebrew original of this verse are discussed by B. G. Wright, *No Small Difference: Sirach's Relationship to its Hebrew Parent Text*, Septuagint and Cognate Studies, 26 (Scholars Press: Atlanta, 1989), 243–5.

[10] See P. W. Skehan and A. A. di Lella, *The Wisdom of Ben Sira: A New Translation with Notes*, Anchor Bible, 39 (Doubleday: New York, 1987), 569–71.

This leaves seven surviving instances of the name Israel in Hebrew MsB. One of these, 45: 22, is fragmentary, only the final ל of ישראל remaining; the word may be reasonably restored on the basis of the Syriac, which here reads 'the house of Israel'. The verse states that Aaron has no inheritance in the Land of Israel along with the other tribes; Greek Sirach and the Latin, however, do not refer to Israel here. Even so, Syriac and MsB most likely are original, inasmuch as Ben Sira quite certainly uses the term Israel with reference to the inheritance of the Land.[11] So much is evident from three other verses which are relatively free of textual problems. First, we may consider 36: 11–12 (Sirach 36: 16–17), where the name Jacob also occurs:

Gather together all the tribes of Jacob: and cause them to inherit (ויתנחלו) as in days of old.
Have mercy upon the people called by Thy Name: Israel, whom Thou didst surname as first-born son (ישראל בכור כיניתה).

For our purposes, three items in these verses should be noted. First, Jacob and Israel appear in parallelism in a prayer which carries with it a distinct *reference to the future*: one is reminded of what Ben Sira will say later about the prophet Elijah (46: 10), appointed by God to establish the tribes of Jacob *for the future*.[12] Secondly, Israel emerges here as the one called by God's Name, a theme repeated at 47: 18, but there with regard to Solomon, whom Ben Sira describes as having been called by the honourable Name which is over Israel. This will engage our attention when we come to treat of the third significant item, the note that God surnamed Israel as His first-born son.

Ben Sira directly relates Israel to the notion of inheritance of the land a second time at 46: 1, telling how Joshua was appointed to make Israel inherit after subduing her enemies. Finally, at 44: 23, having spoken of the covenant which God made with Abraham and Isaac, he notes that the divine blessing rested upon Israel's

[11] On the theme of inheritance in Ben Sira, see O. Rickenbacker, *Weisheitsperi-kopen bei Ben Sira*, Orbis Biblicus et Orientalis, I (Vandenhoeck and Ruprecht: Göttingen, 1973), 139–41, and J. Marböck, 'Das Gebet um Rettung Zions Sir 36, 1–22 (G: 33, 1–13a: 36, 16b–22) im Zusammenhang der Geschichtsschau ben Siras', in J. B. Baur and J. Marböck (eds.), *Memoria Jerusalem. Freundesgabe Franz Sauer zum 70. Geburtstag* (Akademische Druck-u. Verlagsanstalt: Graz, 1977), 109.

[12] Note that Sirach 46: 10 and the Latin version read 'sons of Israel', whereas Hebrew MsB and the Syriac have 'the seed of Jacob'.

head, and that God established him with a blessing and granted to
him his inheritance (ויכוננהו בברכה ויתן לו נחלתו). Such is the
reading of the body of the text of MsB. A highly significant marginal variant, however, in place of 'He established him with the
blessing', reads ויכנהו בבכורה , 'and He surnamed him as first-
born son'. The status of this reading will inevitably occupy us
later; for the moment, however, its affinity with Israel's inheritance
in the land should be carefully noted. It will also be recalled that
the LXX translators of Gen. 32: 22–33 had perceived in those
verses a clear relationship between the meaning of the name Israel,
and the qualifications, strength, and superiority needed by its
bearer for possession of the land to which he was entitled.

All this brings us at last to Ben Sira 37: 25, a verse which apparently offers some insight into what the name Israel might signify.
But this same verse also brings us back to the problem highlighted
at the beginning of the section, since some of the most learned
students of Ben Sira's work regard it as secondary, and difficult in
the way that 17: 17 appears to be difficult.[13] Does this verse truly
represent an addition to the text? Why is it included in extant
manuscripts? And what relationship might it bear to other statements about Israel found in the witnesses to Ben Sira's work which
most likely belong to the original stratum of the Wisdom book?
Some of the complexities involved in attempting to answer these
questions will become all too apparent as we approach this verse.

2. JACOB, ISRAEL, AND DAYS WITHOUT NUMBER

The difficulties inherent in Ben Sira 37: 25 become clear the
moment one sets out the different forms it has assumed in the
manuscripts and versions. It is represented in two Hebrew witnesses, MsB and D from the Cairo Geniza: it is not represented in
the anthology of MsC, which does include some verses from this
chapter.[14] In MsB, according to the critical edition published by
Pancratius Beentjes, the following fragmentary line of Hebrew has
survived:

חיי איש מספר ימים   וחיי עם ישראל [. . . . . .] ישורון

---

[13] See e.g. Segal, *Sefer Ben Sira*, 242; Skehan and di Lella, *The Wisdom of Ben
Sira*, 435, 437.

[14] On the anthological character of Cairo Geniza MsC, see Beentjes, *The Book of
Ben Sira*, 3, 16–17.

which may be taken as meaning: 'the life of (a) man consists of a few days: but the life of the people of Israel . . .' In the margin of the manuscript is written 'Jeshurun', itself almost certainly a variant for the name Israel. The line is placed among verses describing various sorts of חכם. Following the verse enumeration provided by Beentjes, MsB offers the following order of things, given here in a literal rendering:

> 37: 20　And there is a wise man who, when his speech is rejected,
> 　　　　Then all his enjoyable food is diminished (from him).
> 37: 22　And there is a wise man who is wise for himself:
> 　　　　The fruit of his knowledge is (seen) in his own person.

The verse about Israel numbered 37: 25 follows; and then a fragmentary form of 37: 24, of which the only legible words remaining are 'a wise man'; 'enjoyment', and '. . . him'. A gap in the manuscript then precedes 37: 27, which begins: 'My son, in your lifetime test your soul.'

MsD appears to follow a similar verse order, except that a verse not found at all in MsB, and conventionally numbered 37: 26, intervenes between verses 24 and 27. Here we have a continuous legible Hebrew text, in translation running as follows:

> 37: 25　The life of man (אנוש) is for few days:
> 　　　　But the life of Jeshurun is for days without number.
> 37: 24　A wise man for himself is satisfied with enjoyment:
> 　　　　And all who see him shall call him blessed.
> 37: 26　A wise man among the people shall inherit glory (ינחל כבור):
> 　　　　And his name endures in life everlasting
> 　　　　(ושמו עומד בחיי עולם).

Taken together, these two Hebrew manuscripts suggest that the transmission of this verse was confused; and we can thus readily understand why Segal felt that 37: 25 is out of place. He saw it as an addition attempting to explain how the wise man's name stands out publicly in secular life, for which reason in Greek Sirach it stands immediately before a verse telling of the honour the wise man has among his people (see below). Furthermore, says Segal, the verse interrupts the continuity of the whole passage: he explicitly compares it with 17: 17, which, as we have seen already, he regards as an addition to the text of Ben Sira.[15]

The evidence of MsD, however, is informative, since its inclusion of 37: 26, lacking in MsB, possibly provides a reason why 37:

---

[15]　See Segal, *Sefer Ben Sira*, 242.

25 is placed in this section of the book, and what its purpose might be. For the additional verse, 37: 26, tells of one wise among people who shall inherit glory; and here we encounter not only the notion of inheritance, which Ben Sira elsewhere explicitly links to Israel, but also mention of a name enduring to life everlasting, the latter nicely reflecting the 'days without number' ascribed earlier to Israel. Taken on its own terms, MsD's progression of events is quite logical, and could be taken to mean that the wise man's name will endure to everlasting life in the same manner as Israel's days are without number, the not stated, but easily understood, connection between the two things being the fact that Wisdom's residence is none other than Israel's Temple in Jerusalem, and that 'length of days is in her right hand' (Prov. 3: 16). Segal's anxiety about the verse can largely be relieved, therefore, in respect of the MsD tradition. But this very observation raises the question whether the scribe of MsD perceived the same difficulty which Segal was to encounter centuries later, and so ordered the Hebrew as to produce a text which read more smoothly.

Greek Sirach places 37: 25 after 37: 24, a verse which follows it in MsD and (probably) MsB. Next we find 37: 26, which we found to be lacking in MsB, but present in MsD (as translated above) as well as MsC. The Greek version of these two verses reads:

37: 25   ζωὴ ἀνδρὸς ἐν ἀριθμῷ ἡμερῶν,
         καὶ ἁι ἡμέραι τοῦ Ισραηλ ἀναρίθμητοι.

37: 26   ὁ σοφὸς ἐν τῷ λαῷ αὐτοῦ κληρονομήσει τιμήν (many witnesses
         have πίστιν),
         καί τὸ ὄνομα αὐτοῦ ζήσεται εἰς τόν αἰῶνα.

37: 25   The life of (a) man consists in a number of days:
         And the days of Israel are not to be numbered.

37: 26   The man wise among his people shall inherit honour (many
         witnesses have 'faith, faithfulness'),
         And his name shall live for ever.

The Latin version of these two verses is essentially the same as this Greek. Again, if we read these two verses in the light of our observations just made regarding MsD, some of Segal's anxiety about them can possibly be reduced. The Syriac version, however, altogether omits 37: 25, apparently, says Segal, because of Christian hatred for the people of Israel.[16] Segal's explanation for Syriac's omission is certainly possible, although it should be noted

---

[16]   Ibid.

that the Syriac translator seems to have had no difficulty retaining
not only 17: 17, but also 36: 17 (Vattioni 36: 12), with its description of Israel as God's first-born son. That 37: 25 is firmly fixed in
the Greek tradition is admitted by Skehan and di Lella; but they,
in translating this verse in the course of their commentary, place
it in brackets, admitting that in the Hebrew the form of the verse is
unstable.[17] This is so in more than one respect, and, in my view,
that instability tells its own, intriguing story which may account
for the uncertainty surrounding the verse itself, and other parts of
Hebrew Ben Sira. It is to that instability that we must now turn.

3. ISRAEL AND JESHURUN: THE HEBREW BIBLE

According to MsB 37: 25a, the life of אִישׁ, 'man' or 'a man', is for a
few days מספר ימים. MsD has אנוש instead of אִישׁ, which Segal
claims is a better reading, אנוש reflecting more clearly the weak-
ness of humankind as described, for example in Psalm 103: 18.
The expression מספר ימים 'a few days', is found again in MsB as a
marginal reading at 41: 13 where, however, the body of the text
reads ימי מספר. MsD of 37: 25 has ימים מספר, however, a biblical phrase found in Num. 9: 20, and one which the main text of
MsB at 41: 13 may possibly have read originally.

The second part of the verse in MsB has only three words surviving, וחיי עם ישראל, 'but the life of the people of Israel', with
the word 'Jeshurun' written in the margin as a variant for 'Israel' or
'the people of Israel'. This much is intimated by MsD, where the
second hemistich reads וחיי ישרון ימי אין מספר, 'but the life of
Jeshurun is days without number'. Greek Sirach and the Latin of
the first hemistich of the verse could conceivably represent a
Hebrew similar to either MsB or MsD; in the second hemistich,
however, the Greek and Latin clearly read 'Israel', and not 'Jeshurun', and thus differ from the two surviving Hebrew manuscripts.
In the Hebrew tradition, however, the title Jeshurun is clearly
established in both MsB and MsD, and requires elucidation.

Jeshurun is a rare designation for Israel.[18] It is found only four
times in the Hebrew Bible, at Deut. 32: 15; 33: 5, 26; and Isaiah 44:

---

[17] See Skehan and di Lella, *The Wisdom of Ben Sira*, 434.

[18] For modern treatments of Jeshurun, see the useful overview by M. J. Mulder,
article 'ישׁרון', *yᵉšurûn*', in *TDOT*, vi. 472–7, which includes (p. 477) a brief discussion of Ben Sira 37: 25.

2. The first of these texts is ironic in tone, and is best left on one side until the other verses have been considered. We thus begin with Deut. 33: 5, standing at the beginning of the blessing with which Moses blessed Israel before his death. He begins by speaking of God's coming from Sinai, Se'ir, and Paran with myriads of holy ones to give the Torah to Israel through Moses, and continues:

ויהי בישרון מלך בהתאסף ראשי עם יחד שבטי ישראל

which may be rendered: 'and He (either God or Moses) was king over Jeshurun, when the heads of the people are (or: were) gathered together as a union of the tribes of Israel'.[19] In this verse, the title Jeshurun cannot be separated from the tribes of Israel as a united people, accepting the sovereignty of the Torah mediated by Moses and authored by God, who is ultimately King. Although dating from a much later time than Ben Sira, it may be important to record here the view of the Rabbinic Sages set forth in *b. Rosh Ha-Shanah* 32b, that this is one of only three verses in the Pentateuch which can be taken as speaking directly of God as King.[20] Consequently, it finds a celebrated place in the liturgy, being one of the texts employed for *Malkiyyot* of the Musaf service for Rosh Ha-Shanah. Mention of such a thing might be thought superfluous here, were it not for the fact that the only other known appearance of the noun Jeshurun in a text from Second Temple times (apart from Hebrew Ben Sira) occurs precisely in a liturgical text. In the Qumran Daily Prayers document 4Q503 (4QpapPrQuot) *4QDaily Prayers*[a] frags. 29–32. 6, we read [. . .]ישורון [. . .]ל יברך[א. . .], the restored text meaning '[. . . may G]od bless Jeshuru[n'. This Qumran prayer was intended for recitation on the evening of the 16th Nisan, the day following Pesah.[21] Now it was

---

[19] That it was Moses who was king over Jeshurun is the view of many midrashic passages, including *Exod. Rab.* 2: 6; 28: 4; 52: 1; *Lev. Rab.* 1: 3; 31: 4; 32: 2; *Num. Rab.* 15: 13; *Song Rab.* 1. 21. 1; 7. 6. 1; *Eccles. Rab.* 10. 20. 1.

[20] The same Talmudic passage, however, records R. Huna's statement to the effect that R. Jose accepted Deut. 6: 3 as a *malkiyyot* verse, along with Deut. 4: 35, 39; but R. Judah's dissent from R. Jose's opinion with respect to all three of these other verses is also stated.

[21] Cited after García Martínez and Tigchelaar, *Dead Sea Scrolls*, ii. 1000–1. For discussion of this Qumran fragment, see B. Nitzan, *Qumran Prayer and Religious Poetry* (Brill: Leiden, 1994), 50, 56, 70; and for analysis of the prayer formulae used in the manuscript see D. Falk, *Daily, Sabbath and Festival Prayers in the Dead Sea Scrolls* (Brill: Leiden, 1998), 21–43.

precisely at Pesaḥ that the status of Israel as God's first-born son came to the fore in biblical narrative: according to Exod. 4: 22–3, God proclaimed Israel as His first-born, and threatened to kill Pharaoh's first-born son if the latter would not let Israel go from Egypt. As a title for Israel, Jeshurun is almost inseparable from the notion that Israel is God's first-born son, as we shall discover presently.

Toward the close of Moses's blessing of Israel, at Deut. 33: 25, the title Jeshurun recurs in the context of a benediction addressed to the tribe of Asher. The verse which precedes it is of particular interest for our purposes, and we quote both verses in Hebrew followed by an English translation.

33: 25   ברזל ונחשת מנעלך וכימיך דבאך
33: 26   אין כאל ישרון רכב שמים בעזרך ובגאותו שחקים

33: 25   Your bars shall be iron and bronze, and like your days, so shall
          your strength be.
33: 26   There is none like God, O Jeshurun, [or: There is none like the
          God of Jeshurun],
          Who rides on heaven for your help, and whose majesty is in
          the clouds.

The juxtaposition of these verses could lead a reader to the opinion that Jeshurun was somehow connected with Israel's 'days' and with her 'strength', if indeed the rare word דבאך means 'your strength': so LXX understood it (ἡ ἰσχύς σου) some seventy years or more before Ben Sira wrote.[22] The God associated with this title is one who brings help from heaven, and whose majesty is universal by virtue of its heavenly qualities. Furthermore, these verses offer the exegetically agile a possibility of linking the title Jeshurun with length of days as a divine gift for Israel.

At Isaiah 44: 2 Jeshurun is once more set alongside the idea of divine assistance for Israel, who is spoken of as made and formed by the Lord Himself:

Thus says the Lord, your maker and the One who fashioned you from the womb, who shall help you: Do not fear, O my servant Jacob, even Jeshurun, whom I have chosen.

This statement is explicit and straightforward. Jeshurun is a title indicating the privileges granted to Israel as one chosen by God

---

[22] Such is certainly the general Jewish understanding of this rare word: see below, pp. 104–5, for the Targumim; *Num. Rab.* 14: 4; and Rashi's commentary on the verse.

Himself, whose very beginnings testify to the people's election as a unique nation. When, to return to Deut. 32: 15, the title is used in criticism of Israel's wayward behaviour in the desert, one senses something approaching parody in the biblical writer's words, bearing in mind the exalted status of the one who is Jeshurun, fashioned and made by God Himself:

> But Jeshurun grew fat and kicked: you grew fat, you became thick-set, you were covered with fat: and he forsook God who made him, and despised the Rock of his salvation.

No other verses in the Hebrew Bible speak of Jeshurun. Reading them, Ben Sira could conclude that the title itself was one of highest honour, referring to God's creation, formation, and making of Israel as a unique, elect people, constitutionally ordered as a kingdom under His authority embodied in the Torah given through Moses, an order which might be referred to as a יחד or union. Jeshurun might also be associated with strength and length of days, and with a majestic God who is ready to come to the help of this Jeshurun. Besides all this, there is the distinct possibility that, in certain circles, Jeshurun was a title of Israel which could be used in solemn prayer at the season of Pesaḥ, celebrating the Lord's victory over the enemies of His first-born son, Israel. This is not, however, likely to be the whole story about Jeshurun. Above we referred to the LXX Pentateuch, a rendering of the Books of Moses into Greek made probably a mere seventy or so years before Ben Sira wrote his Wisdom book. The translators had a very specific understanding of the title Jeshurun, which Jesus ben Sira could quite easily have known.

4. ISRAEL, JESHURUN, AND THE SEPTUAGINT

On the surface, the name Jeshurun might seem to be derived from, or related in some way to, the Hebrew root ישר, which has the sense of 'be upright, be straight, be right'. One might expect the word, therefore, to mean something like 'the just one; the upright one', and as such to represent, perhaps, a gloss on the name Israel which might be patient of a bad sense if it were understood in the light of Hosea 12: 4–5, as one who wilfully strove with an angel.[23] LXX,

---

[23] See Mulder, art. 'ישרון', 473–4. This same understanding of the name was familiar to the writer of Wisdom of Solomon 10: 10–12, who alluded to Jacob-Israel as 'the just one' guided by wisdom, who showed him God's kingdom and gave him knowledge of holy ones or holy things (a reference to Gen. 28: 10–22 and Jacob's

however, systematically translated the word as ὁ ἠγαπημένος, 'the beloved one'.[24] Significantly, the translators used this word again in Moses's blessing to represent the Hebrew adjective יָדִיד, 'beloved', at Deut. 33: 12, where Benjamin is addressed with the words: 'the beloved of the Lord shall tabernacle safely.'[25] This masculine singular passive participle form is used nowhere else in LXX Pentateuch, except in Deut. 33: 12 and in the three verses which include mention of Jeshurun. It is closely related to the word ἀγαπητός. Both words in LXX are patient of a very particular sense, which Joachim Schaper has delineated as follows: 'According to its common contemporary usage, ἀγαπητός ἠγαπημένος implied the meaning "only son". This may refer to the concept of the only-begotten son of the κύριος. At the very least, the term points to an exalted personality, the "loved one", on whom God bestows the honour of his special attention.'[26] Schaper's comment here is made (at least in part) with reference to LXX Psalm 28: 6, where ἠγαπημένος appears to translate a Hebrew place-name שִׂרְיוֹן (Sirion, another name for Mount Hermon), the translators evidently understanding this word, or interpreting it, as if it were יְשֻׁרוּן, Jeshurun. Furthermore, LXX Psalm 28: 6 compares this 'beloved' with a young unicorn, υἱὸς μονοκερώτων, a striking description which Schaper has discussed in some detail, concluding that it represents an ancient Messianic title.[27]

Although the LXX translation of the Psalms was made some time later than that of the Pentateuch, Schaper's researches are suggestive, and compel us to examine more closely the LXX of the Pentateuchal verses where Jeshurun is found. Of these, Deut. 33: 25–6 stand out as very likely having some direct relevance for the

first visit to Bethel), and who acted as umpire in his strong contest, so that he might know that piety was stronger than any other thing (a reference to Gen. 32: 25–33). For detailed treatment of these verses, see A. Butterweck, *Jakobs Ringkampf am Jabbok. Gen. 32,4ff in der jüdischen Tradition bis zum Frühmittelalter*, Judentum und Umwelt, 3 (Peter Lang: Frankfurt-am-Main, 1981), 59 ff.

[24] See Mulder, art. 'יְשֻׁרוּן', 473–4, including brief notices about the other ancient versions; and C. Dogniez and M. Harl, *La Bible d'Alexandrie, 5: Le Deutéronome* (Cerf: Paris, 1992), 329.

[25] For further comment on the LXX version of this verse, see Dogniez and Harl, *La Bible d'Alexandrie*, 348.

[26] See J. Schaper, *Eschatology in the Greek Psalter*, WUNT 2. Reihe 76 (Mohr: Tübingen, 1995), 92.

[27] See Schaper, *Eschatology*, 113–26; id., 'The Unicorn in the Messianic Imagery of the Greek Bible', *JTS*, N.S. 45 (1994), 117–36.

Ben Sira passage which concerns us. The Hebrew of these verses has been given above. They appear in LXX as follows:

33: 25 σίδηρος καὶ χαλκὸς τὸ ὑπόδημα αὐτοῦ ἔσται καὶ (omitted by
        Codex Vaticanus) ὡς ἀι ἡμέραι σου ἡ ἰσχύς σου
33: 26 οὐκ ἔστιν ὥσπερ ὁ Θεὸς τοῦ ἠγαπημένου ὁ ἐπιβαίνων ἐπὶ τὸν
        οὐρανὸν βοηθός σου καὶ ὁ μεγαλοπρεπὴς τοῦ στερεώματος
33: 25 His sandal shall be iron and bronze: as your days, so shall be
        your strength.
33: 26 There is none like the God of the beloved one: He who rides
        on the heavens is your helper, even the magnificent One of
        the firmament.

The final word of verse 25 in the Hebrew is the rare דׇבְאֶךָ. It is found only here in the whole Hebrew Bible, and LXX, along with Targums Onqelos and Pseudo-Jonathan, took it to signify 'strength'.[28] LXX's choice of Greek ἰσχύς here is striking, inasmuch as 'strength' is fundamental to that version's explanation of the name Israel: at Gen. 32: 29 the translators had declared that Jacob was named Israel with an address from the supernatural being who announced the title: 'because you have strengthened yourself/been strong with God (ὅτι ἐνίσχυσας μετὰ θεοῦ), and with men your are powerful.'[29] In addition, LXX bring the second half of verse 25 into much closer association with verse 26, and its reference to the God of Jeshurun, than does the Hebrew. Whereas the Hebrew of verse 25 speaks of the tribe of Asher, addressing it in the second person throughout and saying 'your bolts shall be iron and bronze, and as your days, so shall your strength be', LXX speak of Asher in the third person, as they have done since verse 24. Thus in the Greek we read that *his*, that is, Asher's, sandal shall be iron and bronze. Suddenly, however, the person changes; and we find ourselves learning: 'as *your* days, so shall *your* strength be.' This enables an interpreter to read LXX Deut. 33: 25 in direct association with the following verse 26, which speaks of the God of Jeshurun in the second person singular, riding on the heavens as *your helper*. If the verses are read in this way, as the LXX seem to have understood them, then Jeshurun can easily be related to

[28] A cognate for this word is known from Ugaritic, and is noted by J. Tigay, *The JPS Torah Commentary: Deuteronomy* (The Jewish Publication Society: Philadelphia, 1996), 333, 411: he gives as translation 'your security'.

[29] See above, pp. 60–6. In the light of Jewish military successes in the Hasmonean period, the LXX interpretation of the name Israel might well have commended itself to a large and growing Jewish constituency at home and abroad.

'days' and 'strength', the latter in any event being LXX's particular fundamental interpretation of what the name Israel means. In this tradition of interpretation of Deut. 33: 25–6, therefore, we have almost certainly uncovered the Scriptural foundation underlying the claim in Ben Sira 37: 25, that the days of Jeshurun, of Israel, are without number.

As we have seen, MsD and the margin of MsB of Ben Sira 37: 25 read 'Jeshurun', while the body of the text in MsB of 37: 25 reads 'Israel'. In respect of this, it may be significant to note that the Aramaic Targumim of those biblical verses which include Jeshurun almost invariably understand the title as a reference to Israel, the house of Israel, or those belonging to the house of Israel. This is the case for Deut. 32: 25 (TO, PJ, TN, FTV, and also Peshitta); 33: 5 (TO, PJ, and Peshitta); and 33: 26 (TO, PJ, TN, FTV, and Peshitta). Targum Jonathan of Isaiah 44: 2 retains Jeshurun (Peshitta has Israel); while TN and FTV of Deut. 33: 5 interpret it as 'those of the house of Jacob'. This evidence permits us to speculate whether a scribe transmitting the text of Ben Sira might not at some point have felt that the word Jeshurun in 37: 25 was obscure, and needed explanation, one such being ready to hand in those exegetical traditions which ultimately informed the Targumim and the Syriac Peshitta, which he then proceeded to copy into the text of MsB. The Targumim also understood the rare Hebrew דבאך of Deut. 33: 25 much as LXX had done. Thus TO took the second half of that verse to mean: 'and like the days of your youth, so shall be your strength.' PJ has: 'and like the days of their youth, so shall they be strong in their old age', an interpretation whose essential aspects are encountered also in TN, FTV, and FTP. The Syriac Peshitta, too, reads 'your strength'.

What I have said here may go some way towards identifying the Scriptural authority undergirding Ben Sira 37: 25, and may also offer some assistance in explaining the textual 'instability', to borrow Skehan and di Lella's term, attendant upon the title Jeshurun. It is possible, however, that my observations on this point may have wider implications, since the text of Ben Sira again shows 'instability' in another verse which describes Israel's status as God's first-born son, a status which is implicit in the title Jeshurun as interpreted by the tradition preserved in LXX, where Jeshurun means 'the beloved one'.

5. ISRAEL AS GOD'S FIRST-BORN SON

Ben Sira 44: 19–23 is a famous section describing God's relations with the three great Fathers Abraham, Isaac, and Jacob. We are told how God Most High entered into a covenant with Abraham (44: 20), a privilege extended to Isaac because of Abraham his father (44: 22). Thereafter, Ben Sira tells us, the blessing rested on Jacob's head; and the Sage goes on to tell of God's further activity in respect of Jacob. In MsB of Ben Sira 44: 23 this reads: ויכוננהו בברכה ויתן לו נחלתו, which may be rendered as 'and He established him with a blessing, and gave to him his inheritance'. In the margin of MsB, however, a variant reading of the first two Hebrew words appears as ויכנהו בבכורה, 'and He surnamed him as first-born'. The Hebrew words of these variants look and sound very similar and may, indeed, represent a play on words, since first-born sonship, according to biblical tradition, should convey blessing. But there had been a well-known disagreement between Jacob-Israel and his elder brother Esau over the matter of first-born sonship and of blessing (Gen. 25: 29–34; 27: 35–6); and the tradents of both Hebrew Ben Sira and Greek Sirach may have been concerned to indicate that Jacob-Israel was the rightful possessor of both. Greek Sirach 44: 23 is closer to the main text of MsB's Hebrew than it is to the marginal note, reading 'He acknowledged him in his blessings, and made a grant to him by way of inheritance', a rendering which the Latin closely follows, both versions suggesting Jacob's right to blessing and inheritance as first-born. The Syriac, however, seems aware of the Hebrew noted in the margin of MsB, and describes blessings resting 'upon the head of Israel whom He called My son, My first-born, Israel', thereby introducing into the text a direct reference to God's words in Exod. 4: 22, בני בכרי ישראל, 'Israel is My son, My first-born'. That the present Syriac text represents an explanatory paraphrase of a statement of the kind found in MsB's margin seems highly probable.

Skehan and di Lella evidently sense that the marginal reading of MsB in this verse represents what Ben Sira is likely to have written, since they reproduce it in the body of their translation of the verse as 'God acknowledged him as the first-born', merely noting the main text of MsB and Greek Sirach's rendering of the verse without further comment.[30] Segal adopts much the same

---

[30] See Skehan and di Lella, *The Wisdom of Jesus Ben Sira*, 503–4.

procedure.[31] Indeed, since 44: 23 begins with a reference to God's blessing of Jacob, a second reference to blessing in the very next breath, so to speak, does seem unimaginative, not to say unpoetic; and this very observation, subjective as it may be, tends to support Skehan and di Lella's decision on the primary nature of MsB's marginal reading. Furthermore, Ben Sira MsB and Sirach 36: 12, along with the Latin and Syriac, speak of Israel as God's first-born son immediately after a verse which prays that God gather the tribes of Jacob and make them inherit as in days of old; so the general idea of Israel as first-born son with rights of inheritance is not one which the Sage is seeking to avoid. This raises acutely the question why the main text of MsB and Sirach should have chosen to speak of blessing here, rather than of Israel as first-born. And might this state of affairs be linked in some way with MsB's marginal reading of Jeshurun at 37: 25, since only-begotten sonship (which by definition must be first-born sonship) is intimately bound up with the earliest explanation of Jeshurun known to us?

To answer these questions, we need to recall that the oldest interpretation of Jeshurun known to us treats the title as signifying 'beloved', ἠγαπημένος, a word which carries with it also the sense of 'first-born son'. As far as Ben Sira's work is concerned, this ancient interpretation points us in two directions. The first leads us back, as it were, towards Israel, explicitly called by God 'My son, My first-born' at Exod. 4: 22, where Israel's status is set in parallel with that of Pharaoh's first-born son. Exod. 4: 22, indeed, provides Moses with the rationale for his demands to Pharaoh: the latter must let Israel go from Egypt, since Israel is the Lord's first-born son. Should Pharaoh refuse this request, the Lord will kill Pharaoh's first-born son, a threat which Pharaoh's obstinacy turns into reality. First-born Israel, however, is protected from the destruction meted out to Pharaoh's first-born by the Pesaḥ offering: most likely this fact of sacred history was uppermost in the mind of the author of Qumran daily prayers in speaking of Jeshurun, the beloved first-born son, in the blessing allotted for the sixteenth day of Nisan during the week of Pesaḥ.

On the other hand, Jeshurun 'the beloved' may point also in the direction of Solomon, the son of David. Ben Sira 47: 18 (MsB) describes Solomon as 'called by the honourable Name which is called over Israel', having earlier spoken of Israel as 'the people

[31] See Segal, *Sefer Ben Sira*, 309.

called by Your Name, whom you surnamed as first-born son' (36:
12). This Hebrew text appears to place Solomon in parallelism
with Israel;[32] and once again LXX may assist us in further explaining this state of affairs. We noted above that ἠγαπημένος, 'beloved',
is very rare in LXX Pentateuch, being found only as a Greek
equivalent for Hebrew Jeshurun and for one other word. That
word is ידיד, 'beloved', whose use in the Pentateuch is confined to
Deut. 33: 12. Now according to 2 Sam. 12: 25, the prophet Nathan
gave to King Solomon a distinctive personal name, a name which is
borne by no other biblical character. It was ידידיה, 'beloved of the
Lord', and was conferred upon him בעבור יהוה ('on account of
the Lord').[33] To anyone with a knowledge of Scripture, this distinctive name could not fail to recall what Moses had said in his
blessing of the tribe of Benjamin at Deut. 33: 12, that the beloved
of the Lord, ידיד יהוה, should tabernacle in safety, ישכן לבטח. In
addition, this Deuteronomic verse is almost invariably understood
in Jewish tradition as referring to the building of Solomon's
Temple, which was located in the territory of the tribe of Benjamin.[34] And there can be little doubt that Ben Sira wishes his
readers to connect Solomon directly with Moses's blessing of Benjamin recorded in Deut. 33: 12, for he alludes to the text of that
blessing fairly directly at 47: 12 in speaking of King David's son:

   [ ]בעבורו עמד אחריו   בן   [ ]שכיל שוכן לבטח

For his sake there stood up after him a [w]ise son, tabernacling in safety.

Like Benjamin, Solomon too will 'tabernacle in safety' according
to Ben Sira, building the sanctuary on Mount Zion and thus
bringing to fruition the divine promise to plant Israel on the
mountain of His inheritance (Exod. 15: 17); and with all this evi-

---

[32] Although not directly named in the text, Solomon implicitly plays a part in
determining what Israel means according to the *Book of Jubilees*: see below, pp.
141–4.

[33] Segal, *Sefer Ben Sira*, 328, rejects any link between Solomon's name Jedidiah
and Ben Sira's statement in 47: 18 that this king was called by the 'honourable
Name'. His view seems unlikely, given the evidence assembled here; but his suggestion that Solomon's name is naturally associated with 'peace', a term which was
later used as a substitute for the Divine Name (e.g. at *Sifre Num.* to Num. 6:24),
makes sense, and in some respects strengthens the present argument.

[34] See TN, PJ, TO, FTV of Deut. 33: 12; *b. Yoma* 12a; *Meg.* 26a; *Sotah* 37a; *Gen.
Rab.* 93: 6.

dence to hand, we may at last be in a position to offer more informed comment on Ben Sira 37: 25 and some of the other textually problematic verses which concern Israel's status and significance for Ben Sira.

6. CONCLUSIONS: JESHURUN AND ISRAEL

The Hebrew manuscripts B and D of Ben Sira 37: 25 used the rare and honorific title Jeshurun to speak of Israel, a title so specific that copyists of the text of Ben Sira's work, and the grandson who rendered his grandfather's book into Greek, might have been tempted to 'explain' it, by replacing it with the more familiar 'Israel' in the manner of the Targumic tradition. In any event, Jeshurun was associated, as we have seen, with the notion of 'strength' through the Scriptural verse Deut. 33: 26 as understood by the LXX translators, who represent the oldest Jewish interpretation of the Books of Moses known to us. 'Strength' was precisely the leading idea in the LXX's particular understanding of the name Israel, as their translation of Gen. 32: 29 had made plain; and thus it was that Jeshurun itself might be closely linked to an interpretation of the name Israel having to do with strength, in respect of angels and men. In addition to all this, the LXX translators understood the word Jeshurun itself to mean the 'beloved one', or the 'first-born son', of the Almighty; this is the oldest interpretation of the word known to us, and it is redolent not only of God's direct statement (in Exod. 4: 22) that Israel is His first-born son, but also of royal status, since the king of the house of David had been directly promised *first-born* status by God, according to Psalm 89: 28. That same Psalm had promised also that this first-born's descendants and throne would endure for ever (Ps. 89: 5, 37), a promise neatly coinciding with the LXX understanding of Deut. 33: 25–6 that the 'beloved first-born', Jeshurun, should enjoy a strength (characteristic of Israel according to LXX) corresponding to his 'days'.

I have attempted to show that those Hebrew manuscripts of Ben Sira which refer to Jeshurun and days without number read rather more smoothly and coherently than many students of the Wisdom book suggest. But among those who transmitted the text of Ben Sira's work there was evidently some uncertainty about how, and where exactly in the book, the material we are considering should be set forth. Corresponding to this, not surprisingly, I pointed to a similar textual 'instability' in verses of Hebrew Ben Sira which speak of Israel either as one surnamed first-born, or as one established with blessing. Both these things were vitally important for those who transmitted the work of Ben Sira, and it would seem that they adopted differing ploys to ensure that both were adequately represented. This was so, it would seem, because Jeshurun, blessing, first-born sonship, and inheritance in their several ways speak of Jacob-Israel as that nation should be, ideally blessed by God and entering into a divine inheritance, an inheritance which includes the Temple service, fully inaugurated in the days of Solomon, who was the 'beloved son' of David and, as king, reckoned as the first-born son of the Almighty and representative of His own blessed first-born, Israel who is called Jeshurun.

In all this, the *future* of the people called Israel is concerned. The different textual witnesses to Ben Sira's work agree that the future 'days' of Israel ought to be, like those of the first-born king of the house of David, like those of the beloved one of God, everlasting or 'without number', in contrast to the common lot of humankind. This forward-looking direction is suggestive, inasmuch as the title Jeshurun will appear, many centuries after Ben Sira's lifetime, in an important section of *Genesis Rabbah* which treats of Israel's name and its meaning; and there, as we shall see, Jeshurun will be named in association with the final redemption of Israel and with the resurrection of the dead.[35] Quite what the links between the material scrutinized here and that Rabbinic midrash might be, it is not possible to say; but some links there most probably were. Thus, mention of Jeshurun in the Qumran daily prayers, composed later than Ben Sira's day but still within the Second Temple period, points to the blessed first-born status of Israel in the context of the Pesaḥ, a festival which in itself conveys some of the most passionate hopes for Israel's future redemption.[36] Another Qumran text, 4Q369, seems clearly to speak of Israel as the recipient of God's inheritance, as His first-born son, and as a prince and ruler over all God's earthly habitation, like the first-born king, the son of David. The surviving manuscript of this text

---

[35] See below, pp. 252–4.

[36] The handwriting of the fragments of 4Q503 is Hasmonean, dating from between 100 and 75 BCE, according to their editor M. Baillet, *DJD. VII. Qumrân Grotte 4 III (4Q482–4Q520)* (Clarendon Press: Oxford, 1982), 105.

appears to date from the Herodian period.[37] In the last resort, all these themes are deeply rooted in the Hebrew Bible, and could be used by any sufficiently sensitive exegete as the need arose; but the possibility that an exegetical tradition which explained the name Israel in terms of Jeshurun was known to Ben Sira, and persisted for many centuries until it appeared again in the Rabbinic midrash in a different dress, should not be discounted.

[37] For the date of the manuscript, see H. Attridge and J. Strugnell, in *DJD. XIII. Qumran Cave 4. VIII*, 354. This text is often referred to as the 'Prayer of Enosh'; but in reality it treats of Jacob and Israel. This has been demonstrated beyond reasonable doubt by J. Kugel, '4Q369 "Prayer of Enosh" and Ancient Biblical Interpretation', where he adduces material from Ben Sira closely related to verses discussed here: see esp. 129–32, 139–40.

4
Jacob Becomes Israel: The Story as Told by the *Book of Jubilees*

At first blush, it would seem that the *Book of Jubilees* offers an account of Jacob's change of name to Israel far removed from the interests of the LXX translators. The writing of the book was most probably completed a century or more after the translation of the LXX Pentateuch, sometime around the middle of the second century BCE; and, whatever and however many the reasons for its publication, its urgent appeal to the Jews to remain true to their ancestral faith in the face of foreign worship is impossible to mistake.[1] Indeed, the proper worship of the One God, and its right conduct in time and space, represent a major preoccupation of the author(s) of this remarkable treatise. *Jubilees* is sometimes classified along with other writings of a similar kind as 'rewritten Bible', a description which seems not inappropriate given its radical re-presentation of those parts of Jacob's story which concern this study.[2] Despite its extensive alterations to the biblical

---

[1] For discussion of the date and composition of *Jubilees*, see G. W. E. Nickelsburg, *Jewish Literature Between the Bible and the Mishnah* (SCM: London, 1981), 78–9; J. C. VanderKam, 'The Putative Author of the Book of Jubilees', *JSS* 26 (1981), 209–17; K. Berger, *Das buch der Jubiläen: Jüdische Schriften aus hellenistisch-römischer Zeit*, Band II, Lieferung 3 (Mohn: Gütersloh, 1981), 295–301; E. Schürer, *The History of the Jewish People in the Age of Jesus Christ*, rev. edn. ed. G. Vermes, F. Millar, and M. Goodman, vol. III. 1 (Clark: Edinburgh, 1986), 311–14; and J. C. VanderKam, article 'Jubilees' in *ABD*, iii. 1030–1.

[2] On 'rewritten Bible', see G. Vermes, *Scripture and Tradition in Judaism*, 2nd edn. (Brill: Leiden, 1973), who was the first to make use of the expression; G. W. E Nickelsburg, 'The Bible Rewritten and Expanded', in M. E. Stone (ed.), *Jewish Writings of the Second Temple Period, CRINT* section 2 (Van Gorcum: Assen, 1984), 89–156 (97–106 for *Jubilees* in particular); J. C. Endres, *Biblical Interpretation in the Book of Jubilees*, CBQMS 18 (Catholic Biblical Association of America: Washington, 1987); and C. A. Brown, *No Longer be Silent: First Century Jewish Portraits of Biblical Women* (John Knox Press: Louisville, 1992). An excellent demonstration of what 'rewritten Bible' meant in practice may be found in J. D. Levenson, *The Death and Resurrection of the Beloved Son* (Yale University Press: New Haven, 1993), 173–99.

narrative, however, *Jubilees* seems to recognize certain exegetical traits already manifest in LXX while ignoring or rejecting others. Given the complexity both of the book and its relationships with older and contemporary Jewish literature, it will be helpful to summarize at the outset some of the major changes it introduces into the biblical story.

First, and most dramatically, *Jubilees* reduces the two accounts of Jacob's change of name (Gen. 32: 25–33; 35: 9–15) to one brief note (*Jub.* 32: 17–20), eliminating altogether the story of his fight with the 'man' and the biblical explanation of the name Israel as somehow bound up with that struggle. Secondly, the book records the note about Jacob's new name in a specially constructed setting, made up of mostly non-biblical tradition: this details Levi's appointment to the priesthood and Jacob's celebration of the feast of Sukkoth for seven days at Bethel, after which he plans to build an enduring sanctuary for God (*Jub.* 32: 1–16). Thirdly, events leading up to the change of name are so presented as to stifle any mention of Jacob's virtual enslavement by Laban; his theft of teraphim; his complaints to Rachel and Leah about Laban's behaviour; and Laban's angry accusations against Jacob (Gen. 29: 1–31: 54). Finally, while Jacob's father Isaac plays no part in the biblical account of these events, *Jubilees* ascribes to him a crucial role in blessing Jacob's two sons Levi and Judah, ancestors of the future priestly and royal houses respectively (31: 8–32). Only when this blessing has been accomplished is Jacob's new name Israel announced to him. Properly to appreciate how the author(s) of *Jubilees* understood the significance of the name Israel, we must look closely at the book's transformation of the biblical narrative, retracing the path followed by Jacob from Paddan-Aram to Bethel.

I. JACOB'S DECISION TO LEAVE LABAN

While he lived in Mesopotamia, Jacob's relations with Laban were not always smooth: so the Bible relates (Gen. 29: 15–31: 21), and *Jubilees* concurs. The immediate cause of Jacob's decision to leave his father-in-law, however, is given in *Jub.* 28: 29–30. Jacob's oxen, sheep, asses, camels, and male and female slaves kept on increasing (see Gen. 30: 43), such that Laban and his sons became jealous; Laban therefore withdrew his sheep from Jacob's care, and watched him with evil intent. This last remark may be a develop-

ment of the comment in Gen. 31: 2, that Laban's countenance was
not favourable to Jacob as it had been before. The note that Laban
withdrew his sheep from Jacob is not found in Genesis, and is
presumably intended to emphasize the sense of Laban's jealousy
of Jacob.[3] Laban is here presented not as a slave-driver, but as a
jealous man, a presentation continued in *Jub.* 29: 1–4. There we
encounter a radical abridgment and restructuring of Gen. 31: 2–21
and other related verses. Thus we are told (*Jub.* 29: 1) that, after
Rachel had given birth to Joseph, Laban went to shear his sheep, a
three days' journey. This brief note is constructed from three separate biblical texts, namely the note of Joseph's birth at Gen. 30:
22–5, a reference to Laban's sheep-shearing in Gen. 31: 19, and a
report 'on the third day' to Laban that Jacob had fled, recorded in
Gen. 31: 22. What *Jubilees* has suppressed in this short note is of
some interest: while Laban shears his sheep, Rachel steals the
teraphim (Gen. 31: 19), and Jacob leaves without warning Laban
(Gen. 31: 20–2).[4]

According to *Jub.* 29: 2, Laban's journey to shear sheep provided Jacob with a pretext to summon Leah and Rachel and
persuade them to leave for the land of Canaan. This differs completely from the biblical account, in which Jacob summons his
wives *before* Laban goes shearing (Gen. 31: 4) and seeks to turn
them against their father by listing the injustices to which he has
subjected Jacob (Gen. 31: 5–13). Neither does the Bible refer to
the land of Canaan at this point: this is named only in Gen. 31:
18. Indeed, *Jubilees* has suppressed for the moment what the Bible
gives as the real reason for Jacob's desired flight, namely, a direct
command of the Lord given in Gen. 31: 3 as: 'Return to the land
of your fathers (אבותיך) and to your kindred (ולמולדתך), and I
shall be with you.' This command does feature in *Jubilees*' account,
but in a somewhat 'lop-sided' way, since the next verse, *Jub.* 29: 3,
makes Jacob tell his wives that he had seen everything in 'the
dream', and that 'He' (presumably God) had told him to return
to his father's house. The biblical order of events has been
disrupted: in Genesis we hear first of the Lord's command to

[3] For the tendency of *Jubilees* to 'whitewash' the Fathers' reputation (even
Laban's) and to 'schematize' the biblical narration of this episode, see Endres,
Biblical Interpretation, 108–11, where the correspondences between the biblical
verses and their counterparts in *Jubilees* are set out in tabular form.
[4] Cf. ibid. 110.

Jacob that he return (Gen. 31: 3), and only later of a dream involving the angel of God urging Jacob to return to the land of his kindred (Gen. 31: 11–13). *Jubilees* has telescoped the two celestial commands, and has taken them quite literally to mean that Jacob should return to the place where Isaac lives, as he eventually did according to *Jub.* 31: 5. The result of this conversation with his wives is then reported: they agree to go with Jacob, saying 'wherever you go, we will go with you' (*Jub.* 31: 5). Their response evokes in the reader memories of Ruth's faithful response to Naomi,[5] that she will go wherever her mother-in-law goes (Ruth 1: 16). So Jacob blessed the God of Isaac and the God of Abraham, a detail not found in the Bible, and taking his wives, children, and possessions, crossed the river into the land of Gilead secretly, without telling Laban. In this way *Jub.* 29: 4 reconstructed Gen. 31: 20–1, with its note that Jacob 'stole Laban's heart' in acting secretly.

What has been achieved by this reconstruction of the biblical narrative? First, Jacob appears as a free man, entirely in control of his actions and in charge of his household. No one, except God, tells him what to do. There is no hint that Laban has enslaved him, or is in some sense his overlord; indeed, Laban's maltreatment of Jacob is minimized. Jacob controls his wives, and makes his decision to leave Mesopotamia without their advice; whereas the Bible has him list Laban's injustices towards him (Gen. 31: 5–10) before he tells them of the angel's order to depart (Gen. 31: 11–13), so that they may recognize that their father has treated them as foreigners and stolen what is rightfully theirs, and that it is therefore proper for Jacob to obey God's command (Gen. 31: 14–16). Secondly, although the divine commands to Jacob are telescoped and altered, it is clear that Jacob's departure is dictated only by God, not by his wives or his own cunning. His enterprise is a pious one, as his formal blessing of the God of his fathers before his departure shows. Finally, there is no hint as yet that Jacob is eventually travelling to Bethel. In the Bible, the angel who speaks to Jacob identifies himself as the God of Bethel, where Jacob has anointed a pillar and vowed a vow (Gen. 31: 13).

---

[5] So Endres, ibid. 110–11. Note that Ruth was the ancestress of King David (Ruth 4: 13–22), a matter of some moment for the author of *Jubilees*, who will make much of the royal status of Israel with possible 'messianic' intent: see further below, pp. 153–4.

Jub. 29: 1–4 suppresses this information, breaking associations between Jacob's time with Laban and his earlier experiences in Bethel. What *Jubilees* wishes to underscore is not Bethel, but *Gilead* as Jacob's secret destination in his flight from Laban (*Jub.* 29: 4).

2. JACOB IN THE LAND OF GILEAD

According to *Jub.* 29: 5, Jacob set out for Gilead on the twenty-first day of the first month, that is, at the end of the celebration of Pesaḥ, 'in the seventh year of the fourth week', being *anno mundi* 2135. The Bible, of course, gives no such date; nor does it indicate when Laban overtook Jacob (*cf.* Gen. 31: 23, 26), which *Jub.* 29: 5 specifies as the thirteenth day of the third month.[6] Both Gen. 31: 24 and *Jub.* 29: 6 agree, however, that God appeared in a dream to Laban; according to the former, God then ordered Laban to speak neither good nor evil with Jacob. *Jubilees* interpreted this to mean that God did not allow Laban to harm Jacob, and that he talked with him.[7]

According to the biblical account, they talked for some time, the section Gen. 31: 26–55 consisting for the most part of a record of their speech. *Jub.* 29: 7–9 reduced this lengthy dialogue to the following brief notice:

And on the fifteenth *day* of the month Jacob prepared a feast for Laban and all those who had come with him; and Jacob and Laban made an agreement that day under oath that neither would cross the highlands of Gilead against the other. And he erected a cairn there *to stand* as a witness: that is why that place is called The Cairn of Witness—after the cairn.

The interest of *Jubilees* is plain to see. The pact between Jacob and Laban is dated precisely to the fifteenth day of the third month, which in the never-changing solar calendar espoused by this book is the feast of Shavuoth, the feast of Weeks or Oaths, the feast of the covenant par excellence, as *Jub.* 6: 15–22 insists at length.[8]

---

[6] Cf. Endres, *Biblical Interpretation*, 111. My observations on the significance of the dates differ from, but do not contradict, his remarks.

[7] See further ibid.

[8] On the significance for the *Jubilees* calendar of the dates given in the verses under discussion, see Annie Jaubert, *La Notion d' alliance dans le Judaïsme aux abords de l'ère chrétienne* (Seuil: Paris, 1963), 90–1; J. van Goudoever, *Fêtes et*

Jacob and Laban make this covenant—for that is what it amounts
to—on the same feast as God made a covenant with other great
Patriarchs, but most notably with Noah and with Moses.[9] Taking
this notice in conjunction with the report of *Jub.* 29: 5, that Jacob
left Mesopotamia on the twenty-first day of the first month, at the
end of Pesah, it becomes evident that *Jubilees*, like LXX, associated Jacob's departure from Mesopotamia with the departure of
Israel from Egypt, and the agreement between Jacob and Laban
with the future covenant at Sinai. This apparent concord between
Jubilees and LXX, however, is of little significance. Unlike LXX,
Jubilees does not develop the themes of Israel's servitude, deliverance from slavery, covenant with God, and eventual possession of
the Holy Land. As we have seen, Jacob's residence with Laban is
not presented as a time of servitude; and the covenant which the
two men make, solemn though it might be, is with reference only to
the land of Gilead. It is nothing more than a solemn contract
between the two men that they should not cross the highlands of
Gilead with hostile intent, a heap of stones being set up as a
witness to the pact.

Thus *Jubilees* strictly limits the significance of the Gilead episode to practical political and military arrangements in respect of
that circumscribed territory. Eliminated altogether are the biblical
verses in which Laban upbraids Jacob for his conduct, accusing
him of ingratitude, deception, and theft of teraphim (Gen. 31: 26–
30); Jacob's reply to these charges (Gen. 31: 31–2) and Laban's
fruitless search for the teraphim (31: 33–5); Jacob's angry recital of
Laban's maltreatment of him (31: 36–42); and Laban's sulky
insistence that all Jacob's property really belongs to him (31: 43). It
is only when they have reached this impasse in their disagreement
that Laban suggests they make a covenant (Gen. 31: 44). *Jubilees*
will have none of this: Jacob must take the initiative and make a
feast, and only then will the two men make the agreement together
(*Jub.* 29: 7). The biblical tale about the making of the cairn and its
Aramaic and Hebrew names is much reduced, while mention of a

Calendriers Bibliques, 3rd edn. (Beauchesne: Paris, 1967), 99–100; and on the sig-
nificance of the feast of Shavuoth for *Jubilees*, see J. Potin, *La Fête Juive de la
Pentecôte*, 2 vols. (Cerf: Paris, 1971), vol. I, 124–31; G. Vermes, *The Complete Dead
Sea Scrolls in English* (Penguin Press: Harmondsworth, 1997), 44, 79–80; and J. C.
VanderKam, *Calendars in the Dead Sea Scrolls* (Routledge: London, 1998), 27–33.

[9] Thus the writer 'elevated this covenant to the peak of solemnity': so Endres,
Biblical Interpretation, 118.

pillar which Jacob set up (Gen. 31: 45, 49) is entirely left out. *Jubilees* says nothing of Mizpah, nor of the meaning of that term (Gen. 31: 49).[10] Instead, we find an insertion of non-biblical material into the story (*Jub.* 29: 9–11), giving Gilead's original name as 'the land of the Rephaim', describing these 'giants', and noting the extent of their land and the seats of their kingdom. They were very wicked; so the Lord destroyed them, and they were replaced by the Amorites. R. H. Charles believed that this insertion represents a form of propaganda, drawing attention to victories won by the Maccabees over the Seleucids; but this view is not without difficulties, since the text does not associate the places named with battles, but with seats of rulership.[11] This non-biblical interpolation seems to me to have a much simpler purpose: it implicitly indicates that Gilead is legally Israelite territory, since both groups of its original inhabitants, the Rephaim and Amorites, were said in Scripture (Gen. 15: 16; Deut. 3: 11–12; Josh. 24: 18) to be destined to be dispossessed of this land. Indeed, *Jub.* 29: 12 notes that after making the agreement Jacob *sent Laban away*, and he went back to Mesopotamia, while Jacob himself returned to Gilead.[12]

3. JACOB CROSSES THE JABBOK AND MEETS ESAU

According to *Jub.* 29: 13, Jacob crossed the Jabbok on the eleventh day of the ninth month: 'And on that day his brother Esau came to him, and was reconciled, and left him for the land of Seir; and Jacob was living in tents.' This brief note is followed by a report of Jacob crossing the Jordan and settling beyond it (*Jub.* 29: 14). From there, he sent clothes, food, and drink to his father and mother, a non-biblical tradition which occupies some considerable space (*Jub.* 29: 15–20). As Endres has noted, *Jub.* 29: 13 represents a 'pithy restatement' of Gen. 32: 3–22; 33: 1–17, omitting vast tracts of biblical material.[13] What is omitted reveals something of the purpose of *Jubilees* at this point. First, and most significantly, all mention of angels, messengers, and 'camps' found in the

---

[10] Further discussion in ibid. 112.

[11] See R. H. Charles, 'The Book of Jubilees', in R. H. Charles (ed.), *The Apocrypha and Pseudepigrapha of the Old Testament* (Clarendon Press: Oxford, 1913), ii. 57.

[12] For the correlation of this note to Gen. 31: 55; 32: 1, see Endres, *Biblical Interpretation*, 113.

[13] See ibid. 114.

biblical text (Gen. 32: 2, 3, 4, 7, 8, 9, 11, 22; 33: 8) is expunged: Jacob makes none of the elaborate preparations for a meeting with Esau so carefully described in Gen. 32: 4–21. Also missing is the Bible's concern with the gifts for Esau 'crossing over' before Jacob himself 'crosses over'.[14] I have already noted the omission of Jacob's fight with the 'man' and his change of name at a place he names Peni'el (Gen. 32: 22–33); also lacking are the details of his encounter with Esau (Gen. 33: 1–10), and the subsequent journeys which Jacob and Esau undertook (Gen. 33: 11–16).

Both the Hebrew Bible and LXX understood Jacob's change of name to Israel as mysteriously, but inseparably, linked to his encounter with a possibly hostile and violent Esau. *Jubilees* absolutely rejected this biblical datum. Implicit also in the Hebrew Bible, and more clearly enunciated in LXX, is the intimate connection between Jacob's new name, won after a struggle, and the title of his descendants to the Land of Israel, to be claimed after a conquest. *Jubilees* also excludes notions such as these. Rather, *Jubilees* presents Jacob as someone completely in control of events, achieving his ends without difficulty, struggle, or opposition. He recognizes no authority other than that of heaven, with the single exception of his parents. Not to Esau does Jacob send presents, but to Isaac and Rebekah, regularly, with almost liturgical precision, four times in the year, on dates corresponding to the four festivals (*Jub.* 6: 23–30) established by Noah after the flood.[15] This piety towards parents contrasts with Esau's wilful behaviour in marrying a foreign wife and leaving his parents (*Jub.* 29: 17–19). Indirectly, this set of circumstances will be related to Jacob's change of name, but in a way quite unknown to Scripture: Jacob's continuing close relations with his parents means that Isaac will eventually bless Jacob's two sons Levi and Judah (*Jub.* 31: 13–22), a necessary preliminary before Jacob can be named Israel.

---

[14] The reconciliation of Jacob and Esau is effected without any planning on Jacob's part. It is as if the author wishes to show how Jacob's progress towards his ultimate goal, the place Bethel, is assured without hindrance, the implication being that God has smoothed the way for this to happen.

[15] See *Jub.* 29: 16; the note on this verse by Ch. Rabin in his revision of the translation of R. H. Charles in Sparks, *The Apocryphal Old Testament*, 92; VanderKam, *Calendars*, 29–30; and the important observations on the house of Isaac and Rebekah as being Abraham's tower (representing fidelity to Patriarchal traditions) noted by Annie Jaubert, *La Notion d'alliance*, 155–6.

The choice of Levi and his descendants for the priesthood (*Jub.* 32: 1–9) forms the immediate setting for Jacob's change of name to Israel. Before telling of Levi's consecration, however, *Jubilees* leaves the reader in no doubt that this man was worthy of such an office. The rape of Dinah by Shechem resulted in bloody vengeance exacted on all the men of Shechem by Jacob's sons Simeon and Levi (Gen. 34). The story is well known, and *Jubilees* perceived in it events which proved beyond doubt that Levi merited the priesthood. *Jubilees* once more substantially altered the original biblical narrative to emphasize Levi's merit. Of the many departures from the biblical text which the book displays, the following are the most salient for present purposes. First, Dinah is presented as a mere child of 12 years of age (*Jub.* 30: 2). Secondly, *Jubilees* omits the discussions between Shechem's father and Jacob's sons following Shechem's request to marry Dinah; the insistence by Jacob's sons that the men of Shechem be circumcised; and their agreement to undergo the rite in the light of the supposed advantages it will bring them (Gen. 34: 4–24). Instead, *Jub.* 30: 3 records the immediate anger of Jacob and his sons on hearing that Shechem had *defiled* Dinah, and their secret planning of revenge. Thirdly, the sudden massacre of the men of Shechem by Simeon and Levi was God's will:

And Simeon and Levi came to Shechem . . . and killed every man they found *there* . . . because they had dishonoured their sister Dinah. And let no Israelite girl ever be defiled in this way again; for judgement was ordained in heaven against them—that all the Shechemites should perish by the sword, because they had committed an outrage in Israel. And the Lord delivered them into the hands of Jacob's sons . . . so that it might not happen again in Israel that an Israelite virgin should be *thus* defiled. (*Jub.* 30: 4–6)

It should be noted particularly that this judgement 'ordained in heaven' had been triggered by 'an outrage in *Israel*'. Dinah had been defiled; and such an irruption of impurity into Jacob's immediate family needed swift and effective countermeasures. Defilement, or impurity, is here displayed as the abomination it is; the judgement of heaven requires radical measures in response to it. The corollary of this is clear. Jacob and his family, here thought of as a group termed 'Israel', are to be holy, and utterly separate from impurity and defilement. They are, in short, to be the 'holy nation' which God requires them to be, according to the law of Exod. 19: 6. The profound influence which this Scriptural verse has exercised on the author of *Jubilees* as regards the meaning of the term 'Israel' will soon become apparent. For the moment, it will be enough to note that *Jubilees* regards the action of Levi, Simeon, and Jacob in removing from Israel the defilement brought about by the Shechem incident as proof that a 'holy nation' is already prepared.[16]

Up to this point in its narrative, *Jubilees* has used the terms 'Israel' and 'Israelite' very sparingly. The first verse of the first chapter of the book refers to the exodus of the Israelites from Egypt as the time when *Jubilees* was revealed to Moses. Obviously, by that time and from the author's perspective, the nation known to the world as Israel has come into existence. The last verse of that same chapter (1: 29) refers to the elect of Israel and their future bliss. Mention of Israel thus creates in that introductory chapter an *inclusio*: we have before us a chapter which, for the most part, consists of a speech by God to Moses about the 'future' of His people. Throughout, this 'people' is described as God's inherit-ance (1: 19–21), the descendants of Abraham, Isaac, and Jacob (1: 7, 28), and are contrasted with the Gentiles whose practices (says God) they will at times follow to their own detriment. What this might mean is made explicit in *Jub.* 1: 10–18. Israel will forsake God's Law and commandments, the festivals of the covenant and the Sabbaths, the holy offerings, the tabernacle and sanctuary, in favour of foreign cults, which *Jubilees* describes in lurid detail (1: 11). They will forget God's precepts, and commit error in respect of new moon, Sabbath, festival, and jubilee (1: 14). Israel, then, is God's chosen people: it observes His Law and commandments, his festivals, the covenant and the Sabbaths, the holy offerings, and the tabernacle and sanctuary; and it keeps his precepts and correctly observes new moon, Sabbath, festival, and jubilee. In the future,

---

[16] See esp. Jaubert, *La Notion d'alliance*, 97, on the fundamental importance of Exod. 19: 6 for the author, and for a general discussion of purity and impurity in *Jubilees*. Exod. 19: 6 is alluded to also at *Jub.* 16: 18; 33: 20, and is discussed further below, pp. 129–30. For the specific notions of purity involved in the author's understanding of Israel as a holy nation, see C. Werman, 'Jubilees 30: Building a Paradigm For the Ban on Intermarriage', *HTR* 90 (1997), 1–22; and, with special regard to the influence of Exod. 19: 6 on the purity ideals espoused by *Jubilees*, see C. E. Hayes, *Gentile Impurities and Jewish Identities* (Oxford University Press: Oxford, 2002), 73–91.

Israel will be truly like this, and God will build his sanctuary in their midst and dwell with them (1: 17). To ensure this, God will circumcise their hearts and create in them a holy spirit: then shall they be his children, and He their Father (1: 23–5), and He will appear in the sight of all and be recognized as God of Israel, father of all the sons of Jacob, and king on Mount Zion forever (1: 28).

The opening chapter of *Jubilees*, therefore, effectively defines 'Israel' as a distinct people in the world, separate from all others, who are under the tutelage of the one and only God, the 'God of Israel'. This people is required to obey God's Law and the commandments it contains: as *Jubilees* will go on to indicate, these commandments offer guidance for every aspect of life. In this opening chapter, however, it is evident that the author was determined to bring to the fore the commandments governing Israel's worship of God. These *in particular*, it would seem, define Israel. This observation may be confirmed with reference to the author's further uses of 'Israel' or 'Israelites' in the earlier chapters of the book. He chooses these terms first and foremost when speaking of Sabbath law (2: 27–9, 33); but they are also used in passages detailing laws of purity affecting admission to the sanctuary (3: 14); the Day of Atonement (5: 17–19); covenant renewal at the feast of Shavuoth (6: 11, 13, 20–2); the calendar regulating the feasts (6: 32–8); the sanctification of Israel through circumcision (15: 27–34); and the laws relating to the feasts of Sukkoth (16: 28–30) and Mazzoth (18: 19). In particular, the covenant of circumcision is singled out by the author as an 'eternal ordinance' (15: 28), indicating God's choice of 'Israel' whom He alone rules, set apart from the Gentiles, who are ruled by angels.[17] Otherwise,

---

[17] *Jub.* 15: 30–2, elaborating an understanding of Deut. 32: 8–9 preserved in LXX, which reads: 'When the Most high divided the nations, when He scattered abroad the sons of Adam, He set the boundaries of the nations according to the number of the angels of God. And the Lord's portion was His own people, Jacob: Israel was the allotment of His inheritance.' Traditionally, it was held that there are seventy angels corresponding to the seventy Gentile nations: see PJ of Gen. 11: 7–8; Deut. 27: 8; 32: 8; Hebrew *Test. of Naphtali* 8: 4–5; *PRE* 24: 4. *Jub.* 15: 30–2 stood somewhat opposed to Scriptural texts like Dan. 10: 13, 20, 21; 12: 1 (stating that Michael is Israel's 'prince'), as noted by R. H. Charles, *The Book of Jubilees* (Black: London, 1902), 112. For an exposition of LXX Deut. 32: 8–9, which is closely related to *Jubilees* at this point, see C. Dogniez and M. Harl, *La Bible d'Alexandrie, 5: Le Deutéronome* (Cerf: Paris, 1992), 325–7; and for the Targum, see R. le Déaut, *Targum du Pentateuque, IV: Deutéronome*, Sources Chrétiennes, 271 (Cerf: Paris, 1980), 266–7.

'Israel' can be used to distinguish God's people from the violent Gentiles (23: 23), and in explication of laws relating to marriage (28: 7).

It will be recalled that *Jubilees* has so rewritten the biblical story that Jacob's change of name to Israel had not taken place before the incident at Shechem. But Gen. 34: 7 had used the term Israel, and *Jubilees* followed suit, taking the opportunity to use the term liberally thereafter in describing this episode. Thus, in the verses following *Jub.* 30: 4–6 we read of what will happen to 'a man in Israel' who marries his daughter to a Gentile: the girl 'shall be rooted out of Israel' (30: 7). No harlot or uncleanness is ever to be found 'in Israel', because 'Israel is holy to the Lord' (30: 8). On the heavenly tablets it is written about 'the stock of Israel' for ever, that a man who causes defilement is to be stoned (30: 9). A man who defiles his daughter by marrying her to a Gentile is to be rooted out before 'the whole people of Israel' (30: 10); and Moses is ordered to issue commandments to 'the sons of Israel' about these matters (30: 11). Given the delineation of 'Israel' in earlier chapters of *Jubilees* as a people bound to the proper worship of God in the festivals with their attendant temple sacrifices and ceremonies, the emphasis on Israel as a pure, undefiled people which is so emphasized in this rewritten account of the Shechem story is entirely appropriate. Indeed, the author of *Jubilees* makes the whole matter explicit:

And Israel will not be free from this uncleanness if anyone has a wife of the Gentiles' daughters, or has given any of his own daughters to a man who is a Gentile. For there will follow plague on plague and curse on curse, and every judgement and plague and curse will fall on Israel if they do this thing . . . or . . . defile the Lord's sanctuary or profane his holy name . . . and there will be no receiving at anyone's hands of fruits and offerings and whole-offerings and fat, nor will the sweet smell of his soothing sacrifices be accepted; and so will every man or woman in Israel fare who defiles the sanctuary. (*Jub.* 30: 14–16)

The purity of the people in themselves is here presented as a necessary corollary to Israel's status as the only group of human beings who have the privilege of worshipping and serving God in company with the two highest orders of angels (2: 30–1; 6: 18–22; 15: 26–8), and to whom God has entrusted the commandments specifying the precise ways in which He should be worshipped on earth. It is hardly surprising, then, that *Jub.* 30: 7 extends the law of Leviticus 21: 9, according to which the daughter of a priest

who plays the harlot shall be punished by burning, to all and any
Israelite women who are given over by their menfolk to inter-
course with the Gentiles. By this means, the author implies that
the rules of priestly purity relating to marriage are binding on
layfolk, and that all Israel is therefore to be regarded as a priestly
nation.[18] God's command given in Exod. 19: 6 that Israel be
ממלכת כהנים וגוי קדוש ('a kingdom of priests and a holy nation'),
is again to the fore. The action of Simeon and Levi at Shechem,
therefore, preserved Israel as a pure and undefiled and priestly
people, and made possible the next stage in the divine plan,
namely, the appointment of Levi and his sons for the priesthood
continually.

   Here we must pause awhile. From the outset of his work, the
author of *Jubilees* suggested to his readers what he meant by
'Israel'. The Shechem episode, however, provided him with a
timely opportunity to develop his understanding of that designation, inasmuch as it allowed him to define 'Israel' as a people
uncontaminated by impurity or uncleanness. Levi is in part
responsible for Israel's remaining pure and clean in a crucial situation. The angel who dictates the book to Moses can therefore
proclaim:

And the descendants of Levi were chosen for the priesthood, and to be
Levites, that they might minister before the Lord (as we *do*) continually;
and Levi and his sons are blessed for ever, for he showed zeal to execute
righteousness and judgement and vengeance on all those who rose up
against Israel. And so blessing and righteousness are inscribed on all the
heavenly tablets as a testimony in his favour before the God of all. And we
(*i.e.* the angels) remember the righteous acts which the man did in his

---

[18] Cf. K. Berger, *Das Buch der Jubiläen*, 471; Endres, *Biblical Interpretation*,
139–47; R. A. Kugler, *From Patriarch to Priest: The Levi-Priestly Tradition from
Aramaic Levi to Testament of Levi* (Scholars Press: Atlanta, 1996), 158–61. All
these writers discuss *Jub*. 30: 9–10 and the interpretation of 'giving one's seed to
Moloch' (Lev. 18: 21) found there, and its relationship to Rabbinic halakhah; but
see further G. Vermes, 'Bible and Midrash: Early Old Testament Exegesis', in
P. R. Ackroyd and C. F. Evans (ed.), *The Cambridge History of the Bible*, vol. 1
(Cambridge University Press: Cambridge, 1970), 214–16, repr. in *Post-Biblical
Jewish Studies* (Brill: Leiden, 1975), 74–6. For the central significance of purity
and a state of holiness as distinguishing Israel from the nations, see E. Schwarz,
*Identität durch Abgrenzung. Abgrenzungsprozesse in Israel im 2. vorchristlichen
Jahrhundert und ihre traditionsgeschichtlichen Voraussetzungen, zugleich ein Beitrag
zur Erforschung des Jubiläenbuches* (Europäische Hochschul Schriften. Theologie:
Frankfurt-am-Main, 1991).

lifetime, at every period of the year: for a thousand generations they will
be recorded, and the blessings resulting from them will come upon him
and upon his descendants after him; and he has been described in the
record on the heavenly tablets as a friend and a righteous man . . . and I
have commanded you to tell the sons of Israel not to commit sin nor
transgress the commandments nor break the covenant that has been
ordained for them, but to keep it and be *themselves* described as friends.
(*Jub.* 30: 18–22)

Before ever *Jubilees* records Jacob's change of name to Israel, it
speaks of his installing Levi into the priesthood (32: 3). In some
sense, therefore, before Israel can become a reality in history it
must possess a priesthood which will endure through time, and
Levi's descendants are marked out by their ancestor's behaviour at
Shechem as priests who shall henceforth minister before the Lord
like the angels, *continually*.[19] This last word indicates that Levi's
priestly descendants are not simply earthly counterparts of the
angels (though they are certainly that). It recalls one of their most
important functions, namely, the offering of the Tamid, the *continual* offering, the daily sacrifice of a lamb each morning and evening
in the Temple Service. For the author of *Jubilees*, it is no
exaggeration to say that this is the most important of all offerings,
instituted in the time of Noah as an act of atonement for every
generation, and perpetually recalling Noah's sacrifice after the
flood and the covenant which that act of worship effected (*Jub.* 6:
1–14, esp. v. 14 for the Tamid). Angelic worship of God is 'perpetual, continual'; and Levi's ministry before the Lord will both
replicate this celestial service and ensure the 'perpetual' offering of
the Tamid on earth. At the same time, *Jubilees* makes it abundantly
clear that Levi and his descendants are worthy of this continuing
priesthood because Levi himself displayed such zeal as to ensure

[19] This qualification serves to distinguish the priesthood of Levi and his sons
from the priesthood exercised by earlier Patriarchs such as Adam (*Jub.* 3: 27),
Enoch (*Jub.* 4: 25; cf. 7: 36–8), Noah (*Jub.* 6: 1–3), and Abraham and Isaac (*Jub.* 15:
2–3; 21: 7–16). Charles, *The Book of Jubilees*, 182–3, seems to regard *Jub.* 30: 18–20
as one of possibly three differing accounts of Levi's *appointment* to the priesthood;
Endres, *Scriptural Interpretation*, 205, speaks more guardedly of this passage as one
in which Levi is 'established' as priest; but J. Kugel, 'Levi's Elevation to the Priesthood in Second Temple Writings', *HTR* 86 (1993), 5–6, 48, certainly believes these
verses record Levi's elevation to that office. In reality, the formal installation of
Levi as priest through the ceremonies of investiture and 'filling of the hands' does
not take place until he and Jacob have gone to Bethel (*Jub.* 32: 3): see Kugler, *From
Patriarch to Priest*, 161–2.

the future purity of Israel.[20] And the last word on the incident at
Shechem is the notice that the dread of the Lord and terror came
upon the neighbouring cities, so that no attempt was made to pursue Jacob and his sons (30: 26). This observation represents a
paraphrase of Gen. 35: 4, describing the trek of Jacob's family to
Bethel. The author has moved it forward in the narrative, the more
to insist upon the significance of Levi's zeal at Shechem, now seen
as the efficient cause of the Gentiles' fear. For the journey to Bethel
is fraught with significance, and it is only proper that its progress
should not be hampered by anxieties on the way about the people's
safety.

5. JACOB'S SECOND VISIT TO BETHEL

The Bible represents Jacob's second journey to Bethel as his
response to a direct divine command to go there, stay there, and
build an altar to the God who appeared to him when he was in
flight from his brother Esau (Gen. 35: 1). *Jub.* 31: 1 introduces
several changes into this straightforward command:

And on the new moon of the month Jacob spoke to all the members of his
household, saying, Purify yourselves and change your clothes, and let us
get up and go to Bethel, where I vowed a vow to the Lord on the day I fled
from my brother Esau, because He has been with me and brought me into
this land in peace; and do you rid yourselves of the foreign gods that are
among you.

Although Jacob still responds to a divine command, he does so
now as it were indirectly: *Jubilees* is intent on portraying him as one
who is faithful, without any prompting, to his vow made on the
occasion of his first visit to Bethel (*Jub.* 27: 27 following Gen. 28:
20–2), to give a tithe of his property to the Lord should he ever
return safely to that place. The time of his announcement and
subsequent journey (*Jub.* 31: 3) is given as the new moon of the
seventh month. In other words, he sets out for Bethel on Rosh
Ha-Shanah, so that he may be resident there during the High

---

[20] For the centrality of the Tamid in *Jubilees*, see C. T. R. Hayward, *The Jewish
Temple: A Non-Biblical Sourcebook* (Routledge: London, 1996), 93–7. Levi's display of zeal at Shechem was evidently a factor in his selection for the priesthood
according to the author of the *Aramaic Levi Document*: see further Kugler, *From
Patriarch to Priest*, 161–2. The extant portions of this last text, however, do not
preserve any association between Levi's priesthood and Jacob's change of name.

Holy Days which follow. He evidently recognizes, again without prompting, the holiness of Rosh Ha-Shanah, by ordering his people at the outset to purify themselves and change their garments, an order which the Bible does not report until after God has spoken to Jacob (Gen. 35: 2). At the same time, this order suggests that both the biblical writer and the author of *Jubilees* viewed Jacob's journey to Bethel as in some measure corresponding to later Israel's assembling at Sinai, where similar ritual purifyings are to be observed before the Lord descends in the sight of all the people (Exod. 19: 10–11). Yet for *Jubilees* the motivating factor in Jacob's activity is his original vow at Bethel, which finds no direct mention in the biblical text of Gen. 35. In this way the author signals to the reader the fundamental importance of Jacob's first visit to and vow at that shrine, which will be further emphasized by Isaac's advice to his son (*Jub.* 31: 29).

The Bible's note that Jacob's family handed over the foreign gods in their hands and the earrings in their ears for Jacob to hide (ויטמן) beneath the oak in Shechem (Gen. 35: 4) is supplemented by *Jub.* 31: 2, which remarks that the cache included idols which Rachel had stolen from Laban, and that all these things Jacob 'burnt, broke in pieces, and destroyed' before hiding them.[21] This is the first of a series of drastic changes to the biblical narrative, which continues with the report that:

Jacob came to Luz which is in the land of Canaan, that is, Bethel, he and all the people who were with him. And he built there an altar, and called the place El Beth El; because there God had been revealed to him when he had fled from before his brother. And Deborah the wetnurse of Rebecca died, and was buried beneath Bethel, under the oak tree; and he called its name 'The Oak of Weeping'. (Gen. 35: 6–8)

Jubilees will postpone notifying the reader of Deborah's death (*Jub.* 32: 30) until the whole revelation at Bethel, and much else besides, have taken place. Rather, we are told (*Jub.* 31: 3) that Jacob:

Went up on the new moon of the seventh month to Bethel. And he built an altar at the place where he had slept, and he set up a pillar there; and he sent word to his father Isaac to come to the sacrifice, and to his mother Rebecca.

Gone are the biblical references to Luz, Canaan, El Beth El, God's

---

[21] While the general sense of this verse is clear, its text presents difficulties, for full discussion of which see J. C. VanderKam, *The Book of Jubilees*, vol. 2, CSCO 511 (Peeters: Louvain, 1989), p. 201.

revelation, and Jacob's flight from Esau. The place of pilgrimage is simply called Bethel, and further specification of it is achieved by cross-reference to Jacob's earlier visit to the place described in *Jub.* 27: 19, 26; Gen. 28: 11, 18–19. Evidently, *Jubilees* understood Jacob's first visit to Bethel as having special significance, and analysis of the author's version of that famous story will engage our attention presently. For the moment, however, it should be observed that a brief biblical mention of Rebecca provided the author with a springboard for a new exegetical development: Rebecca and Isaac can now be brought into the narrative, and that is precisely what the author of *Jubilees* ensures will happen. Thus the remainder of the chapter (31: 4–32) consists of a lengthy account, not found in the Bible, of a visit which Jacob undertakes to his parents at the house of Abraham, in the company of his two sons Levi and Judah. On their arrival Rebecca blesses the two sons with a brief formula (31: 7) before they meet with Isaac, whose blindness leaves him so that he can recognize Levi and Judah for himself. Much, indeed, is made of the circumstance that these two persons are truly sons of Jacob (31: 7, 9–10; cf. 31: 21). At this point, 'the spirit of prophecy' came down on Isaac's mouth, and he took Levi by his right hand, and Judah by his left (31: 12).

Isaac proceeded to bless Levi and his descendants first. What clearly emerges from this prayer is the correspondence between Levi and his sons and the angels: the future priests are earthly counterparts to the two highest orders of angels. They are to be joined to the Lord and also to the sons of Jacob, effectively binding together the earthly and heavenly realms, pronouncing the Lord's blessing upon the sons of Jacob:

> And may the Lord . . . set you and your descendants apart from all man-kind to minister to him and to serve him in his sanctuary like the angels of the presence and the holy ones: like them your sons' descendants shall be accounted glorious, and great, and holy . . . And they shall be judges and princes and chiefs of all the descendants of Jacob's sons. They shall speak the Lord's word in righteousness . . . the blessing of the Lord shall be given by their mouths, to bless all the descendants of the beloved one. Your mother has named you Levi, and rightly she has named you: you shall be joined to the Lord, and be the companion of all the sons of Jacob . . . and blessed be the man that blesses you, and accursed every nation that curses you. (*Jub.* 31: 14–17)

Levi's priestly role is here represented as so crucial for the well-being of the Jewish people that the divine blessing which the Bible ascribed to Abraham (Gen. 12: 3), and which was later uttered (with cursing put first and blessing second) by Isaac himself over Jacob (Gen. 27: 29)—a divine blessing which applied to the whole people of Israel, as the Gentile seer Balaam recognized (Num. 24: 9)—is now pronounced over Levi and the future priests.[22] The character of the priesthood as representative of all Israel is, in this instance, very strongly marked.

Isaac's blessing of Judah is shorter, touching on his strength and power and principality over Jacob's other sons, and on the fear and awe which he will elicit from the Gentiles. This princely son is blessed (31: 18–20) in the hope that he will bring help, salvation, and peace to Israel. We are left in no doubt, however, that Judah is here designated a princely ruler: he and one of his sons will be prince over Jacob's offspring (31: 18), and as he sits on the 'throne of honour' his righteousness will bring great peace (31: 20). It is possible, though not proven, that the author had some kind of 'messianic' hope in mind at this point.[23] What cannot be gainsaid, however, is that this step in the narrative brings us face to face once more with Exod. 19: 6, and its demand for ממלכת כהנים וגוי קדוש. The 'holy nation' has been guaranteed by Levi's zeal for purity during the Shechem incident; Levi has been designated priest continually, and Judah ancestor of princes to come. Here we have kings, priests, and holy nation *in nuce*; and it must be repeated that Jacob's name is not changed until the holy nation is complete, with its future priests and kings provided and ratified by the spirit of prophecy (*Jub.* 31: 12). The reason for all this will be clear if we recall precisely to whom the command of Exod. 19: 6 was addressed. According to Exod. 19:3, Moses was ordered:

$$\text{כה תאמר לבית יעקב ותגיד לבני י שראל}$$

'thus you shall say to the house of Jacob, and declare to the sons of Israel'. The expression 'house of Jacob' occurs in the Pentateuch only here and in Gen. 46: 27; and Exod. 19: 3 is the only Pentateuchal verse in which it is found side by side with 'the sons of Israel'. That is to say, Exod. 19: 6 envisages a complete 'house of Jacob' before speaking of 'the sons of Israel', who are then defined

---

[22] On Isaac's blessing of Levi in *Jub.* 31: 12–17, see further Kugler, *From Patriarch to Priest*, 162–4, and Endres, *Scriptural Interpretation*, 160–1.

[23] See Endres, *Biblical Interpretation*, 161, and Kugler, *From Patriarch to Priest*, 164, n. 181.

as 'a kingdom, priests, and a holy nation'.[24] What *Jubilees* has set before us is the process whereby the holy nation with its kings and priests comes into being. Only one stage remains, and that is the birth of Jacob's twelfth son, Benjamin; it is Jacob's knowledge that this son is about to be born (*Jub.* 32: 3) which brings about the completion of 'the house of Jacob', whereupon the change of name to Israel (32: 17) can go ahead.

Blessings completed, the three men pass the night with Isaac, Levi and Judah sleeping on either side of him; meanwhile, Jacob tells his father all that had befallen him and of God's mercy to him. Isaac's response to all this is to bless God (31: 21–5). In the morning, Jacob tells Isaac of 'the vow he had vowed to the Lord and the vision he had seen', and that he had built an altar and that all was ready for the sacrifice 'to be made before the Lord as he had vowed': Isaac is invited to go with him (31: 26). Isaac refuses, pleading his great age in mitigation, and sends Jacob on his journey with the exhortation (31: 29):

May you prosper and fulfil the vow that you have vowed; and do not put it off, for you will be called to account in respect of it, so make haste and fulfil it now, and may the maker of all things, to whom you have vowed the vow, be pleased.

Once more, this emphasis on the vow directs the reader's attention back to Jacob's first visit to Bethel, so much so that the episode currently being described by the author of *Jubilees* must surely be understood as the completion and fulfilment of that original visit, and as deriving significance from it. That vow, it will be recalled, consisted in a solemn pledge on Jacob's part to render to God a tithe of everything that the Lord should give him (*Jub.* 27: 27; cf. Gen. 28: 22). This tithe will mark the culmination of a process

---

[24] *Jub.* 16: 18; 33: 20 took the somewhat ambiguous Hebrew ממלכת כהנים to mean 'a kingdom, priests' rather than 'a kingdom of priests': see Charles, *The Book of Jubilees* 116. The Ethiopic of *Jubilees* places a conjunction between these words, to give 'a kingdom and priests' as in Rev. 1: 6; 5: 10, Peshitta Exod. 19: 6; see further VanderKam, *The Book of Jubilees*, 98. Thus three discrete privileges are accorded to Israel, in the shape of kings, priests, and a holy people: this is also the understanding of TO, PJ, TN, FT, and Targum Frag. F from the Cairo Geniza of Exod. 19: 6, as noted by M. McNamara, *The New Testament and the Palestinian Targum to the Pentateuch* (Pontifical Biblical Institute: Rome, 1966), 227–30, noting also 2 Macc. 2:17; Philo, *De Abr.* 56; *De Sob.* 66, Symmachus and Theodotion of Exod. 19: 6. Extended discussion is given by J. Potin, *La Fête Juive de la Pentecôte*, vol. i, 218–30.

which began with Jacob's first visit to Bethel and concludes with
the note that Rachel was pregnant with Benjamin, so that Jacob can
offer to the Lord the tithe of his sons (32: 3). Thus it was that
Rebecca and Deborah accompanied Jacob back to Bethel (31: 30),
Jacob remembering Isaac's blessings and being confident that he
had 'an eternal hope', along with Levi and Judah, before the God
of all: 'And so it was decreed concerning the two; and how Isaac
blessed them is recorded on the heavenly tablets as an eternal testimony' (31: 32). Thus equipped, Jacob was ready for his second
encounter with God at Bethel. Not only had Levi now been designated as ancestor of the priests and blessed by Isaac, but Judah had
also been singled out as ancestor of Israel's princes and kings, and
likewise blessed by Jacob's father. At Bethel, Levi dreamt that they
had ordained him and made him 'priest of the Most High God'
along with his sons for ever.[25] The following day was the fourteenth
day of the seventh month (Tishri) and the feast of Sukkoth: on that
day Jacob gave tithes of all he had (32: 2). Now, the author informs
us, Rachel was pregnant with Benjamin, and Jacob counted from
him upwards, and arrived at Levi, who then counted as the tenth of
his sons. Accordingly, he was separated as a tithe and chosen to
minister as priest, his father clothing him with priestly garments
and 'filling his hands'.[26] Jacob then celebrated Sukkoth for seven
days, tithing all clean animals (32: 4–8) in fulfilment of the vow he
had made, that he would give a tenth of everything to the Lord
(*Jub.* 27: 27; Gen. 28: 22). Thus Levi acted as priest, Jacob fulfilled
his vow, and the tithe was instituted and offered as a holy thing
(32: 4–9). The laws of first and second tithe are then set out,
and decreed as eternal laws engraved on the heavenly tablets (32:
10–15).

So it comes about that, before ever Jacob's name is changed
to Israel, Jacob's household is entirely pure, and purified of

[25] Although they do not impinge directly on this study, there are difficulties with
regard to this verse's relationship to the *Aramaic Levi Document* and to the question
when exactly Levi was appointed as priest; these should be noted, as well as discussion of them by Charles, *Book of Jubilees*, 191; Kugel, 'Levi's Elevation', 5–6, 48;
and Kugler, *From Patriarch to Priest*, 164–5.

[26] *Jub.* 32: 3. Charles, *Book of Jubilees*, 191–2, explains the author's system of
computation for reckoning Levi as the tithe-son. A similar sort of tradition is found
in *Test. Levi* 9: 3–4; *PRE* 37: 3, although differences in detail between the accounts
make it difficult to know what the precise relationship between them might be. See
further Endres, *Biblical Interpretation*, 165; Kugler, *From Patriarch to Priest*, 165;
and on *PRE* and other Rabbinic sources below, pp. 288–90.

defilement and foreign idols; the priesthood of the house of Levi has been instituted and blessed as an order of priests for all time to come; Levi himself has officiated at the feast of Sukkoth; Judah has been blessed as ancestor of kings and princes; Levi has been selected as the 'tithe' of Jacob's sons, who are now, with the advent of Benjamin, complete in number; and Jacob has fulfilled his vow to tithe all his possessions for the Lord. The 'holy seed' not reckoned with the Gentiles, 'the Most High's portion', settled in the land that belongs to God, the Lord's special possession out of all nations, the 'kingdom of priests and holy nation' promised by God to Abraham through his son Isaac (*Jub.* 16: 17–19), is the house of Jacob now present in its constituent parts, ready to receive at Bethel the formal designation of Israel. In all of these preparations Jacob himself has played a crucial role: as Robert Kugler has noted, Jacob's part in appointing Levi as high priest serves mightily to enhance his own reputation, as do the accounts of his filial piety, his zeal in the Shechem episode, and his faithful determination to discharge his sacred vow.[27] The stage is now properly set for the house of Jacob to become Israel in the sense the author of *Jubilees* understood the name: 'Israel is a holy nation to the Lord its God, and a special nation of his own, and a priestly and royal nation for his possession' (*Jub.* 33: 20).

6. THE NAME ISRAEL IS CONFERRED

The following night, which was the twenty-second day of the seventh month, Jacob had it in mind to begin building 'that place' at Bethel, to surround the court with a wall, to sanctify it, and to make it holy in perpetuity for himself and his descendants.[28] This non-biblical note, which cannot help but remind the reader of David's plans to build a sanctuary for the Lord (2 Sam. 7: 1–2; 1 Chron. 17: 1–2; 22: 1), is the prelude to a divine vision:

---

[27] See Kugler, *From Patriarch to Priest*, 166–7; and cf. Endres, *Scriptural Interpretation*, 214–17, 228–31.

[28] *Jub.* 32: 16. On this episode, see J. Schwarz, 'Jubilees, Bethel, and the Temple of Jacob', *HUCA* 56 (1985), 63–86; C. T. R. Hayward, 'Jacob's Second Visit to Bethel in Targum Pseudo-Jonathan', in P. R. Davies and R. T. White (eds.), *A Tribute to Geza Vermes: Essays on Jewish and Christian Literature and History* (Academic Press: Sheffield, 1990), 175–92.

And the Lord appeared to him by night and blessed him and said to him: Your name shall no longer be Jacob, but Israel shall be your name. And he said to him again, I am the Lord who created heaven and earth, and I will increase you and multiply you greatly, and kings shall spring from you, and they shall sit in judgement in every land wherever men have set their feet. And I will give to your descendants all the earth that is under heaven, and they shall judge all the nations in accordance with their desires, and after that they shall gain possession of the entire earth and inherit it forever. And he finished speaking with him and went up from him; and Jacob looked [after him] till he had gone up to heaven. (*Jub.* 32: 17–20)

These verses represent a reworking of Gen. 35: 9–13, with many omissions, additions, and other alterations to the original Hebrew, betraying the author's particular understanding and interpretation of the episode. Whereas Gen. 35: 9 tells how God appeared to Jacob, the author of *Jubilees* insists that the Lord was the subject of this vision: the proper name of the God of Israel is evidently required here. The same biblical verse notes that God appeared to Jacob 'again when he came from Paddan-Aram'. The author of *Jubilees* omits the word 'again', and the reference to Paddan-Aram: there must be no hint that Jacob's change of name is connected directly with any previous encounters Jacob may have had with God on his return from Laban. As we have already seen, *Jubilees* removed entirely from its account of Jacob's life the incident at the Jabbok. The geographical and temporal indicators of the episode now described have already been made clear: Jacob is at Bethel, after returning from a visit to his father and mother. Along with these omissions from the Hebrew text of Gen. 35: 9, however, *Jub.* 32: 17 makes one small but telling addition: the Lord appeared to Jacob 'in the night'. Jacob's first encounter with God at Bethel had taken place in the night (Gen. 28: 11, emphasized at *Jub.* 27: 19, 21); and it was presumably 'in the night' that he had woken up from his sleep to declare, in the words of *Jub.* 27: 25, that 'this place is the house of the Lord and I knew it not'.

Next, and most strikingly, it should be observed how *Jubilees* has joined together Gen. 35: 9–10 in such a way that the Lord's blessing of Jacob, reported at the very end of Gen. 35: 9, now consists precisely in his declaration that Jacob's name is Israel. This represents a very particular reading of the Hebrew text, which, given the present verse division handed down by the Masoretes, allows the reader to conclude that the blessing may be a matter quite

separate from the change of name.[29] It would seem, then, that
Jubilees went to some lengths to ensure that the reader would
clearly discern God's blessing of Jacob in the change of name: this
change is reported directly and tersely, to emphasize the point. The
Bible's 'Your name is Jacob: your name shall no longer be called
Jacob, but Israel shall be your name; and he called his name Israel'
(Gen. 35: 10), is thus drastically reduced to 'Your name shall no
longer be Jacob, but Israel shall be your name' (*Jub.* 32: 17). Thus
blessed, Jacob hears what the Lord says to him 'again', a word not
found in the Hebrew of Gen. 35: 11, but supplied in *Jub.* 32: 18,
presumably taken from Gen. 35: 9. The inference is clear: the
change of name constitutes Jacob's blessing, and what is said
afterwards is additional to that blessing, and may be understood as
an explanation of it.

The contents of the Lord's speech to Jacob (Gen. 35: 11–12)
following the change of name is best appreciated if the biblical text
is set alongside the version created by *Jub.* 32: 18–19 and supplied
with labels indicating the various component parts:

Genesis	*Jubilees*
(a) I am 'El shaddai:	(a) I am the Lord who created heaven and earth:
(b) be fruitful and multiply.	(b) and I will increase you and multiply you greatly.
(c) A nation and an assembly of nations will come from you,	
(d) and kings shall go forth from your loins.	(d) and kings shall spring from you and they shall sit in judgement in every *land* (cf. (e)) wherever men have set their feet.
(e) and *the land* which I gave to Abraham and to Isaac, to you I shall give it and to your descendants I shall give *the land*.	(e) And I will give to your descendants all the *earth* that is under heaven, and they shall judge all the nations (cf. (c)) in accordance with their desires, and after that they shall gain possession of the entire *earth* and inherit it for ever.

[29] MT may be rendered: 'And God appeared to Jacob again when he came from
Paddan-Aram: and he blessed him. And God said to him, Your name is Jacob: your
name shall no longer be called Jacob, but Israel shall be your name . . .'

(f) And God went up from him at the place where he spoke with him.	(f) And he finished speaking with him; and Jacob looked after him till he had gone up into heaven. And that night he saw a vision . . .

The message is unmistakable. For *Jubilees*, the name Israel signifies the universal dominion of Jacob and his descendants over the nations, who are here pointedly omitted from among the family of Jacob. The Scriptural authority for this message is equally plain. Twice in Gen. 35: 12 we encounter *the land*, הארץ את, standing at the very beginning and end of the verse. Its repetition and place in the verse have signalled its importance for *Jubilees*, whose author has evidently concluded that the repetition is no redundancy, but the bearer of crucial information: it indicates that Scripture here speaks of the whole earth.

The name Israel is conferred on Jacob in blessing, and without struggle, according to *Jubilees*. This book has already intimated something of what the name means when applied to the descendants of Jacob as a distinct people: in Gen. 35: 9–13, however, the author perceives the significance of the name insofar as it touches on *the land*, that is, the whole earth—for *Jubilees* is in no doubt that the name Israel is invested with a universal as well as 'local' significance. Thus the God who addresses Jacob-Israel in these verses is no longer the 'El Shaddai of Gen. 35: 11, but 'the Lord who created heaven and earth'. This precise title is not common in *Jubilees*, and its use in three other chapters of the book (22: 6; 36: 7; 7: 36) emphasizes its importance here.

At *Jub.* 22: 6 we read that Isaac sent to Abraham, just before he died, a thank-offering by the hand of Jacob; and Abraham ate and drank, and blessed God Most High, 'who created heaven and earth', before uttering a lengthy and comprehensive blessing of Jacob (22: 11–24). It will be noted that, when *Jub.* 32: 19 came to rewrite Gen. 35: 12, mention of Abraham and Isaac was omitted in respect of the land (see section (c) above): by introducing the divine title 'creator of heaven and earth', however, the author was still able to direct attention to Abraham and Isaac, albeit obliquely and for another purpose. He wished the reader to recall, not the promise of land to those two men, but Abraham's blessing of Jacob, which began with a plea to God that he sanctify some of Jacob's sons in the midst of all the earth, a likely reference to the future selection of Levi's sons as priests (22: 11). The eulogy had then powerfully asserted Jacob's sovereignty over the nations, the sons of Seth (22: 15). In this blessing, Abraham ordered Jacob to separate himself from the nations and their idolatrous and impure cults, and to avoid at all costs marriage with a Canaanite woman (22: 16–22).[30] The concluding words of the blessing deserve careful scrutiny, as Abraham says to Jacob:

This house have I built for myself that I might put my name on it on the earth: it is given to you and your descendants for ever; and it shall be called the house of Abraham. It is given to you and your descendants for ever; and you shall build my house and establish my name before God for ever. Your descendants and your name shall endure through all the generations of the earth. (*Jub.* 22: 24)

At Bethel, Jacob will seek to build a house, a sanctuary, for God and will not be allowed to proceed. In the manner of King David noted earlier, he will seek to build a sanctuary for the Lord (*Jub.* 32: 16), only to be told not to undertake the enterprise, but to return to Abraham's house (32: 22). As in the case of David, God will not permit Jacob to construct a sanctuary; rather, God will build a house for him, as promised in Abraham's blessing which the narrator recalls when he makes God reveal himself as 'creator of heaven and earth'. Although the similarities between David and Jacob are not exact (David is forbidden to build a sanctuary because God had never before dwelt in one (2 Sam. 7: 5–7), whereas Jacob is told (*Jub.* 32: 22) that Bethel is not the divinely chosen site of the Temple), a chord is nonetheless struck: for *Jubilees*, the name Israel resonates with royal overtones, recalling the house of David, Nathan's famous prophecy, and, no doubt, the messianic hopes that some Jews attached to that house and that prophecy. Section (a) of God's words to Jacob, as rewritten by *Jubilees*, reveals more than is apparent at first sight. The author's version of section (b) is also dependent on the divine title 'creator of heaven and earth'. *Jubilees* has here turned a biblical command, 'be fruitful and multiply', into a promise uttered by God. God is able to increase Jacob-Israel precisely because He is the creator by whose name everything was made (*Jub.* 36: 7), and who multiplies the fruits of the earth offered to him as holy fourth-year produce (7: 36).

With section (d) we learn that Israel's kings will judge in every

---

[30] For the means used in this blessing to underline the fundamental importance of Jacob as a key partner in the covenant, see Endres, *Biblical Interpretation*, 214–17, 228–31.

land, 'wherever men have set their feet'. An alternative translation of this last clause as 'wherever the foot of the sons of men has trodden' shows more clearly what the author has in mind, which is a covert and somewhat 'slantwise' allusion to Deut. 11: 24–5. In those verses, Moses assured Israel that, if she diligently kept God's commandments,

> the Lord will dispossess all these nations from before you, and you shall inherit nations greater and stronger than yourselves: every place which the sole of your foot treads upon shall be yours—from the desert to the Lebanon, from the river, the River Euphrates, and as far as the western sea shall be your boundary . . . the Lord your God will set the terror and dread of you over all the land on which you tread, as he has spoken to you.

What in Deuteronomy is offered to Israel on condition that the commandments are kept seems in *Jubilees* to have been interpreted as an unconditional grant to Jacob-Israel. Furthermore, for the author of *Jubilees* the words 'every place which the sole of your foot treads upon shall be yours' form the keynote of these verses: their other biblical sentiment, that the jurisdiction of Israel might be geographically limited, is overlooked. Jacob's change of name to Israel, therefore, suggests to the author of *Jubilees* the realization of these words from Deuteronomy: Jacob-Israel embodies an ideal nation, faithful to God's every command, and as a consequence inheriting universal jurisdiction and authority. Already 'the dread of the Lord' had come upon the cities of Shechem (*Jub.* 30: 26), following the zeal of Simeon and Levi for the commandments. Now Jacob-Israel is promised that this dread will be universal, and the author of *Jubilees* felt able to rewrite sections (d) and (e) accordingly.

The name Israel signifies not only the ideal future jurisdiction and power of Jacob's descendants. As God withdrew from Jacob-Israel into heaven, the latter looked up and saw an angel descending with seven tablets, which he gave to Jacob-Israel. On them was written what would happen to his descendants throughout history (32: 21). Jacob-Israel, then, is *one who knows the future of the Jewish people*, a point stressed later in the narrative when he is told to write down all he has seen and read (32: 24). Understandably anxious that he may not be able to remember everything, the Patriarch is encouraged by the angel, who undertakes to ensure that he will indeed recall everything: awaking from sleep,

Jacob-Israel remembered and wrote down all that he had read (on the tablets) and had seen in the vision (32: 25–7). This special revelation is coupled with a command: Jacob-Israel is not to begin building at Bethel to make the place an 'eternal sanctuary' or 'permanent abode', since it is not the place. Readers of *Jubilees* will already know as much, since Zion-Jerusalem has been singled out as the holy place for all eternity (*Jub.* 1: 27–9). Rather, he is to go to Abraham's house and stay there until Isaac dies; the angel predicts that Jacob himself will die in Egypt, but be buried in the Land of Israel with his forefathers (32: 22–3).

This final vision is not reported in the Bible, although a particular reading of Gen. 35: 13 may have provided a starting-point for it. It cannot fail to recall (*mutatis mutandis*) the prophet Nathan's oracle to King David, which restrained him from building a sanctuary and yet promised to him 'a house'. The angelic vision, therefore, may be regarded as a kind of prophetic oracle associated with the divine blessing of Jacob-Israel. The implied parallel with King David's meeting with Nathan is instructive: Jacob-Israel may not build the sanctuary, but God will build for him a 'house' and 'kingdom' which will endure for ever (cf. 2 Sam. 7: 16). It should be noted that Nathan's oracle to David insists that God will appoint a 'place' for Israel who shall be no more afflicted by violent men (2 Sam. 7: 10), while David himself will have rest from his enemies (2 Sam. 7: 11). This promise was not fulfilled in David's lifetime, but in the days of his son and successor Solomon: likewise, Jacob-Israel is told that Bethel 'is not the place' (*Jub.* 32: 22), and the revelation which he received from the angel he eventually handed over to his son, the priest Levi, for the latter's children 'until this day' (*Jub.* 45: 16). It would seem that the author of *Jubilees* is suggesting to his readers an analogy, according to which Levi stands in much the same relationship to Israel as Solomon does to David in the matter of constructing the divinely chosen, permanent sanctuary. And the reader of *Jubilees* would also no doubt recall that David himself had received from the Lord a plan with details of the future Temple (1 Chron. 28: 19), which he handed over to his son Solomon (1 Chron. 28: 11–18) for future realization. One possible implication of what *Jubilees* has told us in the section about Jacob-Israel is that the plans for the future Temple were included in the revelation granted to the Patriarch on the last day of Sukkoth; that he wrote these down and handed them on to Levi; and that they remained, duly copied, in the possession of

Levi's priestly descendants until the time of Moses, who himself was Levi's great-grandson.[31]

Jacob's change of name, God's blessing of him, and the angelic vision just described took place on the night of the twenty-second of the seventh month, in other words, at the conclusion of the feast of Sukkoth, on its seventh day. Following these experiences, Jacob-Israel celebrated an extra day of festival which he called 'Addition' (*Jub.* 32: 27), and which is also written on the heavenly tablets (32: 28–9). This is the feast of the eighth day of Sukkoth, more commonly known as *Shemini 'Atseret*, which the author of *Jubilees* sought to associate with Jacob's change of name to Israel, and the events immediately following. This link between *Shemini 'Atseret* and these events, and the manner in which that link is established, display unusual features which must be explored further.

7. SHEMINI 'ATSERET AND THE NAME ISRAEL

The author of *Jubilees* recorded that, when he awoke from his sleep on that eventful night of the twenty-second day of the seventh month, Jacob-Israel remembered everything he had read and seen, and wrote it all down (32: 26). Immediately follows this note:

And he celebrated an extra day there, and offered sacrifices on it, just as he had on the previous days; and he called it Addition [*or:* Keeping Back], (because it was an additional day), and the previous days he called The Feast. And it was made plain that it should be *so*, and it is written on the

[31] See the genealogy of Exod. 6: 16–20. The fragmentary *Aramaic Testament of Qahat* (4Q542) from Qumran puts into the mouth of Qahat ben Levi (col. 2: 10 ff.) a reference to something which was given to his father Levi and handed on to him: the text is so damaged that what was given to Qahat cannot be discerned; but it goes on immediately to speak of books which Qahat is evidently bequeathing to his son Amram, the father of Moses. Carbon 14 testing of this scroll fragment has dated it to 388–353, or 303–235 BCE: see Vermes, *The Complete Dead Sea Scrolls in English*, 532–33, and Aramaic text in F. García Martínez and E. J. C. Tigchelaar, *The Dead Sea Scrolls Study Edition*, ii. 1083. Col. 1 of this document stresses the purity of Levi, his just deeds, and his refusal to countenance intermarriage with the nations, ideas very close to the heart of *Jubilees'* author: see also A. Caquot, 'Grandeur et pureté du sacerdoce: Remarques sur le Testament de Qahat (4Q542)', in (eds.) Z. Zevit, S. Gitin, and M. Sokoloff, *Solving Riddles and Untying Knots: Biblical, Epigraphic, and Semitic Studies in Honor of Jonas C. Greenfield* (Eisenbrauns: Winona Lake, 1995), 39–44. Likewise, *The Aramaic Testament of Amram* (4Q543–548, 4Q Visions of Amram) seems to envisage the transfer of books from Levi to Qahat and then to Amram (4Q545): see García Martínez and Tigchelaar, *Dead Sea Scrolls*, ii. 1088–91; Vermes, *The Complete Dead Sea Scrolls*, 53; and further Kugler, *From Patriarch to Priest*, 168.

heavenly tablets; and that is why it was revealed to him that he should celebrate it and add it to the seven days of the feast. And it was called Addition because it was recorded among the feast days according to the number of days of the year. (32: 27–29)

This note combines clear prescriptions with a certain reticence. The author leaves us in no doubt that *Shemini 'Atseret* is a divinely appointed feast in its own right, listed along with the other annual feast days, whose celebration requires sacrifices. Its relationship to Sukkoth, however, is not so clear: it constitutes an addition to what is otherwise simply called The Feast.[32] In one sense it is like Sukkoth, in that sacrifice is offered as on the days of that festival; in another sense, however, it is a separate event, an addition emphasized as such. Thus *Jubilees* reflects in some measure the biblical legislation: Lev. 23: 36 and Num. 29: 35–8 order the celebration of an eighth day עצרת to conclude the feast of Sukkoth, but Deut. 16: 13–15 (cf. Ezek. 45: 25), stating laws of that feast, says nothing at all about a concluding eighth day. The Bible itself, therefore, gives the impression that *Shemini 'Atseret* is 'of the feast of Sukkoth but not in it', which *Jubilees* faithfully retains. Indeed, the precise character of the celebration remains somewhat ambiguous up to the present day.[33] Nonetheless, the book agrees

---

[32] The Ethiopic text reads 'addition', whereas the Latin has *retentio*, a 'keeping back': the latter represents one possible rendering of the Hebrew name for the day (עצרת as in Lev. 23: 36; Num. 29: 35; Neh. 8: 18; 2 Chron. 7: 9) as deriving from root עצר 'to restrain, keep back', a view expressed also in *b. Ḥag.* 18a and reported by Charles, *Book of Jubilees*, 195: see also VanderKam, *Book of Jubilees*, 215. Hebrew עצרת with reference to this day means 'solemn gathering' or 'concluding solemnity': see Jacob Milgrom, *The JPS Torah Commentary: Numbers* (The Jewish Publication Society: Philadelphia/New York, 1990), 249, and the sheer oddity of the Ethiopic's rendering 'addition' led H. Rönsch, *Das Buch der Jubiläen oder die Kleine Genesis* (Fues's Verlag: Leipzig, 1874), 148, to suggest that the Ethiopic translator had before him a corrupt Greek text which read ἐπίθεσις, 'addition', rather than ἐπισχέσις, 'holding back': see also Y. Yadin, *The Temple Scroll*, 3 vols. (Israel Exploration Society: Jerusalem, 1977–83), i. 135. The Latin seems the better reading; but note VanderKam's implication (*Book of Jubilees*) that the Ethiopic text might just be defended as a free interpretation related to 32: 28–9, where it is revealed to Jacob-Israel that he should *add* this day to the feast. Some Rabbinic authorities certainly speak of it as an 'addition': see *Pesikta de Rab-Kahana*, trans. W. G. Braude and I. J. Kapstein (Routledge & Kegan Paul: London, 1975), 430.

[33] *b. Sukk.* 47a declares the day in part a festival in its own right, in part a continuation of Sukkoth: see article 'Shemini 'Atseret', in R. J. Zwi Werblowsky and G. Wigoder (eds.), *The Oxford Dictionary of the Jewish Religion* (Oxford University Press: Oxford, 1997), 631. For a summary of the liturgical regulations particular to the day, see L. N. Dembitz, article 'Shemini 'Atseret', in *JE*, xi. 270.

with Leviticus and Numbers that it is a festival which must be celebrated: perhaps the author's insistence on this matter was intended to counter any suggestion that Deuteronomy's failure to record the law signified that *Shemini 'Atseret* was of merely optional or temporary concern for future generations.

Jubilees does not explicitly claim that this 'addition' (to use its own terminology) commemorates Jacob's change of name to Israel, his blessing by God, and his angelic vision. Here we encounter a degree of reticence about the character of *Shemini 'Atseret* which the author does not display when he talks, for instance, about Yom Kippur: the latter is an annual recollection of Jacob's mourning for his abducted son Joseph (*Jub.* 34: 17–19), not unlike the new moon days of the first, fourth, seventh, and tenth months, which are both festival days and 'days of remembrance' of events in the life of Noah (*Jub.* 6: 23–8). Only by implication, however, does the writer suggest that *Shemini 'Atseret* might commemorate Jacob's change of name to Israel and its attendant circumstances. This observation calls to mind a remark by a recent writer on the festival, that it commemorates no historical event.[34] The most that can be said of *Jubilees* is that its author juxtaposed Jacob's change of name to Israel and *Shemini 'Atseret* without further clarification. All this demands explanation.

The Bible itself offers some clues to what may be in the author's mind. Besides the Scriptural verses noted earlier, the eighth day of עצרת features only in 1 Kings 8: 65–66; 2 Chron. 7: 8–10; Neh. 8: 18. The first two of these passages describe the climax of ceremonies at Solomon's inauguration of the newly completed Temple in Jerusalem. The MT of 1 Kings 8: 65 envisages celebrations in the seventh month (cf. 1 Kings 8: 2) which lasted for two seven-day periods, fourteen days in all; then, 'on the eighth day', Solomon sent the people away (1 Kings 8: 66). The textual and other problems inherent in these verses, although important in their own right, need not be discussed in detail here;[35] it is enough to note that the difficulties they raised led the Chronicler substantially to rephrase, as follows:

---

[34] See *The Oxford Dictionary of the Jewish Religion*, 631.

[35] Thus some witnesses of LXX to verse 65 include material not represented in MT, and others omit reference to the second seven-day period making up fourteen days in all: see further J. A. Montgomery and H. G. Gehman, *The Books and Kings* (Clark: Edinburgh, 1951), 199–203; and J. Gray, *I and II Kings: A Commentary* (SCM Press: London, 1964), 216–19.

And Solomon celebrated (*lit*.: made) the feast at that time for seven days, and all Israel with him, a very great congregation . . . and on the eighth day they celebrated (*lit*.: made) a solemn assembly (עצרת), because they had celebrated (*lit*.: made) the inauguration of the altar (חנכת המזבח) for seven days and the feast for seven days. And on the twenty-third day of the seventh month he sent away the people to their tents rejoicing and glad of heart because of the good which the Lord had done for David and for Solomon and for Israel His people. (2 Chron. 7: 8–10)

In both accounts, the 'eighth day' forms the climax of ceremonies inaugurating the Temple Service. The Chronicler, however, is nearer in time to the author of *Jubilees* than the writer(s) of 1 Kings; like *Jubilees*, he insists that the eighth day is significant in its own right, and follows directly on 'the feast' which has occupied the preceding seven days. As Sara Japhet has noted, the Chronicler was mindful of the law of Lev. 23: 34–6, ordering the celebration of the eighth day; consequently, he could not regard that day as simply the moment when Solomon dismissed the people. In the Chronicler's view, Solomon must have observed the law, and therefore must have included the due celebration of the '*atseret*, the solemn assembly on the eighth day.[36] Furthermore, the Chronicler's report effectively clarifies the rather tangled business of dates listed in MT of 1 Kings 8: 65–6 by presenting us with a scheme of great simplicity. First, for seven days Solomon held ceremonies inaugurating the Service; then he celebrated Sukkoth for seven days; finally, he added the statutory eighth day. This last was followed by the twenty-third day of the seventh month, when the people were dismissed.

The final explicit mention of *Shemini 'Atseret* in the Bible is found in Neh. 8: 18, where its observation 'according to the custom' follows a distinctive celebration of seven days of Sukkoth in the time of Ezra and Nehemiah. The event was unusual: the narrator remarks that from the days of Joshua up to that day, the people of Israel had not made booths and dwelt in them (Neh. 8: 17). Throughout the feast, on every day, the Torah was read (8: 18). The eighth day itself was the climax of a 'great assembly' in the course of which Ezra had read out the Torah to all the men, the women, and those who could understand (8: 2–3), while the Levites gave the sense so that the people understood the reading (8: 8). Thus one of the most famous episodes in the early history of Second

[36] See Sara Japhet, *I and II Chronicles* (SCM Press: London, 1993), 611–13.

Temple times was crowned, as it were, by the noted observance of *Shemini 'Atseret*.[37]

First, it should be noted that the calender in *Jubilees* functions in such a way that the day begins (most probably) in the evening.[38] By sunset on the twenty-first day of the seventh month, therefore, the seventh day of Sukkoth would be finished: unconsecrated time would have resumed its dominion, with the advent of the twenty-second day. It was during the *night* of the twenty-second day that Jacob's name was changed to Israel and the angel brought to him the seven tablets (*Jub.* 32: 16). By ensuring that an eighth day was added to Sukkoth, and that *Shemini 'Atseret* was celebrated by Jacob-Israel himself, 'among the feast days according to the number of the days of the year' (*Jub.* 32: 29), *Jubilees* ensures its divinely appointed sacred character, and dramatically arrests the reader's attention. The reader, by this means, is jolted into considering the 'eighth day' and its associations elsewhere in the biblical record. We have seen what these are: the completion of the formal ceremonies inaugurating Solomon's Temple, and the completion of the solemn proclamation of the Torah in the great assembly under Ezra's guidance. In the days of the First Temple, the formal inauguration of the Temple's service represented the realization of all God's promises to David, that Israel should dwell in peace in its own land, unmolested by enemies, and under the secure rulership of a divinely appointed dynasty (2 Sam. 7: 5–16; 1 Kings 5: 5). The solemn agreement of the Jewish people to be subject to the commandments of the Torah in the days of Ezra likewise reaffirmed in the days of the Second Temple God's continued blessing of the Jewish state, now reconstituted, with its Temple rebuilt by a descendant of David in accordance with prophecy (Zech. 4: 1–10; Ezra 5: 1–2).

Given all this, the tradition that Jacob's name was changed to Israel on *Shemini 'Atseret* assumes a mighty significance. We may say with some confidence that Israel, in the mind of the author of *Jubilees*, is a name signifying *formal completion* of qualifications necessary for the house of Jacob to be constituted as a state under God's rule. The author, of course, composed his book at a time when the Temple stood and the Torah's commands were

---

[37] See further, H. G. M. Williamson, *Ezra, Nehemiah*, Word Biblical Commentary, 16 (Word Books: Waco, 1985), 277–97.

[38] See J. C. VanderKam, *Calendars*, 33.

considered binding without question: what he has to say about the historical Jacob is in a sense proleptic. Jacob is like David as presented by the Chronicler, a ruler entrusted with instructions about a Temple which he himself will not build. In linking the name Israel to *Shemini 'Atseret*, the writer of *Jubilees* looks to the future, and uses 'Israel' to designate a nation under the authority of the Torah, worshipping God at the one sanctuary in Jerusalem, whose legitimacy cannot be questioned: all the necessary qualifications for such a nation to come into existence have been met in the life of the Patriarch Jacob, who is Israel.

It is now possible more fully to appreciate why *Jubilees* eliminated any suggestion that Jacob acquired the name Israel as the result of a struggle with some mysterious creature. The name represents the final reward, as it were, for Jacob's fidelity to God throughout his many journeyings; and it is granted even as he starts to build a sanctuary at Bethel, to surround the court with a wall, and to hallow it and make it holy for ever (*Jub.* 32: 16). We have also seen that it betokens universal dominion, and supernatural foreknowledge granted to Jacob of what will befall his descendants in days to come (32: 18–22). Once more, it is seen to represent the *end* of a process, at the same time as it marks the formal beginning of a new phase in the life of the chosen people. The author has so arranged his material as to ensure that the name Israel speaks of the end, the goal, the ultimate destiny of the people, and tantalizes us with questions about his aspirations for the remoter future of Israel. Yet already he has given us clues. In the end, God will ensure that all will be as He wills. His people will hold fast to His commandments after He has circumcised their hearts and purified them (*Jub.* 1: 23–4), and this process will go hand in hand with the construction of His everlasting sanctuary and His revelation as King and God of Israel on Zion for ever (1: 27–8).

The foregoing observations should also go some way towards explaining why *Jubilees* does not speak of *Shemini 'Atseret* as simply a commemoration of some past event. In the author's mind it is much more than that, since it also represents a goal, an end towards which the Jewish people might direct themselves. According to *Jubilees*, all the other festivals commemorate some historical event in the lives of the Patriarchs. *Shemini 'Atseret* certainly recalls Jacob's change of name to Israel, but in a setting which holds before our eyes the whole future of the Jewish people revealed that day on tablets from heaven and entrusted to Jacob-Israel (*Jub.* 32: 21–6). It is Israel's promised destiny, above all else, which *Jubilees* wishes to associate with the 'additional' festival of *Shemini 'Atseret*; and the final realization of that destiny, as the author makes plain from the outset of the book, will come about when:

the heavens and the earth are renewed and *with them* all created things both in heaven and on earth, until *the day when* the sanctuary of the Lord is created in Jerusalem on Mount Zion and all the luminaries are renewed as instruments of healing and of peace and of blessing for all the elect of Israel, and so that it may be from that day on as long as the earth lasts. (*Jub.* 1: 29)

The question that led the writer of *Jubilees* to invest this rather unusual day with so much significance has been answered, in part, through observations on its place in the Hebrew Bible. But there is more to be said on at least two counts in respect of the biblical name of this day, which will undoubtedly have made the author of *Jubilees* consider very carefully what the biblical writers had intended to signify by this 'eighth day of Sukkoth'. First, as we have seen, the Bible calls this day עצרה (Lev. 23: 36; Num. 29: 35). This same word, however, is used by Deut. 16: 8 for the seventh day of the feast of Mazzot, which concludes the season of Pesaḥ. *Jubilees* speaks of Pesaḥ and the seven days of Mazzot indirectly at 17: 15–18: 19 and directly at 49: 1–23, without indicating any awareness of the special status of the seventh day as עצרה. In other words, the specific terminology of Deut. 16: 8 is passed over in silence. One possible explanation for this would be that the author wished to dissociate the minds of his readers from any thoughts of עצרה as relating to Mazzot, and thoroughly to emphasize that עצרה was properly to be regarded as an adjunct to Sukkoth.

This, however, may not be the whole story. Josephus (*Ant.* III. 252) informs us that, in late Second Temple times, the feast of Shavuoth or weeks was known as ἀσαρθὰ, which represents Aramaic עצרתא, the equivalent of Hebrew עצרה. This word, he says, signifies πεντηκοστήν, 'fiftieth' or 'Pentecost'.[39] As we have already seen, the author of *Jubilees* regarded Shavuoth as the feast of the covenant par excellence, all manner of biblical covenants

---

[39] He speaks of the fiftieth day after Pesaḥ ἣν Ἑβραῖοι ἀσαρθὰ καλοῦσι, σημαίνει δὲ τοῦτο πεντηκοστήν. For *'atseret* as a word signifying Pentecost, see also *m. Sheb.* 1: 1; *Bek.* 9: 5; *Ḥag.* 2: 4; *b. Pes.* 42.b; and, alone of the Pentateuchal Targumim, TN of Exod. 34: 22; Deut. 16: 10.

and contracts being located by him on this great day, the fifteenth day of the third month. According to *Jub.* 6: 17–18, it is the feast of the annual renewal of the covenant, and it has been observed in heaven since the day of creation. After the Sabbath, it is the day most highly esteemed by this writing.[40] If, for the sake of argument, we adopt the not unreasonable hypothesis that Shavuoth was popularly called עצרת already in the days when *Jubilees* reached its final form, a number of otherwise disjointed facts and bits of evidence from Second Temple times begin to make sense.

The first fact of interest is the tradition that God had concluded a covenant with Jacob at Bethel. No such information is given by the Bible, which never uses the term 'covenant' in relation to Jacob's two visits to Bethel, nor to any activity in which he was a partner there. Indeed, the only Pentateuchal text which speaks of a covenant with Jacob is Lev. 26: 42, which has God declare:

'And I shall remember my covenant with Jacob, and also my covenant with Isaac, and also my covenant with Abraham I shall remember; and I shall remember the land.'

The extant Palestinian Targum of the verse, which consists of FTP and FTV, along with PJ, specifies that this covenant with Jacob was located 'at Bethel'. The tradition in the Aramaic Targum is ancient, being attested also in the Qumran Temple Scroll: there, God promises to act בברית אשר כרתי עם יעקוב בבית אל, 'according to the covenant which I have made with Jacob at Bethel'.[41] Neither Targum nor Temple Scroll give further *direct* details about this covenant; but the very baldness of their statements suggests that they were simply passing on information which was more or less commonplace in their day. There is, however, some further evidence to suggest that this 'covenant with Jacob at Bethel' was associated with the feast of Sukkoth. Thus the reference to it in the Temple Scroll follows directly the list of sacrifices prescribed for Sukkoth and *Shemini 'Atseret*, after a brief statement about the

---

[40] See J. C. VanderKam, *Calendars*, 30–2; and Jaubert, *La Notion d'alliance* 101–8.

[41] 11QTemp XXIX. 10, Hebrew and English translation as given by Y. Yadin, *The Temple Scroll*, ii. 129. The final form of the Scroll is best dated to the late second/early first century BCE, either late in the reign of John Hyrcanus I or early in the reign of Alexander Janneus. For a convenient digest of views, see L. H. Schiffman, article 'Temple Scroll', *ABD* vi. 349–50.

future Temple which will occupy us presently.[42] Of the Targums, however, PJ alone obliges us with additional information. His version of Gen. 35: 14 makes it plain that he placed Jacob's second visit to Bethel at the feast of Sukkoth, just as *Jubilees* had done; and his interpretation of Gen. 35: 11 introduces unmistakeable allusions to Exod. 19: 6, which at the very least can be understood as a verse with significance for the covenant and which, as we have seen, was never far from the thoughts of the author of *Jubilees*. This verse, in PJ's version, reads:

And *the Lord* said to him: I am El Shaddai. Grow and multiply. A *holy* nation and an assembly of *prophets and priests* shall come from *your sons which you shall beget; and again, two* kings shall go forth from *you*.[43]

All this conspires to suggest that the author of *Jubilees* was aware of a tradition that God had made a covenant with Jacob at Bethel, a covenant associated with Sukkoth and the following *Shemini 'Atseret*. The festival of covenant par excellence for this author, however, was Shavuoth; and if, in his day, this festival was already known as *'atseret* or (Aramaic) *'atsarta*', then one can envisage how easily *Shemini 'Atseret* itself might take on the character of a day with covenant associations. For these reasons, Yadin is probably quite correct to speak of Jacob's covenant at Bethel as linked by the author of *Jubilees* to Sukkoth and *Shemini 'Atseret*, even though neither *Jubilees* nor the Pentateuch itself speaks directly of a covenant with Jacob in that place.[44] For the author of *Jubilees*, however, avoidance of the term 'covenant' in the account of Jacob's visits to Bethel can be explained: in his scheme of things, the visits did not take place at Shavuoth, and the author wished to restrict explicit mention of the covenant of Shavuoth alone.

As we have seen, however, the notion of covenant is only just concealed beneath the surface of Jacob's second visit to Bethel as *Jubilees* presents it. This presentation alludes indirectly to God's covenant with David mediated by the prophet Nathan, according

---

[42] The Temple Scroll's rules for sacrifice on *Shemini 'Atseret* take up col. XXIX lines 101–1 in Yadin's numeration, *Temple Scroll*, ii. 126–7. These are followed by a summary of previous discussion of festivals and sacrifices in col. XXIX. 2–8.

[43] Italics indicate Targum's departure from MT. See further Hayward, 'Jacob's Second Visit', 183–6; and discussion below, pp. 294–5.

[44] Yadin, *Temple Scroll*, ii. 129, states that in *Jub.* 32: 16 ff. 'the covenant [*sc.* with Jacob at Bethel] is linked with the feast of Booths and the Day of Assembly'. What is said here provides supporting evidence for his opinion.

to which God will build for David a house, while his son and successor will build a temple for God.[45] Jacob's desire, like David's, to build a sanctuary features prominently in *Jub.* 32: 16; like David, Jacob is prevented from building by a heavenly command (32: 22). Just as Nathan's message to David forms the basis of a covenant, so we might reasonably conclude that the heavenly commands and vision of Jacob at Bethel set the parameters for a covenant with the Patriarch. This is once more confirmed to some degree by the evidence of the Temple Scroll, which evidently linked the building of the future sanctuary to this covenant with Jacob at Bethel, since God promised Moses:

And I will accept them (?), and they shall be (?) my people, and I will be theirs for ever, [and] I will dwell with them for ever and ever. And I will consecrate my [t]emple by my glory, (the temple) on which I will settle my glory, until the day of blessing on which I will create my temple and establish it for myself at all times, according to the covenant which I have made with Jacob at Bethel.[46]

In this section, the Temple Scroll is most likely speaking of an eternal temple to be set up by God himself at the end of days: *Jub.* 1: 15–17 also predicts God's construction of such an everlasting temple of the end-time, which will involve also (*Jub.* 1: 29) the renewal of the luminaries for healing, peace, and blessing for all the elect of Israel.[47] Yet as Yadin pertinently remarks, neither book declares openly that the future temple's construction fulfils a promise made by the Lord in a covenant with Jacob at Bethel.[48] Indeed, we have already seen that *Jubilees* does not even use the term 'covenant' in respect of Jacob at Bethel, and conveys its thoughts on the subject by alluding obliquely to the story of David and Nathan. That story is not found in the Pentateuch; consequently, the author of *Jubilees* may have felt reticent about applying the language of covenant directly to it, wishing to reserve that word for sacred events recorded in the Torah of Moses. Nonetheless, that allusion to covenant ceases to be oblique and comes to the surface when the writer considers Jacob's relationship to the Sabbath, as we shall see presently.

[45] For what follows, see above, pp. 138–9.
[46] 11QTemp XXIX. 7–10, translated by Yadin, *Temple Scroll*, ii. 128–9.
[47] Thus 'the day of blessing' probably means the end of days: see Yadin, *Temple Scroll*, ii. 129, who also relates it to the future sanctuary of *Jub.* 1: 16ff., and again, i. 183–4.
[48] See ibid., i. 184 and the interesting observations in n. 5 to that page.

Finally, the author of *Jubilees* was very likely aware of a trad-itional explanation of עצרת represented by the Septuagint, which may have contributed to his overall understanding of the term. In the two Pentateuchal verses ordering celebration of *Shemini 'Atseret* itself (Lev. 23: 36; Num. 29: 35), Hebrew עצרת is trans-lated as Greek ἐξόδιον. The same equivalent is used for עצרת of the seventh day of Mazzot at Deut. 16: 8, and for *Shemini 'Atseret* itself at 2 Esdras 18: 18 (= Neh. 8: 18) and 2 Par. 7: 9. These verses account for all the occurrences of ἐξόδιον in LXX save one: it appears also in the heading of Psalm 28 (Heb. Psalm 29), ψαλμὸς τῷ Δαυιδ ἐξοδίου σκηνῆς, the last two words of which are not repre-sented in MT's heading מזמור לדוד. LXX may thereby intend to indicate that the Psalm was used liturgically on *Shemini 'Atseret*, if ἐξόδιον represents Hebrew עצרת and σκηνῆς ('of a tent') is a refer-ence to the feast of Sukkoth, Tents or Tabernacles.[49] The Greek noun ἐξόδιον has a literal sense of 'a finale of a tragedy', and may be used metaphorically of a catastrophe or tragic ending; in LXX it seems to have come to mean 'the final day of a festival'.[50] Com-menting on the use of this word by LXX at Lev. 23: 36, Harlé and Pralon (who translate it as *closure*) remark also on how it recalls, perhaps intentionally, the word 'exodus' and Israel's departure from Egypt.[51]

We may explain the LXX translators' choice of ἐξόδιον to repre-sent עצרת by assuming that they understood the Hebrew noun as related to the verb עצר, 'to restrain, shut up', and perceived in the word a sense of ending, or conclusion. Be that as it may, ἐξόδιον is an unusual choice for them to make to represent a Hebrew word which normally designates sacred assemblies.[52] There are other,

---

[49] So many modern commentators, like C. A. Briggs and E. G. Briggs, *The Book of Psalms*, vol. 1 (Clark: Edinburgh, 1906), 252; A. A. Anderson, *New Century Bible Psalms*, vol. 1 (Oliphants: London, 1972), 232; A. Weiser, *The Psalms* (SCM: London, 1979), 261. The 'tent' to which LXX refer may not, however, signify the *sukkah* used at the Tabernacles, but the Temple traditionally imagined and spoken of as a tent. If so, LXX might have ascribed the psalm not to a liturgical role, but to a 'one off' single historical event, viz., the closing ceremony of Solomon's inaugur-ation of the Temple on *Shemini 'Atseret*. *Massaket Sopherim* 18, however, gives it as a psalm for Shavu 'oth.

[50] See Lust, Eynikel, and Hauspie, *Lexicon*, vol. 1, p. 161.

[51] See P. Harlé and D. Pralon, *La Bible d'Alexandrie, 3: Le Lévitique* (Cerf: Paris, 1988), 191.

[52] See J. B. Segal, *The Hebrew Passover from the Earliest Times to A.D. 70* (Oxford University Press: Oxford, 1963), 208–14.

more common, Greek words to express 'end' or 'conclusion', and we may suspect that Harlé and Pralon have recognized an important influence in LXX's selection of this particular word. Furthermore, the technical sense of ἐξόδιον as the final section of a tragic play should not be lightly passed over, especially when the place and circumstances of the Septuagint are more carefully considered, and in view of the restricted usage of the word by the Greek translators. For it is generally agreed that the Pentateuch was translated into Greek in Alexandria, where Jews represented an influential, prosperous, and cultured element in a cosmopolitan city. The city was a vibrant centre of Greek tragedy, which flourished in Alexandria: there were poets there to write it, and it was regularly performed at the time when the LXX translators were at work. Far from being something foreign to Jews, it was an art form that at least one of them felt called upon to emulate. Indeed, the name of Ezekiel, the Jewish tragedian, is known to students of Greek drama as the major representative of tragedy-writing in the Hellenistic period.[53]

The sense of ἐξόδιον as a formal conclusion to the relation of a grand and elevated recital of formative events in the heroic history of a people fits well with the biblical information about *Shemini 'Atseret*. It fits well, too, with *Jubilees*' description of it as an 'addition', since by the time Jacob comes to celebrate it as a festival the ultimate destiny of his earthly pilgrimage has been achieved with the final emergence *in nuce* of the 'kingdom, priests, and holy nation' which constitutes Israel. The name 'Israel', then, can be 'added to' that of Jacob on the *twenty-second* day of the *seventh* month as a fitting conclusion, ἐξόδιον it may be, to a process which began at creation and culminated on the eve of the *seventh* day in the creation of the *twenty-second* work of creation. Here the words of *Jub.* 2: 23–4 should be recalled:

There *were* twenty-two patriarchs from Adam to Jacob, and twenty-two kinds of created things were made before the seventh day: this *day* is blessed and holy; and Jacob also is blessed and holy; and so the two together are hallowed and blessed. And to Jacob and his descendants it was granted that they should always be the blessed and holy ones of the first covenant and law, even as he had hallowed and blessed the Sabbath on the seventh day.

---

[53] For further discussion, see C. T. R. Hayward, 'The Sanctification of Time in the Second Temple Period: Case Studies in the Septuagint and Jubilees' in S. C. Barton (ed.), *Holiness Past and Present* (Clark: London, 2003), 141–67.

These are compelling words: Jacob and the Sabbath stand in the same continuum of God's creative work, as the climax respectively of his activity in the formation of the cosmos and the genesis of an unique people for his service.[54] Here, too, the covenant makes its appearance in relation to Jacob, and that without vagueness or ambiguity. To avoid all doubt, *Jub.* 2: 31 again emphasizes the irrefragable bond between Sabbath and Jacob, as it speaks of the seventh day:

> And the creator of all things blessed it, but he did not hallow all peoples and nations to keep Sabbath on it, but Israel only: them alone on earth did he allow to eat and drink and keep Sabbath on it.

Here it is specifically Israel, rather than Jacob, who is bound to keep Sabbath, as earlier verses of the same chapter (2: 26–7, 29) have made plain. All this shows, as R. H. Charles noted long ago, that the author of *Jubilees* perceived that Sabbath could not rightly be kept on earth until Jacob's time. His observation, however, may need some refinement in light of what has emerged in this study. It is the conferring of the name *Israel* on Jacob which allows Sabbath to be kept on earth, for it is with the conferral of this name, on the twenty-second day of the seventh month, that Jacob's life as twenty-second patriarch reaches its appointed end, its goal, its destiny.

Here we must speak more plainly. On one level, the writer perceives both Sabbath and Israel as belonging in the realms of history and of this created world: both represent the formal end of a process which finally established the cosmos as God in his great mercy has willed it to be. On another level, however, both Sabbath and Israel are seen as belonging to the supernatural order of things and as pointing forward to, while containing within themselves, the future destiny of the cosmos determined by God in his almighty wisdom. Thus Sabbath is observed on earth by Israel alone, but also at the same time in heaven by the Angels of the Presence and the Angels of Sanctification alone (*Jub.* 2: 17–20). It is in this matter of Sabbath observance that Jacob and his descendants are uniquely singled out by God and specifically designated by Him, according to *Jub.* 2: 20, 'My first-born son': thus Jacob-Israel is 'written into' creation. As James Kugel has remarked, Israel was

---

[54] On the number twenty-two, the Sabbath, and God's choice of Israel being integrated into creation, see further J. C. VanderKam, 'Genesis 1 in Jubilees 2', *DSD* 1 (1994), 315–19.

'conceived' at the time of the very first Sabbath.[55] This seventh
day, then, when properly observed by Israel, ensures that heaven
and earth remain linked together: it is a kind of bridge between the
created and uncreated worlds. Next, I have already observed how
'Israel' points towards the future of the Jewish people and in a
certain manner encapsulates that future. The same is true of Sabbath, which *Jub.* 50: 9 declares as given to Israel by God as: 'A
festal day and a holy day; and this day shall be a day of the holy
kingdom for all Israel among their days forever.' The 'holy kingdom' enduring 'for ever' is the realization of God's promise for the
future made at the beginning of the book and articulated almost as
a programme in *Jub.* 1: 27–8 (emphasis mine):

And [God] said to the Angel of the Presence, Write for Moses the account
from the beginning of creation till *the time when my sanctuary shall be built
among them for all eternity*, and the Lord appear in the sight of all, and all
know that I am the God of Israel and the father of all the sons of Jacob
and King on Mount Zion for all eternity.

Yet more analogies between 'Israel' and Sabbath traced by the
author of *Jubilees* could doubtless be drawn out; the writer's essential message, however, needs no elaboration. His refusal to give a
single etymology of the name is now more readily understood,
since in his view its significance is not limited to one aspect of the
nature of the Jewish people. Nonetheless, it seems almost certain
that the writer was familiar with derivations of Israel from the
word שיר, 'to sing', conveying the notion that Israel is one who (like
the highest angels) sings God's praises and shares in the heavenly
service. Nor can it reasonably be doubted that he was aware of the

---

[55] See J. Kugel, '4Q369 "Prayer of Enosh" and Ancient Biblical Interpretation',
125–6, noting that 'Israel *is* God's firstborn since Israel's existence as a separate
people was set in motion during the first week of creation'. The status of Israel as
God's first-born concerns not only *Jubilees*, but Ben Sira, Philo, the *Prayer of
Joseph*, and other texts explored here. In the same article (pp. 123–6), Kugel demonstrates *Jubilees'* conviction that God, the two highest orders of angels, and Israel
alone observe each Sabbath, while the other angels and nations continue to work,
thus laying to rest notions that God might have kept only the first Sabbath, or that,
having instituted the Sabbath on the first seventh day, He thereafter ceased to
operate and observed Sabbath *in perpetuum*, becoming *Deus otiosus*. Furthermore,
my observations above (pp. 134–6) on universal sovereignty as a crucial element in
the meaning of the name Israel, whom *Jubilees* recognized as God's first-born,
tends to confirm Kugel's analysis of 4Q369 as a document referring to Israel and his
privileges: see his article, 137–40.

tradition surviving in the Aramaic Targums, which understood the name as deriving from שׁרר, 'to be a prince, to rule', intimating that Israel in some manner was a שׂר, that is to say, an angel or prince along with God.

8. SUMMARY

Jubilees offers no explicit etymology of the name Israel, and suppresses completely the biblical account of Gen. 32: 22–33 which tells of the announcing of that name to Jacob, by a man or an angel, after an encounter at the Jabbok. Rather, *Jubilees* tells how God Himself bestowed the name on Jacob, as a blessing, at Bethel: Gen. 35: 9–15 is the author's chosen biblical foundation on which to build his understanding of the name Israel, a text involving no struggle, no obscurity, and a divine promise for the future. *Jubilees* envisaged preconditions on Jacob's part for the reception of this name. First, he had to leave the idolater Laban: he did so as a free man, his wives, like the faithful Ruth, the ancestress of King David, insisting on staying close to him. Secondly, he had to journey from Gilead to Bethel unimpeded, neither Laban nor Esau obstructing him. The land through which he passed was his own: *Jubilees* records no one offering resistance to him, by this means divorcing the events surrounding the conferral of the name Israel from any action on Jacob's part which could be construed as necessary for securing possession of the Land.

Indeed, *Jubilees* had used the designation 'Israel' in narratives placed by the author in the time *before* Jacob had actually received the name. This the author had achieved by failing to provide an account of events at the Jabbok, while retaining the story of the attack on Shechem by Simeon and Levi. This last the author regarded as a wholly praiseworthy episode, publicly displaying an Israel maintaining the highest standards of purity, holiness, and separateness from the surrounding peoples. For *Jubilees*, the events at Shechem proved that Jacob and his sons are truly a 'holy nation', just as earlier references to Israel in the book had indicated: these had already spoken of an Israel involved in the keeping of Sabbath and the proper worship of God.

Jacob's visit to his parents at Abraham's house, an event not recorded in the Bible, gave the author of *Jubilees* the opportunity to expatiate on the necessity of Jacob's return to Bethel for a second visit to pay his tithes promised on his first visit: thus the conferring of the name Israel is eventually to be linked organically to that first visit, when Jacob had seen a ladder linking heaven and earth, and angels ascending and descending. Not only that: Jacob's literal 'return to his father's house', on which the fulfilment of his vow to pay tithes had depended, allowed the author to tell how Isaac had blessed Levi as priest and Judah as royal prince, so that by the time Jacob arrived in Bethel for his second visit (corresponding to the biblical narrative of Gen. 35: 9–15) he was the father of a holy nation, an ancestor of priests, and the originator of a royal dynasty, the earlier allusions to the Book of Ruth coming into their own here. His wife is already pregnant with his twelfth and final son; thus, on his second visit to Bethel, the 'house of Jacob' and the 'sons of Israel' are complete: the holy nation, priests, and kings which constitute Israel according to Exod. 19: 6 are present in the world.

At Bethel, Jacob appointed Levi as priest and celebrated the feast of Sukkoth. At the end of the seven festal days, *Jubilees* tells of his resolve to build Bethel as a sanctuary; but that night he received a divine blessing. He was given the name Israel, which *Jubilees* understood as referring to universal sovereignty and jurisdiction over the earth, rather than simply authority over the Land of Israel. This Israel was one who was told the future of his descendants, and passed knowledge of it to his priestly son Levi. He was not permitted to build Bethel as a sanctuary. The parallels between the figure of the biblical David and the figure of Jacob-Israel as painted by *Jubilees* come clearly to light in this: just as David was not permitted to build the Temple, but was promised a house by God, so Jacob-Israel is not to build Bethel as a sanctuary, but God will assure him of future descendants. God's promises to David had of necessity implied that the king would have a son, who would build the Temple: in its implicit comparison of Jacob-Israel with David, *Jubilees* may have some 'messianic' hope in mind, surely associated with the new name Israel; though what this possible hope might amount to one cannot tell.

Celebrating these things, Jacob-Israel observed the feast of *Shemini 'Atseret*, a biblical institution associated with the inauguration of Solomon's Temple and the public reading of the Torah in the days of Ezra's great assembly. With this feast is the name Israel associated, at once a grand completion of an epic story beginning with the first act of creation into which Israel has been written, and its culmination in Sabbath, and at the same time a new beginning of a formally constituted royal, priestly, holy nation holding authority on earth and keeping Sabbath with the Almighty like the highest angels in heaven. For *Jubilees*, Jacob is the twenty-second head of humanity, corresponding to God's twenty-two works of creation: with Jacob's becoming Israel, there is a sense in which the creative work of the Almighty is fully realized, on the twenty-second day of the seventh, the sabbatical month. No single etymology of the name Israel could possibly encompass such a rich understanding of Patriarch and people, and the author of *Jubilees* refused to be limited by one, even though the Bible had provided it. For that etymology had been part of the tale of Jacob's struggle with an angel, an encounter which would have sat uncomfortably with *Jubilees*' proclamation that Israel and the highest angels shared the same privileges in the presence of the Lord Himself.

5

The One Who Sees God: Israel According to Philo of Alexandria

Philo of Alexandria (*c.*20 BCE—*c.*50 CE), in the course of his many extant writings, regularly explains the name Israel as signifying (ὁ) ὁρῶν τὸν θεόν, '[the] one who sees God', or simply ὁ ὁρῶν, 'the one who sees'. So much is this explanation of the name part of his mental furniture that he sometimes substitutes without further ado 'the one who sees God' or 'the one who sees' for the name Israel when it occurs in Scriptural verses which he is quoting (famously, in his citation of Lev. 15: 31 at *Leg. All.* III. 15; at *QE* II. 38 dealing with Exod. 24:11; and again at *QE* II. 47 in discussion of Exod. 24:17). In similar vein, he is capable of introducing into discussion of biblical verses which themselves have no mention of Israel some reference to 'the one who sees', 'the race which sees', or 'the one who sees God', evidently assuming on the part of his readers some prior knowledge of his usual exposition of the name's meaning (e.g. *De Op. Mun.* 69–71; *De Som.* I. 64–7; II. 226–7).[1] This set of circumstances, when taken together with the fact that nowhere in his writings does Philo offer detailed explanation of how or why the name Israel might mean what he claims it means, suggests that he may have been dependent on an already existing *onomasticon* for this etymology. Some scholars have, in differing degrees, endorsed such a suggestion; and if it be accepted as possible, or even probable, it might not be unreasonable to look for evidence of historical development in the use of the etymology

---

[1] For these references, see E. Birnbaum, *The Place of Judaism in Philo's Thought: Israel, Jews, Proselytes*, Brown Judaic Studies, 290. Studia Philonica Monographs, 2 (Scholars Press: Atlanta, 1996), 77, and further comments of G. Delling, 'The "One Who Sees God" in Philo', in F. E. Greenspahn, E. Hilgert, and B. L. Mack (eds.), *Nourished with Peace: Studies in Hellenistic Judaism in Memory of Samuel Sandmel* (Scholars Press: Chico, 1984), 29–30.

behind and in Philo's writings themselves.[2] In any event, the
description 'one who sees God' represents, for Philo, an individual
who has attained the highest measure of mental and spiritual
development which is possible in this life, and who thereby is
worthy to belong to the fellowship of that privileged society which
Philo calls τὸ ὁρατικὸν γένος, 'the race, or class, which is capable of
seeing'.[3] Since acquisition of the ability to 'see God' constitutes
the very summit of a life devoted to all that is best in philosophical
enquiry, moral striving, and religious piety, it naturally occupies a
central place in Philo's scheme of things. Not surprisingly, therefore, it has attracted the attention of all serious students of the
sage's work, and the literature dealing with it is extensive.[4] A recent
study by Ellen Birnbaum, however, building upon and critically
engaging with earlier scholarship, marks a major step forward in
modern study of Philo's use of designations like 'Israel', 'Jews',
'Hebrews', τὸ ὁρατικὸν γένος, '(the) one who sees (God)', and other
terminology connected with seeing God. Fundamental to this
study is her recognition that the use and meaning of these terms
differs, according to their setting in writings made up of either
allegory, or exposition of Scripture, or questions and solutions of
scriptural texts, or non-exegetical material, or mixed genres. Consequently, she can point with confidence to diverse factors, like the
intended audience of a particular writing, its literary genre, or its
exegetical context, which clearly influenced Philo's discussion of
what it means to 'see God' and the broader question of how such
a vision might correlate with his understanding of 'Israel' in

[2] See e.g. L. L. Grabbe, *Etymology in Early Jewish Interpretation. The Hebrew Names in Philo*, Brown Judaic Studies, 115 (Scholars Press: Atlanta, 1988), 102–3, 172–3; A. Butterweck, *Jakobs Ringkampf*, 65–6; P. Borgen, *Bread From Heaven* (Brill: Leiden, 1965), 115–18; E. Birnbaum, *The Place*, 70–7; E. M. Smallwood, *Philonis Alexandrini Legatio ad Gaium*, 2nd edn. (Brill: Leiden, 1970), 153–5; and the more general discussion in G. J. Brooke, *Exegesis at Qumran: 4QFlorilegium in its Jewish Context*, JSOT Supp., 29 (JSOT Press: Sheffield, 1985), 17–25.

[3] For detailed discussion of this expression, see Delling, 'The "One Who Sees God" in Philo', 28–9, 30–3; and Birnbaum, *The Place*, 94–114.

[4] Only a selection can be given here, in addition to literature cited in n. 2 above. See E. R. Goodenough, *By Light, Light: The Mystic Gospel of Hellenistic Judaism* (Yale University Press: New Haven, 1935), 130–8; *id., The Politics of Philo Judaeus: Practice and Theory* (Yale University Press: New Haven, 1938), 407–14; K. G. Kuhn, article ''Ισραήλ, 'Ιουδαῖος, 'Εβραῖος in Jewish Literature after the OT', in *TDNT*, iii. 359–69; W. Gutbrod, article 'Ιουδαῖος, 'Ισραήλ, 'Εβραῖος in Greek Hel-lenistic Literature' in (ed.) G. Kittel, *Theological Dictionary of the New Testament*, iii, pp. 369–75.

particular instances. In addition, she is able to discern possible earlier and later stages of development in Philo's use of 'the one who sees God' and 'the race/class which is capable of seeing', descriptions used so frequently as to be almost, on the surface of things, commonplace. Likewise, having determined that Philo never refers to 'Israel' as λαός or ἔθνος, but always as γένος, a term meaning not only 'race' but 'class' in the sense of a complete entity before it is broken down into parts, Birnbaum can discern nuances in Philo's use of the phrase τὸ ὁρατικὸν γένος which themselves might be explained as either earlier or more philosophically developed usages.[5]

By drawing attention to this likely process of evolution in descriptions of Israel as 'the one who sees God' or 'the race/class which is capable of seeing', Ellen Birnbaum has ensured that questions about the origin and history of these interpretations of the name Israel are properly confronted. In particular, Philo's relationship in this matter to the Septuagint, normally one of the principal sources of his thought, presents several thorny problems. LXX Gen. 32: 28 (29) offer their own interpretation of the etymology of 'Israel' as set out in the Hebrew text before them, and examined earlier in Chapter 2. Philo, however, does not follow their sense of the name as meaning that 'Israel' is one who is *strong* with God or who has *strengthened himself* with God. Indeed, rarely does he quote this verse directly (*De Mut. Nom.* 44; *De Ebr.* 82), and then to illustrate that Jacob's soul after his wrestling bout was inwardly purified towards God and outwardly clean towards the sensible cosmos, and that his fame is acknowledged by both reason and instruction.[6] The verb ἐνισχύω, which might be said particularly to characterize LXX's interpretation of the verse, is nowhere attested in Philo's work: his direct citation of LXX Gen. 32: 28 (29) reads the simple form of ἴσχυσας, 'you have been strong'.[7]

---

[5] See Birnbaum, *The Place*, chs. 2 and 3, esp. pp. 56–60, 62, 88–9, 120–7.

[6] See below, p. 162. The verse is probably implicit, however, in the discussion at *De Ebr.* 81–2, which partly parallels *De Mut. Nom.* 44 and then presents Jacob as an exemplar of those who guard the laws set by 'right reason' depicted as father, and the customs determined by παιδεία described as mother. Jacob, 'strong with God and with men', fills this role, since 'God' can be understood as the father who is reason, and 'men' as the mother who is discipline: see *Philo* III, pp. 358–9.

[7] On ἐνισχύω in LXX, see above, pp. 59–66 On other occasions, when Philo may be alluding to this verse, he uses the simple form ἰσχύω, the only witness to LXX to do so: see textual apparatus in Wevers, *Septuaginta*, vol. I, *Genesis*, 315, and Butterweck, *Jakobs Ringkampf*, 68.

Likewise, he effectively ignores LXX Gen. 32: 30 (31), expounding the place-name Penu'el by means of Εἶδος θεοῦ because Jacob had there 'seen God face to face', even though the verse would go some way towards providing Scriptural proof and support for his repeated claims that Israel means 'the one who sees God'.[8]

Philo differs noticeably from the LXX accounts of Jacob's change of name in his generous use of language associated with athletics, the gymnasium, and the wrestling arena. LXX themselves at Gen. 32: 25 (26) had understood the rare Hebrew verb וייאבק as 'and he wrestled' (καὶ ἐπάλαιε), thus allowing Philo to picture Jacob as a typical Greek athlete. He was doubtless further encouraged in this enterprise by LXX Gen. 27: 36, which explained Jacob's name with reference to the verb πτερνίζω, 'to trip up', a term used in descriptions of wrestling.[9] Philo himself often speaks of Jacob by using this verb and its related noun πτερνιστής (*Leg. All.* I. 61; II. 89; III. 15, 93, 180, 190; *De Sac.* 42; *De Mig.* 200; *De Mut. Nom.* 81; *De Som.* I. 171), and thereafter can marshal a host of technical terms drawn from the world of the gymnasium and the games in describing Jacob's struggle with his opponent. These include κονίομαι, 'powder oneself' (*De Mig.* 200); τραχηλίζω, 'grasp in a neck-hold' (*De Mut. Nom.* 81); συγκροτέω, 'drill' (*De Som.* I. 251); καταβάλλω, 'throw in wrestling' (*De Mut. Nom.* 85); γυμνάζω, 'train' (*De Sob.* 65); and διαθλέω, 'struggle on' (*De Ebr.* 82). This list does not include words associated with victory in the games, which are a particular feature of Philo's describing the outcome of Jacob's contest.[10]

This state of affairs suggests that Philo has purposefully developed certain definite tendencies in the LXX account of

---

[8] For the use one might expect of this verse in Philo's etymology, see Birnbaum, *The Place*, 70–4. He once quotes LXX Gen. 32: 31 (32) noting that Jacob passed the place τὸ Εἶδος τοῦ θεοῦ (*De Som.* I. 79), the only instance in his entire work where this phrase is recorded, but not in connection with the name Israel. Elsewhere, he tends to keep εἶδος separate from God: see *De Post.* 91–3, where Israel as one who sees is discussed in relation to Deut. 32: 8–9 (as often: see Birnbaum, *The Place*, 137–8, 171–2), and the multiplicity of angels spoken of in those verses representing forms or nations or virtues is contrasted with the one Israel under the direct rulership of God.

[9] On the use of this verb by LXX here and at Hos. 12: 4, Jer. 9: 4, and Mal. 3: 8–9, see M. Harl, *La Bible d'Alexandrie, 1: La Genèse*, 218–19; and for its use as a technical term in wrestling, see H. A. Harris, *Greek Athletics and the Jews* (University of Wales Press: Cardiff, 1976), 69–71.

[10] See further Harris, *Greek Athletics*, 69–72.

Jacob's struggle with his opponent, while applying the soft pedal to other important traits of the version's narrative. Yet on any showing, the element of struggle plays a large, if not dominant, part in Jacob's reception of the name Israel; and this must surely derive from the biblical story recorded in Gen. 32: 22–32 or its interpretation in Hosea 12: 2–6. That said, Philo confines sustained treatment of the Genesis passage to just a few of his writings. These include *De Ebr.* 80–3; *De Mut. Nom.* 44–6, 81–8; and *De Som.* I. 79, 129–31, 171. Even in these sections, however, one senses that Philo is not so much engaged in a systematic commentary on verses of Scripture, as he is setting forth his already formulated understanding of what the wrestling bout at the Jabbok meant. To this end, individual Scriptural verses are cited, often not in narrative order, to emphasize some predetermined message which Philo wishes to convey to his readers. This is evident in the linguistic analysis of Gen. 32: 22ff., which he offers in *De Mutatione Nominum*, and which seems the most logical place to begin detailed study of his thought on the subject.

1. SUSTAINED EXEGESIS OF GENESIS 32: 22–32 IN PHILO'S WORK: MAJOR TEXTS

1.1. *De Mutatione Nominum*

Early on in his treatise *De Mutatione Nominum*, Philo sets forth certain fundamental principles which apply to his exposition of the names Jacob and Israel throughout his writings. Thus we are told (*De Mut. Nom.* 11) that the God revealed to Moses as 'I am the One who exists' (LXX Exod. 3: 14) can properly have no personal name assigned to Him, since His nature is to be rather than to be spoken. Nevertheless, God permits human beings to address Him as 'Lord, the God of the three natures of teaching, perfection, and practice of which Abraham, Isaac and Jacob are recorded as symbols' (*De Mut. Nom.* 12). Sentiments of this sort are found throughout his writings.[11] In this instance, they point to an intimate bond between the Almighty and the Patriarchs in relation to

---

[11] For the textual problem in *De Mut. Nom.* 12, which does not affect what is said here, see notes in *Philo* V, pp. 148–9. That no name can properly be ascribed to God by human beings Philo declares at e.g. *De Vit. Mos.* I. 74–6, which includes mention of the Patriarchs in the manner of *De Mut. Nom.* 12; *Quis Rerum* 170; *De Som.* I, 230; *De Abr.* 50–1; cf. *Quod Det.* 160.

what of the divine Name can be communicated to the world, and
signal a matter of importance which is sometimes overlooked but
which Philo takes most seriously: when Jacob's name is changed,
he asks to be told the name of the being with whom he has
wrestled. The question of the Divine Name itself, therefore, is
never far from Philo's mind as he treats of this episode. Indeed,
what follows in *De Mut. Nom.* 14 is an assertion that not even
God's powers who are His ministers declare His Name: when
Jacob, the man of practice seeking to acquire virtue, asks his
opponent to announce his name (LXX Gen. 32: 29), the request
is refused. Informative is the largely non-biblical reply which
Philo here ascribes to Jacob's opponent, presumably one of those
ministers:

But he said: 'Why do you ask this name of mine?' And he did not reveal his
own and proper name. He said: 'It is enough for you to gain advantage
through my words of good omen ($\epsilon\dot{v}\phi\eta\mu\dot{\iota}as$); but do not seek names,
symbols of created things, alongside of incorruptible natures.'

All that LXX record at this point is the opponent's question, and
the detail that he blessed ($\epsilon\dot{v}\lambda\acute{o}\gamma\eta\sigma\epsilon\nu$) Jacob. Philo's account makes
clear, almost in the manner of a Targum, that the opponent never
revealed his name: so much is evident from the biblical text, but
Philo evidently believes that it requires unambiguous articulation.
The biblical blessing is then represented as $\epsilon\dot{v}\phi\eta\mu\dot{\iota}a$, a word never
used by LXX; in two important passages, however, Philo uses it to
refer to Balaam's blessing of Israel (*De Vit. Mos.* I. 291; *De Mig.*
115), which takes the form of a prophecy setting forth the destiny
of the people. The word can, indeed, have a strongly religious
sense, referring to reverent silence before prayer or some sacred
act; used here, it may imply that the words of Jacob's opponent
had something of the quality of prophecy.[12] The opponent's
words, of course, had been the declaration that Jacob's name was
henceforth to be called Israel. Yet the words quoted above shy
away from names as symbols of created things. As will become
apparent, Philo places Israel firmly in the sphere of the incorruptible, leaving us with the impression that *De Mut. Nom.* 14

---

[12] $\epsilon\dot{v}\phi\eta\mu\dot{\iota}a$ can also express prayer, honour, praise, and, in the best sense of the
word, fame. Philo strongly associates the word with the Patriarch Shem (*De Sob.*
51–2), whose designation in Hebrew means 'name', understood by Philo as
articulating what is good and worthy of praise. On Balaam's oracles, see further
below, pp. 167–8.

represents the change of name as a remarkable blessing, rather than a mere change of designation.

Jacob's struggle next finds mention in a passage beginning at *De Mut. Nom.* 42, where discussion has begun to focus on the twofold duty of the good man towards God and his fellow human being. Philo insists that the soul must be both inwardly and outwardly pure, as Moses taught when he ordered the division of the Tabernacle's courts into two parts, covered the Ark containing the Law with gold both inside and out, and gave two separate robes to the high priest (*De Mut. Nom.* 43).

For these and suchlike things are symbols of a soul pure towards God in respect of inward things, and clean in outward things towards the sensible world and life. So what was said to the victorious wrestler when his head was about to be bound with the crowns of victory was cannily expressed. For the proclamation about him was of this sort: 'You have been strong with God, and (you are) powerful with men.' For to be held in esteem in another order (τάξιν)—that which has to do with the uncreated as well as that which has to do with the created—is a matter for no small mind but for one which (if one must speak the truth) lies as a boundary between the world and God (κόσμου καὶ θεοῦ μεθορίου). On the whole, then, it is fitting for the sensible man (ἀστεῖος) to attend on God, for the governor and father of all things cares for what he has made. (*De Mut. Nom.* 44–5)

Here, the one verse which the Bible offers as an explanation of the name Israel is cited as a clever summing up of what Moses had to say about the double orientation of the worthy soul. Israel is not directly named in this passage; but it would be an ignorant reader indeed who failed to recognize the Scriptural quotation for what it is. Indeed, *De Ebr.* 82 shows some similarities to *De Mut. Nom.* 44 and cites the whole biblical verse, naming Israel explicitly. There is reason to suppose, therefore, that Philo speaks of Israel in *De Mut. Nom.* 45 as μεθόριος, a boundary or border between things earthly and heavenly. It should be noted here that 'cannily expressed' words uttered to Jacob by his opponent have nothing directly to do with sight in respect of his new (but here unexpressed) status as Israel. Rather, Jacob's strength and power are once more noted, and appear to qualify him for a role with respect to God and with respect to men; and Philo makes absolutely certain that this characteristic is firmly founded on an explicitly cited biblical text. It may be noted that elsewhere, too, Philo speaks of the 'sensible man' (ἀστεῖος) as being on a boundary between mortality and

incorruption, so that properly speaking he is neither God nor man
(ὡς κυρίως ἐιπεῖν μήτε θεὸν αὐτὸν ἔιναι μήτε ἄνθρωπον).[13]

Philo, therefore, understands Scripture to state unequivocally
that Jacob, having become Israel after a victorious wrestling-bout
proving his strength, is μεθόριος between God and the world. As
such, Jacob-Israel may be properly compared with other characters, the most exalted of whom is the Logos. Thus in *De Plant.*
10 we read that, since the Flood, the divine Logos acts as μεθόριος
between the various elements which make up the created world, to
keep them separate and to ensure harmony and concord in the
universe. This theme of harmony, often openly related to music,
will occur again in other Philonic discussions of Israel, and is said
to be the happy product of such a 'boundary' (*De Spec. Leg.* II.
157). As μεθόριος, the Logos not only ensures harmony among the
elements of creation, but also exercises a far grander power:

> To the archangel and eldest Logos (τῷ δὲ ἀρχαγγέλῳ καὶ πρεσβυτάτῳ λόγῳ)
> the Father who begat everything has granted a singular gift, that he should
> stand as a boundary (μεθόριος) and separate the creation from the One who
> has made it. But the same Logos is for ever a suppliant (ἱκέτης) to the
> Immortal on behalf of the unquiet mortal, and an ambassador of the ruler
> to the subject. And he rejoices in the gift . . . and says: 'And I stood
> between the Lord and you'—neither uncreated like God, nor created like
> you, but as a middle (μέσος) between extremities serving as a pledge for
> both. To the parent I pledge faith that the thing created should not com-
> pletely refuse the reins, nor rebel and choose disorder over against order;
> to the offspring (I pledge) hopefulness that the merciful God should never
> overlook his own work. For I herald the fruits of peace to the creation
> from God who is for ever guardian of peace. (*Quis Rerum* 205–6)

This remarkable passage permits further definition of Israel as
μεθόριος.[14] The description of the Logos as 'suppliant' is one that
Philo applies also to the Levites (e.g. *De Ebr.* 94; *De Som.* II. 273)
and proselytes (*De Spec. Leg.* I. 309), and thus leads us back again
in the direction of the people Israel. For in one particularly famous

---

[13] *De Som.* II. 230. He says much the same about τέλειος, the 'perfect man', who
stands at the borderline of the uncreated and the corruptible (*De Som.* II. 234–5),
and about the σπουδαῖος, the 'serious man' (*De Virt.* 9). For the relationship of these
'boundary' characters to Philo's notion of covenant, and his application of the word
to parents and the law in the Decalogue relating to them (*De Dec.* 107; *De Spec. Leg.*
II. 224), see Jaubert, *La Notion d'alliance*, 428–9.

[14] For the Logos as archangel and most senior in age and honour, see below,
pp. 207–9.

remark addressed to the Emperor Gaius, he describes Israel as 'the suppliant race which the Father and King of the universe and the (first) cause of all things has assigned as his own portion'; and this description graphically illustrates the liminal character of Israel as a people in the world, yet mysteriously allotted to God whose kingly rule is self-evidently supernatural.[15] In Philo's day the supreme earthly representative of the collective people called Israel was the high priest; and he, too, is not surprisingly described as a 'boundary figure' like Israel itself. Thus in *De Som.* II. 187–8 Philo speaks of his representative character, so that even when he stands alone the high priest may be called a whole people (δῆμος) and, indeed, 'the race of men *in toto*, or rather, if one must speak the truth, a certain boundary, a nature between God and man, less than the former, but greater than man (μεθόριός τις θεοῦ [καὶ ἄνθρωπου] φύσις τοῦ μὲν ἐλάττων ἀνθρώπου δὲ κρείττων)'. In this respect, the high priest is not unlike the First Man, made up of earthly substance and divine breath, himself properly described as 'a boundary between mortal and immortal nature, (θνητῆς καὶ ἀθάνατου φύσεως . . . μεθόριον': *De Op. Mun.* 135).

A summary of the discussion up to this point may be helpful, since we have travelled a good distance from *De Mutatione Nominum*, and need to return to that text with a clear idea of what has been discovered so far. *De Mut. Nom.* 14 strongly implies that Jacob's change of name explained in LXX Gen. 32: 28 is much more than a change of title: it is to be considered a blessing uttered in prophecy, and is inseparably related to the observation that, while God has no proper name made available to human beings, the title 'Lord' and its association with the Patriarchs Abraham, Isaac, and Jacob is given to men as a means for discourse about God and the proper perception of Him. *De Mut. Nom.* 43 uses the same Scriptural verse to establish that Israel is a 'boundary' figure between earth and heaven, standing in the same theological

---

[15] *Leg. ad Gaium* 3, reading: τοῦ ἱκετικοῦ γένους, ὅ τῷ πατρὶ καὶ βασιλεῖ τῶν ὅλων καὶ πάντων αἰτίῳ προσκεκλήρωται. In the very next paragraph, Philo interprets Israel as 'one who sees God'. On this section of the *Legatio*, see Birnbaum, *The Place*, 169–72 with respect to προσκεκλήρωται, which may be rendered either as 'has been allotted' or 'has allotted himself'; and her comments on pp. 60, 106–7, 176–7, and esp. pp. 189–92, where she argues (convincingly, in my view) that Philo here does not declare that Israel is a 'suppliant race' allotted (or allotting itself) to God *because* it sees God. All the evidence suggests that Israel's status and position are determined by Jacob's wrestling with his opponent, as a result of which he emerged as strong with God and powerful with men.

continuum as the Logos, the high priest, and the First Man. Although the name Israel is under consideration in this Scriptural verse, Philo does not here associate it with seeing God. Rather, Israel appears as a kind of 'bridge', linking earthly and heavenly realms.

The results gleaned so far have derived directly from Philo's exegesis of LXX Gen. 32: 28. When he returns to consideration of Jacob's change of name in *De Mut. Nom.* 81–8, after discussing the sense of Abram's change of name to Abraam, and Sara's to Sarra, he does not quote Scripture directly.[16] He opens with an unsupported assertion, that Jacob is called πτερνιστής, 'one who trips up', whereas Israel is called 'one who sees God' (*De Mut. Nom.* 81). His definition of the name Jacob here depends on Esau's assertion in LXX Gen. 27: 36, that his brother had tripped him up twice (ἐπτέρνικεν γάρ με ἤδη δεύτερον τοῦτο). Whereas Esau had intended this declaration in a bad sense and as proof that Jacob had cheated him, Philo took the description as indicating something praiseworthy. From it, he draws the general observation that the 'one who trips up' as he practises virtue is engaged in shaking the solidity of the bases on which the passions are set. The metaphors drawn from athletics and the gymnasium now come thick and fast: the struggle with the passions requires hard, sustained wrestling and gymnastic expertise with throws and neck-locks.[17] The 'one who sees God', Philo insists, must not go forth from the 'sacred stadium' uncrowned, but must take away with him the prizes in victory' (*De Mut. Nom.* 81). Along with the proliferation of athletic metaphors, a tendency to generalize the biblical narrative is also to the fore in this section. It may be assumed that Philo is still talking about Scriptural verses originally speaking of Jacob-Israel, but the language he now uses becomes applicable to any living soul.

So much is evident in Philo's further definition of the victor and his reward (*De Mut. Nom.* 82). The most suitable crown 'for a soul which carries off the prize' (νικηφόρῳ ψυχῇ) is that he should be able to contemplate with sharp-sighted vision the One who exists (τὸν ὄντα δυνήσεται θεωρεῖν ὀξυδερκῶς). These sentiments are not derived from LXX. These translators never speak of Jacob-Israel

---

[16] For his explanation of the names Abram-Abraam, Sara-Sarra, see *De Mut. Nom.* 60–80, where he readily admits that mere adding of letters to a name could be construed as foolish and ridiculous. It is the allegorical and moral lesson conveyed by the change of name which he is concerned to emphasize.

[17] In all this talk of physical combat, however, Philo insists that the real struggle takes place within the soul.

obtaining a crown or wreath. The words νικηφόρος and ὀξυδερκῶς are not found in their vocabulary, and the verb θεωρεῖν and associated forms they never use in their Pentateuch. Furthermore, they do not speak of Jacob as ἀσκητής, 'practiser', one of Philo's favourite explications of his name, and one which he uses immediately after the words of *De Mut. Nom.* 82 set out here; it is right, he says, for the 'ascetic soul' (note the generalizing tone of the words) to receive as reward a 'being-furnished-with-eyes' (ἐνομματωθῆναι) to discern the only One worthy of contemplation (*De Mut. Nom.* 83–4). This expression, too, is entirely foreign to the LXX, but is found elsewhere in Philo's work when he speaks of Israel as 'seeing God'.[18] Indeed, this verb seems to have been used mainly by Philo, and is little attested outside his work.[19] Quite what all this may signify will occupy our attention presently.[20]

Philo next asks why, after Jacob's name had been changed to Israel, he could still be addressed as Jacob—unlike Abraham, who is never again called Abram once his new name has been given. Philo replies that Abraham represents virtue gained by teaching (διδασκαλία), which is more easily retained than the virtue acquired by practice (ἄσκησις): practice needs to 'take a breather', to relax its efforts, like athletes breaking off from training to anoint themselves (*De Mut. Nom.* 83–4). Although he does not say so openly here, Philo may imply that 'seeing God' is a faculty which may be lost, unless the faculties honed by practice retain their sharpness, possibly through continuous training. That, at any rate, seems to be the burden of his further contrastings of Abraham with Jacob-Israel (*De Mut. Nom.* 85–7). Thus the 'taught' man has always the support of his teacher, while the 'ascetic' can rely only on his will, is faced with unrelenting struggle with the passions, and has none to help him. The greatest contrast between the two men, however, is given in *De Mut. Nom.* 87: Abraham was given his new name by the unchangeable God (ὁ ἄτρεπτος θεός) so that his future condition might be solidly founded, while 'an angel, minister of God, a word' (ἄγγελος ὑπηρέτης τοῦ θεοῦ λόγος) renamed Jacob. This was so that it might be acknowledged that 'the things below the One who exists' are not the cause of stability, but of a harmony such as that

---

[18] See further Delling, 'The "One Who Sees God" in Philo', 33–4, quoting also *De Ebr.* 82; *De Som.* I. 164; and note also *De Virt.* 11, where wisdom is said to 'plant eyes' in the soul.

[19] Liddell and Scott cite Philo alone as source for this verb.

[20] See below, pp. 167–9.

produced by a musical instrument. The theme of harmony has already been noted in two of Philo's works noted earlier (*De Plant.* 10; *De Spec. Leg.* II. 157), where it serves to mark out Israel as a 'boundary' figure between heaven and earth.[21] The suggestion here is that the renaming of Jacob as Israel has a good deal to do with the proper ordering of created things, such as they are in agreement with one another, and recognize their creaturely status in terms of the 'boundary' which God's Logos as his minister represents for them. In this matter, it would seem more or less certain that he depended on witnesses of LXX Gen. 32: 24 which specified that an angel wrestled with Jacob.[22]

Somewhat surprisingly, this is the sum total of what Philo has to say about Jacob's change of name in a treatise devoted precisely to the matter of new names. Apart from a passing reference to 'the race/class that can see' in *De Mut. Nom.* 189, with its implied reference to Israel, he has nothing more to say by way of comment on the biblical verses which tell of Jacob's struggle.[23] Indeed, most of what he does have to say in *De Mutatione Nominum* about Jacob becoming Israel is only loosely related to the LXX of Genesis, and uses vocabulary quite foreign to those translators. It is time now to turn to a consideration of what this may betoken. Certainly some of the words he uses here are redolent of the philosophizing which is so much part of his writing: terms like θεωρεῖν, ἀσκητής, ἀρετή, and κατανόησις among many others belong to the realms of common philosophical discourse. In this survey of *De Mutatione Nominum*, however, Jacob's change of name stands revealed as rather more than an allegory of the wise man's struggle against the passions to acquire the sight of something worthy of contemplation. It is certainly that; but it includes also a prophetic character. Jacob-Israel, it will be recalled, gains 'advantage through words of good omen', words which recall the prophetic oracles of Balaam about Israel.[24] Jacob-Israel appears as a 'boundary' figure, 'on the

[21] See above, pp. 162–4.

[22] See Wevers, *Septuaginta*, 314, for the evidence of the MSS and the Church Fathers.

[23] See Birnbaum, *The Place*, 110–11, who concludes that this passage in its present setting may refer either to biblical Israel, or to 'a group of seers whose descent is irrelevant'.

[24] *De Mut. Nom.* 14; see above, p. 161. On Philo's re-presentation of Balaam's oracles as the clear-sighted vision of the unsleeping eyes of the soul, such that Balaam as he prophesies seems to do so *in persona Israel*, see C. T. R. Hayward, 'Balaam's Prophecies as Interpreted by Philo and the Aramaic Targums of the

cusp', as it were, of earth and heaven. The Hebrew prophets would
have understood this well; and they, too, like Jacob-Israel, could be
seen as responsible for ensuring harmony between God and his
creation. But Philo's language seems also to have a personal quality. This is suggested particularly by what he has to say about his
own inspiration in *De Mig.* 35, where he claims to have received
'enjoyment of light, most sharp-sighted vision, very clearest dis-
tinctness of objects such as might occur through eyes as a result of
plainest showing'.[25] This is as good a description as any of what it
might mean 'to be endowed with eyes', and it happens to Philo
through a kind of 'corybantic possession', an external force rendering him unaware of his physical surroundings. Particularly
instructive for our purposes is what follows: the object shown to
Philo is one that is worthy to be contemplated, in this instance the
tree of life (*De Mig.* 36–7). But the one who sees this, remarks
Philo, is the wise man: that is why prophets were once called seers
(he cites 1 Sam. 9: 9), and why Jacob the 'practiser' was keen to
exchange hearing for sight, when he became Israel (*De Mig.* 36–9).
Further attention will need to be given to this remarkable section
of *De Migratione*; for the present, however, it serves admirably to
link Philo's own experience of inspiration with his understanding
of what happened to the Patriarch when he was renamed Israel.

These prophetic-inspirational aspects of the name Israel will
reappear elsewhere in Philo's writings. They should come as no
surprise. Jacob-Israel was credited with prophecy on account of
the famous blessings (Gen. 49: 3–28) which he proclaimed to his
sons, 'the sons of Israel' (Gen. 49: 2) in the course of a biblical
poem which Philo himself regarded as marking out Jacob-Israel as
a prophet (*Quis Rerum* 261). And prophets were once called 'seers',
according to 1 Sam. 9: 9, a point not lost on Philo as his quotations
of this very verse at *Quod Deus* 139 and *Quis Rerum* 78, in addition
to *De Mig. Abr.* 38 cited above, amply testify. These observations
may account, in part, for the generalizing tendency in Philo's exe-

Pentateuch', in P. J. Harland and C. T. R. Hayward (eds.), *New Heaven and New
Earth: Essays in Honour of Anthony Gelston* (Brill: Leiden, 1999), 19–36.

[25] See P. Borgen, *Philo of Alexandria—An Exegete for His Time* (Brill: Leiden,
1997), 18, who describes this as an 'ecstatic experience with loss of consciousness
and with an experience of light'. Philo's theory of inspiration is discussed by
J. R. Levison, *The Spirit in First Century Judaism* (Brill: Leiden, 1997), who also
examines notions of inspiration held by Josephus and Pseudo-Philo: see further
below, n. 35.

gesis of Jacob's name already noted; they may also, again in part, explain his willingness to move far away from close analysis and exegesis of the LXX text. Especially this is so if Philo's personal experience of inspiration has coloured his perception of what happened to the practiser Jacob when he became Israel, the one who sees. The treatise *De Mutatione Nominum*, which one might reasonably expect to throw light on the relationship between Philo's exegesis of Scripture and the particular text which records Jacob's change of name, is nevertheless reticent on these matters, and seems to raise as many questions as it answers. In short, it *explains* very little, being content to assert without further comment the meaning of the name Israel as if everyone knew already what its purport might be. Most striking of all is the fact that this treatise can cite Gen. 32: 28 without any mention of 'seeing God'; when 'seeing God' is under consideration, however, the treatise effectively ignores Gen. 32: 28, and uses mainly non-Septuagintal language to discuss the matter.

1.2 *De Ebrietate 80–3*

Exposition of Gen. 32: 8, cited almost in its entirety, is introduced in *De Ebr.* 82 mainly to illustrate an argument which Philo has been constructing since section 30 of the treatise, where he declares that, in one sense, God is our father and the Wisdom of God is our mother. From another perspective, he can state that our father is philosophy (right reason) and our mother is *paideia*, education or conventional wisdom (*De Ebr.* 34). These 'parents' give rise to four kinds of children, distinguished by their obedience or disobedience towards one parent or both. Jacob-Israel is an example of that child who obeys both parents, observing the laws of father Right Reason (ὁ ὀρθὸς λόγος) and guarding the customs of mother Education (*De Ebr.* 80). The former teaches us to honour the father of all; the latter instructs us not to belittle things commonly esteemed as right (*De Ebr.* 81). Jacob the ἀσκητής, engaged in the contest for virtue, 'was about to exchange hearing for eyes and words for deeds and improvement for perfection' (καὶ προκοπὰς τελειότητος), since God willed to endow his understanding with eyes (αὐτοῦ τὴν διάνοιαν ἐνομματῶσαι) to see clearly what formerly he had received by hearing: for sight is more credible than hearing (πιστοτέρα γὰρ ὄψις ὤτων). At this point, 'the oracles' declare:

Your name shall not be called Jacob, but Israel shall be your name; because
you have been strong with God and powerful with men. (Gen. 32: 28)

Philo now points out that Jacob is the name of learning and
improvement, but Israel the name of perfection (τελειότης), 'for the
name indicates a vision of God' (ὅρασιν γὰρ θεοῦ μηνύει τοὔνομα).
Thus section 82 of the treatise sets the groundwork for discussion,
which the following section takes forward with a rhetorical question: what is more perfect (τελειότερον) of the things associated with
the virtues than the sight of the One who truly is (ἢ τὸ ὄντως ὂν
ἰδεῖν)? The one who sees this good thing (i.e. the vision of the truly
existent), says Philo, is acknowledged as glorious by both parents,
having found strength which is in God and power which is among
men (*De Ebr.* 83).

It is only when we reach the end of section 83 that Philo's motive
for using the Scriptural verse becomes plain: Jacob's name is
changed to Israel because he has been strong with God, that is, he
has obeyed the Father of all who is Right Reason, and because
he has been mighty with men, that is, he obeyed the Mother who is
Wisdom of God or conventional education. Thus he can be
acknowledged by both parents without demur.[26]

What follows (*De Ebr.* 84–7) displays some affinities with *De
Mut. Nom.* 42–3, in that Philo goes on to speak of the child obedient to both parents, Right Reason and Education, as one who
guards not only the laws established amongst humankind, but also
the rules of the Uncreated One. Scripture speaks of this symbolically in telling how Moses covered the Ark with gold both inside
and out (Exod. 25: 10), made two robes for the high priest (Exod.
27: 1; 30: 1), and constructed two altars, one outside the sanctuary,
the other within (Exod. 27: 1; 30: 1). This observation (*De Ebr.* 85)
recalls the twofold duty of the good soul which must be inwardly
pure towards God and outwardly pure and upright towards men,
which Philo discussed in *De Mut. Nom.* 43, although in this last
treatise he substituted the twofold division of the Tabernacle's
courts for the two altars remarked in *De Ebrietate*.[27] But in one
important respect the two treatises are quite different. *De Ebrietate*
does not directly allude to the notion that Israel constitutes
some kind of boundary: this is a central concern of *De Mutatione*

---

[26] The link between Gen. 32: 8 and the wider argument which Philo sets in front
of his readers is not immediately obvious: see *Philo* III, pp. 358–9.

[27] See above, pp. 162–3.

Nominum, and it finds no echoes in the other treatise. Instead, *De Ebrietate* draws further lessons from the imagery of the two parents by associating them with the Scriptural verses Prov. 3: 4; 1: 8; 4: 3, to show how, with his new name of Israel, this particular 'son' stands revealed as obedient to his father and beloved in the sight of his mother.[28] The quoted verses from Proverbs indicate that the 'son' is both obedient to the 'parents' and in turn is beloved, an object of affection. This emphasis on family relationship is quite emphatic and unmistakeable. No sooner is it voiced, however, than Philo turns to his consideration of the Ark, the two high-priestly robes, and the two altars; and this allows him once more to introduce into his discussion the figure of the high priest.

In this instance, the high priest represents the 'wise man', who must be adorned with 'good sense which is more valuable than gold'; like the high priest when he enters the Holiest Place on Yom Kippur wearing only a robe of pure linen (see Lev. 16: 4, 23–4); so when he worships the One he wears the unembroidered robe of truth. In everyday affairs, however, there is complexity, and, like the high priest ministering at the outer altar of burnt offering, the wise man assumes clothes of many colours, representing his mastery of the many facets of life in society (*De Ebr.* 86). Similarly, his ministry at the altar of burnt offering outside the Holy Place has to do with the bodies of sacrificial victims, while the service of the inner altar, on which incense is offered, is to do with rational things which may be compared with the incense (*De Ebr.* 87). Although some distance removed from the citation of Gen. 32: 28, these sentiments suggest that Philo has again sought to present Israel as sharing certain attributes and characteristics of the high priest, a sacral figure who lives, as it were, in two worlds.

We may summarize Philo's exegesis of LXX Gen. 32: 28 in this section by noting, first, that he has used the verse *primarily* to illustrate the kind of 'personality' whose father is God and whose mother is the Wisdom of God. At no point in his discourse does he show how or why the name Jacob refers to practice, while Israel refers to sight; these are matters which he appears to take for granted, without need of explanation. Secondly, in his exposition of the Scriptural verse Philo is less concerned with the names Jacob and Israel and what they might signify, than he is determined to show how the kind of personality he describes is obedient

---

[28] See *De Ebr.* 84; and *Philo* III, p. 503.

both to divine and human instruction. It is Jacob-Israel's power
with both God and men which seems to lead to the quotation of the
verse in the first instance, as illustrating the personality who obeys
both parents (*De Ebr.* 80–1). Thirdly, obedience plays a further role
in providing the *reason* why Jacob's name was changed to Israel;
but it does not, of itself, explain either name. Finally, although the
image of 'boundary' applied to Israel in *De Mut. Nom.* 44–5 is
lacking here, Philo's continuing insistence on the double-sided
character of the personality he describes, one side turned to God,
the other to the world of the everyday, is once more grounded in
language drawn from the world of the Temple and the life of the
high priest.

1.3 *De Somniis I. 79, 129–31, 171*

De Som. I. 79 is part of an extended discussion of four allegorical
senses which Philo ascribes to the word 'sun' in different Pentateuchal passages, namely: the human mind; sense perception; the
divine Logos; and God himself. Here he quotes LXX Gen. 32: 31
to illustrate his opinion that the 'sun' may, in certain circumstances, symbolize sense perception which has the effect of banish-
ing incorporeal images from the mind, replacing them with objects
of sense. Thus when Moses says of Jacob-Israel, after his
encounter with the angel and his reception of the new name, that
'the sun rose for him when he passed by the Form-of-God (τὸ εἶδος
τοῦ θεοῦ), we are to understand that Jacob-Israel no longer
remained with 'the holiest forms which are also as it were incorporeal images'.[29] Rather, he turned elsewhere and was led by a light
corresponding to sense perception, which compared with healthy
reason is little better than darkness. This 'sun' arouses the senses,
and turns into sleep the higher virtues of prudence, righteousness,
knowledge, and wisdom. It should be observed that Philo makes
no attempt directly to expound the phrase 'Form-of-God', but
simply invites the reader to conclude that it is something associated
with incorporeal realities and the principal virtues, which the
senses can overwhelm and banish from a person's consciousness.
Once more, he seems concerned to show how easily and quickly
Jacob's night-time experience, when he is named 'the one who sees

---

[29] Philo's citation of this verse differs slightly from the critical edition of LXX
prepared by Wevers, *Septuaginta*, 316, which reads: ἀνέτειλεν δὲ αὐτῷ ὁ ἥλιος ἡνίκα
παρῆλθεν τὸ Εἶδος τοῦ θεοῦ.

God', may vanish in the 'light' of sense perception. It will be recalled that he has said something of the same sort in *De Mut. Nom.* 83–7.

We may now turn to *De Som.* I. 129–31. Although Jacob's encounter with the incorporeal world is once more central to the argument Philo sets out there, his direct quotation of LXX Gen. 32: 25 comes as something of a surprise. This verse follows hot on a paraphrase of Jacob's fight with an opponent who turns out to be the divine Logos (129); and this paraphrase, in turn, is itself set within a lengthy exegesis of Jacob's first visit to Bethel as recorded in Gen. 28: 10–22. In their different ways, both LXX and *Jubilees* had contrived to associate Jacob's change of name to Israel with events set in train by that first visit to Bethel; these have already been noted elsewhere.[30] Philo's ploy, while it may well owe something in general terms to this history of exegesis, is nonetheless rooted in his own very particular reading of Gen. 28: 11, with its note that, at Bethel, Jacob took one of the stones of the *place*, put it under his head, and slept in that *place* (*De Som.* I. 120). Philo at once understands these words to refer to Jacob's life of hard work and endurance, which he contrasts with sensual lives of self-indulgence (121–3). The latter cannot be acquainted with the holy Logos; this privilege is available only to those who have been toughened by the self-imposed austerities and deprivations which necessarily accompany the attempt to acquire virtue, a matter which he dwells on in some detail (124–5). The point of this lengthy treatment of the verse is revealed in *De Som.* I. 126, where Philo winds up his description of Jacob's frugal, demanding, and austere way of life and speaks of him as 'the athlete of excellent pursuits'. From this moment on, therefore, Philo can intertwine details of the athlete Jacob's wrestling with the angel into his account of Jacob's first visit to Bethel.

On reaching Bethel, the Bible informs us, Jacob lighted upon the place (Gen. 28: 10). The word 'place' is found some six times in the LXX of Gen. 28: 10–22, and has already featured in Philo's commentary: in *De Som.* I. 115–19 he tells us that it represents, in this instance, an immortal Logos, a 'word' which may also be described

---

[30] Thus LXX Gen. 28: 20 made Jacob offer a prayer (MT has him vowing a vow) that God allow him to return in safety to his 'father's house', which may be understood as Bethel; and *Jub.* 31: 1, 3, 29 insists on Jacob's need to return to Bethel to fulfill the vow he made on his earlier visit.

as an angel.[31] Thus in arriving at the 'place', Jacob arrives at a holy
land full of incorporeal 'words', and these are souls (*De Som.* I.
127). Indeed, the stone which Jacob took to sleep upon was one
such 'word', which Jacob set close to his mind and on which he
rested, laying all his life upon it (128). At this point, Philo gives a
dramatic twist to the exegesis by drawing upon Jacob's change of
name to Israel:

He (the Logos) gladly hearkens to and receives the athlete as one who first
of all will be a disciple; then, when he has accepted the fitness of his
nature, he binds his hands in a manner of a trainer and calls him to the
athletic exercises, leans upon him and compels him to wrestle until he has
prepared in him an invincible bodily strength: he changes ears into eyes
with divine inspirations, and calls him, when he has been newly engraved
as a new character (τύπος), Israel, the one who sees.[32]

This passage does not cite Scripture directly; but throughout it
Philo draws on his particular reading of LXX Gen. 32: 28 in the
light of Greek athletic practice. Something of the same sort we
have already met in our reading of *De Mut. Nom.* 81, although in
that treatise Philo remarks (82) that the prize awarded to Jacob in
the wrestling bout is contemplation with sharp-sighted vision of
the One who exists.[33] Familiar also are Philo's words about the
change of ears into eyes. What we have not encountered so far,
however, is the suggestion that Jacob's change of name involves a
more radical alteration of the Patriarch's personality. The words
quoted above indicate that Jacob's wrestling with the Logos leads
to the latter's re-formation, μεταχαραχθέντα καινὸν τύπον Ἰσραήλ,
'newly engraved as a new character of Israel'. This language
smacks of the artisan or metalworker, restamping, remoulding, or
reminting a metal or other substance into a new form. In particular, it may refer to the reminting of coinage, as in *De Mig.* 39,
where once again Philo uses it to describe Jacob's change of name
to Israel as one who sees; in this instance, the object of his seeing is
the divine light, that knowledge which opens the eye of the soul.[34]

---

[31] For Philo's discussion of God in relation to the notion of 'place' and the
Logos, see R. Goulet, *La Philosophie de Moïse. Essai de reconstitution d'un commentaire préphilonien du Pentateuque* (J. Vrin: Paris, 1987), 292–339.

[32] *De Som.* I. 129.

[33] See above, pp. 165–6.

[34] For Philo's use of μεταχαράσσω with respect to the reminting of coinage, see
also *Quod Det.* 152; *De Conf. Ling.* 159; *De Mut. Nom.* 123; and *Quod Omnis* 98.

Elsewhere, too, Philo takes up the verb μεταχαρασσεῖν to express change of character consequent upon a new name, as in the cases of Abraham and Sarah (*De Cher.* 4) and Joshua (*De Mut. Nom.* 121). The verb itself, then, is one which Philo can readily adopt when he has to write about changes of name; but his only pretext for introducing it here, into what is principally an exegesis of Gen. 28: 10–22, is a rather remote one. For those verses say nothing at all about Jacob's name. It is only their reference to the stone, which Philo allegorically interpreted as Logos, which allowed his line of thought at all. In consequence, his exegesis here led him to envisage Logos as fighting with Jacob. This is unexpected, to say the least, inasmuch as what we have seen of his writings so far suggested Jacob's wrestling resulted in his becoming a 'boundary figure', who might properly be compared with the Logos, not set in opposition to it.

Equally unexpected is what follows in *De Som.* I. 130. Here at last we find a direct quotation from Scripture (LXX in Gen. 32: 25) telling how, after Jacob's wrestling bout, 'the broad part (of his thigh) became numb'. This, it seems, represents the crown of victory which Jacob achieved in the fight! Here the prize for victory in the fight is neither clear-sighted vision of the One who exists (*De Mut. Nom.* 82); nor Jacob's elevation to the status of a boundary figure (*De Mut. Nom.* 45); nor his acknowledgement as obedient son of the two parents, 'right reason' and 'conventional education'; but a 'numbness' which Philo takes to be a voluntary renunciation of the power which the soul might rightly claim, so that it still falls short of incorporeal beings (*De Som.* I. 131). Jacob-Israel's lameness in the aftermath of the fight leaves him in the realms of this world, even though his victory rightfully entitled him to associate with incorporeal beings.

The differences between this account of things in *De Somniis* and the other Philonic writings examined here should not, however, be exaggerated. In this essay, Philo's prime purpose is to provide an exposition of Jacob's first visit to Bethel and his vision of angels ascending and descending a ladder linking earth and heaven. In Philo's view, these angels are incorporeal beings, souls, who may be called 'logoi'. When he introduces the story of Jacob's wrestling bout into this exposition, he does so knowing that Jacob's opponent was an angel: this much is evident from his explanations of the wrestling bout found elsewhere in his writings. It is not difficult for him, then, in this particular essay, to envisage the angel opponent as a 'logos', akin to those 'logoi-angels' ascending and descending the ladder. Jacob's vision of those beings vanished when he awakened, just as his wrestling opponent would later vanish with the dawn (LXX Gen. 32: 31), leaving Jacob in the world of common sense-experience, yet in some measure transformed inwardly.

In other words, the character of the narrative in Genesis 28 has largely determined Philo's presentation of Jacob's wrestling bout in *De Som.* I. 129ff., in that both Philo and the biblical author have understood the dream of angels and ladder as evanescent, but of an inspired, even prophetic kind; for later on, in *De Som.* I. 141, Philo will speak of the angels as 'daimons', who provide access to the divine.[35] Indeed, when Philo comes to the end of expounding that dream sequence, he is at pains to indicate that the new name Israel is not evanescent at all, thus correcting the impression he had given earlier in the essay. For in *De Som.* I. 171 he contrasts what Jacob saw vaguely in dream-fashion with the clear sight accorded to him by his change of name:

> However, if this practiser runs vigorously to the goal, and sees clearly the things he dreamed of obscurely, and is transformed with a better character and is named Israel (the one who sees God) in place of Jacob (the one who trips), he no longer registers as his father Abraham (the one who learns) but Isaac, the one who was born sensible by nature.

He also makes clear his reason for making this observation here: proper exegesis of the biblical passage under his consideration demands nothing less. As he explains (*De Som.* I. 168–70), in Gen. 28: 13 God had addressed Jacob as 'the Lord God of Abraham your father, and the God of Isaac', pointedly calling Abraham, but not Isaac, the father of Jacob. For Philo, this can mean only one thing: at that point in the Scriptural narrative Jacob was still 'son of Abraham', that Patriarch who represents virtue as acquired by learning instilled through teaching. Jacob is the son of this Abraham, Jacob the 'practiser', who strives to acquire virtue

---

[35] 'These the other philosophers are accustomed to call daimons, while the sacred word calls them angels, using a more suitable designation; for they announce the Father's orders to his children, and the needs of the children to their Father.' See Levison, *The Spirit*, 43–5, for a detailed comparison of this and other Philonic passages with Plato's discussions of daimons in his *Symposium* 202E–203A, and their role in inspiration. Observe also what Philo had said about the Logos as boundary figure in *Quis Rerum* 205–6, cited above, pp. 162–3.

by mastering the passions. Both he and Abraham have to put effort into their attaining of virtue. Later in the Scriptural record, however, we hear (at Gen. 46: 1) that 'Israel' offered sacrifice to the God of his father Isaac. This 'oracle', says Philo, in a manner uncannily reminiscent of the author of *Jubilees*, is 'inscribed on the sacred tablets', and speaks not of mortal men, but of 'facts of nature' (*De Som.* 172). The upshot of it is this: Israel, the one who sees God, has as his father Isaac: this father has for his guide a nature which is self-hearing and self-taught (168), and is 'the one who was born sensible by nature' (171). Thus Jacob is son of Abraham, while Israel is the son of Isaac; and the latter represents a higher stage than the former in the acquisition of virtue.

1.4 *Israel As One Who Sees God and the Septuagint Pentateuch: Summary*

The results of this survey must necessarily be tentative and suggestive rather than definitive; but certain aspects of Philo's thinking are fairly clear. In his extensive writings we should not always expect consistency, and a tendency on his part not always to offer the same 'prizes' to the athlete Jacob has already caught our attention. The following points, however, seem to stand out, and prepare the way for the next task in hand.

First, Philo never directly quoted a verse of the LXX version of Gen. 32 or of Gen. 35 to *demonstrate*, directly or indirectly, that the name Israel had to do with seeing. He nevertheless quoted Gen. 32, often embellishing it with references to the wrestling arena, mainly to speak of Jacob's victorious struggle with an angel, the reward for which was 'vision'; to prove that Israel is the beloved son of right reason and convention; and to show how Israel acts as a harmonious boundary between heaven and earth.

Secondly, Philo seems to have regarded Gen. 28 as the key biblical text displaying how it is that Israel signifies 'the one who sees God'. He directly associated this chapter with Jacob's change of name, and was careful to record how and why he did so. It should be recalled that both Gen. 28 and Gen. 32 in Philo's LXX included mention of angels (28: 11, 15; 32: 24) and repeated references to 'place' (Gen. 28 six times; Gen. 32 and 35 four times between them). He also understood the angels at Bethel as 'logoi', one of whom was responsible for wrestling with Jacob and for conferring the name Israel upon him. In *De Som.* I. 141 he designated angels as 'daimons', who communicate divine knowledge to humanity.

This last item points directly to our third observation, concerning Philo's exegesis of those biblical verses which he did quote directly. Here he introduced the notion of *prophecy* and *prophetic inspiration* to the reader's attention more than once, and in a variety of ways. These allusions to prophecy helped to give coherence to his various statements about Israel as a 'boundary' at the limits of earth and heaven; as receiving 'words of good omen'; as a visionary 'endowed with eyes'; and as one who has been changed into another character: this last was exactly what happened to King Saul, who was 'turned into another man' under the influence of prophetic inspiration (1 Sam. 10: 6, 9).

Fourthly, throughout his exposition of these biblical passages, Philo reiterated the twofold character of Israel as one turned now towards God, now towards the world: see particularly Gen. 32: 28 as interpreted in *De Mut. Nom.* 44–5. The principal symbol of this is the high priest. The latter represents the whole Jewish people; and this suggests that whenever Philo spoke of Israel as 'one who sees God', he always had in mind the Jewish people as a whole, whoever else he might be considering. He may have had in mind some non-Jews as well. Recent studies by John R. Levison of Philo's theories of inspiration, especially his illuminating monograph *The Spirit in First Century Judaism*, have underlined Philo's awareness and use of models of inspiration current in the Graeco-Roman world of his time. From the Bible, Philo knew that God could make use of Gentiles as seers, the prime example of this being His inspiration of the wicked Balaam. Taking these two observations together, we may begin to explain why Philo could speak approvingly of non-Jews whom he labelled 'seers', occasionally describing them in terms not unlike those he used to speak about Israel.[36]

Philo's interpretation of Israel as 'one who sees God' cannot, however, be properly appreciated unless some attempt is made to examine the matter from God's point of view, if we may so speak. Perhaps understandably, this aspect of his concern with the name Israel attracts much less attention than the matter of seeing God. Yet the very words themselves indicate a divinity who is willing to be seen in some sense; and they may have a very particular point, if we set them alongside the LXX Pentateuch's repeated assertions that the sanctuary which Moses constructed, the prototype of the

---

[36] See Birnbaum, *The Place*, 94.

Jerusalem Temple, was the place above all others where God might be seen. At various places within the sanctuary, according to the LXX translators, God might appear to Moses, to Aaron the high priest, and to other rightly ordered individuals, in a manner at once majestic yet intimate. As we shall see, Philo was not unaware of this in his estimate of Israel as 'one who sees God'.

2. PHILO'S ISRAEL AND THE WORSHIP OF GOD

This journey through Philo's writings has allowed us to establish some bearings regarding his use of LXX; and it has also showed themes in his thinking which recur more or less regularly, and which serve to station Israel as 'one who sees God' in a position between the created and uncreated, between earth and heaven, between the human and the divine. So many are the ramifications of Israel's position, that we must now attempt to discern whether they form a pattern, which itself can bring into focus what Philo had in mind by so often stressing the character of Israel as 'one who sees God'. I shall suggest that a powerful influence on his thought has been exercised by LXX Pentateuch, which speaks of the Sanctuary as a place where God may be seen. Such an understanding of the Sanctuary's function expressed in his text of Scripture, coupled with Philo's own acceptance of a tradition that Israel is 'one who sees God', is a powerful combination of ideas which demands investigation.

2.1. *The Sanctuary As the Place Where God Is Seen*

According to the Hebrew of Exod. 25: 8, God commanded Moses that Israel should make for Him a Sanctuary, so that he might dwell in the midst of the people.[37] The LXX translators represented this verse as a command to Moses, as follows: 'And you shall make for me a sanctuary, and I shall be seen among you (καὶ ὀφθήσομαι ἐν ὑμῖν).' This is the text of Scripture which Philo knew.[38] The very distinctive translation was no accident: it accords with the LXX version of the closing words of Gen. 22: 14, after Abraham had offered up the ram in place of his son Isaac on

---

[37] The Hebrew has: 'and let them make for me a sanctuary, that I may tabernacle among them'. For comment on the LXX translation, see A. Le Boulluec and P. Sandevoir, *La Bible d'Alexandrie, 2: L'Exode* (Cerf: Paris, 1989), 252.

[38] See further Borgen, *Philo of Alexandria*, 38–41, 46–62.

Mount Moriah which, as the translators very well knew, was the designated site of the future Jerusalem Temple. The words in question are put into Abraham's mouth, and he is made to remark: 'on the mountain the Lord has been seen.'[39] That the Sanctuary, whose final and permanent earthly location is Jerusalem, constitutes the place where God might be seen is clear from two further LXX passages. At Lev. 16: 2 the translators make the Lord Himself state that *He will be seen* in a cloud from within the Holy of Holies on Yom Kippur; and at Gen. 31: 13 Jacob was confronted with the God who *appeared* to him in the place of God, a passage which was discussed above.[40] In all these verses, LXX speak of God—not His Glory, His majesty, or His splendour—being seen or appearing. The translators did not specify what they thought this might mean. They merely recorded the fact.

One general point might be noted here. The people responsible for translating the Law of Moses into Greek would certainly have been aware that non-Jews might now have access to the lawgiver's teachings, including his words about the Sanctuary. Educated Greeks, reading or hearing that the Jewish Temple was the place where God might be seen or appear, might conclude that the religion of Israel had something of the quality of the non-Jewish so-called mystery religions, in which the sight of ineffable religious secrets played a dominant role. With the proper safeguards in place, Philo seemed happy to collude with such an idea. As we shall see, he does indeed present Israel's religion as a mystery, with Moses as its hierophant; and there can be little doubt that LXX's

---

[39] The Greek translates here an ambiguous Hebrew יֵרָאֶה יְהוָה בְּהַר. The verb may be read as either *qal* or *niphʻal*, and translated respectively either as 'on the mountain the Lord shall see', or 'on the mountain the Lord shall be seen'. LXX appear to have opted for the latter. The translators would have been familiar with the fact that Mount Moriah, the mountain in question here, was the place where Solomon was to build the Temple, according to 2 Chron. 3: 1.

[40] According to the Hebrew of Lev. 16: 2, the Lord declared: 'I shall be seen in the cloud upon the ark-cover', and the LXX retained that sense. On Gen. 31: 13, see above, pp. 42–3. The Hebrew of that verse identified the speaker as 'the God of Bethel', Bethel signifying 'house of God' and carrying with it very strong Temple connotations. The LXX have here introduced a notion of God's being seen which is lacking from our current MT; and the 'place' of God also may allude to the Sanctuary: see esp. Jer. 7: 12, and the Deuteronomic formula relating to the place where the Almighty will make His Name dwell, Deut. 12: 5; 15: 20; 17: 10. For a convenient survey of 'place' as Sanctuary in biblical literature, see J. Gamberoni, article 'מָקוֹם *māqôm*', *TDOT* viii, 532–44.

portrayal of the Sanctuary as a place of God's appearing had something to do with his willingness to use expressions drawn from the mysteries. The mysteries were also the means whereby initiates learned hitherto concealed truths, and they consorted well with Philo's notion of Israel as a status which the 'practiser' arrives at after instruction and lengthy training.

For Philo, then, Israel is one who sees God, and the Sanctuary is the place where God may be seen. These two considerations he explored in *QE* II. 51, commenting on Exod. 25: 8. The literal meaning of this verse, he noted, indicates that the Sanctuary spoken of in this Scriptural verse is the archetype of the Tabernacle.[41] Its deeper meaning, however, is to the effect that God always appears in His work which is most sacred, that is to say, the world. His beneficent powers are seen in all its parts, since as saviour God is beneficent and kind, and wishes to distinguish the 'rational race' from all other living creatures. The 'rational race', suggests Marcus, may refer either to Israel, or to pious people in general.[42] To these God grants a special gift, which consists in His appearing. But this appearance of God is dependent on there being a suitable place for Him to appear, a place purified by holiness and every kind of purity. A mind filled with pleasures and passions cannot see the intelligible sun; but if it is worthily initiated, consecrated to God, and in some sense an animate shrine of the father, then it will see the First Cause and be awakened from the deep sleep which had hitherto been its portion:

Then will appear to thee that manifest One, Who causes incorporeal rays to shine for thee, and grants visions of the unambiguous and indescribable things of nature and the abundant sources of other good things. For the beginning and end of happiness is to be able to see God. But this cannot happen to him who has not made his soul, as I said before, a sanctuary and altogether a shrine of God.

This exposition is valuable, in that it allows us to draw together motifs and ideas which have already occupied our attention. First, there is Philo's understanding that God has two temples, the universe and the rational soul, whose sensible copy is the Temple in Jerusalem (*De Som.* I. 125). Secondly, Philo's sense that the rational soul is a temple allows him to describe it as worthy of

---

[41] For what follows, see the translation of this passage by R. Marcus, *QE*, 97–9.

[42] See ibid. 98. The original Greek appears to have read τὸ λογικὸν γένος, which could refer either to a race or to a class of people.

consecration and purification, states which require labour and effort to achieve and maintain. The business of Jacob struggling with the passions, although not explicit in this particular exposition, is certainly of a piece with it. Finally, the 'rational race' is one which sees God, whose being seen is indissolubly linked with His expressed desire to be seen in a temple and confer benefits on those by whom He is seen. That race is distinguished, excepted, set apart from other living creatures; and it brings to mind those texts discussed above in which Israel as one who sees God was described as specially allotted to the Creator.[43]

By so intimately bonding together the seeing of God with the Sanctuary, Philo compels his readers by his language of consecration, initiation, and purification to consider *holiness*, which is the special characteristic of the God of Israel, of His Temple, and of the Jewish people. These matters Philo pondered in *De Praem.* 120–3 as part of an extended reflection on the nature of the mind of the serious man housed in a well-built body: a mind which is purified, initiated into divine mysteries, and which accompanies the circuit of the heavenly chorus. Already these words recall his musings on the Logos as 'boundary', an association confirmed at *De Praem.* 122, where he describes this same mind as drinking the wine of God's beneficent powers. This mind, Philo continues (*De Praem.* 123), is one

in which, says the prophet, God walks about as in a royal house, for indeed a wise man's mind is a royal house for the One who exists, and a house of God. Of this house, the God is called peculiarly God of all; and again, a chosen people is this, not belonging to successive rulers, but to the one true Ruler—a holy (people) of a holy (ruler) (ἁγίου ἅγιος).

Although this is a description of the serious man's mind, it is also a description of Israel, among whom God walks about (LXX Lev. 26: 12) and for whom this people was constituted as a royal house (βασίλειον), a house of God, a chosen people ruled by God alone. The 'royal house' is an allusion to LXX Exod. 19: 6, which decreed that the house of Jacob and the sons of Israel are to be βασίλειον ἱεράτευμα καὶ ἔθνος ἅγιον, a royal house, priesthood, and holy nation. Israel is a 'chosen people' (λαὸς ἐξαίρετος), delivered from Pharaoh, as Philo goes on to say in *De Praem.* 124; and this is a

---

[43] See above, p. 164.

deliverance from the passions and lusts.[44] Israel is ruled by God alone, not by angels, a point made with some effect by LXX Deut. 32: 8–9. The climax of all this is the designation of the people as holy, belonging to a holy ruler.

In one sense, it is evident that Philo has here applied characteristics of Israel to the mind of the serious man, who is also called the wise man.[45] This may lead us to suppose that Philo implied that Israel as one who sees God might include not only the Jews, but also others who had acquired the necessary qualifications for seeing God. Students of Philo have sometimes drawn this conclusion, and it has something to commend it. Yet Philo's insistence on the holiness of the serious man, who provides for God a royal house, is very striking; and the God who is seen in this royal house is the God of all, not merely in the sense that He is the God of every human being, but precisely in the sense that He is the God of 'the chosen people'. It is of interest to recall at this point that the title 'God of all' was also used by the author of *Jubilees*, to speak of the one universal deity worshipped by Israel alone.[46] When we turn to *De Abr.* 50–8, this matter forces itself on us again, as Philo considers the 'royal house' of God spoken of in Exod. 19: 6; but on this occasion he further introduces discussion of the Name of God, knowledge of which, on any showing, is granted to the Jewish people alone. At the very start of this chapter I noted that Philo had alluded more than once to the Divine Name in treating of Jacob's change of name to Israel; and the passage I examine next will show something of his reasons for bringing these two names so closely together.[47]

His exegesis begins in earnest at *De Abr.* 48, where Philo alludes to the trio Abraham, Isaac, and Jacob as athletes in the truly sacred games, athletes who train the soul to gain victory over the passions. These all belong to the same house and race or class of people, and Philo dubs them 'Godlovers' and 'Godloved' (*De Abr.* 50). Their love of God, says Philo, was rewarded when God united His own

---

[44] See LXX Exod. 3: 8, where God commissioned Moses ἐξελέσθαι Israel from Pharaoh's power, such that the people is said quite properly in Philo's words to be ἐξαιρετός.

[45] See also *De Cong.* 116, where Philo speaks of the Tabernacle's structure as including the whole of wisdom, which is the court and royal house of the head of all, the only King and sole Ruler.

[46] See above, pp. 124–5.

[47] See above, pp. 160–2.

name (τὸ ἴδιον ὄνομα) with theirs, as is shown by the biblical verse Exod. 3: 15, declaring that God's eternal Name is 'the God of Abraham and the God of Isaac and the God of Jacob' (*De Abr.* 51). At once Philo asserts that God needs no name (ὀνόματος γὰρ ὁ θεὸς οὐ δεῖται); but he grants to human beings a Name so that they may pray and supplicate the deity. On a deeper level, says Philo, the words of Scripture refer to different types of soul (*De Abr.* 52), such that Abraham is symbolic of virtue acquired through teaching, Isaac of that gained through nature, and Jacob of what is obtained through practice. Although ascribed to separate individuals, these symbols complement one another, Philo comparing them with the three Graces of Greek mythology, and remarking that they signify not men but potentialities which are of eternal value.[48] Next, Philo adds to the first group of three another trio, the 'royal house', 'priesthood', and 'holy nation' of LXX Exod. 19: 6. Abraham, Isaac, and Jacob were the progenitors of this trio, which has a special name:

> And the name discloses its power: for in the language of the Hebrews the nation is named Israel, which interpreted means 'one who sees God'. Now the sight of the eyes is the best among all the senses, since through it alone the best of all existing things is comprehended . . . and sight through the ruling principle of the soul excels the other powers which are in it: indeed, this is prudence, which is the sight of the mind. (*De Abr.* 57)

In this scheme of things, the three characteristics represented by Abraham, Isaac, and Jacob, with whom God associates His own Name as given to human beings to use in prayer and supplication, are excelled by one other quality. This quality is also represented by a threefold title; but unlike the others, it can be summed up under the single name Israel. It consists in the vision of God. Philo's words in *De Abr.* 50–7 strongly suggest that, just as the three names Abraham, Isaac, and Jacob are inseparably bound up with the Divine Name given to human beings, so also the single name Israel is to be associated with the Divine Name. He does not state this explicitly; but it is a natural inference from what he has said here and in other places in his writings.[49]

In short, Philo is implying that Israel, the royal house, priesthood, and holy nation, is associated with another Name of God, but one which human beings do not commonly use to address

[48] See *De Abr.* 54–5; *De Mut. Nom.* 11–14; and above, pp. 160–2.
[49] See above, pp. 166–9.

Him, and one which is as much superior to the title 'Lord God of Abraham, Isaac, and Jacob' as Israel is superior to Jacob, as sight is superior to hearing, as the dominant faculty of the soul is superior to its lower qualities. This Name must surely be the only other formal title which Philo regularly uses to speak of God, namely ὁ ὤν, 'He who Is'. As is well known, these two Greek words were chosen by the LXX translators to represent the Hebrew אהיה אשר אהיה of Exod. 3: 14, which is often put into English as 'I am who I am'.[50] This expression God offered to Moses as an amplification of His title 'God of Abraham, God of Isaac, and God of Jacob' which He had already revealed to the lawgiver (Exod. 3: 6). From the human point of view, this first person name 'I am who I am' is represented by the four consonants יהוה, as Exod. 3: 15 makes plain. This is the ineffable Name, the Tetragrammaton, as Philo called it (*De Vit. Mos.* II. 115), a Name which, by a custom already old in Philo's own days, might lawfully be articulated with its proper vocalization only in the Temple at Jerusalem, and nowhere else. Only at the very centre of Jewish life, in the place where the people Israel solemnly and formally serve the One God as 'a royal house, priesthood, and holy nation' to use LXX's words, might this Name be proclaimed and directly invoked. Indeed, it was engraved upon the golden plate attached to the high priest's headdress as he ministered in the Temple; reporting this, Philo reminded his readers that it is a Name 'which only those whose ears and tongues are purified may hear or speak in the holy place, and not in any other place at all'.[51]

This section of the *De Abrahamo*, it would seem, offers for those with eyes to see a hint of a higher world beyond the reach of conventional philosophy. There is here a strong sense that access to the most elevated realms to which the human soul might rise is to be found in Judaism, and in Judaism alone. It is indeed the case in this passage that Philo speaks of the soul in general, possibly implying that non-Jews might aspire to 'see God' in the manner he describes. The same might be said of his remarks in *De Sob.* 62–7, which expound LXX Gen. 9:7, Noah's prayer that God may dwell in the *houses* of Shem. Philo treated Shem as a root of moral goodness from which sprang Abraham, a tree bearing the sweet fruit

[50] On the LXX translation and interpretation of the Divine Name in Exod. 3: 14, see Le Boulluec and Sandevoir, *La Bible d'Alexandrie*, 92.
[51] *De Vit. Mos.* II. 114, translated by F. H. Colson, *Philo* V, 505.

Isaac the self-taught, from whom arose Jacob the athlete, wrestling with the passions. This last was the source of the twelve tribes—Israel, though Philo does not use the name here—who make up the 'royal house, priesthood, and holy nation' of LXX Exod. 19: 6, a plural designation leading back to the plea that God dwell in the *houses* of Shem. This royal house, Philo declares, is 'the sanctuary in reality, and alone inviolate' (ἱερὸς ὄντως καὶ μόνος ἄσυλος: *De Sob.* 66). Once more, it seems that the royal house marks a stage beyond, an advance on Abraham, Isaac, and Jacob.

What comes next is illuminating. For LXX Gen. 9: 27 is ambiguous, and may be understood, as Philo has so far understood it, as a prayer that God dwell in Shem's houses. The verse, however, could be read as a plea that Shem's brother, Japheth, who is also named in the blesing, dwell in the houses of Shem. In Philo's scheme of things, Japheth represents the kind of philosophy which holds that riches, health, and some other material things are a form of the good. Such a kind, he insists, has no part in the houses of Shem (*De Sob.* 67): the soul is the only place where the treasures of the houses of Shem can be appreciated. Rather, the serious man will pray with 'the prophetic word' the prayer 'turn to me', the prayer of Jacob-Israel addressed to his son Joseph recorded by LXX Gen. 49: 22. This particular prayer, says Philo, is a request that the one for whom it is uttered should receive beauty as the only good, and leave behind notions of the good which are wrong-headed. He should dwell in the houses of the soul of the one who declares that moral goodness is what matters supremely (*De Sob.* 68). Although this section also might be construed as referring in general terms to any human being, another reading is possible. For Japheth might represent the Gentiles, non-Jews who might feel inclined to live in the houses of Shem. To these, then, Philo would be addressing words of Jacob-Israel, 'turn to me', possibly in the sense of an invitation to them to convert to Judaism.

Both the texts examined here speak of Israel, explicitly in the *De Abrahamo*, implicitly in the *De Sobrietate*, as 'royal house, priesthood, and holy nation' in keeping with LXX's translation of Exod. 19: 6. Both texts, therefore, inevitably carry with them the sense that God is present in His Temple, which is a place where God may be seen, as the LXX translators made plain. 'Israel' represents a stage beyond the world of Abraham, Isaac, and Jacob, who are linked with God through a divine title in which they themselves feature. 'Israel', however, is implicitly associated with a Name for

God which is beyond the conventional, an idea which brings us back to the Temple, the only place where the Tetragrammaton may be pronounced in full. Israel, 'the one who sees God', is thus bound up with the priesthood, with purity, with holiness, and with the service of the Almighty; and this is the next topic which needs to be addressed.

2.2. *Israel and the Service of God*

On many occasions as he comments on Israel as the 'one who sees God', Philo has some reference to the Levites or to Num. 3: 12–13, the Scriptural verses declaring that God has consecrated to Himself the Levites as first-born; but for our purposes *De Sac.* 118–20, 134 and *Quis Heres* 124 are of special interest. Philo's treatment of the Levites adds considerably to our knowledge of what he intended to convey by saying that Israel is 'one who sees God'. In *De Sac.* 118 he noted that the Levites were selected in place of the first-born to serve God, and as a ransom for all the other first-born of Israel. He then cited at length Num. 3: 12–13, and went on to explain that, in these verses, the Levite signifies 'reason' which has taken refuge with God and has become His suppliant. Reason, he declared, is taken from the governing element in the soul; and God allotted it to Himself, and deemed it fitting for it to be the allotted portion of the eldest son. This needs to be said, since Scripture, as Philo's readers very well know, does not reckon Levi as the first-born son of Jacob. This honour goes to Reuben. Indeed, Philo had to admit that Reuben was the first-born son of Jacob; but Levi, he informs us, was the first-born son of Israel, and it is this Levi who holds the seniority in worth and power (*De Sac.* 119). Not for the first time in this discussion, we must register Philo's talk of the seniority and status of the first-born son. Philo then explains that Jacob represents toil and development: his son is Reuben, a name taken to indicate natural ability; and he is presented as the natural offspring of a Jacob whose life is one of toil and labour.[52] Philo then explains Levi's status in the following words: 'But the fount of contemplation of the only wise One is the service of that same One: according to that contemplation Israel is ordered; and Levi is a symbol of service' (*De Sac.* 120). It is important to be quite clear

---

[52] Philo almost invariably represented Reuben as a symbol of natural ability. As well as the text discussed here, see *De Mut. Nom.* 97–102, 210; *De Ebr.* 94; *De Som.* II. 33; and *De Fuga* 73.

about what Philo is saying in this passage. He is asserting that the source and origin of contemplation (θεωρία) of the One God, according to which (καθ'ἥν) Israel is ranked or ordered (τέτακται), is the service or worship of that God (τὸ θεραπευτικῶς ἔχειν αὐτοῦ), and that Levi is a symbol of this. With this statement, Philo has brought into relationship with Israel two highly significant terms, 'contemplation' and 'service'. The first is a central, technical word in the language of the philosophers; the second is an expression he uses often to speak of the worship of God. So central to Philo's thought is contemplation that he devoted to it a separate treatise, the *De Vita Contemplativa*, perhaps the best-known of all his writings; it is given over to discussion and praise of contemplation, and includes a description of a unique group of Jewish contemplatives whom Philo calls Therapeutae (θεραπευταί), which may be translated as 'worshippers' or 'healers'. For this extraordinary group, the whole business of rank and order is of the greatest importance: they modelled their religious-philosophical way of life on the priestly service of the Temple, Philo tells us, and uttered praise of God in hymns and other poetic compositions. To illustrate this, Philo gives over a large section of his treatise to accounts of the worship of the Therapeutae (see especially *De Vita Cont.* 66–87); this includes a 'banquet' which, Philo explicitly states, was modelled on the service of the Temple (*De Vita Cont.* 81–2). He leaves his readers in no doubt that these Therapeutae represent the highest and most excellent philosophy, both in contemplation and in practice.[53] They have brought contemplation and worship, which is service and healing of the soul, to perfection; and they are all of them Jews. Indeed, it is hard to see how these Therapeutae, if they were not Jews, could have attained to the heights of perfection which Philo ascribed to them.

What Philo has to say about Israel's rank in *De Sac.* 120 seems to echo his words about the Therapeutae and their contemplation and service of God; and it serves to strengthen the bonds between Philo's Israel as 'one who sees God' and the Jewish people among

[53] For expositions of Philo's account of the Therapeutae, see E. Schürer, *The History of the Jewish People*, ii. 591–97; Daumas's commentary on the relevant sections of the treatise in F. Daumas and P. Miguel, *De Vita Contemplativa. Les Oeuvres de Philon d'Alexandrie*, 29, ed. R. Arnaldez, C. Mondésert, and J. Pouilloux (Paris, 1963); and C. T. R. Hayward, article 'Therapeutae', in L. H. Schiffman and J. C. VanderKam (eds.), *Encyclopedia of the Dead Sea Scrolls*, 2 vols. (Oxford University Press: New York, 2000), ii. *ad loc.*

whom he lived and wrote. In truth, we have seen Philo applying to the 'sensible man' and to the 'serious man' in general many or most of the things which he tells us characterize Israel as 'one who sees God'; and to this extent he holds out the possibility that non-Jews who are 'sensible' or 'serious' might themselves 'see God', and in some measure count as Israel. Yet the question remains whether any non-Jews, however 'sensible', 'serious', or otherwise devoted to contemplation, can ever fully or perfectly claim membership of Israel, 'the race which is capable of seeing', without becoming a Jew in reality by converting to the people of Abraham, Isaac, and Jacob. The question retains its force, because the knowledge and discipline, the rites and ceremonies, the religious teachings and traditions, and the sacred duties enshrined in the Law of Moses which Philo holds most dear—all of these are God's gifts to the Jews, and must be acquired by anyone who seriously hopes to 'see God' in the sense Philo himself intended. Insofar as he holds out the possibility of the vision of God to non-Jews, Philo most likely envisages their conversion to Judaism, a subject on which he holds very positive views.[54]

Such a state of affairs is in part suggested by Philo's words here and elsewhere, words which include the notion of 'perfection'. For he goes on to say (*De Sac.* 120) that Levi, as well as symbolizing the service of God, the very source of contemplation according to which Israel is ordered, also represents a life of perfect virtue (ἀρετῇ τελείᾳ). Philo had already taught us in *De Ebr.* 82 that Israel is the name of perfection (τελειότης), because the name indicates vision of God; and the way to this vision is through following Moses. What he had to say in *De Conf. Ling.* 95–7 is illuminating at this point: the special characteristic of those who worship the One who Is (literally, the 'Therapeutae' of the One who Is), Philo asserted, consists in their ascension to the ethereal height, with *Moses* as their leader on the road. Then they see the 'place', who is in fact the Logos;[55] they see the place where God stands, as the

[54] See L. H. Feldman, *Jew and Gentile in the Ancient World: Attitudes and Interactions from Alexander to Justinian* (Princeton University Press: Princeton, 1993), 294–9, 313–14, 348–9.

[55] The Logos, it will be recalled, is a boundary figure having a portion in both the heavenly and the earthly worlds: note how Philo brings to an end his discourse on the Therapeutae by describing this group as 'citizens of heaven and of the cosmos' (*De Vita Cont.* 90), after telling his readers about the final act of their worship-service, a prayer for 'good times, truth, and sharp-sighted reasoning' (ibid. 89). On the quality of sharp-sightedness, see above, pp. 165–7.

Scriptural verse Exod. 24: 10 proclaims in the LXX version: then they see Logos and his most perfect work, which is this very cosmos itself (τελειότατον ἔργον τόνδε τὸν κόσμον). These sentiments should be compared with what he said about the Therapeutae in *De Vita Contemplativa*: they are worshippers of God who have been taught to see and desire the vision of the One who Exists, who mount up above the sensible sun, and never leave their rank which leads them to perfect happiness (*De Vit. Cont.* 11). These associations of the worship of God with perfection are too strong to be accidental; and they take on added significance when considered in the light of Philo's presentation of Judaism as the highest and most solemn of all the mysteries, of which Moses is the hierophant.

Philo was evidently as well versed as a learned Jew could be in his knowledge of the Eleusinian mysteries, and he compared the teaching of the Hebrew prophets with the instructions imparted to candidates in the so-called 'lesser mysteries': the teachings of Moses constituted the 'greater mysteries' (*De Cher.* 49; *De Sac.* 62), in such a way that, for Philo, Moses could fulfill the role of the hierophant, the supreme revealer and teacher of mystical knowledge (*Leg. All.* III. 151, 173; *De Sac.* 94; *De Mig. Abr.* 14; *De Som.* II. 29). Such was the secrecy surrounding the Eleusinian mysteries that even today not a great deal is known in detail of the rituals and their explanations; but this much has always been certain, that the climax of the celebrations consisted in a brilliant *vision* granted to the initiates. In the words of one modern writer on the subject:

Moments pass. Suddenly, the Anaktoron opens, and the hierophant stands in the doorway, silhouetted against a brilliant light streaming from the interior. The initiates enter, passing from darkness into an immense space blazing with extraordinary light, coming from thousands of torches held by the Epoptai.[56]

Philo's choice of words to speak of Moses was in part determined by his desire to insist that the Jewish lawgiver was acquainted with the most profound mysteries: as hierophant, his place was within the adytum, not outside it like some postulant (*De Post.* 173; *De Gig.* 54). It is precisely for this reason that Moses is the one who can lead people to 'the hidden light of sacred words' and reveal the

[56] See K. Clinton, 'The Sanctuary of Demeter and Kore at Eleusis', in N. Marinatos and R. Hägg (eds.), *Greek Sanctuaries: New Approaches* (Routledge: London, 1993), 110–24. The quotation is on p. 118.

great mysteries, as Philo was at pains to point out in *De Som.* I. 164–5.[57] The consequences of all this are clear. If Philo's description of Moses as hierophant, and his portrayal of the lawgiver's teachings as the greater mysteries have any force at all, it must follow that the worship of the God of Israel is a *sine qua non* for true initiation into these mysteries, and that all Philo's talk of Israel as 'one who sees God' must, in the last resort, be inseparable from the beliefs and practices of Judaism as he knew it. For him, vision is the highest of the senses; vision is the high point of the mysteries; Israel is one who sees God; the Jewish sanctuary is the place where God may be seen and served aright; Israel is the name of perfection; and perfection depends on the right service of God of which those contemplatives called the Therapeutae are the most excellent celebrants.

Naturally, God alone can produce perfection, as Philo explained in a few sentences devoted to the characteristics of learning (*De Fuga* 172). The beginning of the perfection of learning, he wrote, is nature inherent in the pupil; but it is God alone, the most excellent nature, who can produce the summit of perfection. Perfection, that is to say, is in reality a quality of God Himself (*Quod Deus* 26; *Quis Rerum* 121). Nonetheless, at *De Fuga* 113–15 Philo had already reminded his audience that the high priest in some manner represented the noblest kind of perfection; and the tenth of the tithes which the Levites received represented allegorically the perfection of that group of God's servants (*De Mut. Nom.* 2). Mention of high priest and Levites brings us back again to Israel, whose name represents perfection, with its ordered service of God set out in the books of the lawgiver, Moses the hierophant.

---

[57] For discussion of Philo's use of the vocabulary of the mysteries, initiation, and mystic revelation, and on his description of Moses as hierophant, see E. R. Goodenough, *By Light, Light: The Mystic Gospel of Hellenistic Judaism* (Yale University Press: New Haven, 1935), 189–96, and the nuanced and critical treatment of H. A. Wolfson, *Philo: Foundations of Religious Philosophy in Judaism, Christianity, and Islam,* 2 vols. (Harvard University Press: Cambridge, Mass., 1948), i. 36–8 (on Philo's fundamental disapproval of the pagan mysteries), and 41–55 (analysing Philonic passages which speak of Judaism in terms of mystery). It should be clear from the evidence assembled here that Israel as 'one who sees God' possesses this status as a result of real conflict with the passions and a determined decision to live and worship according to the norms revealed by the One who Exists. Any ecstatic or supernatural experience accorded to 'one who sees God' would be impossible without these prerequisites.

3. CONCLUSIONS

Philo's designation of Israel as 'one who sees God' encapsulates favourite themes and ideas which appear throughout the sage's writings: it is much, much more than an etymological device, touching as it does on some of the philosophical and religious ideas which Philo holds most dear. Perhaps it was precisely because the expression encompassed so much which is central to his thinking that Philo did not seek to 'prove' the etymology of the name Israel with reference to one or more verses of the LXX Pentateuch, but preferred to use those Scriptural verses which tell how Jacob became Israel as demonstrating the character of Israel as a boundary figure, an earthly being yet associated with angels, or 'daimons' as he calls them. This 'one who sees God' is a visionary endowed with the eyes of prophetic inspiration, turned now towards this world, now towards heaven, like the high priest and the Logos.

For Philo, Israel is most particularly one who sees that God is, that He truly is 'the One who Exists'. For this reason, proper understanding of the name Israel, in his view, is involved in the larger matter of correct understanding of the Divine Name made available to human beings. He seems to envisage two distinct levels of revelation here: the name 'Lord God of Abraham, of Isaac, and of Jacob' is appropriate to those natures representing teaching, perfection, and practice; while Israel, the one who sees God, perceives that God is the Existent One, a theological truth expressed by the Tetragrammaton, the sacred, ineffable Name whose utterance is confined to the Temple in Jerusalem. This Temple is the permanent counterpart of that mobile desert Sanctuary which God had ordered Moses to make so that He might be seen therein: thus had LXX Exod. 25: 8 ordained, and so Philo believed. God's being seen within the Sanctuary and the Temple goes hand in hand with the service offered within that shrine, a service ordered by the Almighty Himself, and duly prescribed in the writings of Moses the lawgiver. Philo saw nothing improper, therefore, in describing Moses as a hierophant: like the holder of that office in the mystery cults of Philo's day, Moses was responsible for inducting initiates into the mysteries, leading them from darkness to light, to a point where *they are enabled to see*. Israel, as the one who sees God, is the highest and noblest example of the one initiated into the only true mysteries, the service of the God of Israel, the One who truly Is.

Since these things are so, Philo must speak of Israel in terms of the Levitical family, the 'suppliant race' whose prime duty is the service of God. But this race, the priestly family, was chosen by God (according to the Book of Numbers) as representing the first-born; and with this observation Philo brings us back full circle, as it were, to contemplation of Israel, the one who sees God, as the first-begotten, the one whose name is borne also by the Logos, described as the most senior of the angels and first-born of God in *De Conf. Ling.* 146. This Israel has a distinctly heavenly aspect to his character; he is at home with angels, yet remains a boundary figure with earthly responsibilities, among them the constant need to seek after perfection through that form of seeing which is called contemplation. The Therapeutae, those sharp-sighted, seeing Jews in Egypt whom Philo singles out as the highest and noblest example of the contemplative life, are both servants and worshippers of the One who Is, ordering their worship in conformity with the service of the Temple: they are citizens of both earthly and heavenly worlds, and offer us perhaps the best example of what Philo meant by speaking of Israel as one who sees God.

The angelic traits alluded to in the character of Israel as Philo sets it forth are especially marked in those passages from his writings discussed in the second part of this chapter. Some further and deeper appreciation of them may be possible if they are examined in the light of a post-biblical Jewish writing called the *Prayer of Joseph*, which also defined Israel in terms of one who sees God. This fragmentary and difficult writing will provide the topic for the next chapter.

6

The Name Israel, Philo, and the
Prayer of Joseph

Philo's explanation of Israel as 'one who sees God' or 'the one who sees' *tout court* stands revealed as a convenient shorthand expression, as it were, for some of the author's most elevated thoughts about the character of the Jewish people and about the inner dispositions, both intellectual and spiritual, of the individual 'philosopher' who strives for virtue as Philo understood it. We have seen that Philo does not take his explanation of the name directly from the Septuagint, although he could quite easily have done so. Some aspects of his complex relationship to LXX in this matter have already been considered. Others point us ultimately in the direction of the mysteries, Israel as 'one who sees God' representing those who are illuminated by and initiated into a discipline which grants access to a supernal world, such that the one seeing and contemplating the mysteries is a citizen both of earth and of heaven. This is the point at which it will be proper to address a complex and difficult matter, namely: one must try to elucidate the part which may have been played in Philo's thought by traditions extant in a peculiar, unique, and fragmentary work commonly called the *Prayer of Joseph*. Its possible relevance for what Philo has to say about Israel was explored before the Second World War by Edmund Stein, and in more recent times it has featured in important studies by J. Z. Smith and Ellen Birnbaum.[1] Here it will be in order, first, to give a brief account of this enigmatic writing and the circumstances of its preservation, before

---

[1] See E. Stein, 'Zur apokryphen Schrift "Gebet Josephs"', *Monatsschrift für Geschichte und Wissenschaft des Judentums*, 81 (1937), 280–6; J. Z. Smith, 'The Prayer of Joseph' in J. H. Charlesworth (ed.) *The Old Testament Pseudepigrapha*, vol. 2 (Darton, Longman & Todd: London, 1985), 699–714; E. Schürer, *The History of the Jewish People in the Age of Jesus Christ*, vol. III.2, rev. and ed. G. Vermes, F. Millar, and M. Goodman (Clark: Edinburgh, 1987), 798–9; and E. Birnbaum, *The Place*, 73–7.

attempting to discuss whether it should be considered pertinent to Philo's works.

1. THE PRAYER OF JOSEPH

A writing known as the *Prayer of Joseph* was apparently quite well known in ancient times: in his *Stichometry*, Nicephorus noted a document of this name as having some 1,100 lines. Our earliest witness to it is Origen (*c*.185–*c*.254 CE), who evidently held it in some regard and attests to its use by Jews of his day.[2] As J. Z. Smith tellingly records, Origen's extant works preserve only three fragments of the composition, consisting of nine Greek sentences, or 164 words.[3] The longest fragment is found in the commentary *In Ioannem* II. 31.25; the two other fragments, both very short, appear in the *Philokalia*, and one of them is little more than a part-paraphrase of the longest fragment.[4] The original language of the work is in doubt. To quote Smith, 'the majority of commentators have abstained from hazarding an opinion', although either Greek or Aramaic are suggested as the main contenders.[5] In any event, we may note Smith's observation that these tiny Greek quotations contain no fewer than three *hapax legomena*, and that the largest number of significant linguistic and theological similarities are to be found with Egyptian, Greek, and Coptic Jewish and Christian texts.[6] In considering whether Philo was aware of traditions attested by this work, the question of its original language is evidently important. If the *Prayer* had been composed originally in Aramaic, was a Greek version of it available to Philo? And even if its original language had been Greek, had the *Prayer* been written when Philo began his literary enterprise? While these questions cannot be answered with anything approaching certainty, they nevertheless help to focus the student's mind on the nature of the

---

[2] This and further detailed information can be found in Smith, 'The Prayer', 699–700. For Origen's estimate of it, see Schürer, *History*, 798.

[3] See Smith, 'The Prayer', 699–700.

[4] Of the two smaller fragments, the first is preserved by Origen in his *In Genesim* III. 9 (to Gen. 1: 14) and by Eusebius, *Praeparatio Evangelica* VI. 11, 64; the second fragment, which paraphrases what is found in the other two surviving texts, is quoted in the *Philokalia* (33: 19). For the Greek text of the *Prayer*, I have used that set out by Schürer, *History*, 798–9. Translations are mine.

[5] See Smith, 'The Prayer', 700.

[6] See ibid.

extant Greek text, and ensure that statements made about the *Prayer* are properly cautious.

What survives of the *Prayer* consists of a speech (or speeches) by Jacob in the first person; and it may be worth noting at the outset that nowhere in Philo's writings does Jacob-Israel speak in such fashion as we find in the *Prayer*. The longest fragment of the *Prayer* is easily subdivided; and it will be simplest to translate it, and to record key expressions in the original Greek *en passant*, noting the while its affinities or lack of affinities with Philo as they occur. Thus the *Prayer* opens with Jacob addressing his audience:

(1) For I who speak to you am Jacob, namely, Israel: I am an angel of God and a sovereign spirit (ἄγγελος θεοῦ εἰμι ἐγὼ καὶ πνεῦμα ἀρχικὸν).

In the well-known section 146 of his treatise *De Confusione Linguarum*, Philo spoke of the Logos as many-named: he is called 'beginning', and 'name of God', and 'Logos', and 'the man according to His image'. The final name is 'the one who sees', Israel. In that same passage, Philo had already declared that the Logos occupied the most senior position among the angels (τὸν ἀγγέλων πρεσβύτατον). Although he never speaks of Jacob-Israel as an angel without further qualification, Philo does openly assert here that the Logos is the most senior angel, and that one of his names is Israel. Insofar as Philo implies that Israel is the senior angel, his idea concurs with that of the *Prayer*, in the course of which it will emerge that Jacob-Israel is the chief *chiliarch* among the sons of God, and first minister before the face of God, as we shall see presently. On the other hand, Philo never used the expression πνεῦμα ἀρχικὸν.

De Confusione Linguarum has a good deal to say about the name Israel and its meaning, and section 146 is just one of a number of passages (*De Conf. Ling.* 36, 56, 72, 92–3, 147–8) where it crops up in discussion. I have earlier commented on Philo's association of Israel as one who sees God with a *harmony* which pervades the universe: this sentiment finds a place in *De Conf. Ling.* 56, and a little later the reader is reminded that the name Jacob is symbolic of hearing, Israel of sight, both of which the oppressing Egyptian Pharaoh intended to destroy (72). By the time he reaches sections 91–3 of the treatise, therefore, Philo has prepared the ground for further observations on Israel: these centre on the notion of sonship, since the expression 'children/sons of Israel' is used in the Scriptural verses (Exod. 1: 11; 2: 23) which concern him at that point. Summarizing his words, we learn that the children of the race that has vision have been forced by the Pharaoh to make bricks: this means that the eye of the soul which alone may lawfully look upon God is incarcerated, and is thus justifiably sorrowful. The sons of Israel groan for freedom from these labours; thus do the wise seek respite from labour to serve God. In the following paragraphs (94–7) Philo insists that those who serve God ascend to the ethereal height, having Moses as their leader on the way. Then they will see the place, which is the Logos, where the immutable God stands with the word of our senses beneath His feet, symbolized by the sapphire pavement-work described in Exod. 24: 10. The wise man desires to see (if he can) the One who Exists; if this is not possible, he wants to see God's image, which is the most sacred Logos.

Much of this discussion will be familiar from the preceding chapter of this book. The message is clear: it is the sons of Israel, the one who sees, who alone are capable of acquiring such privileges. All this is essential for gaining a proper perspective on *De Conf. Ling.* 146, which is preceded by a blunt reminder (145) that only those who have knowledge of the One may rightly be called 'sons of God'; and anyone aspiring to such a privilege who is yet unworthy of it should be eager to be assigned to (κοσμεῖσθαι) the Logos, who is the most senior of the angels. The language here is redolent of the gymnasium, the κοσμητής being the magistrate who was in charge of youths during their time of training.[7] Finally, Philo notes (147–8) that any who have yet to become worthy to be 'sons of God' might nonetheless aspire to be sons of His invisible image, the most sacred Logos, who is the most senior angel of God; and he remarks that the biblical phrase 'sons of Israel' signifies hearers, that is, sons of the one who sees, receiving teaching which derives from clear light.

I have laboured this matter to show beyond reasonable doubt that Philo's main concern in *De Conf. Ling.* 146 is not so much a characterization of Israel as an angelic being, but a determination to instruct his readers in how to become sons of God or sons of

---

[7] On the language of the gymnasium, see above, pp. 159–60. It will also be important to bear in mind throughout the following discussion motifs which have already appeared, and which will continue to appear, as Philo discusses Israel. The most important of these are: the Logos conceived of as Place; the Logos and Israel as a boundary; the Logos and Israel as responsible for harmony; and expressions relating to sonship and other familial relationships.

Israel, both of which expressions he is at pains to explain. The Logos, not Israel, plays the decisive role in this, and dominates the discussion. This Logos is called Israel only in passing; and Israel's equation with an angel is made indirectly via this Logos, who is the most senior of those beings and image of God. The extant portions of the *Prayer of Joseph*, however, do not describe Jacob-Israel as the image of God.[8] Even so, Philo's thought in this treatise assumes that Israel has angelic traits. The 'sons of God' he describes have such characteristics themselves, and his words in section 145 leave little doubt that the sure way to acquire these features lies through a gymnastic encounter with the Logos. This, of course, was exactly what Jacob endured in order to be renamed Israel, most graphically described, perhaps, in *De Som.* I. 128. While observing some similarities of sentiment between Philo's thought and ideas found in the *Prayer*, one should note also sharp differences in language and expression, Philo using words and phrases not found in the *Prayer*, while the latter is apparently unfamiliar with terms such as Logos and 'image'.

(2) Both Abraham and Isaac were made before ($\pi\rho o\epsilon\kappa\tau i\sigma\theta\eta\sigma\alpha\nu$) any work.

Philo says nothing of the kind about Abraham and Isaac; and it is difficult to envisage how a notion of this sort might have contributed to his ideas about the name Israel. On the other hand, the statement is certainly germane to development of ideas in the *Prayer*, which will go on to speak of Jacob-named-Israel as 'first-born of all living vivified by God'. This remarkable assertion receives fuller treatment below; for the moment, it is enough to note that it seems to trace Jacob's human ancestry to Abraham and Isaac, both of whom are brought into existence in a supernatural manner.

What the *Prayer* has to say is complicated by its use of the verb $\pi\rho o\kappa\tau i\zeta\acute{\alpha}o\mu\alpha\iota$, which is unattested outside this text and the writings of the Christian Fathers.[9] The fact that such a rare verb is here

---

[8] In *De Conf. Ling.* 146, the Logos is named not only 'Israel', but also 'the man according to the image (of God)', $\acute{o}$ $\kappa\alpha\tau'\epsilon\grave{\iota}\kappa\acute{o}\nu\alpha$ $\mathring{\alpha}\nu\theta\rho\omega\pi o s$.

[9] Smith, 'The Prayer', 700, cites its appearance in Didymus of Alexandria, *De Trinitate* 3: 4 and Gelasius Cyzicus, *Historia Concilii Nicaeni* 2: 16. In Rabbinic texts, the idea that Israel was created before the world is attested in *Midrash Tehillim* on Ps. 72: 17; but it is not found in earlier writings which list items created before the world was made (*b. Pes.* 54a; *Ned.* 39b; *Yalqut* on Jer. 298). I am not aware of any Rabbinic text from Talmudic times or before which speaks of Abraham and Isaac as pre-mundane creations. The belief that the world was created for the sake of Israel, and that Israel was in God's mind as His first-born son during the creative process,

used of Abraham and Isaac might be held to suggest that we are
here in the presence of a text either influenced by Christianity, or
reflecting Jewish attempts to respond to Christian assertions that
Jesus Christ pre-existed the foundation of the cosmos (Col. 1: 17;
1 Cor. 8: 6). Such may very well be a present *consequence* of the
Greek wording of the *Prayer*; but it may not necessarily explain its
genesis. For Scripture states both that God Himself declared
Israel to be his first-born son (Exod. 4: 22), and that Israel is the
son of Isaac (Gen. 46: 1) and the son of Abraham (Gen. 28: 13).
Here we have a difficulty confronting even the most casual reader
of the Bible.[10] How might these radically different statements be
reconciled, or properly understood? One possible solution might
be the very tactic adopted by the *Prayer*, which involves a frank
acknowledgement that Jacob is a human being who is at the same
time God's first-born, and thus has a kind of angelic status. Since
this angelic status requires further comment, it becomes important to note the extraordinary status of Jacob's human forebears.
The widely known and respected *Book of Jubilees* had also maintained that Jacob was, as it were, 'written into' the very process of
creation (*Jub.* 2: 23), precisely in his character as God's first-born
son, who will keep Sabbath with the Angels of the Presence and
the Angels of Sanctification (*Jub.* 2: 19–20).[11] In other words, the
data contained in the various Scriptural verses, and traditional
notions already expressed and popularized by the *Book of Jubilees*,
could have been combined to produce the kind of picture of
Jacob's character and ancestry which confronts us in the *Prayer*.
The whole development, therefore, might be a purely Jewish
affair, thus making it unnecessary to posit anti-Christian sentiment to explain the origin of the statements about the Patriarchs.
Once Christianity had arrived, however, a writing of this kind
might have been considered useful to help counter some of its
claims.

But was Philo aware of such problems relating to Jacob's ancestry as reported by the Bible, assuming that the *Prayer* existed in his

however, is well known from pre-Rabbinic texts: see Kugel, '4Q369 "Prayer of
Enoch" ', 125–7, citing Bar. 3: 32–4:1; Test. Moses 1: 12; 4 Ezra 6: 55–6, 59; 7: 11;
LAB 28: 4. See further, J. Kugel, *Traditions of the Bible* (Harvard University Press:
Cambridge, Mass., 1998), 86–7, 90–1.

[10] MT of Exod. 4: 22 has God state: בני בכרי ישראל, which LXX translated as υἱὸς
πρωτότοκός μου Ισραηλ. See further Smith, 'The Prayer', 703–4.
[11] On these verses of *Jubilees*, see Kugel, '4Q369 "Prayer of Enoch" ', 123–6.

day? One small point may be of some interest, and possibly of importance, in this regard. LXX Exod. 4: 22 had spoken of Israel as God's πρωτότοκος, his 'first-born son'. The *Prayer*, by contrast, describes Jacob-Israel as πρωτόγονος. Philo uses this word only six times in his writings, always to speak of the Logos (*De Conf. Ling.* 63, 146; *De Som.* I. 215), Israel as a first-born (*De Post.* 63; *De Fuga* 208), or Israel in the character of the Logos (*De Agr.* 51). He never speaks of the Logos as πρωτότοκος; indeed, his use of this last word seems almost entirely dictated by Scriptural verses he is quoting or considering.[12] That he applies πρωτόγονος to the Logos on five out of the six occasions he uses the word does, on the other hand, appear significant. For the Logos is a supernatural reality, whose traits as a 'boundary' figure between earth and heaven have already been discussed.[13] When Philo calls Israel πρωτόγονος, therefore, it may be that he has in mind once again a being who belongs both on earth and in heaven; and just such a being is described with this very word in the *Prayer*, even though the latter also uses words and phrases with which Philo is not familiar.

(3) Now I am Jacob, the one who is called by men Jacob; but my name is Israel, the one who is called by God Israel, 'a man seeing God'; because I am the first-born of all living vivified by God.

The two names are here explained in parallel expressions in the Greek, which I have tried to reproduce in English translation. Jacob is so called by human beings; this statement may bear the double sense that he was given this name by human parents, and was thereafter known to human beings by it. Likewise, we may understand the *Prayer* to mean that he was given the name Israel by God, and was thereafter known to God by that title. Here, the *Prayer* not only reflects obvious Scriptural data, but may also be trying to offer its own explanation of why two names continue to be used of the Patriarch in Scripture: once Abram was named Abraham, his former name was no longer spoken, whereas Jacob

---

[12] For numbering the occurrences of these two words, I have made use of G. Meyer's *Index Philoneus* (de Gruyter: Berlin, 1974), 251–2, which lists 39 appearances of πρωτότοκος. The majority of these are found in direct quotations of Scripture, or in comments which arise directly out of these Scriptural verses. The word may refer either to animal or human first-born, and sometimes provides a springboard for allegory, as in *De Sac.* 126. It does not appear to be used in connection with angels or other supernatural beings.

[13] See above, pp. 161–4.

continues to be known by his 'old' name. The *Prayer*'s comment on this Scriptural conundrum seems plain: Jacob is an earthly name, Israel a heavenly one. And Israel is explained as 'a man seeing God'.

It has been noted many times that Philo never explains Israel as '*a man* seeing God': for him, Israel is never ἀνὴρ ὁρῶν θεόν.[14] For the purposes of the *Prayer*, however, we shall see presently that the precise designation of Israel as *a man* who sees God is crucial. Indeed, the *Prayer* tells us why Israel is called 'a man seeing God': it is because (ὅτι) he is 'first-born of all living vivified by God'. This is an astonishing statement, meriting several observations. First, it flatly contradicts Scripture, according to which Jacob was given the name Israel on earth because he had struggled with a mysterious being called a 'man' and had been victorious (Gen. 32: 25–32). The *Prayer* as quoted by Origen will go on to tell of this struggle, but will make it clear that Jacob already knew that he was Israel before the struggle took place. What remains of the *Prayer* does not even hint that the 'man' who struggled with him proclaimed his name as Israel. Rather, we shall find a certain emphasis on the fact that Jacob already knew his opponent's name and his precise status, another detail which flatly contradicts the Scriptural story, according to which Jacob asked to know the identity of his opponent (Gen. 32: 29).

Secondly, it will be evident that, in this matter, the *Prayer* stands poles apart from Philo's repeated assertions that Jacob's name was *changed* to Israel as the *result of his struggle* with an angel. Almost everything that Philo has to say about Israel as 'one who sees God' is based on that struggle. In the *Prayer*, Jacob's name is not changed, and the struggle with his opponent serves a purpose which Philo does not envisage. Thirdly, the name Israel is made dependent on its owner's status as first-born, a status which is not straightforward, as a glance at Genesis shows. For it was Esau, not Jacob, who was born first to Isaac and Rebekah: the men were twin brothers, and Jacob acquired the status of first-born through his own actions (Gen. 25: 24–34; 27). This does not trouble one whit the author of the *Prayer*, who seems to take Jacob's first-born rank as self-evident. In this regard, the *Prayer* recalls Hebrew Ben Sira MsB 44: 23 margin; Greek Sirach

---

[14] For possible explanations of this, see Birnbaum, *The Place*, 76–7; Delling, 'The "One who Sees God" ', 38–9; and below, pp. 204, 212–13.

36: 12; Pseudo-Philo *LAB* 18: 1; and the tenor of 4 Ezra 6: 58, all
of whom regard Jacob as first-born: behind the *Prayer*, there evidently lies a tradition justifying Jacob's claim to this status.[15]
Such a tradition may even show itself in Philo's own writings, as
in his *De Post*. 63, where he remarks of Israel as 'one seeing God'
that he is first-born son (πρωτόγονος) in honour, even though he is
younger in age. This is so because, by seeing God, Israel is honoured as the τοῦ ἀγενήτου γέννημα πρώτιστον, 'the very first child
of the uncreated One'. With this, we are returned to the *Prayer*
with a blaring of trumpets, *De Post*. making virtually the same
claim as the *Prayer* that Jacob-Israel is 'first-born of all living
vivified by God', because he sees God. This kind of talk, indeed,
seems to reverse Philo's more usual claim that Jacob needs to
become Israel *in order to* see God. This point must be given due
weight.

What stands revealed here is a very complex situation. Enough
evidence has been presented to show beyond reasonable doubt
that, whatever may be the date and circumstances of the *Prayer*'s
composition, Origen has preserved for us a fragment that depends
for what it has to say on earlier traditions. The heavy emphasis
which the *Prayer* puts on Jacob as the first-born of all living
because he sees God virtually rules out Christian authorship of
this fragment; for the Christians had been taught that no man, not
even Jacob, had seen God at any time (John 1: 18), and that the
first-born of all the living was Jesus Christ himself (Rom. 8: 29;

---

[15] See esp. the important insights of H. Jacobson, *A Commentary on Pseudo-
Philo's* Liber Antiquitatum Biblicarum, 2 vols. (Brill: Leiden, 1996), i. 585–7 discussing *LAB* 18: 6, where the status of Jacob as first-born is bound up with his
struggle with the angel. Among the Rabbinic texts he cites, *Tanhuma B*. 3.12a and
Num. Rab. 4: 8 are of particular interest. Given the importance of Uriel in 4 Ezra, it
is perhaps striking that Israel is referred to as first-born in that writing at 6: 58. For
brief comment and a summary of the textual problems in that verse, see A. L.
Thompson, *Responsibility for Evil in the Theodicy of IV Ezra*, SBL Diss. Ser. 29
(Scholars Press: Missoula, 1977), 191, 315, 347. See also P. W. Skehan and A. A. di
Lella, *The Wisdom of Ben Sira*, Anchor Bible, 39 (Doubleday: New York, 1987),
422. Also significant are those sources which speak of Jacob-Israel as God's first-
born 'by dint of discipline', a phrase used by James Kugel, '4Q369 "Prayer of
Enoch" ', 126–31, with special reference to 4Q504 (Words of the Luminaries) iii. 2–
7; Sirach 17: 17–18; Pss. Sol. 18: 3–4; *LAB* 16: 5; but note carefully Kugel's observation (p. 131) that, according to these texts, 'Israel was not *born* God's firstborn . . .
instead, "firstborn" here was a title that Israel received after it was already in
existence'.

Heb. 1: 6). It may, of course, still be the case that the *Prayer* represents a Jewish text written with Christianity in view; but my examination of it so far has suggested that this is not a necessary explanation of it. In truth, one of the most peculiar claims of the *Prayer*, that Jacob is one who sees God because he is the first-born of all living vivified by God, we have seen effectively claimed for Judaism before the genesis of Christianity by Philo's dramatic statement in *De Post*. 63.

Philo's own relationship to what is found in this *Prayer*, though, is still problematic. While we have noted some remarkable similarities between his writings and aspects of this peculiar text, we have also recorded striking divergences; and the latter are significant enough for us to pronounce, with some confidence, that Philo did not solely depend on traditions which may have informed the final text of the *Prayer* for all that he has to say about Israel as one who sees God. On the other hand, we may also discern another aspect of something already suggested by Ellen Birnbaum, namely, that Philo's description of Israel as 'one who sees God' may vary in significance depending on the kind of work in which it appears; and we may now add to her observation the possibility that Philo, when it suits his purposes, might draw on traditional material about the meaning of the name which is not entirely consistent with some of his other remarks about it.[16] For his argument in *De Post*. 63, it is important that Israel should signify 'one who sees God' by nature, as it were; Philo could not, in this section of his work, remind his readers that Jacob obtained his new name after a struggle without impairing the case he is trying to put forward. It is interesting, to say the least, that he here resorts to an explanation of the name which bears such astonishing resemblance to that found in the *Prayer*, and represents such a departure from his usual view that Jacob's seeing God is dependent on becoming Israel.

Origen's quotation of the *Prayer* appears to leave out some material following the sections which we have just examined. How much material he has omitted is impossible to say. He merely remarks: 'and he (or: "it", that is, the text he is quoting) continues', before citing another portion of Jacob's speech.

---

[16] Note also the judicious remarks of Delling, 'The "One Who Sees God"', 37–8. Birnbaum seems not to have discussed *De Post*. 63, even though it would strengthen her thesis that Philo may have known traditions now incorporated in the *Prayer*.

(4) But when I came from Mesopotamia of Syria, Uriel the angel of God went out, and said that I had descended onto the earth and that I had encamped among men, and that I had been called by name Jacob.

This section of the *Prayer* corresponds to very little in Philo's writings, beyond the general identification of Jacob's interlocutor as an angel. Thus Philo does not refer to the place called Mesopotamia of Syria, which is, however, of some importance for the author of the *Prayer*, since the exact words of Jacob given there in Greek (ἐγώ δὲ ὅτε ἠρχόμην ἀπὸ Μεσοποταμίας τῆς Συρίας) closely reflect LXX Gen. 48: 7 and 35: 9, and serve to link those two verses with Jacob's change of name as described in Gen. 32. These passages may, indeed, already be implicitly linked by the Hebrew Bible itself.[17] Next, we may record that Philo never speaks of an angel called Uriel; nor does he suggest that Jacob had descended to earth. The *Prayer* further states that Jacob had encamped (καὶ κατεσκήνωσα) amongst men: Philo's single use of that verb is with reference to the wise man's encamping in the Tent of Meeting, which represents Wisdom (*Leg. All.* III. 46). This section of the *Prayer*, furthermore, helps us to understand why the document interprets Israel as *a man* who sees God. From the point of view of the author of this composition, Israel is an angel who assumes the form of a man, but whose angelic status allows him to be a man in a category of his own, retaining the ability to see God, a privilege which is fatal for any ordinary 'man'. We may also recall that the Bible had spoken of Jacob's supernatural opponent as a 'man', and by using this word specifically of Israel, the *Prayer* draws attention to the angelic character of Jacob-Israel in another, more complex manner.

The fact that the *Prayer* understood Jacob's opponent at the Jabbok to have been an angel, however, is of undoubted significance. This is indisputably an old tradition, since it is attested by Demetrius the Chronographer.[18] The compiler(s) of the *Prayer* have considerably elaborated this, providing the angel with a name, a status, and a reason for confronting Jacob. It is worth recalling here that this tradition, although not unknown to witnesses to the text of LXX Gen. 32: 24, is only weakly represented within the Greek Bible text tradition prior to Origen, and may not have been

---

[17] See discussion by Smith, 'The Prayer', 710.
[18] See above, p. 58; J. Hanson, 'Demetrius the Chronogropher', in *Old Testament Pseudepigrapha*, ii. 849; and Delling, 'The "One Who Sees God" ', 38, n. 69.

present in the text of LXX known to Philo.[19] The *possibility* that Philo drew upon a tradition standing outside LXX for the identification of Jacob's opponent cannot, therefore, be discounted. At some point between the time of Demetrius and the composition of the *Prayer*, someone took it in hand to elaborate the simple angel into the figure of Uriel as pictured in the *Prayer*, a being claiming superiority over other angels. Philo accepts that Jacob's adversary is the most senior of the angels; but the *Prayer* has a twist to this story, to which we must now turn.

(5) The Greek of this section is ambiguous, and two separate translations need to be considered: (a) He was jealous of me and fought with me and wrestled against me, saying that his own name was superior above my name and that of the angel who is before all; (b) He was jealous of me and fought with me and wrestled against me, saying that His own name and that of the angel who is before all was superior above my name.

Again, we are struck by the radical differences between the *Prayer* on the one hand, and Philo and the Bible on the other. For the former, the name of the angel is central to the drama which is unfolding, whereas LXX state clearly that the angel's name was never revealed to Jacob. Philo may hint that Jacob was aware that the angel was the Logos (e.g. *De Mut. Nom.* 87; *De Som.* I. 127–9), but does not suggest that his name might be Uriel. The Bible gives no motive for the supernatural attack on Jacob. Philo regards the 'attack' in an entirely good sense, as a contest from which Jacob emerges as victor over the passions to merit the name Israel. The *Prayer*, however, attributes the attack to jealousy, and adds something entirely foreign to both the Bible and Philo: what is at issue between the two combatants is their relative status as angels, and their exact positions within the celestial hierarchy. In the first translation offered above, Uriel is presented as vying for position in the order of archangels with Jacob-Israel and with another celestial being, 'the angel who is before all'. In the second, Uriel associated himself with the 'angel who is before all', saying that they are both superior to Jacob-Israel. It should also be noted that the *Prayer* has already altered the drift of Scripture by making Uriel declare that his opponent's name was Jacob, *while failing altogether to state that his name will henceforth be Israel*. The main function of Jacob's opponent in the Scriptural narrative, has, in the *Prayer*, been suppressed.

---

[19] For the evidence, see Wevers, *Septuaginta*, vol. I: *Genesis*, 314, and above p. 58.

That the angel's attack on Jacob had been motivated by jealousy is a notion which may be present in Targum Neofiti of Gen. 32: 25–30, and in other Rabbinic texts commenting on those verses.[20] Philo, however, lends no support to any such idea; nor, indeed, can he afford to do so, since in his view of things those who 'see God' have, by definition, removed themselves far beyond the world of the passions in which jealousy plays so prominent a role. The very suggestion that angels, or mortals who are privileged to 'see God', might be stirred to base feelings of envy would be unthinkable for Philo. Furthermore, given the part which Philo ascribed to the Logos in Jacob's change of name to Israel, jealousy is doubly inadmissible, since the Logos is one whose business is specifically to promote harmony between heaven and earth, the uncreated and the created. Yet another difference between the *Prayer* and Philo's account of the struggle is apparent if translation (a) cited above is given its full weight, since this interpretation of the Greek suggests that Uriel implicitly admits that 'the angel who is before all' claims superiority over all the other angels, including himself. Philo, on the contrary, is convinced that Jacob's opponent was the most senior angel, a view which the *Prayer* might, perhaps, admit as a theoretical possibility if translation (b) is read with such a sense in mind. Nonetheless, the overall message of the *Prayer* is concerned to *deny* Uriel's somewhat ambiguous claim to be chief angel: this will be made clear in the following section of the text, where Uriel's claims are dismissed by Jacob, and the angel is put firmly in his place.

(6) And I (Jacob) told him his name, and of what degree (πόσος) he was among the sons of God: 'Are you not Uriel, the eighth below me; and am I not Israel, chief angel of the power of the Lord (ἀρχάγγελος δυνάμεως Κυρίου), and chief *chiliarch* among the sons of God? Am I not Israel, the first minister before the face of God; and have I not invoked my God by the unquenchable name?'

By asserting that Israel knows Uriel's name and position in the heavenly hierarchy, this section demonstrates the Patriarch's power

---

[20] These are discussed below, pp. 252–306. The *Prayer*, however, differs from Targum Neofiti in not stating explicitly that the angel who opposed Jacob was responsible for singing hymns before God. It is Israel who is later called 'first minister before the face of God', which may imply that he was in charge of heavenly worship. Does the *Prayer* intend to exclude Uriel from this ministry?

and superiority over Uriel. The very form of the text proclaims Israel's assured position as first in rank and chief among the celestial beings. Israel asks two balanced questions, both beginning with οὐχί, and both having almost the same number of Greek words, sixteen in the first question, and seventeen in the second. Although the first question opens with words about Uriel, it is soon made plain that the questions are really assertions about Israel, who is quickly named in the first question, and dominates the second. The only thing said of Uriel here is that he is 'eighth'. In stark contrast, Israel is 'first' or 'chief' in some respect: in the course of these few Greek words, he emerges as ἀρχάγγελος, ἀρχιχιλίαρχος, and πρῶτος. The earlier part of the text has paved the way for this: already he has been called πνεῦμα ἀρχικὸν and πρωτόγονος. We may note how matters of precedence and priority dominate this short text: it is said even that Abraham and Isaac, the progenitors of Jacob-Israel, were made before any work, προεκτίσθησαν πρὸ παντὸς ἔργου.

It is evident that what has survived of the Greek text of the *Prayer of Joseph* represents a polemic of some sort, directed against a view of the heavenly world in which Uriel, or, just possibly, another angel 'who is before all', claimed to be chief of the angelic hierarchy.[21] This fundamental concern of the *Prayer* is worlds away from Philo and his interpretation of Israel's name as 'one who sees God'; yet even here the individual Greek expressions used to define Israel may repay further examination. Uriel we may pass over, since Philo does not speak of him. Israel, however, is here called ἀρχάγγελος, chief angel or archangel, a title which Philo in *De Conf. Ling.* 146 used to qualify the Logos, who is also called Israel. What he has to say in that treatise I discussed earlier; but here a few further details must be added. First, it should be recalled that *De Conf. Ling.* 146 begins by calling the Logos the most senior of angels, and then adds by way of qualification the note ὡς ἂν ἀρχάγγελος, 'as it were an archangel/a chief-angel/a ruler-angel'. This word is not common. It is not found in LXX,

---

[21] Insofar as Jacob-Israel might be considered human, the *Prayer* would represent angelic jealousy directed against a man, of the sort represented in texts assembled and analysed by P. Schäfer, *Rivalität zwischen Engeln und Menschen*, Studia Judaica, 8 (de Gruyter: Berlin, 1975), 75–218: see pp. 164–92 for texts revealing angelic hostility to Israel in particular. Angelic jealousy of Israel's precedence in the worship of God is well represented in the *Hekaloth* texts: see P. Schäfer, *Der verborgene und offenbare Gott* (Mohr: Tübingen, 1991), 45–9.

and occurs just three times in Philo's writings.[22] Apart from its appearance in *De Conf. Ling.* 146, it is found only in *Quis Rerum* 205, where it once more describes the Logos, this time as a boundary (μεθόριος) between the creator and the created world,[23] and in *De Som.* I. 157, to speak of the Lord himself as ruler of the angels witnessed by Jacob in his dream at Bethel. This last pictures the Lord controlling the whole created order, like a charioteer (ἡνίοχος) guiding his chariot, or a pilot directing his ship.

It is also *possible* that yet another detail in the *Prayer* may be redolent of Philo's thinking. This is the description of Israel as 'chief angel' or archangel 'of the power of the Lord'. Perhaps one of the best-known of Philo's interpretations of Scripture is his understanding that the two cherubim set over the Ark of the Covenant symbolize God's two chief 'powers', the creative and the royal: so he remarks in *De Vit. Mos.* II. 99. LXX Exod. 25: 21 state that God would speak with Moses 'from above the mercy-seat, in the midst of the two cherubim'; and in *De Fuga* 101 Philo expounded this verse to show how the divine Logos, being the image of God and most senior of all intellectual beings, is the charioteer (ἡνίοχος) of these powers which the cherubim represent, being above them and placed nearest to God Himself.[24] Similarly, in *De Cher.* 27–8, Philo speaks of the Logos as standing between and uniting the two cherubim, which here represent the powers of God's rulership and his goodness. Does the *Prayer*, with its talk of a chief angel of the power of the Lord, breathe the same kind of air as Philo's writings when he speaks of the two powers presided over by a Logos who is also styled 'archangel'? This question becomes more urgent when Philo's extended comment on LXX Exod. 25:

---

[22] Outside Philo, it is found twice in the New Testament (1 Thess. 4: 16; Jude 9); 4 Ezra 4: 36; 1 Enoch 20: 7 (Greek a1, a2); and becomes more frequent after the first century CE. See L. Stuckenbruck, *Angel Veneration and Christology*, WUNT 2, Reihe 70 (Mohr: Tübingen, 1995), 79–81, 192–200; and G. W. E. Nickelsburg, *1 Enoch 1. A Commentary on the Book of 1 Enoch Chapters 1–36; 81–108* (Fortress Press: Minneapolis, 2001), 207.

[23] See above, p. 163.

[24] Although there is some difficulty in construing Philo's precise meaning here (see *Philo* V, p. 584), the Logos is still represented as being 'between' the two cherubim, and as separated from God by virtually no μεθόριος, since the Logos and God are in the same chariot. In a passage very similar to this (*Quis Rerum* 166), it is God Himself, rather than the Logos, who stands between the powers. For a definition of the 'powers' of God as spoken of by Philo, their significance, and their relationship to the Logos and to God Himself, see Wolfson, *Philo*, 217–61.

21 in his *QE* II. 68 is brought into play. There, he develops a view of the Logos as part of a sevenfold hierarchy of powers which have their source and origin in God Himself. Viewed 'from the top down', so to speak, God may be seen as the Speaker who communicates with Moses through the Logos located between the cherubim of the Ark. God Himself, Logos, and the two powers represented by the two cherubim make up four members of this hierarchy, which is extended by two further powers, the beneficent and the punitive, deriving from the creative and royal powers respectively: the Ark represents the world of ideas, the intelligible world, and constitutes the seventh member of the group.[25] Might it be significant that Israel, in the *Prayer*, declares the angel Uriel to be the *eighth* in rank? If, for the sake of argument only, we temporarily set together side by side the *Prayer* and Philo's words in *QE* II. 68, might we understand the *Prayer* to be declaring that Uriel is so low in rank as to be outside the 'charmed circle' which has access to God? Indeed, might not Israel's claim to have invoked God 'by the Unquenchable Name' be another device adopted by the *Prayer* to suggest that Israel has direct access to God in a way which Uriel does not?

Interesting as this hypothetical argument may be, it remains entirely hypothetical. For once again we encounter a now familiar problem: both Philo and the *Prayer* either use the same sort of language with quite different ends in view; or the one uses words and phrases which are foreign to the other. The 'archangel of the power of the Lord' may *sound* like Philonic terminology; but its relationship to Philo's own thinking is far from clear, and may be non-existent. Similarly, for Philo, the number eight, far from representing something lowly and junior in rank, is an exalted number whose praises are recounted at length in his *Questions and Answers on Genesis* III. 49, where he explains why Jewish boys must be circumcised on the eighth day. After listing seven properties which indicate the excellence of the number eight, he declares that the nation commanded to circumcise males on the eighth day is called Israel, which means 'seeing God'. Then, without delay, he reiterates the supreme importance of the number eight in God's act of

---

[25] *QE* II. 68 states: 'The Speaker first, and the Logos second, and the creative power third, and the ruling (power) fourth, and then, below the creative, the beneficent (power) fifth, and below the royal, the punitive (power) sixth, and the world of ideas seventh.' Translation by R. Marcus, *QE*, 118.

creation, much as he has done in *De Opf. Mun.* 93–110. The qualities of this number have a good deal to do with harmony and equality, notions which elsewhere, as we have seen, he associates with the Logos and, indirectly, with Israel.

What, then, of the title *archichiliarch* which the *Prayer* applies to Israel? The word is foreign to LXX and Philo, although the latter uses the word *chiliarch*, a military term whose meaning is literally 'commander of a thousand men', at *De Cong.* 110, *Vit. Mos.* I. 317, and *Leg. ad Gaium* 30. The *Prayer*, however, evidently applies the word to the angelic hosts, while Philo's *chiliarchs* are human soldiers. J. Z. Smith compares it with the term ἀρχιστράτηγος, found in some Jewish Hellenistic sources as a title of the archangel Michael.[26] Perhaps we should also consider the rank of ταξίαρχος, 'squadron commander', to which Philo once (*De Spec. Leg.* I. 114) allots the high priest as one who has been assigned (προσκεκληρωμένος) to God: what he commands in this capacity is 'the sacred order', τῆς ἱερᾶς τάξεως γεγονὼς ταξίαρχος. The notion of Israel as commander among the 'sons of God' is not in itself far removed from what Philo has to say about Israel *qua* Logos and high priest, although his manner of speaking of it is not that of the *Prayer*.

Although Philo does not directly describe Israel as 'first minister (λειτουργός) before the face of God', his use of the word λειτουργός is nonetheless revealing. Most commonly it refers in his writings to priests carrying out their duties in the Temple Service (*De Som.* II. 186, with allegorical interpretation; *De Vit. Mos.* II. 94, 149, 276; *De Spec. Leg.* I. 152, 249; IV. 191); but two passages in particular serve to recall the language of the *Prayer*. In *De Virt.* 73 he speaks of ἄγγελοι λειτουργοί, 'ministering angels' as comprising, along with men, an audience when Moses sang his song recorded in Deut. 32; these angels he describes as expert in music, who watch over (ἔφοροι) the song to discern any hint of discord. Here the theme of harmony, elsewhere in Philo's works connected with Logos, high priest, and through them with Israel, comes to the fore yet again. In *De Som.* II. 231 he speaks of the high priest when he enters the Holy of Holies on Yom Kippur: at that moment, Philo remarks following his reading of LXX Lev. 16: 17, the high priest 'will not be a man until he comes out'. This means, Philo asserts, that at this point he is neither man nor God, but God's λειτουργός, and occupies a μέσην τάξιν, 'an intermediate rank', until he emerges from the innermost shrine into the world of 'body and flesh'. All this is highly suggestive, though its precise relationship to material in the *Prayer* is far from clear, and is at least 'one remove' from statements Philo makes about Israel. It will require further consideration below.

The last claim which Israel makes in this *Prayer* is that he has invoked God 'by the unquenchable Name'. The expression is very unusual, is not found in Philo's writings, and is of uncertain inter-pretation. As suggested earlier, it may be intended as a snub to Uriel, carrying the implication that Israel knows and makes use of God's ineffable Name (the Tetragrammaton as pronounced with its vowels), whereas the angel is unacquainted with this, the most sacred of all Names.[27] With this observation, the exercise of com-paring and contrasting the subject-matter of the *Prayer* with Philo's work is complete. Some assessment of the relationship between them is now pressing. To assist that evaluation, the date and provenance of the *Prayer* must first be addressed.

2. A POSSIBLE DATE AND PROVENANCE OF THE PRAYER OF JOSEPH

From the evidence set out above, the following conclusions may be drawn with a certain degree of confidence. First, the *Prayer of Joseph* was not composed by Christians. Not only does Origen explicitly assert (*In Ioannem* II. xxxi. 25. 189) that it was used by Jews in his own day, but the content of the *Prayer* has nothing specifically Christian about it. Furthermore, the description of Abraham and Isaac as created before any work, the idea that Jacob is the first born of all living by God; and the assertion that the angel Israel had descended to earth, encamping among men as Jacob, hardly serve to bolster the claims of the Church. The

---

[27] The adjective ἄσβεστος, 'unquenchable', is nonetheless appropriate if the author of the *Prayer* wishes further to contrast Israel and Uriel. Israel can call on the Name; but Uriel, as an angel, is a mere 'minister of flame and fire', to use the language of the Bible (Ps. 104: 4; Dan 7: 19), who could be extinguished by the divine will. According to some Rabbinic texts, new angels are created each day to sing the Creator's praises, and then die: see *b. Ḥag.* 14a (R. Hiyya b. Rav); *Gen. Rab.* 78: 1 and *Lam. Rab.* III. 23: 8 (both R. Helbo); *Exod. Rab.* 15: 6, and discussion below, pp. 259–64, and comments below, pp. 275–9, on *b. Ḥull.* 91b, which asserts Israel's privilege of uttering the Divine Name after only two prefatory words, whereas angels must utter three of these.

insistence that Israel is 'a man who sees God' contradicts John 1: 18; and the suggestion that Jacob-Israel is the highest of all angels is not something to be expected from a group seeking to minimize the role of angels (see especially Heb. 1–2). Finally, the exaltation of Jacob-Israel which the *Prayer* expresses fits uneasily with second-century Christianity, some of whose representatives showed a tendency to promote Esau at the expense of Jacob.[28]

Was then the *Prayer* composed by Jews as a counterblast to Christianity, emphasizing the heavenly status of Israel, and thereby implying that such a status belonged as of right to Israel, and not to Jesus or his followers? The answer to this question must be given in two parts, the first dealing with second-century Christianity after, let us say, 130 CE. In this period it is almost certain that no Jew would have composed a text of this sort as an answer to Christianity's claims. In my scrutiny of the *Prayer*, I noted how often it departed from the Scriptural text, and ended up contradicting the Bible. Thus, according to the *Prayer* Jacob is not given the name Israel by his adversary; he already knows his adversary's name; he is called 'a man seeing God', because he is first-born of all living; and he is object of envy on the part of his opponent. All this, and much more besides, is foreign to Scripture. In his *Dialogue with Trypho*, written probably around 160 CE, Justin Martyr makes it plain that Jews had for some time been pointing out to Christians that the Church's texts of Scripture were inaccurate, and therefore provided no solid basis for many Christian claims.[29] This was evidently a powerful argument in Jewish–Christian debate; and the commissioning of Aquila's revision of LXX by the Jewish authorities, which Emanuel Tov dates to around 125 CE, indicates the degree of seriousness attaching to the matter on the Jewish side from the early part of the century at least. Given this, it is almost unthinkable that any Jew from 130 CE onwards (or perhaps even from 110 onwards) should set out to compose a document like the *Prayer* with a specific anti-Christian intention.[30] All the Christians would need to do would be to point to the *Prayer*'s radical contradiction of the Scriptures to have it laughed

---

[28] See esp. Tertullian, *Adversus Ioudaeos* 1; M. Simon, *Verus Israel: A Study of the Relations Between Christians and Jews in the Roman Empire AD 135–425*, tr. H. McKeating (The Littman Library of Jewish Civilization: London, 1996), 170–1.

[29] See Justin, *Dialogue*, 68. 7; 71. 1; 72–4.

[30] See E. Tov, *Textual Criticism of the Hebrew Bible* (Fortress Press: Assen, 1992), 146; cf. Simon, *Verus Israel*, 55–60.

out of court; and that, so far as we know, is something which never occurred.

Part two of the question concerns the period from (say) 40 CE to 130 CE. Here again, it is highly improbable that any Jew would have composed the *Prayer* at this time as a counter to Christianity. The *essential* Christian claims, that Jesus was the Messiah; that his death and resurrection, foretold in detail by the Scriptures, had effectively put an end to the kingdom of Satan which had hitherto dominated the world; and that adherence to this Christ, and nothing else, would ensure everlasting bliss for the believer on the Great Day of God's Judgement of the world, are left untouched by this *Prayer*. There, Israel is opposed not by Satan, but by Uriel, who remains part of the angelic hierarchy: he may be jealous of Israel, but he does not belong to the realms of evil. Indeed, his very name places him in the realms of light.[31] Furthermore, Uriel's encounter with Jacob happened when he came from Mesopotamia of Syria; the *Prayer* presents it as an historical event which manifests a heavenly truth, rather than a victory over the cosmic forces of evil which for ever alters the relationship between God and His world. Central to the *Prayer* is the question of who is *first*, or *chief*, in the heavenly hierarchy, Israel or Uriel? As a piece of specially composed anti-Christian polemic, the *Prayer* simply does not work, since it fails to engage with the most fundamental elements of Christian preaching. Aspects of it may have proved useful for Jewish controversialists in certain situations; but to say that is to say nothing about its origins.

Up to this point, my arguments have been mainly negative. On the positive side, however, it may be said with some assurance that this is a Jewish composition. Several observations support such a view. First, the author is familiar both with the Jewish Scriptures and with Jewish tradition. Close reading of the text has shown the author's knowledge not only of Gen. 32, but also of material in Gen. 35 and 48. Uriel, too, is the name of a high angel known to us from Jewish writings outside the Bible. Second, a simple and compelling *raison d'être* for one important aspect of the *Prayer*'s composition is provided if Jewish authorship is granted: the work represents an attempt to reconcile conflicting Scriptural

---

[31] On the name Uriel and its interpretation, see Y. Yadin, *The Scroll of the War of the Sons of Light against the Sons of Darkness* (Oxford University Press: Oxford, 1962), 237–40.

statements about the origin and status of Jacob-Israel, whom the
Bible variously describes as son of Abraham, son of Isaac, or
God's first-born son, by using information provided by Scripture
itself and tradition. Third, angelic jealousy engendered by God's
preferring Israel is known to us from other Jewish writings, notably the *Hekhaloth* texts; and it should be recalled that the theme
of jealousy is explicit in this *Prayer*. We have noticed how Uriel
loses no opportunity to 'downgrade' Jacob, as it were. Fourth, the
Prayer's description of Jacob as first-born of all living whose con-
verse is with angels is strongly redolent of traditions preserved in
the *Book of Jubilees*, according to which Jacob-Israel, as God's
first-born son, is 'written into' creation, and keeps Sabbath on
equal footing with the highest orders of angels. Interestingly, both
Jubilees and the *Prayer* agree also in eliminating the biblical claim
that Jacob received his name Israel from an 'angel' as the result of a
struggle or wrestling bout. Finally, Israel's claim in the *Prayer* to
be the first minister before God's face, invoking God by the
unquenchable Name, stakes a claim for the Jewish people as having
direct access to God, especially, it may be, in worship, if the
expression λειτουργὸς πρῶτος is to be understood as indicating
Israel's priestly character. This claim is made against the pretensions of the angel Uriel, and carries more than a hint that Israel's
service of God is superior to that of the highest angels, a matter
which receives some attention in *b. Ḥull*. 91b–92a and the Aramaic
Targumim of Gen. 32: 25–31.

Jewish authorship of the *Prayer* is indicated most dramatically,
however, by the interpretation of the name Israel as 'a man who
sees God'. No Christian familiar with John 1: 18 or 1 Cor. 2: 10–16
is likely to have written such a thing. In addition, this explanation
of the name almost certainly rules out Gnostic authorship of
the *Prayer*, since the status it accords to Israel, and thereby to the
Jewish people, gives the lie to the fantastic pretensions of the
Gnostic teachers. The reader is left in little doubt that direct knowledge of God (including his unquenchable Name) and the heavenly
world is given to Israel, not to self-appointed teachers, often ped-
dling vicious anti-Jewish propaganda, who lay claim to mysterious
secret knowledge of the realms above.

The *Prayer*, then, is almost certainly a Jewish writing. Beyond
that, however, it is difficult to go. Origen knew it, in Greek form,
sometime in the third century. There is no reason to dispute
his statement that it was then being used by Jews; and it is not

overstretching the evidence to suggest that those Jews probably regarded it as a traditional text of some value. If it was composed in a language other than Greek, it may have been some years before it was translated, and its point of origin could be pushed back into (say) the mid-second century. But all this is speculation; we do not know its original language if it was not Greek; nor do we know where or how it was produced.

This conclusion, however, may not be as bleak as it appears. It will have been noted that Philo has not figured in this section of my discussion, and that deliberately. It has been essential to try to discern what could be known of this *Prayer* without recourse to Philo, before once more returning to our principal author and the contents of the *Prayer*. It has been important to try to establish that the *Prayer* is a Jewish writing without reference to Philo, in order to avoid any hint of circular reasoning. With the probable Jewish origin of the *Prayer* in mind, we can consider once more Philo's interpretation of the name Israel, and the wide range of ideas associated with this designation in his thought.

3. OLD TRADITIONS AND NEW INTERPRETATIONS

The *Prayer of Joseph* and Philo's writings now concur, now disagree, about the character of Jacob-Israel. For the sake of clarity and simplicity, a brief summary will prove helpful. The differences between the two will be considered first.

(a) The *Prayer* uses terms never found in Philo's writings to speak of Jacob-Israel. These are: 'angel of God' *tout court*; 'sovereign spirit'; 'a man seeing God'; '*archichiliarch*'; and 'first minister before the face of God'.

(b) The *Prayer* contains elements which disagree not only with Philo, but also with the Bible. These are: the pre-creation of Abraham and Isaac; the identification of Jacob's opponent as Uriel; Uriel's statement that Israel had descended to earth and encamped among men under the name Jacob; the notion that Jacob's opponent was jealous of him; Jacob's knowledge of his opponent's name and rank in the angelic hierarchy; and Jacob's own extended explication of the name Israel.

(c) Philo seems to echo some of the terminology of the *Prayer* in *De Conf. Ling.* 146. Yet this passage has also much that is

not found in the *Prayer*. Its main concern is description of
the Logos, which does not feature in the *Prayer*. The Logos
is given several names, of which the final one is Israel: it
may, therefore, be reasonable to consider the other names as
designations of Israel as well. But these include terms not
found in *Prayer*, namely: 'most senior of angels'; 'beginning'; 'name of God'; and 'the man according to the image'.

These differences are weighty, and allow us to conclude with some
confidence that a direct, literary relationship between the *Prayer*
and Philo's writings is highly improbable. To express the matter in
other words: if the *Prayer* was well known to Philo (something
which, as we have seen, cannot be demonstrated), then he has not
drawn upon it directly for his interpretation of the name Israel. At
this point, however, equally weighty considerations attract our
attention in another direction. They have been set out in order
above, but it will be important to gather them together in summary
form here to get a proper overall appreciation of them.

(a) Both Philo and the author of the *Prayer* agree in ascribing to
Israel the status of highest angel. They arrive at this conclusion by different routes, but the conclusion is the same.
Thus Philo speaks of the Logos, whom he also calls 'archangel' or 'chief angel', and whom he further identifies as
'Israel': this same being is, to use his own words, 'the most
senior of angels'. In the *Prayer*, Israel himself declares that
he is chief: *chief* angel of the Lord's power, *chief* chiliarch
among the sons of God (i.e. angels), *first* minister before the
face of God.

(b) Whereas the Hebrew Bible described Jacob's opponent as 'a
man', both Philo and the *Prayer* state that he was an angel.
This angel is of highest rank: Philo identifies him as the
Logos, the *Prayer* as Uriel; and in the *Prayer*, Uriel claims to
be the highest angel, and *would be accepted as such*, were it not
for Israel's prior knowledge that he is, in fact, eighth in the
hierarchy. As we have seen, the number eight may not necessarily be intended to demote Uriel too drastically: Philo
himself witnesses to the noble properties of this number.

(c) Both Philo and the *Prayer* interpret the name Israel with
reference to seeing God.

(d) Israel's seeing God is related in some manner to his status as
first-born. According to the *Prayer*, Israel sees God because

he is first-born of all living vivified by God; and Philo in *De Post.* 63 remarks that, because Israel sees God, he is honoured as first-born, the very first child of the Uncreated One. Both Philo and the *Prayer* use the word πρωτόγονος rather than πρωτότοκος to describe Israel's first-born status.

(e) The phrase 'archangel/chief angel of the Lord's power' used in the *Prayer* calls to mind Philo's use of 'archangel' to describe the Logos, who presides over and unites the two chief powers of God. Philo also envisages a heavenly hierarchy, of which the Logos is a part, consisting of seven elements. The *Prayer*'s relegation of Uriel to eighth position may reflect a view of the heavenly world of the sort set out by Philo in *QE* II. 68.

(f) In the *Prayer*, Israel is *chiliarch* among the angels; Philo represents the high priest, whom on occasions he is capable of assimilating to the Logos and Israel, as *taxiarch* of the sacred order.

(g) The *Prayer* describes Israel as first λειτουργός before God, who invokes the Divine Name. This very probably has high-priestly connotations. Philo in *De Som.* II. 231 speaks of the high priest as representative of Israel ministering in the Temple Service on Yom Kippur (when, famously, the Divine Name was shouted aloud) as a λειτουργός who is neither man nor God, but occupying an intermediate rank.

I have argued that the *Prayer of Joseph* is most likely a Jewish writing composed sometime before the end of the second century CE, and that Philo did not draw upon it directly for his exegesis of the name Israel. The seven points listed above, however, allow us to advance a little beyond this, and to suggest that the peculiar similarities between this *Prayer* and some of Philo's writings indicate the existence of a tradition of Jewish reflection on the significance of the name Israel which is older than both writers, and on which both have drawn in different ways for their own distinctive purposes. In an earlier chapter I observed how the *Book of Jubilees* insisted on Israel's intimate association with the highest angels as characteristic of his status as God's first-born son; eliminated from its narrative any hint that Jacob received his new name as the result of a struggle; forged a direct link between the granting of the name Israel and the institution of the priesthood; and presented Israel as possessed of knowledge beyond that of ordinary mortals. All these things we encounter, *mutatis mutandis*, in the *Prayer of Joseph*. In addition, close reading of the LXX version of Gen. 32: 10–22 has revealed how the translators have made an association between Jacob 'strengthening himself' and becoming Israel so that he saw God 'face to face', and the angels of God who, according to LXX Deut. 32: 43, are likewise to 'strengthen themselves' along with God. The same translators had already presented Jacob's vision of angels at Bethel as an epiphany, language they reserve in their Pentateuch for the Priestly Blessing, and the appearance of angels in Deut. 33: 2. Both LXX and the *Book of Jubilees* enjoyed wide circulation among Jews, and leave little doubt that reflection on Israel's name was thriving among Jews from the third century BCE onwards. Much of the material in the *Prayer of Joseph* is clearly of a piece with this kind of reflection, even though it also ploughs its own furrow. To suggest that some of it, especially those parts of it which cohere so closely with Philo's observations, belong to a world of exegesis traditional in Philo's own lifetime is not, it seems to me, to claim too much.

The upshot of all this is twofold. First, it tends further to confirm Ellen Birnbaum's suggestion that Philo derived his etymology of Israel as 'one who sees God' from earlier Jewish tradition: we have already seen that he appears not to use LXX to support this meaning of the name, even though that version would have been his most obvious port of call. His reliance on tradition for the meaning of the name may also be connected with another aspect of Philo's work which Birnbaum has perceived, namely, his moulding of material to suit his own needs in his different kinds of treatise. For example, one important element in Philo's analysis of 'Israel' as 'one who sees God' which appears in *some* of his writings is his association of this name with the angels, and with the Logos or high priest as boundary figures between earth and heaven. LXX Pentateuch alone did not provide Philo with sufficient evidence for such a portrait of Israel. *Jubilees* offered him rather more; but it was precisely the sort of thinking still preserved for us in the *Prayer* that could allow what he had to say about Israel to gain a hearing. Without some traditional material of this sort, his linking of Israel to the Logos, in particular, might have seemed to some to border on wishful thinking, or even fantasy. As it was, should his views have been challenged, he could have invoked the tradition in his favour.

Second, the existence of a tradition of this kind helps to explain and support Philo's linking of Israel with the Logos depicted as *chief* of the angels. This association is otherwise not so easy to account for, since the Bible, when talking of Jacob's meetings with angels, strongly implies that they are superior to him. Not even *Jubilees* states that Jacob-Israel is the chief of the angels, but is content to accord him a status parallel and equal to theirs. But the presence in earlier non-biblical Jewish tradition (like that still found in the *Prayer*, for instance) of a notion that Israel was highest angel would have encouraged Philo to develop his material as he did, without too much fear of counter-argument from detractors of his work. Furthermore, his persistent failure to define Israel as '*a man* who sees God', which is the etymology of the name given in *Prayer*, may be intended precisely to confirm his view of Israel as yet another name for the Logos and the High Priest; for the latter, it will be recalled, is said by Philo *not* to be a 'man' (ἄνθρωπος), when he encounters the Divine Presence in the Holy of Holies (*De Som.* II. 231; cf. *Quis Rerum* 84). In other words, an older tradition of the sort still preserved in *Prayer* smooths the way for Philo to develop the notion of Israel 'seeing God' qua Logos and high priest to the heights that he does.[32]

It would seem that both the LXX and traditional Jewish exegesis of Scripture have had their part to play in Philo's exposition of Israel as 'one who sees God'. Such traditional material as Philo knew may reasonably be deduced from sources still available to us; and it would seem that it was to those sources in particular that Philo was indebted for his perceptions of Israel's angelic characteristics. These in their turn allowed him to speak as freely as he did, and apparently without fear of misunderstanding, about Israel's religion in terms of the 'mysteries' so popular among non-Jews in his own days: these Jewish 'mysteries', he could declare, are those which truly initiate a person into the highest realms of knowledge, into the very presence of that light discerned by the one who sees God, the only source of vision for both angels and human beings. The *Prayer of Joseph*, or rather the traditions out of which it was composed, may cast some light on all this; and it certainly indicates that angelic jealousy of Israel, which comes to the fore in Rabbinic texts soon to be discussed, was a matter for serious reflection on the part of Jewish thinkers long before the redaction of the Talmuds and midrashim.

[32] See again Birnbaum, *The Place*, 76–7; and cf. also P. Harlé and D. Pralon, *La Bible d'Alexandrie, 3:Le Lévitique* (Cerf: Paris, 1988), 153.

7
Jacob Becomes Israel: The Account of Flavius Josephus

The first detailed, sustained, and dateable reflection on the significance of the name Israel after the defeat of the Jewish armies in the Land of Israel following the great war against Rome (66–70 CE) comes from the pen of Flavius Josephus, whose celebrated account of that same war was supplemented around 93–4 CE by his *Jewish Antiquities*.[1] This work, in twenty books, relates and retells the whole course of biblical history, continues that history into the post-biblical period, and concludes with the declaration of the war in 66 CE. This *magnum opus* was aimed explicitly at non-Jews: to quote the revisers of Schürer's *The History of the Jewish People in the Age of Jesus Christ*, 'that its main purpose was to elicit from the cultivated world respect for the much calumniated Jewish people, is clear enough from its character and is declared emphatically by Josephus himself, *Ant.* xvi 6, 8'.[2]

Against the background of this stated aim of Josephus in writing the *Antiquities*, his explanation of the name Israel, which was bestowed on the ancestor of all the Jewish people, will inevitably be a matter of great moment. Indeed, vital clues to the essential character and ethos of the nation, which only twenty years

---

[1] For the Greek text of Josephus' writings, I have used that printed in the Loeb Classical Library edition of the complete works, ed. and trans. H. St. J. Thackeray, R. Marcus, A. Wikgren, and L. H. Feldman (Harvard University Press: Cambridge, Mass., 1963–76). Translations are mine. For introductions to Josephus as a writer and historian, see esp. R. Laqueur, *Der jüdische Historiker Flavius Josephus* (Munchow: Giessen, 1920); T. Rajak, *Josephus: The Historian and His Society* (Duckworth: London, 1983); E. Schürer, *The History of the Jewish People in the Age of Jesus Christ*, vol. 1, rev. and ed. G. Vermes and F. Millar (Clark: Edinburgh, 1973), 43 f.; and L. H. Feldman's important survey in his article 'Josephus', *ABD*, iii. 981–98. On the date of Antiquities, see Schürer, *The History*, i. 48; Rajak, *Josephus*, 237–8.

[2] See Schürer, *The History*, i. p 48.

previously had been overcome by the Romans with dreadful carnage, might be offered to pagan readers by Josephus' exposition of that ancestral name, which the people of his own day still bore as בני ישראל, 'the sons of Israel'.[3] It is not unlikely that his representation of the biblical account of Jacob's reception of the name Israel will have raised some eyebrows, especially among his Greek and Roman readers. Jews who chanced upon the *Antiquities*, however, might have found themselves reading what he has to say about Israel over and over again, perhaps in some astonishment. For to many Jews of Josephus' own generation, and to many Jews today, the historian is a highly problematic figure, a traitor to his own people and a man of doubtful integrity.[4] His comments on the Scriptural account of Jacob's change of name serve only to complicate the portrait of Josephus; but they do convey to us some startling information from a period when the Jews were at last beginning to 'find their feet' after the disaster of 70.

The two accounts of Jacob's change of name to Israel given in the Genesis story Josephus condenses into a single, carefully crafted paragraph set out in *Ant*. I. 331–4. This paragraph occurs at the point in Josephus' narrative where we might expect him to deal with Gen. 32: 23–33, following his account of Jacob's treaty with Laban and journey back to his homeland (*Ant*. I. 324–30); and, as we shall see presently, it includes his version of Gen. 35: 9–15, or at any rate his version of the miniscule amount of those verses that he chose to record. This second biblical account of Jacob's change of name we might expect to find reproduced at *Ant*. I. 341–2, were Josephus following strictly the order of events told in Scripture. In reality, however, he effectively omits those verses altogether, and in so doing

[3] Josephus himself is somewhat sparing in his use of the expression 'Israelites'; by this term, he indicates the historical and political reality of the Jewish people formally constituted as a God-centred society according to the Torah's commandments: see especially *Ant*. III. 189; IV. 50, 180; V. 316, 318, 355. For the descendants of Jacob, Josephus tends to use the term 'Israelite' rather than 'Israel': see G. Harvey, *The True Israel: Uses of the Names Jew, Hebrew and Israel in Ancient Jewish and Early Christian Literature* (Brill: Leiden, 1996), 125–6.

[4] See e.g. the judgements passed by modern historians in Schürer, *The History*, i. 57–8. Already in his own lifetime he was accused and effectively convicted of having distorted his own role in the war against Rome, as the extant fragments of the work of Justus of Tiberias testify: see ibid. 34–7.

radically alters the biblical account of things. It is worthwhile reminding ourselves here of what those verses have to say. They record an appearance of God to Jacob while the latter is still in Paddan-Aram, and His blessing of the Patriarch; God's announcing that Jacob shall from now on be called Israel; a divine command to Israel to be fruitful and multiply, with the concomitant promise of a nation, a company of nations, and kings as Israel's descendants; and the granting to Israel and his descendants of the land which had been already given to Abraham and Isaac. The episode ends with the note that God went up from Jacob in the place where He had spoken to him. With the exception of the last note, and a very general reference to Israel's descendants which he gives in *Ant.* I. 334 and 333 respectively, Josephus passes over these biblical verses in silence. The effects of this silence will have to be assessed in the light of Josephus' presentation of Gen. 32: 23–33.

1. JOSEPHUS AND THE BIBLICAL NARRATIVE

The Greek words and phrases which Josephus uses to introduce his account of Jacob's change of name appear openly to invite the reader to recall LXX Gen. 32: 23–33. This quasi-biblical introduction to *Ant.* I. 331–4, and Josephus' carefully positioned words and phrases recalling other parts of the LXX narrative, are presumably intended to invest what he has to say with some kind of authority. This will be clearer, perhaps, in the light of the translation set out below, where significant original Greek expressions are given in brackets, and will be the object of further discussion.

(331) Having set these things in order during the course of the whole day, when night came on he [Jacob] moved those who accompanied him; and when they had crossed a certain torrent called Jabokchos (καὶ χειμάρρουν τινὰ Ἰάβακχον διαβεβηκότων), Jacob, being left behind (Ἰάκωβος ὑπολελειμμένος) met a phantasm and wrestled (φαντάσματι συντυχὼν διεπάλαιεν). The latter began the fight, and he prevailed (ἐκράτει) over the phantasm, (332) which also then used a voice and words addressing him, exhorting him to rejoice in the things that had happened, and not to suppose that he had prevailed over a small opponent (καὶ μὴ μικρὸν κρατεῖν ὑπολαμβάνειν);[5] rather, he had conquered a divine angel (ἀλλὰ θεῖον ἄγγελον

---

[5] Some witnesses read μικρῶν, indicating that Jacob should not suppose that he had prevailed over small men or small things.

νενικηκέναι), and should regard this as a sign of great good things to come, and that his nation would never cease (ἐκλείψειν), and that no human being at all would be triumphant over his strength (μηδὲ ὑπέρτερον ἀνθρώπων τινὰ τῆς ἰσχύος ἔσεσθαι τῆς ἐκείνου). (333) He also ordered him to call himself Israel:[6] this signifies, according to the Hebrew language, an opponent of an angel of God.[7] Indeed he predicted these things at Jacob's request, for he perceived that he was an angel of God, and besought him to signify what fate should hold for him (τίνα μοῖραν ἕξει σημαίνειν παρεκάλει). (334) And the phantasm said these things, and became invisible. Now Jacob was delighted with these things and named the place Phanuel, which signifies 'face of God'. And since as a result of the battle he suffered pain around the broad sinew, he himself held off from the eating of this thing; and on his account it is something which we also do not regard as fit for eating.

As I have already remarked, the opening note that Jacob crossed the Jabbok recalls at first blush the language of LXX, especially their version of Gen. 32: 24–5, καὶ διέβη τὸν χειμάρρουν καὶ διεβίβασεν πάντα τὰ αὐτοῦ. (25) ὑπελείφθη δὲ Ιακωβ μόνος, καὶ ἐπάλαιεν ἄνθρωπος μετ᾽ αὐτοῦ . . ., 'and he [Jacob] crossed over the torrent; and he brought across all his possessions. And Jacob was left alone, and a man wrestled with him . . .'. The specific reference to wrestling is characteristic of the LXX version; and the appearance of the word 'angel' also recalls the use, by some LXX witnesses and Demetrius the Chronographer, of this appellation. There is also direct mention of Jacob's strength, which might remind the reader of LXX's exposition of the name Israel as one who strengthens himself or makes himself strong. Now, all this may beguile the unwary reader into imagining that what will follow will be a *reprise* of the Scriptural story; yet nothing could be wider of the mark.[8] Even the most unobservant of readers would be arrested by the word 'phantasm', which in Josephus' account of things does duty for the mysterious 'man' of the Hebrew and Greek biblical texts of Gen. 32: 25. This peculiar expression is nowhere used in LXX Pentateuch; and in the rest of the Greek Bible it is found only at Codex Alexandrinus Job 20: 8 to represent Hebrew הזיון 'vision';

[6] Translating the Loeb edition's text ἐκέλευέ τε καλεῖν αὐτὸν Ἰσράηλον. For καλεῖν, some MSS and the Latin translation read καλεῖσθαι, 'be called' (passive) or 'call himself' (middle).

[7] This is the only occasion on which Josephus uses the noun ἀντιστάτης, 'opponent'. A minority of witnesses read ἀντιστάντα, 'one who opposes'; but the sense is the same.

[8] For the LXX material, see above, Ch. 2, pp. 50–70.

again in the Alexandrinus at Isaiah 28: 7; and at Wis. 17: 15.[9] Its sense I shall discuss presently. Equally, Josephus reports that Jacob met (Greek συντυχὼν) the phantasm: this again is language not found in LXX Pentateuch, the Greek translators confining their use of this verb to 2 Macc. 8: 14, significantly in a setting of military struggle.[10] Thus, in what is superficially a retelling of a biblical story in old, familiar language, Josephus contrives to introduce strange and disturbing new things.

Foremost among these is the notion that the phantasm began a battle or fight (μάχη) with Jacob, a notion also alien to LXX, who neither speak of such a thing in Gen. 32: 23–33, still less of the 'man' as the one who intiates it; nor do they use words in any way similar to those of Josephus. The latter also speaks twice of Jacob's prevailing over the phantasm using the verb κρατεῖν, which LXX never use in this narrative, and which indeed is found only four times in the whole LXX Pentateuch (Gen. 19: 16; 21: 18; Deut. 2: 34; 3: 4). According to Josephus, the phantasm exhorted (παραινοῦν) Jacob to rejoice (χαίρειν): not only is this sentiment foreign to the LXX, but the verb παραινέω occurs nowhere in LXX Pentateuch. Other Greek words which Josephus uses in this short account are also not attested in the LXX version of the narrative, and some are also very rare in the version as a whole: for example, the word 'suppose', ὑπολαμβάνειν, is not found at all in LXX Pentateuch; ὑπέρτερον, translated above as 'triumphant over', is altogether unknown to LXX, as is μοῖρα, 'fate'; ἄλγημα, 'pain', is lacking in LXX Pentateuch; σημαίνω, 'to signify', occurs in LXX Pentateuch only at Exod. 18: 20 and Num. 10: 9; while the noun ἀντιστάτης, 'opponent', and the verb προλέγω, 'to predict', are found only once in LXX, at Judith 2: 25 and Isaiah 41: 26 respectively.

We are confronted by an account of things, therefore, which initially seeks to present itself in the familiar guise of a well-known

---

[9] LXX Codex Alexandrinus Job 20: 8 describes the evanescence of the wicked in terms of a night phantasm which is not found in the morning; at Isa. 28: 7 Alexandrinus has phantasm as a description of the perverted vision and judgement of drunken priests and prophets; and at Wisd. 17: 15 (Rahlfs 17: 14) it describes monstrous apparitions terrifying the Egyptian magicians on the departure of Israel from Egypt. For those conversant with the Greek Bible in one or other of its recensions, therefore, the word would have mostly negative connotations. On the phantasms described in Wisd. 17: 15, see C. Larcher, *Le Livre de la Sagesse ou La Sagesse de Salomon*, vol. 3 (Gabalda: Paris, 1985), 971–2.

[10] The word describes Nicanor's hostile meeting with Jews, which had resulted in their capture and subsequent sale into slavery.

story from the Greek Bible, but which soon radically departs from any Greek translation of Genesis now known to us. For the versions of Aquila, Symmachus, and Theodotion, insofar as fragments of them have survived, offer no verbal correspondences with Josephus' version of the story, with one exception only: Symmachus, whose work dates from a century or more after Josephus' death, represents the Hebrew place-name Peni'el at Gen. 32: 31 as $Φανουήλ$,[11] which agrees with Josephus' transcription of the name at *Ant*. I. 334. Apart from this solitary instance of concord with the Greek versions, Josephus' retelling of the biblical narrative diverges widely from the LXX, such of the later Greek versions as are known to us, and, indeed, from the Hebrew text which forms the basis of all those Greek translations. Further inspection of his narrative reveals that he has omitted material represented both in the Hebrew and Greek accounts of Jacob's change of name; that he has added details not present in those accounts; and that he has altered the drift of such elements of the biblical story (in either Hebrew or Greek form) which he has chosen to retain. Each of these changes will be examined in turn; and throughout the following investigation I shall ask whether there is precedent in Jewish exegetical tradition for what he has done.

2. JOSEPHUS OMITS SCRIPTURAL DATA

If we follow the biblical narrative as we find it unfolding in MT (and LXX), it becomes clear that Josephus has omitted some fourteen details from his account of Gen. 32: 25–33. Thus, in dealing with Gen. 32: 25, he says nothing about Jacob's being left *alone*; omits the note that Jacob's opponent engaged *with him*; and fails to indicate that the engagement went on *until dawn arose*. In treating the next verse, Josephus makes no attempt to reproduce the ambiguous biblical statement that 'he saw that he did not prevail', nor does he say that Jacob's adversary touched the broad part of Jacob's thigh: he offers a version of this last detail at the very end of his account (*Ant*. I. 334) which carefully avoids the direct statement given in the Bible. He omits almost entirely Gen. 32: 27. MT reads: 'And he said, Send me away, because the dawn has

---

[11] See A. Salvesen, *Symmachus in the Pentateuch* (Victoria Press: Manchester, 1991), 50, 216, 267 (noting Jerome's rendering Phanuel).

arisen. And he said, I will not send you away unless you bless me.'
All that survives of this in Josephus' narrative is the reference to
saying, in the report that the phantasm 'used a voice and words'
addressing Jacob; otherwise, all talk of sending away, the dawn,
and blessing has vanished from the scene. Completely expunged
from the story is Gen. 32: 28: 'And he said to him, What is your
name? And he said, Jacob.' Josephus also removes the detail in
Gen. 32: 29 that the Patriarch shall *no longer* be called Jacob; suppresses Jacob's question asking his opponent's name (Gen. 32: 30);
omits the note that 'he blessed him' (Gen. 32: 30); and ignores
Jacob's expression of relief that his life has been preserved after he
has seen God face to face (Gen. 32: 31). Finally, Josephus fails to
record that the sun arose for Jacob when he passed by Penu'el
(Gen. 32: 32).

In considering these omissions, what should first strike the
reader most forcibly is Josephus' removal of all direct speech from
his account of things. The biblical account is lively and graphic,
with dialogue, questions, answers, and conversation. Josephus has
transformed this into indirect speech, such that there is no real
conversation between Jacob and his opponent. Indeed, it is evident
from the beginning that Josphus seeks to portray Jacob has having
been in control of these events from the start and throughout: he
prevails over the phantasm at once, perceives that it is an angel, and
takes advantage of his superiority to request knowledge of the
future for himself and his descendants. There is something rather
perfunctory about the event, which seems *prima facie* to be very
much a happening in this world.

Secondly, it should be particularly observed that Josphus has left
out of his account all three biblical references to the dawn or daybreak (Gen. 32: 25, 27, 32). The wrestling bout takes place at night
(*Ant*. I. 331), but by suppressing all mention of the daytime
Josephus contrives to imply that Jacob's fight was a brief one. He
quickly establishes control over the phantasm: he certainly didn't
wrestle all night long; and the appearance of dawn has nothing
whatever to do with phantasm's departure. Closely allied to this is
Josephus' removal from the story of the detail that Jacob's opponent engaged *with him* (Gen. 32: 25), and the opponent's request to
be sent away (Gen. 32: 27). Once more, Jacob is shown as being in
charge of things: the phantasm begins a fight, only to find that
Jacob at once establishes his dominance. Hence, Josephus ignores
the ambiguous Gen. 32: 26, informing the reader that 'he saw that

he did not prevail': the subject of the verbs in this verse is unclear, both in MT and LXX, and for Josephus its presence can only obscure what, to the historian, is crystal clear. Jacob was in control. Given this fact, Josephus feels able to ignore Gen. 32: 31, where Jacob expresses relief that he has been preserved, since there is no question in Josephus' mind that Jacob's life was ever under threat. So much in command is Jacob, that Josephus even hesitates to ascribe directly to the phantasm the injury he sustains to his thigh, reducing the account of this to a remark that Jacob has suffered pain or injury during the fight. Only indirectly is it implied that the phantasm may have been responsible for this.

Equally sweeping is Josephus' removal from the narrative of anything which speaks of *blessing*. Twice the Bible introduces this idea (Gen. 32: 27, 30); and it features again in Gen. 35: 9, during the second biblical account of Jacob's change of name. As we have seen, Josephus fails to report this second account; and the notion of blessing included in it thus sinks without trace. Josephus is at pains to show that the events at the Jabbok have nothing to do with blessing. The name Israel, therefore, should not (in his view) be understood in relation to blessing. Its conferral, even, cannot be construed as a blessing; and it is noticeable that Josephus' suppression of most of Gen. 35: 9–15 ensures that his narrative does not include the clear biblical report of Gen. 35: 9–10 that God blessed Jacob, and conferred the name Israel upon him.

In passing over Gen. 32: 28, where the opponent asks Jacob what is his name, Josephus reveals his further concern to eliminate altogether from his narrative as much as possible concerning *names*. The biblical narrative, both MT and LXX, uses the noun *name* on some five occasions in this short section of text (Gen. 32: 28, 29, 30 twice, 31). By contrast, Josephus restricts all mention of name to a single verb, commenting that Jacob 'named' ($\mathring{o}\nu o\mu\acute{a}\zeta\epsilon\iota$) the place where he met the phantasm as Phanuel (*Ant.* I. 334). This is an extraordinary ploy on Josephus' part, in his rewriting of a biblical passage whose evident aim is to explain how the ancestor of the Jewish people came by the new name Israel, and what that name means. Josephus merely records that the phantasm ordered Jacob to *call* himself, or to be *called* ($\kappa\alpha\lambda\epsilon\hat{\iota}\nu$ or $\kappa\alpha\lambda\epsilon\hat{\iota}\sigma\theta\alpha\iota$) Israel; and we have already seen that he carefully omits the biblical note that he shall *no longer* be called Jacob (Gen. 32: 29). All that remains with direct reference to name in Josephus' reworking of this biblical passage is thus the place-name Phanuel. Josephus seems concerned to take the term Israel out of the realm associated with the noun 'name': gone is all the biblical dialogue between Jacob and the opponent which centres so much on the question of name. Indeed, Josephus seems here to treat 'Israel' simply as a designation applied to Jacob on this particular occasion. As such, he makes the point that it was the phantasm-angel, not God, who ordered Jacob to call himself Israel, a name which Josephus defines very pointedly with reference to angels as 'an opponent of an angel of God'. This matter will require further investigation.

3. JOSEPHUS ADDS DETAILS NOT FOUND IN SCRIPTURE

Certain items in Josephus' account of Jacob wrestling at the Jabbok represent additions to the Scriptural narrative, and pave the way for a deeper perception of the author's purpose in so reconstructing the story. The first such addition occurs at the end of *Ant.* I. 331, where we learn that the phantasm began the μάχη ('battle, fight') with Jacob. LXX avoid using the word μάχη to describe what was going on at the Jabbok, and the Hebrew Bible likewise has no word corresponding to 'battle, fight'. But the notion of a fight colours Josephus' account, to the extent that at the end of his narrative (*Ant.* I. 334) he speaks of the fight or battle during which Jacob had suffered pain or injury. Also important is his explicit statement that the phantasm began the fight (ἐκείνου προκατάρχοντος τῆς μάχης, *Ant.* I. 331). No reason is given for this fight. It may be important to note here, however, that according to the *Prayer of Joseph*, Jacob was engaged in a fight (ἐμαχέσατο) with the angel Uriel, and the text strongly suggests that Uriel had initiated that fight. That some notions similar to ones extant in the *Prayer of Joseph* might have been in Josephus' mind is strongly suggested by his direct interpretation of Israel as 'an opponent of an angel of God', which points to a struggle with a supernatural being as the enduring characteristic of 'Israel'.

For Josephus, therefore, Jacob was engaged not only in a wrestling bout, but in a battle, an opinion which allows him to make a second addition to the biblical story. Jacob gained the victory (νενικηκέναι) over a divine angel (*Ant.* I. 332), language foreign to the Bible. Here the unspoken assumption is that Jacob has (somehow or other) aroused the hostility or jealousy of at least one angelic being, who consequently has picked a fight with Jacob and, by implication, has sought to crush, defeat, or even kill him. The sense that the world above numbers among its inhabitants some power hostile to Jacob is at least suggested; indeed, in this respect the fact that the phantasm identifies himself as an angel is significant.

In this regard, we may observe that the battle begun by the phantasm-angel is not explained as having arisen out of Jacob's failure to carry out divine commands (as in the Aramaic Targumim) or to obey some moral precept. Rather, Josephus reveals the battle's purpose in his third addition to the biblical story: Jacob's victory over his opponent is viewed as a sign (σημεῖον) of great good things to come (*Ant*. I. 332). Having subdued the opponent, Jacob can beseech him to signify (σημαίνειν) the future. As Annelise Butterweck has rightly noted, the effect of Josephus' addition is to turn the biblical story into a prophetic oracle.[12] The whole episode becomes a *sign*, inasmuch as Israel 'signifies' (σημαίνει) one who opposes an angel of God, and the place where this happened is Phanuel, which 'signifies' (σημαίνει) the 'face of God'. Not blessing, which Josephus has rigorously excluded from his version of the story, but revelation is the keynote here. In yet another addition to the biblical story, Josephus states that the phantasm-angel 'predicted' (προύλεγεν) things at Jacob's request. And this revelation, in which things are signified, is overwhelmingly verbal. At the very beginning of the episode Josephus tells us that the phantasm used 'a voice and words' to communicate the revelation; at the end he reminds us that the phantasm 'said these things and became invisible' (*Ant*. I. 334). Biblical references to seeing he either omits, as in the case of Gen. 32: 26, or transforms, as in the case of Jacob's famous declaration in Gen. 32: 31 that he has seen God face to face. This last survives in drastically altered form as the place-name Phanuel which, Josephus tells us, 'signifies' the face of God. Further emphasis on the verbal character of the revelation is provided by other additions to the biblical story, when Josephus remarks that the angel 'predicted' things at Jacob's request, and Jacob had 'besought' him to 'signify' what fate might hold.

The content of this verbal revelation, this quasi-prophetic oracle, is threefold. Jacob is assured of great good things to come; that his nation would never cease; and that no human being would

[12] See Butterweck, *Jakobs Ringkampf*, 53–4. Her discussion of the Josephus material as a whole may be found on pp. 52–6. On Josephus' use of the term φάντασμα to speak of angels, see L. H. Feldman, 'Josephus's Portrait of Jacob', *JQR* 79 (1988–9), 140.

ever be triumphant over his strength. The second and third parts of this oracle are best understood as Josephus' interpretation of biblical material, and will be dealt with below. The assurance of 'great good things to come', however, Josephus seems to have added to the story. It appears to be based on Gen. 32: 9, where Jacob recalls God's promise made to him: 'Return to your country and to your kindred, and I will do good to you.' This verse Josephus seems to have related to Gen. 32: 2–3, which tells how Jacob, going on the journey that will shortly lead him to the Jabbok, met angels of God at a place he named Mahanaim. Interestingly, Josephus (*Ant.* I. 325) seems to have combined these two verses of Scripture and to have interpreted them to mean that Jacob, while going forward to Canaan, encountered *phantasms* which dictated good hopes about things destined to be for the future. This is Josephus' own distinctive contribution: it is non-biblical information, and his use of the term 'phantasm' in the Jabbok episode allows him to link this earlier episode involving phantasms with the 'prophetic oracle' given by the phantasm at the Jabbok. It also invites us to consider the possibility that the phantasm which fought with Jacob was but one of a larger number of phantasms which had been with him for some time; and this may explain Josephus' reluctance to declare that Jacob had been alone at the Jabbok.

One final point concerning the 'good things' predicted for Jacob is especially significant. The phantasm's prediction takes up an earlier promise made to Jacob by God Himself, according to *Ant.* I. 281–2. In this section, Josephus offers his version of Jacob's vision at Bethel described in Gen. 28: 10–22, where the Patriarch saw a ladder fixed on earth and reaching to the heavens, with angels ascending and descending, and with the Lord present at the top of the ladder. According to Josephus, God in the course of this vision promised Jacob 'great good things', and a fate or portion ($\mu o \hat{\iota} \rho a$) no less than that granted to Abraham and Isaac. But in contrast with his account of Jacob's experiences at the Jabbok, Josephus here (*Ant.* I. 279) speaks of the presence of 'visions' ($\ddot{o}\psi\epsilon\iota s$), and goes on to speak about God's gift of the land to Jacob and his descendants, whose numbers will be very great (*Ant.* I. 282). The designation *Israel*, we shall see, has nothing to do with land in Josephus' retelling; yet *Jacob* is promised that his descendants will inherit the land occupied by the Canaanites.

The remaining additions Josephus makes to the biblical story consist in the phantasm's command to Jacob to rejoice in the good things to come, and the note that Jacob was delighted with the predictions of the phantasm. The whole emphasis here is placed on rejoicing and celebration: Josephus truly gives us a 'happy-ever-after' ending to his account. So much is this the case that Jacob's naming the place Phanuel, 'face of God', is directly related by Josephus to this joy and gladness occasioned by the 'prophetic oracle' uttered by the phantasm-angel. In all this, the 'face of God', at any rate, seems to be understood in direct relation to Israel, and to an Israel promised a good future, everlasting existence, and triumph over human enemies.

4. JOSEPHUS INTERPRETS ELEMENTS OF THE SCRIPTURAL NARRATIVE

Two matters concern us here. The first appears to involve a major rearrangement of the Biblical story for which Josephus has been responsible. The Bible indicates that the 'man' who opposed Jacob first told him that henceforth his name would be Israel, and only subsequently did the 'man' explain what the new name signified. Josephus seems to reverse this order of things. First, the phantasm explains that Jacob has conquered an angel of God and predicts his destiny, explaining this in terms of a sign; and only then does the phantasm proclaim the title Israel, understood as an opponent of an angel of God. Thus Jacob is informed that he has prevailed over no small opponent, and this is a sign of good things coming, and that his nation will never cease, and that no human being will ever triumph over his strength *before* he is bidden to call himself Israel. The point of this apparent alteration of biblical order is disclosed by other interpretative stratagems which Josephus here brings into play. These make up the second matter for consideration here.

The 'man' of the Hebrew Bible becomes, in Josephus' account, both a 'phantasm' and an 'angel'. The angelic identity of the 'man' is, of course, very ancient, being attested already by Demetrius the Chronographer and some witnesses of LXX. What is remarkable about Josephus' version of the biblical story, however, is that it presents the angel openly proclaiming his angelic status to Jacob. The one Jewish source so far examined which retails any information remotely similar to this is, once again, the *Prayer of Joseph*, where it is evident that the angel Uriel identifies himself, and that the conflict between him and Jacob is occasioned by his concern for

his angelic status. Here, however, the essential ambiguity of
Josephus' presentation of this event is at its most apparent: while,
in all probability, he draws on pre-exisiting Jewish tradition to
describe the opponent of Jacob as 'angel', with the term 'phantasm' he steps outside Jewish tradition into the world of Greek
philosophy. The word φάντασμα is common in learned treatises of
the Graeco-Roman period, and refers to an image presented by an
object to the mind, a dream, or a vision.[13] The sense of the word as
dream or vision heightens the prophetic quality of the narrative
which, as Butterweck shows, is one of Josephus' main aims.[14]
Indeed, three times Josephus refers to the figure as a phantasm,
whereas only once does the Hebrew Bible define it as a 'man'. The
notion of phantasm is thus crucial for Josephus, and, as we have
seen, it serves to relate this event to another, earlier episode in
Jacob's life when phantasms had accompanied him.

In explaining the difficult Hebrew word רַיֵּאָבֵק of Gen. 32: 25 as
referring to 'wrestling', Josephus has followed in the footsteps of
LXX; but, as we have seen, he supplements this traditional interpretation also with language of fight or battle, which is not found
in LXX. This fight Jacob wins: according to Josephus, he 'prevailed over' (ἐκράτει) the phantasm, a victory which the phantasm
itself acknowledges, saying that Jacob should not suppose that he
had prevailed (κρατεῖν) over a small opponent, but had conquered a
divine angel. Now in all of this it would seem that Josephus has
drawn on traditional Jewish exegesis of the Hebrew of Gen. 32: 29,
where Jacob is named Israel and his opponent explains that name
as meaning 'you have struggled with God and with men and you
have prevailed'. The exegetical possibilities inherent in this
explanation have been discussed earlier; all we need to note here is
Josephus' affinities with both LXX and Targum.[15] On the one
hand, Josephus is aware that *struggle, fight, and conflict* is part and
parcel of the name Israel. So much he will have known from LXX
and other traditional sources which understood Gen. 32: 29 to

---

[13] Thus in the good sense of an image presented by an object to the mind,
φάντασμα is used by Plato, *Phaedo* 81D; *Theaetetus* 167B; and Aristotle, *De Anima*
III. 3. 9. Yet in philosophical discourse the word can often have a pejorative sense
of something which is unreal, an appearance only, as in Plato, *Republic* 598B. This is
a highly ambiguous word: its use in the Greek Bible, as we have seen, hardly
recommends it for description of one who brings good news to Jacob.

[14] See Butterweck, *Jakobs Ringkampf*, 53–4.

[15] See above, Ch. 2 and below, Ch. 8.

mean that Jacob had been strong, exerted himself, persisted, or struggled with God, looking to the Hebrew root שׂרה as affording authority for such explanation. But Josephus, as we see here, also used the verb κρατεῖν to explain Jacob's activity. This verb has the sense of 'rule; be lord, master, chief; hold sway; be sovereign'. When construed with the genitive, as it is at the end of *Ant*. I. 331, it has the sense of 'be lord of; be master of': Josephus says that Jacob ἐκράτει τε τοῦ φαντάσματος, 'was also lord/master over the phantasm'. The verb may also mean 'conquer; prevail; be superior'. In short, Josephus here shows close correspondence with the Aramaic Targumim, all of which interpret Gen. 32: 29 to mean that Jacob has 'been a prince, ruler, lord, chief' with God or with an angel or with angels of God. This traditional material seems to inform Josephus' interpretation of much of the episode; but only a close reading of what Josephus has to say, allied with some previous understanding of Jewish biblical interpretation, reveals what underlies the historian's choice of words.

Further evidence of traditional Jewish interpretation and its influence on Josephus may perhaps be perceived in the phantasm's statement that no human being at all would be triumphant (ὑπέρτερον) over his strength. While the mention of strength here may recall LXX Gen. 32: 29, which explains the name Israel as meaning 'you have shown yourself strong' or 'you have strengthened yourself' (ἐνίσχυσας), the word ὑπέρτερον is not found at all in LXX. It means 'over, above', and by extension is employed metaphorically, as here, to mean 'higher, nobler, stronger, more excellent'. When followed by the genitive case, as in this instance (ὑπέρτερον ἀνθρώπων), it means 'victorious, triumphant'. The sense here is very strong: Jacob is promised superiority over his human opponents. For all the world, this recalls once again the exegesis of LXX at this point, even though Josephus is using non-Septuagintal language to express himself. It will be recalled how this version strongly emphasizes the superiority of Jacob over human foes.

For those with some knowledge of the Jewish exegetical tradition, therefore, it turns out that Josephus has not altered the order of the biblical narrative as much as it might seem at first sight. What he has done, rather, is to put into the phantasm-angel's mouth a traditional interpretation of the Bible's explanation of the name Israel given at Gen. 32: 29, but without indicating what he has done. Indeed, everything that the phantasm-angel says about

Jacob as subject of the verb κρατεῖν can be understood as a definition of Israel as chief, lord, or prince, and corresponds almost exactly with the exposition of Gen. 32: 29 offered by the Aramaic Targumim. It would take an educated Jew fully to understand what was happening in this re-presentation engineered by Josephus, which turns out to be no less complex than it is informative. For his Gentile readers, however, Josephus presents Israel as a designation of Jacob almost as an afterthought, and (seemingly) attaches to it only one meaning: Israel is an opponent, not of earthly powers, but of 'an angel of God' in what appears to be a single, isolated event. The isolated nature of this same event is further strengthened if, as is most likely, what Josephus wrote in his definition of Israel was indeed τὸν ἀντιστάτην ἀγγέλῳ θεοῦ, since the noun ἀντιστάτης, 'opponent', is confined to this one place in his writings. Israel then turns out to be an unique opponent of angelic power.[16] Here once more, however, the influence of Jewish exegetical tradition in respect of Gen. 32: 29 כי שרית עם אלהים makes itself felt, the words this time being taken to mean that Israel signifies 'because you have exerted yourself with angels'.

The phantasm's prediction that Jacob's nation would never cease is not represented in Gen. 32: 25–33. Josephus has probably developed this out of God's promise to Jacob-Israel in Gen. 35: 11, that 'a nation and an assembly of nations . . . and kings' should arise from Jacob. These words seem to indicate a future for Jacob stretching into the distance. Although Gen. 35: 11 may provide the Scriptural basis for the phantasm's words, this pointed denial that Jacob's descendants will ever cease goes beyond the general sense of the Bible, and itself is likely to owe something to post-biblical tradition. Thus in the Hebrew text of Ben Sira 37: 25 we read:

> The life of a human being is for a few days:
> But the life of Jeshurun is for days without number.

Translating his grandfather's work into Greek, Ben Sira's grandson substituted 'Israel' for 'Jeshurun', since the latter is a poetic name for Israel attested in biblical passages such as Deut. 32: 15; 33: 5, 26.[17] Again, we read in 2 Macc. 14: 15 that when pious Jews were threatened with defeat and exile by Nicanor, they prayed to

---

[16] See above, n. 7.

[17] See discussion of this matter in Ch. 3 above, pp. 91–111; and Skehan and di Lella, *The Wisdom of Ben Sira*, 436–7.

God 'who had established His people for ever' (τὸν ἄχρι αἰῶνος
συστήσαντα τὸν αὐτοῦ λαόν). Both of these documents are concerned
to promote the idea that Israel will never cease to be a nation, and
concur with the prophetic oracle of Jer. 31: 35–7, that the very
order of creation would have to be undone before God would make
Israel cease to be a nation before Him. For according to Jeremiah,
Israel is as much a part of the divinely constituted order of creation
as are the rules governing the sun and moon and sea. The promise
or oracle given to Jacob by the phantasm, that his nation would
never cease, implies not only a continuing nation, but a populous
one; in this regard, we should recall that Josephus, in re-presenting
to his Gentile readers the oracles of the Gentile seer Balaam, puts
into the seer's mouth a prediction that the land of Canaan will be
too small to hold the descendants of a single father (Jacob), even
though Jews will continue to possess that land. Rather, whole con-
tinents and the islands of the sea will be populated by Jews, who
will be more numerous than the stars of heaven (*Ant.* IV. 115–16).

Josephus was not alone in understanding the events of Gen. 32
as relating to the indestructible nature of Israel, divinely predicted. A near-contemporary writer, the so-called Pseudo-Philo
who composed the *Liber Antiquitatum Biblicarum*, makes exactly
the same point. This complex work was most probably composed
in the latter part of the first century CE, and reflects Jewish concerns about the political situation arising out of conflict (of one
sort or another) with the Roman power. *LAB* 18: 4–6 retells the
story of Balaam, and re-presents his oracles about Israel's future:
the author uses this opportunity heavily to underscore the divine
guarantee about Israel's future as the unique, chosen people.[18]
Pseudo-Philo depicts God reminding Balaam of the exalted and
privileged status that Israel as a people enjoys. The author thus
tells how God sharply drew Balaam's attention to Abraham, and to
the divine promise given to that Patriarch that his progeny should
be like the stars in number. He speaks of Isaac, who was returned
safely to Abraham after being offered in sacrifice, and whose blood
confirmed God's choice of Israel as His people. Finally, he speaks
of Jacob, whom God named as first-born son, and who wrestled
with the angel and received the blessing. The blessing in this
instance refers to Israel's continuing status as God's people, since

[18] See further H. Jacobson, *A Commentary on Pseudo-Philo's* Liber Antiquitatum
Biblicarum, i. 241–2, 596–7; ii. 622, 665, 809.

the author of *LAB* concludes by asking whether Balaam imagines that he can curse those whom God has chosen. Elsewhere in *LAB*, the author is at pains to point out very clearly that God has not chosen Israel *in vanum*, 'for nothing; to no purpose' (*LAB* 18: 11; 23: 12; cf. 28: 5); nor has He chosen any nation other than Israel (see *LAB* 20: 4; 30: 2; 31: 5; 35: 2). Both Josephus and the author of *LAB* understand that Jacob faced a real enemy at the Jabbok in the shape of the angel; and both writers see the outcome of Jacob's victory over that enemy in terms of an assurance that Israel shall never cease to exist.

Although, according to Josephus, the designation Israel signifies 'an opponent of an angel of God', the battle which Jacob fights is not just a 'supernatural' engagement. It is a struggle in this world of history and event. Annelise Butterweck and Louis Feldman suggest that Josephus, in presenting the events at the Jabbok as he does, is intent on minimizing the political significance of the event, hinting instead at its eschatological sense.[19] Certainly, hopes for the future of the Jewish people occupied Josephus' mind as he composed this passage; so much should be evident from what has been set out for inspection here, and Butterweck and Feldman are right to draw attention to it. But the very fact that Josephus seems intent on looking to the future indicates that he regards the present as one of hope. The defeat of the Jews in the great war against Rome does not seal the fate of Israel for ever. After all, Jacob, the ancestor of all the Jewish people, was designated Israel because he had overcome a supernatural foe, who signified that no human being would ever be superior to the Jacob who is bidden to call himself Israel. Feldman has convincingly demonstrated that Josephus, elsewhere in his writings, presents Jacob very much as a military figure of great prowess; and this must surely have political connotations.[20]

5. CONCLUSIONS

The short section of Josephus' writing which tells how Jacob received the title Israel stands revealed as a composition of great complexity. Taking as the foundation of his account the two biblical passages in Gen. 32: 25–33 and 35: 9–15, Josephus omitted material, added extra information of his own, and, by one means or

---

[19] See Butterweck, *Jakobs Ringkampf*, 55–6; and Feldman, 'Josephus's Portrait', 136–7.

[20] See Feldman, 'Josephus's Portrait', 110–11.

another, interpreted the verses of Scripture which seemed most
important for his needs. The result is a narrative which can be
understood on different levels, depending on whether the reader is
a pagan Greek or Roman, a Gentile with some knowledge of the
Bible in Greek translation, or a Jew versed in Scripture and its
interpretation. His 'message' runs somewhat as follows—and it
will doubtless have evoked widely different responses from different kinds of readers. Indeed, when we bear in mind that he wrote
his *Antiquities* principally for non-Jews, some of the things he has
to say are surprising. We may summarize as follows:

(a) At the beginning of his account of how Jacob acquires the
title Israel, and at various points in the body of that account,
Josephus uses words and phrases which would have been familiar
to Jews and non-Jews who could read the Bible in Greek translation. In this way, he seems to claim for his account a certain authority, and suggests that this is the *proper* way of understanding the
episode. Those with no knowledge of the Bible would naturally not
be aware of how Josephus was using Scriptural language; but the
authoritative nature of his account would be suggested to pagan
readers particularly by his use of the supernatural phantasm and
his oracular sign, and the indication that the phantasm had predicted Jacob's *fate* or future destiny. Josephus' choice of the word
'fate' or 'portion' here would be significant for pagans, who could
easily have interpreted the episode as an event announcing Jacob's
personal allotted role in life.

(b) Josephus is very clear about what the events at the Jabbok *do
not say* about the title Israel. By omitting Scriptural data, he insists
that 'Israel':

(i) has nothing to do with land granted by God to the
Patriarchs;
(ii) has nothing to do with blessing;
(iii) has nothing to do with dawn or daybreak;
(iv) has nothing to do with seeing God; and
(v) has nothing to do with a replacement name for Jacob.

Furthermore, the title Israel is ordered for Jacob *not* by God Himself, but by a phantasm; and insofar as there is any reference to
'seeing' in Josephus' narrative, it is confined to the figure of the
phantasm, who is a 'vision' or 'apparition' by definition. Even so,
what the phantasm does is to speak; his appearance is incidental to
his main function in Josephus' narrative, for which see below (d).

(c) Throughout the events Josephus describes, *Jacob is in control*. His opponent is both phantasm and angel; his struggle is both battle and wrestling bout. From the very outset, Jacob is victorious. His earthly victory involves superiority over a supernatural foe. He becomes ruler, chief, or lord of the angel. It is therefore impossible for the angel to bless him, since the angel has been shown to be his inferior. His is no small victory. The phantasm identifies himself as nothing less than a divine angel; and Jacob makes capital out of this by extracting from the angel a knowledge of present and future. Jacob is in control; and the keywords are 'prevail', 'conquer', 'strength'; 'be ruler', 'be chief', 'be lord'.

(d) Victory over the phantasm-angel is a *sign* for Jacob. This sign, a quasi-prophetic oracle, is the prize for Jacob's victory over his opponent. Although 'phantasm' refers to a vision or apparition, *the sign is entirely verbal in form*, consisting in promises of future good things, a nation that will never cease, and assurance that no one will triumph over Jacob's strength. There is, perhaps, subtlety here: the first and third promises could be understood as restricted to Jacob himself, without reference to the people who descend from him. The second, however, clearly looks forward to a continuing people, the Jews, of whom Josephus himself is a living representative, confirming the truth of the phantasm's prediction. Josephus here could be implying a distinction between Jacob the man who is given the title of Israel, and the descendants of the man Jacob who are known collectively as Israel. That such may be the case is indicated by what follows.

(e) Jews versed in Scripture and tradition would recognize that Josephus is drawing on a range of traditional Jewish understandings of the name Israel, and traditional interpretations of Gen. 32: 29, to build up his account of the episode in respect of items (c) and (d) above. Non-Jews, however, would be most unlikely to discern this. For such readers, Josephus introduces the title 'Israel' almost *en passant*. He avoids suggesting that it is a 'name'; and he gives no hint at all that Jacob is no longer to be known by his old name Jacob, but from now on is to be named Israel. The title, in Josephus' account, can be understood simply as *an additional designation for Jacob relating only to this one episode in his life*: for Israel 'signifies' an 'opponent of an angel of God', and there is nothing in the narrative to suggest that Jacob goes on opposing angels and fighting with them. A pagan reader, having no knowledge of Scripture and tradition, might well understand Josephus in this way. And that, one might say, would suit Josephus well. He can admit that Israel is a word redolent of struggle and opposition; indeed, any pagan who could read LXX would find out that much for himself. But that struggle and opposition, Josephus deftly points out, is directed towards angelic powers, not earthly ones. The earthly might of Rome need have no fear of Israel, whose battle is not with earthly powers. And learned Jews themselves, reading this definition of Israel, considering traditions lying behind materials preserved for us in *LAB*, the Aramaic Targumim, and the *Prayer of Joseph*, would acknowledge that Josephus' restricted definition of the title Israel was not without authority. It is the setting which Josephus has created for that definition which might well cause concern for Jewish readers.

(f) As we have already hinted, Josephus' use of the word μοῖρα, 'fate', to describe Jacob's destiny is somewhat ambiguous. On the one hand, he seems to be underscoring the authoritative nature of his narrative for pagan readers: Jacob's fate, his whole future, is determined not by chance, but by a divine messenger foretelling his good fortune and strength. This could be construed as a personal privilege, inasmuch as what the phantasm says could be understood as relating to Jacob alone. But the Jewish reader might be privy to a wider sense of what Josephus has written, inasmuch as the superiority ascribed to Jacob, who is to be called Israel, is understood in Jewish tradition as a characteristic of Jacob's descendants also.

(g) Josephus tells how Jacob named the place where his 'fate' was explained to him as Phanuel, declaring that this word signifies 'face of God'. The Bible's explanation of this place-name he omits, as we have seen: there is no reference to Jacob's naming the place Peni'el because he has seen God face to face, and his life has been preserved. On the surface, Josephus offers by implication only one explanation of the place-name: Jacob was delighted with 'these things', namely, the predictions made to him by the phantasm-angel. The reader is left to her or his own devices to ascertain how the 'face of God' might be connected with 'voice and words' from the phantasm, which make up the lion's share of the story, predict Jacob's fate, and order that he be called Israel. Josephus has eliminated the astonishing biblical proclamation that Jacob has *seen* God face to face, but compensates for this by emphasizing what Jacob has *heard*. Josephus seems to be saying that the promises given to Jacob, promises which may (depending on how one reads what he has to say) refer also to the future of his descendants, in some mysterious manner express the 'face of God' in this world of political and historical reality. It is a *place* which is given this name; and it calls to mind the prediction that great good things will happen to Jacob; that his nation would never cease; and that no human being would ever triumph over his strength.

Perhaps the most dramatic aspect of Josephus' re-presentation of the biblical story is his apparently radical separation of the title Israel from anything to do with God's gift of land or blessing to Jacob. He knows that the title has to do with struggle, with strength, and with Jacob's superiority; but for obvious reasons he wishes to avoid too close an association of these things with Jacob *qua* ancestor of the Jewish people. To suggest to Roman or Greek readers in 93–4 CE that the main characteristic of the Jewish people in the person of their ancestor Israel was opposition to or struggle with earthly authority, coupled with claims to a specific land and the promise of divine blessing expressed in terms of victory over foes, would have been unwise in the extreme, and we have seen how he avoided saying all these things, at any rate directly. But the careful reader would no doubt discern that the 'good things' and continuing posterity promised by the phantasm at the Jabbok might not be entirely unconnected with 'good things' and posterity promised to Jacob at Bethel, as Josephus recounts that episode; and in the latter there is a clear statement of Jacob's claim to the land in a vision granted by God Himself.

According to Josephus, Israel is a title conferred on Jacob which points to his status in respect of angels, and his descendants' continued existence by divine promise. The Israel which Josephus has in mind spreads over the face of the known world; it is not confined to the 'land of Canaan', and it can never be destroyed.

8
Jacob's Change of Name Expounded in Rabbinic Texts

The accounts of Jacob's change of name do not feature so prominently in the classical Rabbinic sources as might be expected. With the exception of the Aramaic Targumim, which by their very nature cannot avoid treating each verse of the biblical material which concerns us, the precise meaning of the name Israel granted to the Patriarch Jacob was not a topic which engendered extended discussion and debate. This state of affairs, however, cannot conceal profound concerns on the part of the Rabbinic authorities, as with each passing generation they sought to articulate Israel's place in a world where imperial Rome in both west and east, and the power of Persia further to the east, could never be far from their thoughts. The Bible itself tells of Jacob's change of name in the course of a narrative describing the cunning machinations of Jacob's opponents from east and west, first Laban from Mesopotamia, then Esau from the land of Seir. By the time the earliest Rabbinic texts were completed, Esau had come to represent the wicked and oppressive rule of Rome.[1] This symbolic identification of Jacob's often ill-intentioned brother initially with the Roman Empire and later, by extension, with the Christian Church is assumed throughout the Rabbinic texts I shall examine here; it is rarely directly expressed, but its influence is unmistakeable.

[1] On the identification of Esau with Rome in Rabbinic texts, see H. Hunzinger, 'Babylon als Deckname für Rom und die Datierung des I. Petrusbriefes', in H. Reventlow (ed.), *Gottes Wort und Gottes Land: Festschrift für H.-W. Hertzberg* (Göttingen, 1965), 67–77; G. D. Cohen, 'Esau as Symbol in Early Medieval Thought', in A. Altmann (ed.), *Jewish Medieval and Renaissance Studies* (Harvard University Press: Cambridge, Mass., 1967), 19–48; S. Zeitlin, 'The Origin of the Term Edom for Rome and the Christian Church', *JQR* 60 (1969), 262–3; L. H. Feldman, 'Josephus's Portrait of Jacob', *JQR* 70 (1988–9), 130–3. Not all Rabbinic references to Rome as Esau-Edom were hostile, however: see L. H. Feldman, *Jew and Gentile in the Ancient World* (Princeton University Press: Princeton, 1993), 102 and 493–4, n. 56, 57; 181 and 512, n. 14.

I. THE MISHNAH AND TOSEFTA: THE SINEW OF THE THIGH

The Mishnah and the Tosefta, which are the oldest Rabbinic documents to refer to the events of Gen. 32: 23–33, are not so much
interested in Jacob's new name as in the law of גיד הנשה, 'the
sinew of the thigh' (Gen. 32: 33), for which the story of Jacob's
struggle with a supernatural opponent provides the rationale. The
basic discussion of the halakhah may be found in *m. Ḥull.* 7: 1–6,
supplemented by *tos. Ḥull.* 7: 1–8, where several important questions are raised. Of these, two are specifically related to the text of
Gen. 32: 33, namely, whether the law applies both to right and left
thighs of animals (*m. Ḥull.* 7: 1; *tos. Ḥull.* 7: 1); and whether the
law includes beasts both clean and unclean (*m. Ḥull.* 7: 5; *tos. Ḥull.*
7: 8).[2] Both of these see R. Judah adopting views which differ from
the rest of the Sages. The latter insist that the sinew of both right
and left thighs of animals are forbidden, whereas R. Judah, implicitly in the Mishnah, explicitly in the Tosefta, restricts the prohibition to the right thigh.[3] Reasons which could support R. Judah's
opinion emerge in *b. Ḥull.* 91a, where four separate authorities
bring proof that Jacob's right thigh was injured. First, Rava intimates here, and also at *b. Pes.* 22a, that the use of the definite article
to define the thigh in Gen. 32: 33 (הירך) indicates the principal, that
is, the right thigh; then R. Joshua b. Levi is credited with the view
that the verb ויאבק describes a wrestling lock in which the right
hand of the opponent seizes the other's right thigh; R. Samuel b.
Nahmani argues that Jacob's opponent was a heathen, and that
following Rabbinic advice that an Israelite should always let a heathen (who might be assumed to be predisposed to attack a Jew)
walk on his right-hand side, Jacob was indeed attacked from the

---

[2] Other questions occupying the Sages and arising indirectly from the biblical
text include: whether the law applies to embryos; whether butchers are trusted to
have removed גיד הנשה (*m. Ḥull.* 7: 1); how much of it must be removed to satisfy the
requirements of the halakhah (*m. Ḥull.* 7: 2); how much may be eaten before one is
liable to punishment (*m. Ḥull.* 7: 3); and the consequences of its being cooked and
thereby imparting flavour to a dish (*m. Ḥull.* 7: 4, 5: see also discussion at *b. Pes.*
22a).

[3] Although neither the Mishnah nor the Tosefta specify the source of Jacob's
injury, Rabbinic texts generally understood Gen. 32: 29 with its note that Jacob had
struggled with אלהים to mean that he had fought with an angel of some kind: see P.
Schäfer, *Rivalität zwischen Engeln und Menschen. Untersuchungen zur Rabbinischen
Engelvorstellung*, Studia Judaica, 8 (de Gruyter: Berlin, 1975), 155, n. 199, and
comments below, pp. 266–70, on *Gen. Rab.* 78: 3.

right;[4] and finally R. Samuel b. Aha in the name of Raba b. 'Ulla suggests that the opponent appeared to Jacob as a scholar, and consequently Jacob, again following the code of Rabbinic good manners, walked on the left of this 'sage' only to be attacked on his right side.[5]

Gen. Rab. 78: 6 further attempted to provide Scriptural justification both for R. Judah's opinion, and for that of R. Jose, who is named as arguing that Jacob's left thigh was dislocated. This text, however, suggests that גיד הנשה of both thighs is prohibited as food.[6] This might well be construed as a sign of Israel's concern for maintaining holiness; for the difference of opinion between R. Judah and R. Jose is introduced by a remark of R. Huna to the effect that the 'ramification' of the sinew, the mass of tissue surrounding it, was not forbidden as food: 'but Israel are holy, and treat it in practice as forbidden.' *Gen. Rab.* 78: 6 may intend us to regard the two thighs in a similar light: Scripture says that only one was injured, but in practice Israel avoids eating the sinew of both.

The Talmudic discussion of this matter ends with two important notices. First, the Rabbis state that the angel attacked Jacob

[4] See *b. Abodah Zarah* 25b. The heathen should walk to the right of a Jew, so that, if attacked, the latter may offer a ready defence.
[5] The rule is given by Mar: one who walks on the right-hand side of his teacher is a boor. Consequently, Jacob walked to the left of this 'sage'.
[6] *Gen. Rab.* 78: 6 opens with R. Judah's opinion, that Jacob's opponent 'touched only one of them (Jacob's thighs); consequently, one of them is forbidden. R. Jose said: He touched only one of them, but the two are forbidden. One Tanna states: The weight of evidence inclines to the view that it was the right one (thus according to R. Judah's words); but another Tanna states: The weight of evidence inclines to the view that it was the left (thus according to R. Jose's words). The one who says it was the right thigh (can adduce in support the verse) "And he touched the hollow of his thigh" (Gen. 32: 26); and the one who says it was the left thigh (can adduce the verse) "For he touched the hollow of Jacob's thigh" (Gen. 32: 33).' This is far from clear. Scripture seems to indicate that only one of Jacob's thighs was injured: both verses quoted in the midrash use the singular form 'thigh', and it may be that R. Judah is making the plea that the biblical law in fact refers only to one thigh. Rabbinic law, by contrast, refers the prohibition to both thighs: this may be R. Jose's point. The views of the two Tannas suggest Scriptural support for maintaining that either right or left thigh could be meant; perhaps the mention of 'his' thigh in Gen. 32: 26 was taken by one Tanna to indicate Jacob's principal thigh, that is, his right thigh (by analogy with the interpretation of '*your* hand' in Deut. 6: 8 as meaning your right hand, according to *Sifre Deut.* 35; *Mekhilta de R. Ishmael Pisḥa* 17. 130–9). Since evidence can be adduced for injury to either thigh, both are prohibited.

from behind and dislocated both his thighs. Consequently, it is implied, גיד הנשה of both right and left thighs is prohibited. Secondly, what of the meaning of ויאבק, which R. Joshua b. Levi had understood as a technical term relating to a wrestling hold, and the implications of that interpretation? The same Rabbi, we are told, had another explanation of the word based on the noun אבק, 'fine dust': the combatants, he said, had thrown up the dust of their feet such that it reached the Throne of Glory![7] In this way, the accepted halakhah is supported and reinforced. Although R. Judah's view is not accepted, it was clear that it could be supported and was known at the time when the Mishnah was completed. Interesting in this connection is PJ of Gen. 32: 33, which reproduces the Bible's prohibition of the sinew without comment; adds a note found also in *m. Ḥull.* 7: 1 that the law applies both to domestic and wild animals; and reproduces R. Judah's view that the angel dislocated Jacob's right thigh. No other Targum of the verse addresses these matters. What PJ seems intent on doing is preserving the opinion of R. Judah as a view of some importance.

Ought this Targum to be read with *Gen. Rab.* 78: 5 in mind? In that section, R. Judah's opinion is set out very clearly: the angel touched Jacob's right thigh, and only the right thigh of animals is consequently forbidden as food. R. Jose objected. Accepting that the angel touched only one of Jacob's thighs, he insists that the nerves in both thighs of an animal are forbidden, prohibition of both nerves being the accepted custom. At this point, however, the Midrash presses into service the views of two Tannas, one of whom suggests that the weight of evidence inclines to support R. Judah's view, while the other disagrees, taking the evidence as a whole as supporting the view that Jacob's left thigh was injured—

---

[7] In support of this, R. Joshua cited Nahum 1: 3, 'The Lord is patient and great in strength, and will surely not acquit (the guilty): as for the Lord, His way is in the storm-wind and the tempest, and the cloud is the dust of His feet, וענן אבק רגליו'. That the noun 'fine dust' might explain the nature of Jacob's encounter with his opponent was known to Aquila in the second century CE, when he translated ויאבק with ἐκονίετο, 'he became dusty'. *LAB* 18: 6, probably dating from the century before Aquila, assumes the same sense of the Hebrew verb, speaking of the time when Jacob 'wrestled in the dust' (*cum luctaretur in pulvere*) with the angel: see H. Jacobson, *A Commentary on Pseudo-Philo's Liber Antiquitatum Biblicarum,* i. 587. Through the prophecy of Nahum, R. Joshua is able to link Jacob's struggle with dust beneath God's feet and thus the Throne of Glory, which has Jacob's image engraved upon it: see further below, pp. 268–9.

an opinion which is now attributed to R. Jose, but had not been so attributed earlier in the discussion. In light of this, can it be said that PJ, by agreeing with R. Judah that Jacob sustained injury in his right thigh, also hinted agreement with R. Judah's view that the nerve of the left thigh may therefore be permitted as food? The Targum's (deliberate?) vagueness on this point means that it is impossible to decide; yet all the debates about the right thigh as opposed to the left in PJ, the Bavli, and Midrash Rabbah centre implicitly on R. Judah's view and on details of the biblical narrative itself which, it would seem, were under discussion and scrutiny at the time when the Mishnah was undergoing its final redaction.

Be that as it may, earlier Jewish discussions of Gen. 32: 23–33 for the most part seem unconcerned with these matters. Thus LXX, *Jubilees*, Philo's treatises, *Wisdom of Solomon*, the *Prayer of Joseph*, and other writings dating from before the Rabbinic period do not address them. The only pre-Rabbinic Hebrew text to do so, as far as I am aware, is the Qumran fragment of reworked Pentateuch 4Q158, whose contents were set out and discussed above.[8] This document, dating most probably from the second half of the first century BCE, shows that at least two of the Mishnah's concerns were 'live issues' in the period of the Second Temple: it states explicitly that both thighs are prohibited as food, and makes the prohibition binding on Jacob himself and, by implication, his immediate descendants as well as for future generations.[9] Evidently, 4Q158 would not have felt it necessary to express matters in such a direct way if there had not been opposing views at the time it was composed. Its direction that both thighs be avoided conforms to the mishnaic halakhah, against R. Judah's view that only one thigh is prohibited; its order that Jacob himself abstain from

---

[8] See above, pp. 34–7.

[9] This seems likely, in that a divine command given to the father would be understood as something which had to be passed on to his sons. The milieu in which 4Q158 was preserved understood this very well, since it was a principle embodied in the *Book of Jubilees*, a writing held in the highest regard by the Qumran group: see especially the general rule concerning the handing on of teaching given to individuals from generation to generation set out in *Jub.* 7: 37–9, and the principles underlying Abraham's commands to Isaac, *Jub.* 21: 10. That 4Q158 envisaged future generations keeping this commandment is evident from the appearance in line 13 of the words 'unto th[is day . . .]', the key section of Gen. 32: 33 detailing the continued observance of the custom.

the sinew requires observation of the law from his day onwards, in agreement with R. Judah's opinion that this ruling was observed before Israel assembled at Sinai. Unfortunately, 4Q158 gives no reason for its understanding the law in this way. It simply rewrites the relevant biblical verses to conform to what it regards as the norm.[10]

For R. Judah, and possibly for other authorities in his day, the precise interpretation of Gen. 32: 33 has become highly significant. It seems that R. Judah holds that the precise manner of putting into effect the law of the sinew should depend on determining what exactly happened to the Patriarch at the Jabbok and the replication of this, so to speak, in the application of the law among his descendants. This suggests that, as far as R. Judah was concerned, the detailed observance of this law was tied to the historical aspects of Jacob's struggle, so that Jewish abstinence from the sinew may be seen as a fairly precise 'reminder' or 'commemoration' of what really happened to Jacob when he became Israel, a victory achieved after a mighty struggle.

At this point we need to examine more closely another aspect of R. Judah's halakhic position. According to *m. Ḥull.* 7: 6, the law of the sinew applies only to clean animals. R. Judah disagreed with this, because the sinew was forbidden to the children of Jacob at a time when unclean beasts were still permissible as food, that is, before the giving of the Torah at Sinai. In other words, this was a single divine commandment made known centuries before the days of Moses. The same Mishnah presents unnamed scholars, simply designated 'they', as challenging R. Judah, arguing that the commandment, though written down in Scripture as part of Jacob's story, was as a matter of fact not promulgated until the rest of the Torah was given at Sinai.[11] Once more, R. Judah's understanding seems to focus on the life of the Patriarch: he wrestled and became lame in one of his thighs, as a direct result of which a commandment at once became binding on his children. To say this, however, is to admit that individual commandments could have been

[10] Such procedure seems to have constituted general practice in non-polemical legal documents at Qumran: see A. Shemesh and C. Werman, 'Halakhah at Qumran: Genre and Authority', *DSD* 10 (2003), 104–29.

[11] *Tos. Ḥull.* 7: 8 records that the argument against R. Judah's position is confirmed by Gen. 32: 33, which does not state that the children of *Jacob* (namely Reuben and Simeon) shall not eat the sinew, but that the children of *Israel* shall not eat of it, that is, the Israelites who were present to receive the Torah at Sinai.

revealed before the Torah was given to Moses; and, while the authors of *Jubilees* or 4Q158 might find no difficulty with such a notion, it might fit uneasily with general Rabbinic teaching. There is the further implication in what R. Judah says that 'Israel' existed before the giving of the Torah. In one sense it did, inasmuch as 'Israel' was the name conferred on Jacob when the sinew of his thigh was dislocated. But R. Judah's opinion may also invite the view that 'Israel' as a nation had existed when Jacob had wrestled at the Jabbok, and we have seen that even *Jubilees* found such an idea unacceptable. In the case of the latter document, it will be recalled, Jacob's change of name is not recorded until the point is reached in the biblical narrative where all twelve sons of Jacob are in existence.[12]

Why, then, did R. Judah adopt this stance with regard to the law of the sinew of the thigh? His apparent insistence that this commandment must be related in detail to the life of the Patriarch may provide us with a tentative clue to this question, and may be expressed as follows. The Sage may not have been unsympathetic to interpretations of Gen. 32: 33 which he regarded as having ancient authority, and which specifically related the Jews' present practice to the life of their illustrious ancestor. Such interpretations would, no doubt, claim the support of Gen. 32: 33 itself, which states that Israelites do not eat the sinew of the thigh *because* (כִּי) Jacob's opponent touched him there. This seems to be the purport of 4Q158, lines 12–13; and we may also recall what Josephus had written not a century before R. Judah's day, that since Jacob 'as a result of the battle suffered pain around the broad sinew (of the thigh), he himself held off from eating of this thing; and on his account it is something which we also do not regard as fit for eating' (*Ant.* I. 334). This 'rewriting' of the Bible adds two important elements not present in Gen. 32: 33. First, we learn that

---

[12] That divine commandments were granted to the Patriarchs before the days of Moses was evident from the Bible itself; and the Sages explained the matter simply. Thus at *Song Rab.* 1. 2: 5 we find the commandment of the sinew given to Jacob listed along with others in pre-Sinaitic days: e.g. the commandment of circumcision given to Abraham, and the law of the *levir* given to Judah. Parables are given to explain this. A king with a cellar full of wine gives his guests (like Abraham, Jacob, and Judah) individual cups to drink; but he grants the whole cellar only to his son (Israel, at Mount Sinai). A king will give rewards to his soldiers through individual officers: thus Abraham was entrusted with the commandment of circumcision; while through his son (Israel) he will grant all rewards; and so on.

Jacob himself, in the days before Moses, put into practice the commandment about the sinew: according to 4Q158, he was specifically commanded to do so. Secondly, contemporary Jews do not eat this sinew on account of Jacob himself. The Greek is not precise, and Josephus may mean that Jews do not eat the sinew, either because of the injury Jacob sustained, or because they follow Jacob's example in not eating it. In either case, and throughout this little portion of text, it is Jacob who is the deciding factor, much as he is in R. Judah's interpretation of the law. R. Judah may thus represent an old interpretation of the law which he is unwilling to relinquish entirely; and both 4Q158 and Josephus, in their different ways, bear witness to its antiquity and to discussions about it which can be traced back into the second century BCE. Whether R. Judah was keen to preserve his opinion because it commemorated and bore witness to Jacob's victory in a struggle with an angel who is actually Esau's guardian, and thus the heavenly representative of the Roman Empire, neither the Mishnah nor the Tosefta say; but it is a subject which will need further attention.[13]

2. THE TOSEFTA AND MEKHILTA DE RABBI ISHMAEL: THE NAME ISRAEL

The Tannaitic midrashim say little about Jacob's change of name. Indeed, only the *Mekhilta de Rabbi Ishmael* alludes to the narrative, and that in order to deal with an obvious question posed by the biblical record. Jacob was not alone in being granted a new name; but why, after his name was changed to Israel, was he still spoken of and addressed as Jacob? Commenting on this, R. Simeon b. Yohai explicitly contrasted the cases of Abraham and Sarah with that of Jacob. Their original names of Abram and Sarai, he declared, were removed or given up (עבר), while their new names of Abraham and Sarah were established or endured

---

[13] J. Neusner has noted that the Mishnah never refers to Rome under the code-names of Esau, Edom, or Ishmael, and that only one comment in the Tosefta might be construed as a cryptic reference to Rome: see his *Judaism in the Matrix of Christianity* (Fortress Press: Philadelphia, 1986), 73–87. Although the Mishnah is silent on this matter, in the first century Josephus seems already to express the equation of Rome with Esau in his *Ant.* 1. 275: see Feldman, 'Josephus's Portrait of Jacob', 130–3. It is interesting that R. Judah's exegesis of Gen. 32: 33 may have some affinities with Josephus' treatment of the same verse, given his possibly covert anti-Roman interpretation of events at the Jabbok.

(נתקיים). In the case of Jacob, however, he quoted Gen. 32: 29, 'And he said: Your name shall no longer be called Jacob', remarking: הראשון נתקיים לו והשני נתוסף לו, 'the first name endured in his case, while the second was added to it'.[14] No further comment or explanation is offered.

One might assume that what R. Simeon means is this: whereas in the cases of Abraham and Sarah the 'first' names Abram and Sarai disappeared altogether from use, in Jacob's case the 'first' name Jacob continued in use and then had another, 'Israel', added to it. Indeed, such is the opinion set out in *Gen. Rab.* 78: 3, and ascribed to R. Zechariah in the name of R. Aha, that Jacob is the 'root' name (עיקר), and Israel a supplement (טפל) which is added to it. R. Simeon's words in *Mekhilta*, however, are ambiguous. Which really is the 'first' name, and in what circumstances? He does not tell us in so many words. This is significant, since in *tos. Ber.* 1: 10 (see also *b. Ber.* 12b–13a) we read an exposition, not of Gen. 32: 29, but of Gen. 35: 10, running as follows:

In similar manner you interpret 'Your name shall no longer be called Jacob, but Israel shall be your name, etc.', (Gen. 35: 10). This does not mean that the name Jacob was 'uprooted' from him, but that Jacob should be added to Israel: Israel was the root (name), and Jacob an 'attachment'.[15]

Immediately before this explanation, Ben Zoma had suggested that in the days of the Messiah no mention will be made of the Exodus from Egypt in reciting Shema`. This opinion he based on the prophecy of Jer. 23: 7–8, that in Messianic times 'they will no longer say, As the Lord lives, who brought up the Israelites from Egypt', but will refer to His deliverance of Israel from the foreign kingdoms.[16] The other Sages insisted that this prophecy does not mean that Egypt will be 'uprooted' (שנתעקר), that is, omitted from

[14] See J. Z. Lauterbach, *Mekilta de-Rabbi Ishmael*, 3 vols. (The Jewish Publication Society of America: Philadelphia, 1933–5), vol. 1, tractate *Pisḥa* 16, lines 79–81.

[15] כיוצא בו לא יקרא עוד שמך יעקב כי אם ישראל וגו׳. לא שיעקב שם יעקב ממנו. אלא שיהא יעקב מוסף על ישראל, ישראל עיקר ויעקב טפילה as given by S. Lieberman, *The Tosefta According to Codex Vienna: The Order of Zera'im* (Jewish Theological Seminary of America: New York, 1955), 4. For discussion of the scriptural quotations and Rabbinic authorities named in *tos. Ber.* 1: 10 and in the parallel sources, see also S. Lieberman, *Tosefta Ki-Fshuta: A Comprehensive Commentary on the Tosefta: Order Zera'im, Part I* (Jewish Theological Seminary of America: New York, 1955), 13.

[16] On the identification and extent of the Jeremiah quotation, see Lieberman, *Tosefta Ki-fshuta Order Zera'im, Part I*, 13.

recitation of Shema` rather, mention of the Exodus will be added to the reference to foreign kingdoms, such that the latter becomes the root or essence (עקר) of the prayer, and the Exodus an addition or attachment. Similarly in the case of Jacob: once the name Israel was conferred, this became the principal name, and the other an attachment to it. If we now return to *Mekhilta*, we find that R. Simeon b. Yohai's comment is part of a larger discussion including this same prophecy of Jer. 23: 7–8. Thus at *Mekhilta Pisḥa* 16, lines 61–4, R. Eleazar b. Azariah explained the prophecy through a parable: a king who at first has only a daughter will initially swear oaths by the life of that child (understand Israel's Exodus from Egypt); but when he has a son, he will swear by his son's life (understand Israel in the days of Messiah).

This parable, however, offers an interpretation of the prophecy different from that found in the Tosefta, and prepares the way for R. Simeon's observation, based on a parable of his own, that more recent troubles lead a person to forget earlier ones. The changes of Abram's and Sarai's names are a case in point; and then the matter of Jacob's new name is introduced. This does not fit well with what R. Simeon has said earlier; rather, it appears almost as a piece of traditional material which has found a home here because of the subject-matter under discussion, but which could be left out of this part of *Mekhilta* without damage to the flow of the argument. Its place in *tos. Ber.* 1: 10, by contrast, is absolutely crucial to the argument there. The language of the Tosefta underscores this point, with its wordplay on the verb עקר in the sense of 'uproot, abrogate, abolish', and the noun עיקר, meaning 'root, reality, essence, chief matter', and it is preserved in the further discussion of Ben Zoma's teaching found in *b. Ber.* 12b–13a. Certainly, in both *tos. Ber.* 1: 10 and in *b. Ber.* 12b–13a the emphasis is placed on Israel as the essential name once it has been conferred. Both documents, however, are clear that the name Jacob remained in use; and *b. Ber.* 13a stressed the point by noting that this is so in the case of Jacob, while by contrast whoever persists in calling Abraham or Sarah by their old names is guilty of transgressing a commandment.[17]

In Jacob's case, however, the Talmud notes that Scripture brings back to him his old name, when God addresses him as Jacob at Gen. 46: 2, long after the events at Jabbok and Bethel.

[17] According to bar Qappara, the commandment is a positive one; while R. Eliezer argues that it is negative.

Gen. Rab. 78: 3 offers a similar solution to this difficulty. There, bar Qappara's contention that calling Abraham 'Abram' after his change of name represents a transgression of a positive command is strengthened by R. Levi, who demonstrates that it also transgresses a negative command. No such stricture exists on calling Sarah 'Sarai', however, since only Abraham was forbidden thenceforth to use that name. The question is then asked whether one who calls Israel 'Jacob' has transgressed a positive commandment. To this, the midrash replies: 'it was not the case that the name Jacob should be "uprooted" (שיעקר), but Israel was to be the essential ("root") name (עיקר), and Jacob an "attachment" (טפל).' This indeed corresponds to Tannaitic tradition as represented by *tos. Ber.* 1: 10. At once, however, the text of *Gen. Rab.* 78: 3 introduces the opinion of R. Zechariah noted above, that *Jacob* is the essential name, and Israel an attachment to it, thus bringing into the open a matter concealed beneath the surface in *Mekhilta*'s account. The final word of *Gen. Rab.* 78: 3 on the matter, therefore, leaves things unresolved: we may understand the name Israel as essential and fundamental, a name in form like that of the great angels Michael, Gabriel, Raphael, and Uriel, Jacob being a secondary supplement to that name; or we may view 'Jacob' as the term which expresses the essence of Patriarch and people, Israel being an additional name, conferred by divine blessing after a struggle. The majority Rabbinic opinion seems to incline to the former position, and presents us with Patriarch and people whose essential character is not unlike that of the highest angels; presently, we shall see what *Gen. Rab.* in particular made of this, in somewhat dramatic fashion. Yet this same midrash points also in another direction. Jacob, for some Sages, evidently remains the 'essential' name, Israel being the additional designation granted after Jacob's victory in a battle with Esau's guardian. Such a view might envisage a fight yet to occur between Jacob and the angel, who according to *Gen. Rab.* 78: 3 is Esau's celestial representative.

Unlike his grandfather and grandmother, therefore, Jacob retained his former name when he became Israel. This is a biblical fact which the Tosefta, the *Mekhilta*, the *Bavli*, and *Genesis Rabbah* sought to account for in their several ways. The use of this Scriptural datum by some of these texts to illustrate the correct interpretation of Jer. 23: 7–8 is of some interest, inasmuch as it emphasizes that God's initial choice of the Jews, and His first redemption of them from Egypt, will not be forgotten in the final redemption when the Messiah comes; and that initial choice and redemption has its parallel, as it were, in the name Israel conferred on to Jacob, whose original name is not to be abrogated in the future. *Genesis Rabbah*, however, also draws attention to the other perspective. Israel is the essential name, and is used to describe Jacob from the time of his victory over his opponent at the Jabbok, Jacob remaining as a supplementary name. Even so, R. Zechariah sounds a warning note, which sets the name Jacob once more in the forefront. This may simply arise from the Rabbi's recognition that the Bible continued to refer to Jacob by his old name; on the other hand, R. Zechariah may have more particular reasons for highlighting the name Jacob. To discover whether this might be so, we must examine the *Genesis Rabbah* material as a whole.

3. GENESIS RABBAH

The oldest midrashic collection of more or less continuous commentary on the biblical passages dealing with Jacob's change of name is to be found in *Gen. Rab.* 77–78, 82. Parallels to some of the material preserved there are to be found in the later collections of *Song Rab.* 3 and *Lam. Rab.* 3: 7–8, and will be discussed below.[18] The exegetical stance adopted by the redactors of *Genesis Rabbah*, however, is given a distinctive flavour by its introduction, which is not paralleled elsewhere in the *Midrash Rabbah*, although it appears in *Yalqut Shim'oni* בראשית 132 shorn of all names of Rabbis represented in *Gen. Rab.* 77: 1. This introduction opens with the lemma 'And Jacob was left alone, etc.' (Gen. 32: 25), followed at once by a quotation of Deut. 33: 26, אֵין כָּאֵל יְשֻׁרוּן. This Hebrew sentence may be read in a number of different ways. First, it may be taken to mean: 'There is none like God, O Jeshurun', an address to Israel under that rare and highly

---

[18] The date of the final redaction of *Gen. Rab.* is given as the first half of the fifth century by H. L. Strack and G. Stemberger, *Einleitung in Talmud und Midrasch*, 7th edn. (Beck: München, 1982), 259–60; a somewhat later date in the sixth century was proposed by L. Zunz, *Die gottesdienstlichen Vorträge der Juden historisch entwickelt*, 2nd edn. (Frankfurt-am-Main, 1892), 84–7. A brief commentary of the sections of *Gen. Rab.* discussed here may be found in J. Neusner, *Genesis Rabbah: The Judaic Commentary to the Book of Genesis. A New American Translation*, 3 vols. (Scholars Press: Atlanta, 1985), iii. 117–27, 165–70.

significant biblical title discussed ealier.[19] Secondly, it might be read as yielding the sense: 'There is none like the God of Jeshurun', a statement of the incomparability of Israel's God similar to sentiments expressed elsewhere in the Bible, as at Exod. 15: 11; Isaiah 40: 18, 25; 46: 5. Finally, the words may be construed as a question and answer, to yield: 'Is there none like God? (Yes!) Jeshurun.' It is this third way of reading the text which the midrash took up:[20]

[R. Berekhiah in the name of R. Jehudah b. R. Simon: There is none like God; and who is like (the) God (of) Jeshurun?] The most distinguished and praiseworthy who are among you. You discover that everything that the Holy One, blessed be He, is destined to do in the world to come He has anticipated and already done through the agency of the righteous who are in this world. The Holy One, blessed be He, revives the dead, and Elijah revives the dead. . . . the Holy One, blessed be He, makes sweet what is bitter with what is bitter, and Elisha makes sweet what is bitter with what is bitter. R. Berekhiah in the name of R. Simon said: There is none like (the) God (of) Jeshurun; and who is like God? Jeshurun—Israel, the Patriarch. Just as it is written concerning the Holy One, blessed be He, 'And the Lord alone לבדו shall be exalted in that day' (Isa. 2: 17), so also it is written concerning Jacob, 'And Jacob was left alone, לבדו' (Gen. 32: 25).

The exposition begins by understanding the title Jeshurun in the light of the common word ישר, 'upright, perfectly straight', to suggest that, insofar as anyone might be 'like God', it is the noblest and most distinguished in Israel. Then at once the exegete's thoughts turn to the world to come: some of the extraordinary and incomparable blessings of that world have already been realized, by special divine privilege, in the actions of the righteous in Israel's own history. The midrash particularly singles out Elijah and Elisha and, among other activities common to God and these prophets, notes (in the section not quoted here) the withholding of the rain; the blessing of what is small in compass; and the visitation of barren women, to grant them children. But the title Jeshurun itself Scripture applied to Jacob who is Israel: so Isaiah 44: 2 attests, and we have already seen how a good deal was made of this either by Ben Sira himself, or by those who were responsible for handing on the Hebrew text of his work.[21] It is this that R. Berekhiah in R. Simon's name enunciates at the end of the

---

[19] See above, pp. 102–6.
[20] *Gen. Rab.* 77: 1, translated from the critical edition of J. Theodor and Ch. Albeck, *Bereschit Rabba mit kritischem Apparat und Kommentar* (Berlin, 1912–29).
[21] See above, pp. 102–6.

exposition, sensing a Scriptural question, 'Who is like God?', to which the answer is Jeshurun, Israel the Patriarch. The exposition itself, however, relates the title to extraordinary events in Israel's history which are manifestations of the world to come: through the agency of the righteous, God has already anticipated the mighty events of the coming age. The title Jeshurun, it would seem, is redolent of the world to come when nothing, least of all opposing forces, will stand in the way of God's sovereignty. As *Gen. Rab.* unfolds the meaning of Jacob's reception of the name Israel, concern with that world to come can be discerned as never far below the surface of the midrash. The connection of the title Jeshurun with Israel's victory over her enemies in the last days is certainly relevant here; it is a subject which may have interested Ben Sira, and which certainly engaged those responsible for transmitting the Hebrew text of his work. In this respect, then, the proem of *Gen. Rab.* 77: 1 may belong to a tradition of interpretation with very ancient roots, although we now lack the evidence to trace its progress down the centuries.

This introductory exegesis also draws attention to the nobility of the people called Israel, and the privilege granted to the best of them to be empowered by the Creator to perform actions which He Himself alone is able (in normal circumstances) to accomplish. Just as God is 'alone', so Israel is alone: such is the implication of the proem, which speaks of Jacob being 'alone', on his own, before the struggle out of which he emerges as Israel. Israel is an unique nation (אומה יחידה) according to *b. Sukk.* 55b and PJ of Num. 29: 6, following the biblical teaching of 1 Chron. 17: 1, a verse which itself asks of God the rhetorical question: 'And who is like Thy people Israel, a nation unique (אחד) on the earth?' Implicit throughout this introduction, and further developed as the midrash runs its course, is a sense that the bestowal of the name Israel has to do with the relationship between God and the world He has created; and that the appearing of Israel the Patriarch as one who, like God, is 'alone' cannot be separated from the Jewish proclamation of God's unity and uniqueness in a world hostile now, but destined to be subjected to His 'upright' and 'perfectly straight' dominion.[22]

---

[22] For the Unity of God and the uniqueness of Israel as 'two sides of the same coin', see further *b. Ber.* 6a; *Ḥag.* 3ab; *Mekhilta de R.Ishmael Shirta* 2, lines 13–16; PJ of Deut. 26: 17–18, and discussion of the matter in E. E. Urbach, *The Sages: Their Concepts and Beliefs*, trans. I. Abrahams, 2 vols. (Magnes Press: Jerusalem, 1979), i. 528–30.

3.1. *The Character of Jacob's Angelic Opponent*

Throughout *Gen. Rab.* 77–8, 82, it is assumed that Jacob's opponent was an angel. From the outset, this otherworldly being plays a vital role. By implication, the midrash first raises the question of why Jacob was left alone on that night. In answering, the text tells how Jacob's being left 'alone'—a crucial matter for the proem—was in fact determined by the angel, whether with good or evil intent. Indeed, *Gen. Rab.* 72: 2–3 offers differing evaluations of the angel's character and motives. In R. Huna's opinion, which opens *Gen. Rab.* 77: 2, the angel appeared to Jacob as a shepherd with sheep and camels like Jacob, and they agreed to take their respective possessions across the Jabbok. Jacob then returned, 'and saw that he had forgotten some item', whereupon the angel wrestled with him. In this case the angel appeared benign; and the illustration following suggests as much. It concerns R. Hiyya the Elder, R. Simon, and R. Simeon b. Gamliel, who, engaged in the silk trade at Tyre, followed Jacob's example of going back to where they had been, only to discover a bale of silk. The implication is clear: Jacob's return also resulted in benefit for him, the new name Israel; and inasmuch as the author of that return was the angel-shepherd, the angel had Jacob's good in mind. This exposition implicitly agrees with the view of the Tosefta and the *Mekhilta* that one or other of the names Jacob and Israel represents something in addition for the Patriarch, an extra bonus, as it were.

By contrast, the Rabbis made the angel into an arch-brigand with sheep and camels who was intent on enervating and terrifying Jacob. He took Jacob's possessions across the Jabbok 'in the twinkling of an eye', while Jacob, having agreed to bring the brigand's possessions across, found more and more items to bring on each successive journey, and accused his companion of being a magician (פרמקוס).[23] According to R. Pinchas, Jacob

---

[23] For the various spellings in the MSS of this Greek loan-word, see Theodor and Albeck, *Bereschit Rabba*; Jastrow, *Dictionary*, p. 1230; and S. Krauss, *Griechische und lateinische Lehnwörter im Talmud, Midrasch und Targum*, 2 vols. (Berlin, 1897, 1899), ii. 490. The Greek word itself was used by LXX to speak of the Egyptian sorcerers involved in Pharaoh's schemes with hostile magic against Israel: see Le Boulluec and Sandevoir, *La Bible d'Alexandrie, 2: L'Exode*, 36–7. In the Christian Apocalypse of John 18: 23, Rome, under the code-name Babylon, is represented as deceiving nations by her sorcery (ἐν τῇ φαρμακείᾳ). Of all New Testament writings, the Apocalypse is perhaps the most strongly Jewish in its content; and it may indicate an association in Jewish minds of Rome with sorcery as early as the first century CE.

countered the magic by stuffing a tuft of wool into the magician's throat, and reminding him that sorcerers were ineffectual at night. R. Huna, however, presented the angel as remaining incognito, and seeking to frighten Jacob by putting his finger to the ground so that fire flashed forth from it. Unimpressed, Jacob reminded his opponent that he himself was entirely constituted of fire, by quoting the prophetic verse Obadiah 1: 18, 'and the house of Jacob shall be a fire'. This quotation is apposite, in that documents from the Cairo Geniza demonstrate use of the Book of Obadiah as *haftarah* for the *parashah* וישלח. This prophet had thoroughly denounced Esau and Edom; and the identification of Esau-Edom as Rome is crucial here, given the biblical information (Gen. 32: 7) that Esau with 400 troops was advancing on Jacob.[24] The angel who appears in this setting as arch-brigand, therefore, is a thinly disguised celestial counterpart of Rome, perceived as a sorcerer.

As if to confirm all of this, *Gen. Rab.* 77: 3 opens with a frank statement of R. Hama b. R. Haninah that Jacob's opponent was Esau's angel; this is supported by Gen. 33: 10, where Jacob says to Esau: 'I have seen your face as one sees the face of God, and you have accepted me'. As we have seen, the significance of this verse was not lost on the LXX translators, who implied that the one who wrestled with Jacob was something to do with Esau. But as they perceived, this verse suggested also that any danger had passed by the time Jacob met Esau: the two embraced peaceably and that, the midrash implies, was because Jacob had already defeated Esau's angel. This point is illustrated once Gen. 33: 10 has been quoted: 'It was like an athlete who stands up and wrestles (ומתגשש) with a king's son. He lifted up his eyes and saw the king standing beside him, so he surrendered himself to him' (*Gen. Rab.* 77: 3). The language of wrestling is explicit here, just as it was in LXX; in this case, however, the athlete is not Jacob, but the angel, who gave up the wrestling bout when he saw the king, the Shekhina, in attendance.[25] Lying behind this imagery is perhaps an understanding of Gen. 32: 29 to the effect that Jacob had struggled in the company of God with men, that is, with Esau, and had

---

[24] See Jacob Mann, *The Bible as Read and Preached in the Old Synagogue*, 3 vols. with Prolegomenon by Ben Zion Wacholder (Ktav: New York, 1971), i. 260–6.

[25] See Theodor and Albeck, *Bereschit Rabba*, for witnesses to the text which include an additional statement that the Shekhina was present.

prevailed.[26] The ambiguities of the biblical account, however, were not lost on the Rabbis contributing to this midrash. Who was speaking to whom? Who won the fight? Thus *Gen. Rab.* 77: 2 concluded with R. Berekhiah's words, that from the words of the Bible we would not know which party was victorious, the matter being finally elucidated only by careful consideration of the words ויאבק איש עמו, 'and a man engaged with him'. Who was the one covered in dust, אבק, asks R. Berekhiah? It was the man who wrestled with Jacob; and he came off the worse.

3.2. *Esau's Angel Did Not Prevail*

Gen. Rab. 77: 3 continues with an interpretation of Gen. 32: 26, 'and he saw that he did not prevail'. Having established that it was the angel who realized his failure, R. Hanana bar Yitzhaq apostrophized him: 'He [Jacob] came to you with five amulets suspended on him: his own merit, the merit of his father, the merit of his mother, the merit of his grandfather, and the merit of his grandmother. Measure yourself to see if you can stand even against his merit.' This comment clearly assumes that Jacob was doing battle against demonic power. The evil associated with the sorcerer who appeared in the guise of an arch-brigand was uppermost in the Rabbi's mind; Jacob, therefore, would need to be armed against such power with appropriate countercharges. When *Genesis Rabbah* was being composed, amulets were widely used as such protective devices, written incantations invoking some character or event from the Bible or traditional writings, and seeking to apply the powers at work therein to overcome a present threat or misfortune. Frequently angels are invoked to aid the afflicted party. The Cairo Geniza has preserved abundant material shedding light on this custom, whose efficacy is probably assumed by R. Hanana:[27] the merits of Jacob and his progenitors—their pious deeds, faithfulness, acts of charity, fulfillment of *mitzvot*, sufferings, and acts of repentance—are written down, assumed, and

---

[26] See above, p. 62, where it was noted that the Hebrew of Gen. 32: 29 might be construed as declaring to Jacob 'for you have struggled in the presence of God even with men, and have prevailed'.

[27] See L. H. Schiffman and M. D. Swartz, *Hebrew and Aramaic Incantation Texts From the Cairo Geniza: Selected Texts from Taylor-Schechter Box K1* (Sheffield Academic Press: Sheffield, 1992); M. D. Swartz, *Scholastic Magic: Ritual and Revelation in Early Jewish Mysticism* (Princeton University Press: Princeton, 1996), 197–9.

invoked as protection by Jacob in his hour of need. The midrash strongly implies that the amulets protecting Jacob do not contain the names of angels, as so many contemporary amulets did.[28] The reason for this will become clear in the next section: the names of the angels are in a constant state of flux, altered by God at a moment's notice. Little help would be gained, therefore, from invoking such beings by names which may not even exist in a time of dire threat. Such beings are inherently unstable and transient, unlike the enduring merits of Jacob and his forefathers.

Thus the presumption of Jacob's angelic opponent is criticized, though also explained: faced with such overwhelming odds against him, the angel was able to attack Jacob only because a higher power permitted it. In respect of this, the Rabbi introduced a similitude of a king who had a wild dog and a tame lion: the latter the king used to make his son courageous as he battled with it. Should the wild dog then attack the king's son, the king can then inform the dog that the lion could not hurt his son. Likewise, should the nations attack Israel, the Holy One can remind them that their angel did not prevail over Jacob, and leave them to draw the consequences. Thus the midrash brought the biblical narrative into the present: despite Rome's apparent dominion, that rule will be temporary, and the Jews should understand that Israel's ultimate victory under God's protection is assured. On this view of things, Jacob's victory over the angel was as much for the benefit of future generations as for himself. With this in mind, the midrash moves on: ' "And he touched the hollow of his thigh"—he touched the righteous who were destined to arise from him: this refers to the generation of the persecution, זה הדור דור השמד.' The persecution in mind was that unleashed by the Emperor Hadrian at the time of the Second Revolt against Rome (132–5 CE). *Midrash Ha-Gadol* comments at length on this verse, the virtues of the great heroes of the persecution being celebrated; but the note here in *Genesis Rabbah* is impressive in its brevity, a brevity designed to draw out the implications of the angel's identity as Esau's counterpart. The sufferings of the Second Revolt were somehow anticipated in Jacob's battle with Esau's angel long ago. In touching Jacob's thigh and injuring him, Esau injured those descendants of Jacob who would

[28] Swartz, *Scholastic Magic*, 74–81, provides graphic evidence for the use of angelic names as means of protection for human beings engaged with the heavenly world.

suffer in Hadrian's persecution. Once more, however, the comment is placed firmly in a setting which has no doubt of Israel's ultimate victory over Rome, a victory anticipated in the events at the Jabbok. As a result of the flight, the hollow of Jacob's thigh was dislocated (Hebrew ותקע). This rare word required explanation. R. Berekhiah and R. Eleazar understood it to mean that the angel 'flattened' the limb, and a tradition in the name of R. Assi explained that 'he split it like a fish'. R. Nahman adduced Ezek. 23: 18, where the word occurs in the sense of 'alienate, separate', to suggest that the angel separated the hollow of his thigh. Finally, R. Haninah b. Yitzhaq insisted that Jacob and the angel were engaged in hand-to-hand combat through the night; but that as soon as the column of the dawn arose, the angel asked to be sent away. With this, the midrash marks a transition to a new section, which opens in *Gen. Rab.* 78: 1 with a new introduction.

The chapter just reviewed has presented Jacob's struggle with the angel as a violent physical contest in which Jacob, although sustaining an injury, was ultimately victorious over the heavenly representative of Esau, who stands for the power of the Roman Empire. The force of the opening homily about Jeshurun has become more apparent: Jacob the Patriarch was the ancestor of an unique people through whose righteous representatives God works His miracles in this world. Whatever God will do in the world to come, He has already anticipated through the agency of those righteous ones; and that anticipation includes the most astounding of all miracles, the resurrection of the dead. The victory over Rome is yet to come; but this is assured, just as the other miracles listed in the opening section of the midrash are assured. That victory itself, indeed, was anticipated in Jacob's victory over Esau's angel, and his consequent reception of the name Israel.

3.3 *Where Do Angels Come From, and What Is Their Status?*

If Jacob could defeat Esau's angel, and if that defeat could portend the eventual end of Rome's power, what precisely is the status of the angels? *Gen. Rab.* 78 addresses this question, once again using discussion of the redemption of the Jewish people, the resurrection of the dead, and the Hadrianic persecution as the setting. *Gen. Rab.* 78: 1 introduces the topic with what are now understood to be the angel's words in Gen. 32: 27, 'Send me away, for the dawn has arisen', putting them alongside Lam. 3: 23, חדשים לבקרים רבה אמונתך, 'new each morning, great is your faithfulness'. Almost at once we shall be told that each new day the Lord creates new angels to praise Him; but this matter is not addressed before two authorities are quoted as linking this verse to the redemption and the resurrection of the dead:

R. Simon b. Abba said: Because you renew us each morning, we know that great is your faithfulness to redeem us. R. Alexandri said: Until you renew us each morning, we know that great is your faithfulness to revive the dead for us.

This twin concern with the redemption and the resurrection points to a deeper concern of the midrash, namely, the whole matter of *change*. Redemption and resurrection involve change in status and character; this section of Scripture speaks of a change of name for Jacob; and, at first sight perplexingly, the midrash will tell us that the angels change: they do not remain constant. Significantly, however, we shall learn that the very highest angels, notably Michael and Gabriel, never change. Michael is the traditional heavenly representative of Israel;[29] and Gabriel announces God's mighty deeds. Other angels are altered, as is Esau's angel. The midrash will eventually explain that, even if he had been able to tell Jacob his name at the time of their conflict, that name would soon have changed. Thus *Gen. Rab.* 78: 4 made Rabbi, in the name of Abba Jose ben Dosai, explain why the angel refused Jacob's request to know his name (Gen. 32: 30): angels have no fixed name, since God changes their designation at will, and an angel's name today will not be the same tomorrow.[30] But Jacob, as Israel, will have gained power over Esau's angel; and, unlike the transient celestial beings of whom Esau's guardian is one, Israel has permanent status, for the midrash will tell us that his likeness is engraved upon the Throne of Glory. Before reaching this point, however, the commentators take us on a journey.

---

[29] Michael as Israel's heavenly representative is a biblical datum: see Dan. 10: 13, 21; 12: 1. For the *creatio continua* of the other angels from the 'river of fire' beneath God's throne, see below, p. 261; cf. further *b. Ḥag.* 14a; *Lam. Rab.* III. 23 §8, discussed below, p. 279; and P. Schäfer, *Rivalität*, 51–4.

[30] Initially, two Scriptural verses were brought in support of this: 'He tells the number of the stars, and calls them all by name' (Ps. 147: 4), and 'He who brings forth by number their host: he calls them all by name' (Isa. 40: 26). These verses indicate that angels have no fixed names, a point confirmed by Judg. 13: 18, where the angel says to Manoah: 'Why do you ask my name, seeing that it is marvellous?' The angel in dispute with Jacob thus does not know what his name will be changed to at any given time.

R. Samuel b. Nahman said in the name of R. Jonathan: There is no band [of angels] on high which utters praise and then does so again. R. Helbo said: Every day the Holy One, blessed be He, creates a band of new angels, and they utter a song and depart. R. Berekhiah said: I objected to R. Helbo by saying: But it is written, 'And he said, send me away, for the dawn has arisen'. He said to me: Strangler! How do you propose to strangle me [with your arguments]? Michael and Gabriel are indeed angels of the highest rank: all [the rest] of them are exchanged; but these are not exchanged.

The opinion that each company of angels praises God on one occasion only, and then departs to be replaced with a newly created band, will form the basis of R. Joshua b. Hananiah's forthcoming debate with the Emperor Hadrian. It is central to the development of the midrash, and R. Berekhiah's objection to it needs to be considered carefully.

The Rabbi quotes the angel's words in Gen. 32: 27, 'send me away', and suggests that this being—identified as Esau's angel at *Gen. Rab.* 77: 3 and again at *Gen. Rab.* 78: 3—was regularly involved in the praise of God, and that the dawn's appearance meant that he needed urgently to return to heaven to fulfill his duties at the allotted time. This is exactly the view of some of the Aramaic Targumim to this verse. According to TN, the angel identified himself as Sariel, 'the chief of those who utter praise': his need to return to lead the heavenly service is thus obvious and explicit. FTP and *CG* also identified the angel with the same words as TN, although they did not name him. These Targumim, however, neither suggested nor implied that the angel who fought with Jacob was the celestial counterpart of Esau. Was R. Berekhiah, perhaps, also arguing that Jacob's opponent was nothing to do with Esau, but was the leader of the heavenly service? Whatever the answer to that question, it is certain that the Rabbi understood Gen. 32: 27 *in particular* as proving the enduring importance and status of the angel: so much is evident from his own words, and from R. Helbo's reply to him, which had to admit that at least two of the highest angels remain without change. Indeed, if the angel who fought with Jacob was due to be 'exchanged' after a day had passed, what would it matter whether Jacob let him go or not? R. Berekhiah apparently argued that the angel's request truly *meant* something, and that R. Helbo's view of a perpetually changing angelic host had deprived Gen. 32: 27 of its meaning. R. Berekhiah may also have subscribed to the idea that the angels are not 'exchanged', but utter praise only at more or less widely spaced intervals, or only once in the whole of time. Such possibilities are discussed at *b. Ḥull.* 91b; but there is no statement in that source that the angels are ephemeral.

That God creates new bands of angels to praise him each day, and that those who have uttered their praise depart and give way to new angels was taken by the Emperor Hadrian as the starting-point for his discussion with R. Joshua.[31] One possible implication of this is that Esau's guardian angel has long ceased to exist or has failed to maintain his original character. Where, Hadrian asked, did these superannuated angels go? The Rabbi told him that they returned to the place of their creation, which is the נהר די נור, the 'river of fire' which, like the River Jordan, flows day and night; and it issues from the sweat of the Living Creatures which bear up the Throne of God.[32]

This discussion, which leaves the reader in no doubt about the transient nature of angels, leads to a question about their worth relative to Jacob, who is Israel, in a series of observations closing this section of the midrash. The angels are truly the appointed guardians of Israel, as Psalm 91: 12 declared:

R. Meir and R. Jehudah and R. Simeon. R. Meir said: Who is greater, the guardian, or the one who is guarded? Learn from what is written: He shall command His angels in respect of you to guard you. You have to admit

---

[31] R. Joshua b. Hananiah is presented as often involved in theological discussion with the Emperor Hadrian (reigned 117–38 CE); see W. Bacher, *Die Agada der Tannaiten*, vol. 2 (Strassbourg, 1890), 123–7; R. Loewe, 'Gentiles as Seen by Jews after CE 70', in W. Horbury, W. D. Davies, and J. Sturdy (eds.), *The Cambridge History of Judaism*, Volume 3, *The Early Roman Period* (Cambridge University Press: Cambridge, 1999), 254–5. Urbach, *The Sages*, i. 181–2, notes that Justin Martyr (*c*. 100–*c*.165 CE) recorded a similar tradition about the ephemeral nature of some 'ordinary' angels and the eternal existence of others, and suggests that this 'downgrading' of the angels by some of the later Tannaim and the early Amoraim should be related to the tendency of those Sages to subordinate the importance of the heavenly *Beth Din* to the earthly academy. The downgrading may also be inspired by Rabbinic antipathy towards Gnosticism, especially in those texts where angels are depicted as jealous of, or hostile to, human beings or Israel: see Schäfer, *Rivalität*, 83–5, 219–20.

[32] This puts all the lesser angels firmly in their place, and subordinates them to the mysterious living creatures which bear the divine Throne, the Merkavah, according to Ezek. 1: 5–14. The notion that such angels are created 'new every morning' may indicate a reserve on the part of Rabbis cited in this midrash towards the mystics and their attempts to delineate precisely the functions of named angels in the various heavens: see Schäfer, *Rivalität*, 54–5.

that it is the one guarded who is greater than the guardian. R. Jehudah said: Who is greater, the one who carries, or the one who is being carried? Learn from what is written: They [the angels] shall bear thee in their hands. Behold, the one carried is greater than the bearer. R. Simeon said: Who is greater, the one who sends, or the one who is sent? Learn from what is written: And he said, Send me away. You have to admit that the one who sends is greater than the one who is sent.[33]

Jacob here is shown to be greater than the angel: the former has power to send the angel away, and the latter is consequently the one sent, and in an inferior position. Psalm 91, used to prove this point, is famous as an anti-demonic prayer. It expressly notes God's protection of the one who is under the covering of the Most High and the shadow of the Almighty (verse 1), and is remarkably apt for Jacob's situation, promising deliverance from terror in the night: לא תירא מפחד לילה, 'you shall not be afraid of the night's terror' (verse 5). The psalm may have been chosen to illustrate Jacob's superiority over the angel precisely because it was used as a protection against evil: as we have seen, the five amulets which Jacob carried in this struggle indicated that his adversary was demonic and malicious. But the psalm served another purpose, being quoted to show that Jacob was superior to those same angels sent by God as His messengers and as doers of His will. Here we may note a marginal gloss to Targum Neofiti of Gen. 32: 27. The body of the manuscript text here identifies the angel as 'the chief of those who utter praise', while the gloss depicts the angel as 'the chief of the messengers', who begs to return to heaven because the time has come 'for the angels of the height to be sent forth'. This Targumic fragment is arresting, confirming Jacob's power and superiority over one who might otherwise be required to do the bidding of the Holy One! It is the most dramatic illustration of the central contention of R. Simeon's statement in *Gen. Rab.* 78, that the sender is superior to the one who is sent.

Gen. Rab. 78: 2 unambiguously moved the discussion to the question of angelic worship of God, and Jacob's effect on this. Lurking beneath the surface of the text, this topic now emerges

[33] Parallels to this midrash are found in *Yalqut* וישלח 133; *Mid. Pss.* 91. 6; 104. 3; *Yalqut* Psalms 843; *Yalqut Makhiri* Ps. 91. 23; and *Midrash Ha-Gadol* on Genesis 32: 27. For tradition-historical discussion, see Schäfer, *Rivalität*, 192–5, who notes that all these texts stress the present superiority of the righteous over the angels, the question why this is so being answered most clearly by the *Midrash Ha-Gadol*: the righteous possess the Torah.

into the light of day. The angel's request is accompanied by a reason: the time has come for those who utter the heavenly praise to do so. Jacob retorted that the angel's colleagues should do the praising; but the angel's reply indicated that, should he miss his turn in praising God today, God would note the fact, and prevent him from praising on the morrow. None of this affected Jacob, whom the midrash now presents as demanding a blessing from the angel, citing for a reason the fact that the angels sent to Abraham granted him a blessing. The angel replied that those angels had been sent for that express purpose, whereas he had not been so commissioned, a response dismissed by Jacob in the same terms as he had waved aside the angel's complaint that his failure to praise on the correct day would result in his not being able to take part in the heavenly service. At this point, R. Levi reported a tradition in the name of R. Samuel b. Nahman, according to which the angel complained to Jacob:

> The angels of the service, because they revealed the mysteries of the Holy One, blessed be He, were cast down from their [heavenly] divisions: if I listen to you, how much more will I be cast down from my division! [Jacob]said to him: Have you finished? Are you done? I will not let you go unless you bless me.

Three times, then, was Jacob involved in verbal 'wrestling' with the angel, each time taunting him with a colloquial expression recalling the exasperated tones of a preparatory schoolmaster to a tiresome pupil: 'Have you *quite* finished?' This battle of wits was evidently going on at the same time as the physical struggle between Jacob and the angel, and it served to emphasize Jacob's intellectual superiority as well as his physical strength. In fact, according to R. Huna, it forced the angel into a resigned disclosure of what was about to happen to Jacob:

> I will disclose [things] to him; and if the Holy One, blessed be He, says to me: Why have you revealed [things] to him? I shall say before Him: Lord of all the worlds, your children issue decrees and you do not stop their decrees—then can *I* stop their decrees? He said to him [to Jacob]: He [God] is intending to be revealed to you at Bethel and to change your name; and I shall be standing there, as it is said: At Bethel he found him, and there he shall speak with us. 'With you' is not written here, but 'with us'.

It will be recalled that Josephus had shown Jacob taking advantage of his opponent's plight to gain knowledge of the future. R.

Huna's interpretation of the episode is similar, but only in broad terms; and it has very different aims in view. The powerlessness of the angel is here quite frankly portrayed. He tells Jacob what will happen, as having no option, knowing that God Himself will confirm Jacob's decrees; indeed, he envisages Jacob's sons, the sons of Israel, sitting in the *Beth Din* and issuing authoritative rulings ratified by the Holy One. This the Rabbi is able to prove in a most significant manner, by uniting into one magisterial comment all three Scriptural texts which speak of Jacob's experiences accompanying his change of name. Thus, the name Israel will be divinely conferred on Jacob at Bethel: Gen. 35: 10 says as much, and that verse is here recalled. The prophecy of Hosea 12: 5 is understood as involving at Bethel the same angel as fought with Jacob at the Jabbok, an angel who knows what authority the sons of Israel bear in issuing decrees.

Gen. Rab. 78: 2 tells how Jacob struggled with an angel not only physically, but verbally and intellectually. He was victorious in both contests. Angels, with the exception of the very highest in rank such as Michael and Gabriel, are transitory creatures. Jacob takes precedence over them, and can to some degree exercise control over them in their chief functions as messengers of God and as chanters of the heavenly service. They are created beings: this is heavily emphasized by the midrash, for they are pictured as originating in the sweat of the Living Creatures who bear up the Throne of the Living God. They depart daily to the River of Fire; their identity is changed; and, like the stars, they may be called by any name at all as the Almighty wills. Among their number is Esau's angel, the guardian of the mighty Roman Empire; this creature is no exception to the rules governing other angels, and the midrash makes the Emperor Hadrian himself a witness to the ultimate infirmity of his empire's custodian who, like the rest of his kind, returns to the River of Fire beneath the Throne of God.

Such was Jacob's strength in the battle with this angel that the latter was compelled to disclose God's plan to confer on Jacob a change of name to Israel. This plan Jacob forced out of the angel resigned to the fact that the decrees of Israel are in any case accepted by God. This plan Jacob insisted on hearing about before the angel departed; and, as far as the midrash is concerned, it more or less constituted the blessing which Jacob had requested of his opponent (Gen. 32: 27, 29), on the grounds that angels had blessed his grandfather Abraham. At any rate, the angel's words appeared sufficiently to satisfy Jacob to allow him to release the angel. Yet in reality the angel could not bless Jacob-Israel, for the midrash has proved that Jacob was superior to the angel! Consequently, the midrash made no allusion to blessing in repect of the sections of the two Scriptural verses which refer to it, Gen. 32: 27, 30. For it is God who blessed, blesses, and will bless Jacob, with an abundance of prosperity and gifts. This much will be made plain at *Gen. Rab.* 82: 2, commenting at length on the note at Gen. 35: 9 that God was revealed to Jacob at Bethel *and blessed him*, at the same time changing his name to Israel. This part of the midrash will refer back explicitly to the angel's words given in *Gen. Rab.* 78: 2 and cited above: the angel had told Jacob in advance what God would do in Bethel, when the very same angel will again be present.[34] In respect of Jacob who is to be named Israel and his descendants, therefore, the angelic band is inferior in authority, in status before God, in liturgical function, and, by implication, in power to bless.

3.4 *The Interpretation of the Name Israel*

The midrash now needed to turn to detailed consideration of the name Israel and its meaning. Consequently, *Gen. Rab.* 78: 3 opens with a discussion of the relative status of the names Jacob and Israel which I reviewed earlier.[35] Then the biblical explanation of the name Israel, 'for you have engaged/struggled with God and with men and have prevailed' (Gen. 32: 29) was quoted and expounded as follows:

You have wrestled (ויתגששתה) with those above and have prevailed over them; with those below, and you have prevailed over them. 'With those above' refers to the angel. R. Hama in the name of R. Haninah said: It was Esau's angel, according to what Scripture says: 'I have seen your face as

---

[34] *Gen. Rab.* 82: 2 repeated the angel's prediction for an additional reason, namely, to prove that God carries out the counsel of His angels, as is stated by Isa. 44: 26. What the midrash had put into the angel's mouth at *Gen. Rab.* 78: 2 is fully realized at *Gen. Rab.* 82: 2, which makes the further point that if in this single matter God performs what His messengers have said, then He will more surely do so in the case of Jerusalem, about whose future so many prophets had spoken. See also *Pesiqta Rabbati* 17: 2.

[35] See above, pp. 250–2. In my quotation of the midrash below, note how Jacob's opponent is assumed, without debate, to be an angel. The assumption was based on interpretation of the words of Gen. 32: 29, that Jacob had struggled with 'God', א׳להים, the term being taken to refer to some kind of angel: see Schäfer, *Rivalität*, 155, n. 199.

one sees the face of God, etc.' Just as 'the face of God' refers to judgement, so also 'your face' refers to judgement: just as 'the face of God'
implies 'None shall appear before Me empty handed', so they shall not
appear before your face empty handed. 'With those below, and you have
prevailed over them': this refers to Esau and his troops. Another explanation: 'For you have persisted with God'—you are the one whose likeness
is engraved on high.

Two differing explanations of the biblical interpretation of the
name Israel are offered here. In the first, the midrash follows a
sense of 'you have engaged' which is as old as the days of LXX,
understanding it as 'you have wrestled'. Given that almost everything said about Jacob's encounter with the angel up to this point
has been understood as a fight, the midrash could now provide a
rationale for its exegesis. The wrestling is first 'with God', and
then 'with men'. The biblical 'with God' is taken as meaning 'those
above', more specifically the angel, once again identified as Esau's
guardian as in *Gen. Rab.* 77: 3. Once more Gen. 33: 10, with its
record of Jacob's words on meeting Esau that he has seen his face
as if one saw the face of God, is brought in in support of the
identification, but further significant exegetical details are now
added.

   First, R. Hama noted that the phrase 'the face of God' in
Gen. 33: 10 refers to judgement: this is so, because the divine title
אלהים, 'God', is traditionally understood as signifying the
Almighty's attribute of justice, מדת הדין.[36] Jacob's encounter
with the angel is thus first portrayed as a kind of lawsuit with Esau,
in which Jacob was judged to be the victorious party. But the
phrase 'the face of God' also occurs in the biblical commandment
that all Israel should appear before God three times each year with
appropriate offerings (Exod. 23: 14–17). Likewise, Jacob had sent
offerings to Esau (Gen. 32: 13–21) as the latter was advancing to
meet Jacob with his troops. On that occasion, too, Jacob had prevailed. In all this, the exegete has understood that Jacob became
Israel because he had persisted (Hebrew root שרה) or had been
firm (Hebrew root שרר) with God: such is his reading of the
Hebrew of Gen. 32: 29, כי שרית which I have translated in the
midrashic quotation as 'because you have engaged'.

   The midrash, however, offered another explanation of 'for you have engaged', which understood the Hebrew verb as deriving from the root שרר, 'to be a prince, to rule'. From this root comes the noun שר, 'a prince', a word used by the Bible to describe angelic beings: thus Dan. 10: 21; 12: 1 had spoken of the chief angel Michael as 'prince'. Jacob-Israel is a 'prince', inasmuch as his own likeness is a heavenly reality, engraved on the Throne of Glory. He is a prince with God already, a matter emphasized also by Targum Onqelos of Gen. 32: 29 in particular and by the other Targumim of that verse in general. As we shall see presently, the Targumim were determined to present Jacob-Israel as having a princely-angelic status with God.[37] What for them was a primary concern, however, was presented in *Gen. Rab.* 78: 3 simply as 'another explanation'. It did not again feature in that section of the midrash, and *apparently* had little influence on the exegesis recorded before it. Indeed, up to this point *Genesis Rabbah* has been determined to demonstrate Jacob's superiority to angels, both as messengers and as worshippers of God. He was superior in particular to Esau's angel, the representative of Roman power, defeating him and acquiring the name Israel, whose likeness is engraved on God's Throne. For all its apparent downplaying of the angelic dimension of the name Israel, the midrash, in this one brief note, recalls its fundamental importance to the reader's mind.

But Esau's angel will not tell Jacob-Israel his own name. He cannot, since it is changed by God, many times and without warning. This we learn in what follows at *Gen. Rab.* 78: 4, a passage examined earlier in respect of the question whether Jacob was the Patriarch's essential name and Israel an addition to it, or vice-versa.[38] The mutability of angelic names, including the name of Esau's angel, is expressed by the midrash in bold contrast to, and cheek by jowl with, the permanence of Jacob-Israel's likeness engraved on the Throne of Glory. Furthermore, the majority opinion of the Rabbis that 'Israel' is the essential name, Jacob being an attachment to it, now stands revealed as bringing into prominence 'another explanation' stating that Jacob's likeness is engraved upon the Throne of Glory. For this other explanation gives to the name Israel a permanent status from days of eternity, and must be regarded as anything but an exegetical afterthought; rather, it now emerges as central to the discussion. *Gen. Rab.* 82: 2 pursued the

[37] See below, pp. 282–304.
[38] See above, pp. 250–2.

matter further. Commenting on Gen. 35: 9's words that God appeared to Jacob and blessed him, R. Isaac remarked that if one who builds an altar to the Lord's Name is blessed (Exod. 20: 21), how much the more was it right that God should be revealed to Jacob and bless him, since his likeness was engraved on His Throne? R. Levi concurred: if one who offers an ox or ram to the Lord gains the privilege of divine revelation and blessing, how much more should Jacob merit such things, whose likeness is engraved on the Throne? The permanence of that likeness would guarantee the continuing presence of God and blessing for Israel.[39]

But the permanence of Israel's name is part of a larger continuum: it parallels that permanent status accorded to those who experience the redemption, and the resurrection of the dead to everlasting life. *Gen. Rab.* 78: 1 has already been noted as setting out both these things at the beginning of its exegesis, contrasting the final change of all which will lead to permanent glory and blessedness for Israel with the perpetual change and alteration to which the angels are subject, their daily return to the River of Fire and designation by whatever name the Almighty chooses to give them being destined to go on and on without end.[40] For the end of days is certainly in mind, as *Gen. Rab.* 78: 8 makes plain, beginning with R. Berekhiah's comment on Gen. 32: 32 and its notice that the sun arose for Jacob as he passed by Penu'el:

R. Berekhiah said: The sun shone only to heal him; but for others it shone to give its light. R. Huna in the name of R. Aha said: Just as the sun effected healing for Jacob, but burning up for Esau and his troops, so the sun will be healing for your children, but burning up for the nations. 'Healing' in respect of the former, as it is said: 'But for you that fear My Name shall the sun of righteousness arise, with healing in his wings' (Mal. 3: 20); 'burning up' in respect of the nations, 'For behold, the day comes burning, etc.' (Mal. 3: 19).

---

[39] M. Fishbane, *Biblical Myth and Rabbinic Mythmaking* (Oxford University Press: Oxford, 2003), 247–9, analyses *Gen. Rab.* 78: 3, and the related texts *Gen. Rab.* 47: 7; 82: 13; the tantalizing exegesis of Gen. 33: 20 in *b. Meg.* 18a which apparently styles Jacob 'god'; and the *MHG* on Gen. 28: 13, in terms of the mystical traditions: 'each in its own way instructs us how the components of the divine world could be personalized or interiorized in the heart and mind of a seeker after the concrete reality of God—be that a matter of knowledge or presence' (p. 249). See also his comments later, pp. 340–1.

[40] See above, pp. 260–4. For discussion of the context of Rabbinic ideas in general concerning the creation of the angels, see esp. Schäfer, *Rivalität*, 51–5.

R. Berekhiah's interpretation has no necessary reference to the end of days, although his comments on Jeshurun in *Gen. Rab.* 77: 1 indicated that he was prepared to understand that name in the light of what God will do for Israel in the future. R. Huna's does, and implicitly introduces the twin notions of redemption and resurrection as well. The explanation offered in the name of R. Aha is particularly adroit: the sun's rising or shining (Hebrew זרחה of Gen. 32: 32) is juxtaposed with the sun of righteousness arising or shining (Hebrew וזרחה) in Mal. 3: 20, a famous prophecy predicting the final day of the Lord: this will be heralded by the prophet Elijah (Mal. 3: 23), whose duty it will be to gather together the twelve tribes of Israel for the final redemption and the resurrection of the dead. That final day will also see the fire which consumes the wicked, and which will eat up the descendants of Esau, the Roman imperial power. Nevertheless, the midrash will not permit its readers to dwell too long on this future hope without some qualification. The sun had shone for Jacob, as it will in future in the manner foretold by Malachi; yet, when the sun had shone on the Patriarch, 'he was limping on his thigh'.

> R. Joshua b. Levi went up to Rome. When he came to Akko, R. Haninah went out to meet him. He found him limping on his thigh. He said to him: You are like our Patriarch—'and he was limping on his thigh'. (*Gen. Rab.* 78: 5)

Rome is here identified with Esau, whose angel fought with Jacob long ago. Esau in the shape of Rome still conflicts with Israel. Even the saintly Joshua b. Levi, Israel's representative, did not escape entirely unharmed and unmarked from the clutches of Esau-Rome, but returned home limping. Whatever hopes for the future might be intimated in the biblical narrative of Jacob's victory over the angel, the short account of R. Joshua reminds all Jews that Rome is a present reality which has to be dealt with day by day, and which can still cause injury and distress.

3.5 *Jacob's Second Visit to Bethel and the Name Israel*

Gen. Rab. 82: 1–6 comments extensively on Gen. 35: 9–14, which tells how God conferred on Jacob the name Israel during the Patriarch's return to Bethel. This section of the *Midrash Rabbah* offers no further direct interpretation of the name Israel, and some of what it has to say has already been noted above. Thus we have seen how the note in Gen. 35: 9, that God appeared to Jacob and blessed

him, had been taken to refer to the rich blessings which the
Patriarch received from God, both before and after his sojourn
with his father-in-law: for proof of this, *Gen. Rab.* 82: 1–2 invoked
Psalm 26: 17, referring it to Jacob in terms of blessing and
divine comfort. *Gen. Rab.* 82: 3–5, however, concentrated on two
particular details: the significance of God's appearing to Jacob
'again' (עוד), and the promise that 'a nation and an assembly of
nations', גוי וקהל גוים, should arise from Jacob (Gen. 35: 9, 10).
R. Jose in the name of R. Haninah explained that 'again' meant

as on the first occasion: just as on the first occasion (He appeared) by the
agency of an angel, so on the second occasion by the agency of an angel.

The Rabbi referred back to Jacob's first visit to Bethel, when he
had experienced a vision of angels in attendance on the Lord (Gen.
28: 12–13). The incident at the Jabbok is apparently not under
consideration here; and, insofar as the bestowal of the name Israel
is in the commentator's mind at all (and the verse which deals with
it, Gen. 35: 10, is not cited in this part of *Genesis Rabbah*) it is
associated with Jacob's visits to Bethel. *Genesis Rabbah* at this
point, however, in no way emphasized the granting of the name
Israel, nor its meaning, in relation to this episode at Bethel: in this
respect, it is quite unlike the writings of Philo and the *Book of
Jubilees*, for whom the place Bethel and the events associated with
it were presented as central to proper appreciation of what it meant
for Jacob to become Israel.

By contrast with those older texts, *Gen. Rab.* 82: 4–5 attempted
to resolve problems raised by God's words to Jacob after the conferring of the new name: the command to be fruitful and increase;
the prediction of a nation and a congregation of nations destined to
go forth from him; and the promise of kings descended from him
(Gen. 35:11). Only in *Gen. Rab.* 82: 5 was the name Israel itself
under review; and then, as it happens, through a quotation of 1
Kings 18: 31.

R. Judan and R. Aibo (and R. Ashian b. Nagri) said in the name of R.
Johanan: Your sons are destined to make a nation among a congregation of
peoples. Just as the 'congregation of peoples' offer sacrifice on the forbidden high places, so your sons will offer on the forbidden high places. Abina
b. Shila in the name of R. Johanan inferred it from this Scriptural verse:
'And Elijah took twelve stones according to the number of the tribes of the
sons of Jacob as the Lord spoke to him, saying, Your name shall be Israel'
(1 Kings 18: 31); for from the hour that this name was given to him it was

declared to him: 'a nation and a congregation of nations shall come forth from you.' R. Simlai inferred it from this Scriptural verse: 'And they called Leshem, Dan, according to the name of his father, Dan' (Josh. 19: 47) ['who was born to Israel' (Judges 18: 29)]; for from the hour that this name was given to him it was declared to him: 'a nation and a congregation of nations shall come forth from you.'

These comments do not portray the naming of Jacob as Israel and its aftermath in the best of lights: the sons of Jacob from that time onwards appear among the Gentiles, offering sacrifice in illicit sanctuaries, and even venturing in the direction of idolatry. Sin is to the fore in this comment, dramatically contrasting with other texts expounding the name Israel. R. Simlai in particular indicates that Jacob himself, when his name was changed to Israel, knew that in the future the idolatrous shrine of Dan would be set up; indeed, the sense that Jacob was party to information about what his descendants would do is very strong here. In some general respects, it is reminiscent of the knowledge which Jacob was granted of the future according to the *Book of Jubilees*, although the religious deviations specified here do not feature as such in the older writing. R. Johanan's comment, with its reference to Elijah's victory over idolatry, somewhat ameliorates the dark predictions of this passage; but as a whole, it speaks of sin on part of the tribes, and the liability of tribe and nation for such sin.

Gen. Rab. 82: 4–5, then, seems more concerned about the people who issued forth from Jacob *qua* Israel, than about the name Israel itself granted to that Patriarch; and it sees God's words as somehow alerting Jacob in advance of calamities which will befall his descendants in the time to come. This is hardly surprising, given the content of the verses it undertook to interpret. The section contains no significant references back to the biblical story of Jacob's struggle with the angel in Gen. 32: 22–33 and the commentary on those verses already given in *Gen. Rab.* 77–8; no quotations or discussions of Hosea 12: 3–6; and no hint, even indirect, of concern with Esau, the Roman Empire, or the Christian Church. But the commentary which immediately preceded this rather dark analysis of Gen. 35: 11 included a reminder from R. Isaac that Jacob's likeness is engraved upon the Throne of Glory (*Gen. Rab.* 82: 2), and R. Berekhiah's statement in the name of R. Levi that the angel who fought with Jacob at the Jabbok had revealed to the Patriarch that his name would be changed by God, and that he would be present when that event occurred at Bethel (*Gen. Rab.* 82:

2 end). These observations must be linked with the comment at the end of this discussion of Jacob's second visit to Bethel. There, at *Gen. Rab.* 82: 6, we read:

'And God went up from upon him, etc.' (Gen. 35: 13). R. Simeon b. Laqish said: The Patriarchs, they constitute the Merkavah, as it is said: 'And God went up from upon Abraham' (Gen. 17: 22), 'And God, went up from upon him', and 'Behold, the Lord was stationed over him' (Gen. 28: 13).

The Scriptural report of God's going up 'from over' Jacob-Israel (Gen. 35: 13, וַיַּעַל מֵעָלָיו אֱלֹהִים and Abraham (Gen. 17: 22, וַיַּעַל אֱלֹהִים מֵעַל אַבְרָהָם) indicated for R. Simeon b. Laqish that the Patriarchs form the Throne of God itself, enduring for ever, bearing the divine presence, and ensuring Israel's access to the Almighty. Not for nothing is Jacob-Israel's likeness engraved upon this Throne: in a manner of speaking, the living creatures of Ezekiel's vision might be said to bear up his likeness, while mere angels are daily altered, and have no part in the constitution of the Merkavah.

4. BABYLONIAN TALMUD ḤULLIN 91A–92A

There is a single, extended discussion of Gen. 32: 22–33 in the Babylonian Talmud, and this is in tractate *Ḥullin* 89b–92a, where the general topic of debate is גִּיד הַנָּשֶׁה, 'the sinew of the thigh', as treated by *m. Ḥull.* 7: 1–6. In the first instance, the Talmud is interested in Jacob's struggle with the angel and its outcome primarily as source for further understanding the commandment of the sinew of the thigh. Thus in earlier discussion of the mishnaic material we have already had recourse to the Talmud, to throw light on questions raised in the Mishnah, and also in the Tosefta, including the question whether the right thigh, the left thigh, or both thighs of an animal be prohibited. This is debated in *b. Ḥull.* 91a, the precise details of Jacob's encounter with his opponent being used as arguments illustrating or proving the several views which the Sages adopted.

Two short, homiletic passages follow this discussion. The first explains why Jacob was left on his own (Gen. 32: 25). R. Eleazar explained that he had returned to fetch small jars left behind, showing that the belongings of just persons, rightly acquired without robbery, are dearer to them than their own bodies. The second (*b. Ḥull.* 91ab) derived from the Scriptural note (Gen. 32: 25) that Jacob's opponent struggled with him until daybreak the general rule that a scholar should not go out alone at night: so R. Isaac opined, although other authorities derived the same rule from other biblical verses. A third haggadic passage, however, serves to introduce into discussion Jacob's first visit to Bethel, and his vision of a ladder with angels going up and coming down. R. Akiba reports that he once asked R. Gamaliel and R. Joshua whether the verse reporting that the sun arose for Jacob after his struggle with the angel (Gen. 32: 32) meant that it had arisen only for him, and not for the whole world. R. Isaac explained the verse with reference to Jacob's first visit to Bethel:

> It indicates that the sun which had set on his account arose on his account, as it is written, 'And Jacob went out from Beer-Sheba, and went towards Haran' (Gen. 28: 10); and it is written, 'And he lighted upon the place' (Gen. 28: 11). When he arrived in Haran, he said: Is it possible that I have passed by the place where my fathers prayed, and I have not prayed myself? When he had set his mind to go back, the earth contracted itself for him, and at once 'he lighted upon the place'. When he had prayed, he sought to return. The Holy One, blessed be He, said: This righteous man has come to My dwelling place; and is he to depart without lodging for the night? At once, the sun set.

The basic elements of this exegesis were well known, and may be found also in *b. San.* 95ab; *Gen. Rab.* 68: 10; PJ, FTP, and FTV of Gen. 28: 10; *PRE* 35, and other sources.[41] In this section of Talmud, however, they clearly serve to forge a strong bond between the account of Jacob's vision at Bethel recorded in Gen. 28 and the account of his struggle with the angel at the Jabbok. The key element linking these accounts, as far as this passage is concerned, is the matter of the sunrise, the appearing of daybreak, which can be contrasted with the setting sun or night in both Scriptural narratives. At Bethel, Jacob had seen angels: *b. Ḥull.* 91a gives the width of the ladder on which they stood, and notes that there were at least two of them going up and coming down. Their size is given, in the manner of a mystical treatise. What were these angels doing?

A Tanna taught: They were going up and observing the likeness above, and coming down and observing the likeness below. They sought to

---

[41] See B. Grossfeld, *Targum Neofiti 1: An Exegetical Commentary to Genesis* (Sepher-Hermon Press: New York, 2000), 201, and comments by M. Maher, *Targum Pseudo-Jonathan: Genesis*, The Aramaic Bible, vol. 1b (Clark: Edinburgh, 1992), 99.

expose him to danger: immediately, 'And behold, the Lord was stationed over above him'. R. Simeon b. Laqish said: If it were not so written in Scripture, it would be impossible to say it—it was like a man fanning his son.[42]

The Tanna assumed that the engraving of Jacob's likeness on the Throne of Glory was common knowledge (see above, on *Gen. Rab.* 78: 3), and that the angels were going to compare it with the living Patriarch's form. They were also jealous; and we have here been presented *in nuce* with a notion which we have seen was as old as the *Prayer of Joseph*, which explained Jacob's fight at the Jabbok as arising from the rivalry of an archangel. But there is much more than a hint of rivalry here. The angels resent Jacob's privilege, and the Lord Himself protects Jacob, R. Simeon effectively giving the reason for this. Whatever the status of the angels, Jacob is really Israel, whom the Lord has called 'My son, My first-born' (Exod. 4: 22).

Next, God's promise of the land to Jacob (Gen. 28: 13) was graphically illustrated by R. Isaac: God rolled the Land of Israel up into a bundle and put it beneath Jacob, and he lay down upon it. *b. Ḥull.* 91b–92a now returns to Gen. 32: 27, and the wrestling angel's plea to Jacob to let him go, 'because the dawn is coming up'.

He (Jacob) said to him: Are you a thief or a gambler that you are afraid of the dawn? He said to him: I am an angel; and from the day I was created my time has not yet arrived to utter the Song, until now. This supports the opinion of Rab Hananel in the name of Rab. Rab Hananel reported that Rab had said: Three groups of angels utter the Song every day. One group says 'Holy'; and another group says 'Holy'; and another group says 'Holy Lord God of Hosts'. They raised an objection: Israel are more beloved before the Holy One, blessed be He, than the angels of the service; for Israel utter the Song every hour and the angels of the service utter the Song only once a day. Some say, once a week; and some say once a month; and some say once a year; and some say once every seven years; and some say once in a jubilee; and some say once in the whole of time. Also Israel make mention of the Name after two words, as it is said: 'Hear, Israel, the Lord, etc.'; whereas the angels of the service make mention of the Name only after three words, according as it is written: 'Holy, holy, holy Lord of

---

[42] The tradition cited by the Tanna here existed in a number of forms, some of which were obscure, and betray a complex transmission history: see Schäfer, *Rivalität*, 205–7, for the parallels, and proposed solutions to the problems of tradition-history they pose.

Hosts, etc.' Nor do the angels of the service utter the Song on high until Israel recite it below, as it is said: 'When the morning stars made a joyful noise together, and all the sons of God shouted for joy,' Rather, one group says 'Holy'; and another group says, 'Holy, holy'; and another group says 'Holy, holy, holy Lord of Hosts'. But is there not also to be considered the matter of 'Blessed [be the Glory of the Lord from His place]'? 'Blessed' is said by the Ophanim; or, if you prefer, one may say that once authority has been granted, it has been granted.

This discussion established the superiority of Jacob-Israel and his descendants the children of Israel over the angels in their chanting the *Q^eduššah* in its various forms in the recital of the Liturgy; and at the same time it underscored the privilege of Israel's access to the Divine Name in the recital of Shema`, when Israel on earth proclaim the uniqueness of the Almighty.[43] They do this 'when the column of the dawn arises', at the time when the angel left Jacob in possession of his new name Israel. The primary concern of the Talmud at this particular point, then, is liturgical, featuring Israel's relationship to the heavenly service of the celestial retinue. It is at once followed, however, by a more ambiguous section, which concludes the tractate's dealings with this episode in Jacob's life. It is introduced by Hosea 12: 5: 'He struggled with an angel and prevailed; he wept and he made supplication to him.' The anonymous interpreter noted that we do not know who prevailed over whom; it is only with Gen. 32: 29, when the angel says to Jacob, 'you have struggled with God and with men, and you have prevailed', that we know for certain that Jacob was made prince over the angel, that is, he himself is revealed as a prince, שׂר, with angelic status of his own, but superior to that of his opponent.[44] Similarly, we do not know who wept towards whom making

[43] The Sages' insistence that Israel's chanting of the Song of the Service takes precedence over that uttered by the angelic bands may have been intended as a counterblast to certain apocalyptic writings which went out of their way to describe and highlight the liturgical songs and poems uttered by the angels in the worship of God: see E. E. Urbach, *The Sages*, i. 150–2; ii. 750. For the place of the *Q^eduššah* in heavenly and earthly worship, see D. Flusser, 'Sanktus und Gloria', in *Abraham unser Vater: Festschrift für Otto Michel zum 60. Geburtstag* (Brill: Leiden, 1963), 129–52; on Israel's privileges over angels in reciting *Shema*, see further Schäfer, *Rivalität*, 171–4; and for this emphasis on Israel's privileges as balancing the roles accorded to angels in some of the *Hekhalot* texts, see Schäfer, *Rivalität*, 231–2.

[44] The Talmud states: יעקב נעשה שר למלאך, 'Jacob was made prince over the angel', an understanding assumed by all the Aramaic Targumim: see below, pp. 283–4.

supplication, until Gen. 32: 27 is taken into account, where we learn that the angel begged Jacob to let him go. This implies that the angel wept towards Jacob. Then we read:

'For you have struggled (with God and with men)'. Rabah said: He hinted by intimation to him that two princes were destined to go forth from him: the Head of the Diaspora which is in Babylon, and the Nasi who is in the Land of Israel. From this also is derived an intimation of the exile.

The verses in Gen. 32 appear to interest the authorities participating in the discussion for several reasons. First, the fact that Jacob was alone at night, contravening the rules of conduct that the Sages expect him to have observed as a scholar, is explained and justified.[45] The fact that it is night, and that an angel is present, serves to ensure that the episode is taken in conjunction with Jacob's first visit to Bethel, at night, when angels appeared to him. It also brings into relief the matter of dawn or sunrise, which is equally important in both accounts of Jacob's doings: at Bethel he woke in the morning to recognize that the Lord was in that place, and at the Jabbok the sunrise corresponded to his awareness that he had seen God face to face, and that his life had been preserved. In other words, Jacob's being alone at night was not a sign of scholarly indiscipline, but divinely arranged. R. Isaac was further concerned to use the Bethel episode to prove that Jacob was not only a scholar, but also a man of prayer: it is as a man of prayer that he was anxious about having passed by Bethel, 'the place where my fathers prayed'.[46] Jacob thus exemplifies study and prayer, those twin cardinal virtues of Rabbinic Judaism. Even when he breaks the rules about being alone at night set down for scholars, the breach of etiquette has a divinely arranged reason: the scholar Jacob is brought into the divine presence, and miracles are done for him to expedite his journey to the place of prayer and to grant him a night of rest.

The Talmud's discussion thereafter, however, is dominated by the theme of rivalry. The likeness of Jacob engraved upon God's Throne is not primarily a proof of Jacob's eternal and enduring

---

[45] Jacob was a pious student, who attended the *Beth Ha-Midrash*: see *Gen. Rab.* 63: 10; TO, PJ, TN of Gen. 25: 27.

[46] That Jacob prayed at Bethel is derived from the note in Gen. 28: 11, ויפגע במקום, which is usually rendered into English as 'and he lighted upon the place'. The general view of the Rabbis, however, is that the verb 'to light', Hebrew פגע, refers to prayer and intercession: see *b. Ta'an.* 7b; *San.* 95b; *Soṭ.* 14a; *yer. Ber.* 4: 1.26; *Sifre Deut.* 26; *Gen. Rab.* 68: 9.

significance as it was in *Genesis Rabbah*, but a matter of curiosity for the angelic beings, who go down to Bethel to compare this likeness with the man Jacob. The Talmud's observation is brief: 'they sought to expose him to danger'. This particular interpretation of the events at Jacob's first visit to Bethel is yet another bond joining Bethel and the Jabbok, where Jacob was certainly injured, most probably by angelic activity. The Talmud's very brevity at this point heightens the dramatic tension. Jacob confronted a terrible threat motivated by jealousy, and was preserved only by the presence of the Almighty Himself. But the change of Jacob's name is nowhere in the forefront of discussion here; rather, it is assumed that the name Israel is known for what it is, a name of the sort borne by Michael and Gabriel and ascribed by the Almighty to one designated 'My son, My first-born' (Exod. 4: 22). Only at the end of the discussion does the anonymous authority interpreting Gen. 32: 29 state clearly that this verse and its explanation of the name Israel signify that Jacob was made prince over the angel. That is to say, Jacob proved himself of superior rank to the angel.

The granting of the Land of Israel to Jacob is certainly part of the divine promise made to him when his name was changed (Gen. 35: 12). However, the Talmud section reviewed here focused not on this verse, but on Gen. 28: 13 as supporting Jacob's title to the land as verified by a miracle, once more confirming the central importance of Jacob's first visit to Bethel in the interpretation of events at the Jabbok, a matter already noted in Philo's treatment of the latter. The Talmud, too, emphasized Gen. 32: 27, where the angel demanded to be sent away because the dawn had arisen. Other interpreters preferred to pass over this verse, as we saw in examining *Gen. Rab.* 78: 4. There, it will be recalled, R. Berekhiah had to 'rescue' the verse. For the Talmudic debate, it is important as compelling the angel to acknowledge his identity, and in such a way that *Israel* (not Jacob) can prove his superiority in the chanting of the divine service and, most significantly, in having the right to utter the Divine Name after only two prefatory words, one of which is the name Israel itself, שמע ישראל יהוה אלהינו יהוה אחד, 'Hear, Israel, the Lord our God the Lord is one'. When it comes to the formal, liturgical worship of God, and to the proclamation of the Divine Unity, Israel takes precedence of the angels: the Talmud insists on this matter.

Unlike the exegesis of *Genesis Rabbah*, which set its understanding of the name Israel in discussions of the redemption, the future hope of the Jewish people, and the world to come which shall last for ever, *b. Ḥull.* 91b–92a was more concerned with Israel's status in this world, the world of the Head of the Diaspora in Babylon and of the Nasi in the Land of Israel. Superior to celestial beings by virtue of his overcoming the angel at the Jabbok, this Israel is God's first-born son, protected by God Himself from the rivalry and jealousy of angels, and having precedence over them all in the chanting of the service and the uttering of the Divine Name. With such privileges, it is implied, the Jews have little to fear in this world.

5. LAMENTATIONS RABBAH AND SONG RABBAH

Lam. Rab 3: 23 § 7–8 is very similar to *Gen. Rab.* 78: 1, which itself opened with a comment on Lam. 3: 23, 'new every morning, great is Thy faithfulness'. The whole section is concerned with the creation and destiny of the angels, and the Emperor Hadrian's question. Little here affects discussion of the name Israel, although it may be noted that *Lamentations Rabbah* begins like *Gen. Rab.* 78: 1 by setting the discussion in terms of resurrection of the dead (R. Alexandri), but without allusion to redemption (R. Simon b. Abba, *Gen. Rab.* 78: 1). Redemption is mentioned as having in part a this-worldly dimension: R. Simon b. Abba follows mention of resurrection with an address to God affirming that because each morning Israel knows that God renews the worldly kingdoms (in their successive manifestations as world rulers), His redemption is certain. The remainder of the commentary is so close to *Gen. Rab.* 78: 1 as to require no further comment here.[47]

Song Rabbah is a work drawing on a number of sources, including *Genesis Rabbah*, and dating in its present form from the mid-sixth century CE at the earliest.[48] Indeed, *Song Rab.* 3: 6 § 3 reproduces parts of *Gen. Rab.* 77: 2–3, but with significant differences which are doubtless dictated by the Scriptural verse being expounded:

---

[47] The final redaction of *Lam. Rab.* is probably to be dated to the first half of the fifth century CE, and quite possibly post-dates *Gen. Rab.*: see Strack and Stemberger, *Einleitung*, 265.

[48] Some students have dated it as late as the ninth century CE: for its dating, and the sources used in its composition, see further Schürer, *The History of the Jewish People*, i. 94–5; Strack and Stemberger, *Einleitung*, 289–300.

Who is this who ascends from the wilderness, like columns of smoke, perfumed with myrrh and frankincense from every powder of the merchant? (Song 3: 6)

The preceding section (*Song Rab.* 3: 6 § 2) referred the phrases 'perfumed with myrrh' to Abraham, 'and frankincense' to Isaac, and 'from every powder of the merchant' to Jacob. This last phrase in Hebrew reads מכל אבקת רוכל, and the middle word, 'powder, fine dust', provided the exegetes with a link to Gen. 32: 25 and its note that Jacob 'engaged with' (Hebrew ויאבק) his opponent, which I have already noted was understood by some ancient interpreters as meaning that he 'made himself dusty'. The exegetes did not reveal this verbal link between the verse of Song under discussion and Gen. 32: 25, but assumed it throughout. They began by noting that Jacob's bed and descendants were without defect before God. R. Tanhum compared the merchant's box with all kinds of perfumes with Jacob's descendants, who included priests, Levites, and kings. All that Isaac had he gained from Abraham; but Jacob's profits were derived entirely from the 'powder, fine dust', אבק, beneath his feet. To the power of this same 'powder, fine dust', R. Judan attributed Israel's wordly success in merchandise and business, and R. Azariah Israel's prowess in war and in Torah study. The section ends:

R. Berekhiah and R. Simon in the name of R. Abbahu: The Holy One, blessed be He, took that powder, and set it beneath the Throne of His glory, as it says: As for the Lord, in the whirlwind and in the storm is His way; and the clouds are the dust of His feet. (Nahum 1: 3)

This preamble shows us a successful Jacob in this world, as a result of his conflict with the angel, the dust of that conflict reaching the Throne of Glory and establishing Jacob's success. That the dust reached the Throne of Glory we have already learned from *b. Ḥull.* 91a, where, however, despite the quotation of the same proof-text Nahum 1: 3, the combatants themselves were seen as responsible for its ascent. Despite this heavenly dimension of Jacob's struggle, what follows in *Song Rab.* 3: 6 §2 is far more concerned with Jacob's status in the here and now. Its re-presentation of *Gen. Rab.* 77: 2–3 lacks entirely the whole proem speaking of Jeshurun, the redemption, the resurrection, and the world to come. Rather, we hear first of R. Berekhiah's statement in the name of R. Helbo (paralleling *Gen. Rab.* 77: 3), quoting Gen. 32: 25 that a man 'engaged/got dusty' with Jacob, and noting that we should not know who had authority over whom: at once the midrash moves to tell us, on the basis of Gen. 32: 27 where the angel requests to be sent away, that Jacob had authority over the celestial being. This will prove the key to all that follows: Jacob was in control throughout the episode at the Jabbok, the midrash implying that Jacob's descendants are likewise in control, under divine providence, of all that will happen to them.

Having from the very beginning established that the angel was under Jacob's control, only then does the midrash ask in what manner he appeared to Jacob. Again, the answer comes without hesitation, R. Hama in the name of R. Hanina reporting that he appeared as wicked Esau's angel, Gen. 33: 10 being given as proof. Thus the celestial representative of Rome is from the outset put in his proper place; and the midrash can turn to a suitably simplified version of the parable of the tame lion and savage dog. And the lesson is urged upon the reader at once: Jacob could cope with a lion, so he will feel able to defeat a mad dog! Similarly, God will say to nations disposed to attack His son that their angel could not succeed, so how could they? R. Huna's description of the angel as a shepherd assisting Jacob to transfer sheep across the Jabbok follows; but, unlike its parallel in *Gen. Rab.* 77: 2, his account lacks any 'magical dimension', and concentrates solely on Jacob's return across the river to see if he had forgotten anything. This introduces the story told by R. Hiyya and his colleague about the bale of silk at Tyre, now used explicitly to illustrate Jacob's outstanding success in business matters—the very concern with which this whole midrashic exposition began! Evidently, *Song Rab.* at this point sensed that Israel's material prosperity required some explanation, and set out to provide it.

Magic does make its appearance, however, with the description of Jacob as a chief brigand: R. Pinhas relates how Jacob countered the angelic sorcerer; but *Song Rab.* added to the parallel in *Gen. Rab.* 77: 2 the angel's declaration in Aramaic that he was 'not going to let this man [Jacob] know with whom he was dealing', perhaps to reinforce his occult powers. The end is the same as in *Gen. Rab.*, the angel producing fire from the rock, and Jacob reminding him that he is entirely constituted of this element, as the prophet Obadiah had declared. Indeed, magic has no power of any kind over Jacob. *Song Rabbah* altered *Gen. Rab.* 77: 3 quite dramatically when it came to presenting R. Hanina b. Yitzhaq's report that Jacob was armed with five amulets in his struggle with the angel. In the account in *Song Rabbah*, the Holy One began by expressing

amazement that Esau's angel was 'still standing' at all after Jacob
had come against him with those amulets of merits of his forebears! The angel thereupon 'measured himself' and saw that he
would not prevail over Jacob. Likewise, R. Levi confirms the
angel's powerlessness: like a chief brigand wrestling with a king's
son, who looks up to see the king standing by, so the angel saw the
Shekhina, and gave up the unequal struggle with Jacob. For good
measure, the text repeats R. Levi's assertion. And that, as far as
this section of *Song Rabbah* is concerned, is really the point. Jacob
is successful and strong in this world.

Although the comparison of this section of *Song Rabbah* with
the material in *Gen. Rab.* 77: 2–3 has been necessarily brief, clear
differences between the two documents are immediately apparent.
Jacob's encounter with the angel and change of name are associated in *Genesis Rabbah* with Rome and its hostility to the Jews.
There is a struggle going on between Rome and the Jews, although
the future is assured for the latter because Jacob's victory at the
Jabbok, and his new name, are anticipations of what the Holy One
will do for Israel in the world to come. *Song Rabbah*, by contrast,
seems more or less content in this world, where Jacob is successful
in all kinds of ways, where magical arts present no threat, and
where it is quite astonishing that the Roman authority still stands,
after the humiliating defeat its angelic representative had sustained
at the Jabbok. Whereas *Genesis Rabbah* offered an explicit interpretation of the name Israel, however, *Song Rabbah* did no such
thing. What is implicit is that *Israel's* prosperity in this world arises
from that dust which *Jacob* kicked up in his struggle with the angel,
and which the *Holy One* placed beneath the Throne of His Glory.

6. THE ARAMAIC TARGUMIM

We have complete Aramaic Targum for those verses of Genesis
which concern us in Targum Onqelos (= TO), Targum Neofiti 1
(= TN), and Targum Pseudo-Jonathan (= PJ).[49] For some of these

---

[49] These three Targumim are cited according to the following critical editions: A.
Sperber, *The Bible in Aramaic, I: The Pentateuch According to Targum Onkelos* (Brill:
Leiden, 1959); A. Díez Macho, *Neophyti 1 Targum Palestinese Ms de la Biblioteca
Vaticana*, vol. 1, *Génesis* (Consejo Superior de Investigaciones Científicas: Madrid–
Barcelona, 1968); E. G. Clarke, W. E. Aufrecht, J. C. Hurd, and F. Spitzer, *Targum
Pseudo-Jonathan of the Pentateuch: Text and Concordance* (Ktav: Hoboken, 1984).
Translations of these, and of all other Targumim, are mine.

verses, TN offers additional Targum in the form of marginal and interlinear glosses.[50] The Fragment Targumim of mss Paris 110 (= FTP) and Vatican 440 (= FTV) yield interpretations of Gen. 32: 26 in part, the whole of Gen. 32: 27, and of Gen. 35: 9, this last with a long haggadic expansion.[51] Targum of Gen. 32: 22–9; 35: 9–15 is represented also in Cairo Geniza Ms *CG*.[52] Targum Jonathan of Hosea 12: 3–6 is also a complete Targum.[53]

The complete Pentateuchal Targumim display certain common features in their interpretations, which are shared also by *CG*. First, they specify that Jacob's opponent at the Jabbok was an angel (TO of Gen. 32: 31; PJ of Gen. 32: 25, 27, 29, 31; TN of Gen. 32: 25, 27, 29, 31; *CG* of Gen. 32: 25, 27, 29), as distinct from the Hebrew Bible, which throughout this narrative refers to the opponent as a man.[54] In accord with this, these same Targumim interpret Gen. 32: 29's explanation of the name Israel ('because you have striven with God', כי שרית עם אלהים) by having recourse to the Aramaic form רב, 'great one, prince, mighty one' (so TO) or רברב, 'be prince, chief; be mighty; claim superiority over' (so TN, PJ, and *CG*). Thus the angel tells Jacob that his name will henceforth be Israel, 'because you are a prince before the Lord' (TO); 'because you have been prince with the angels of the Lord' (PJ); 'because you have been prince with angels from before the Lord' (TN); 'because you have been prince with holy angels from before the Lord' (*CG*). In all these cases, a correct, alternative translation of the Targumim would indicate that Jacob was to be Israel because he was a chief or superior one before the Lord (TO), or because he had achieved superiority over the angels (PJ, TN, *CG*). In short, these Targumim, like *b. Ḥull.* 92a, note that Jacob as Israel was made a prince over his angelic opponent: as Hebrew

---

[50] On these glosses, see S. Lund and J. Foster, *Variant Versions of Targumic Traditions within Codex Neofiti 1*, SBL Aramaic Studies, 2 (Scholars Press: Missoula, 1977), esp. 100, 106, 141, 148–9.

[51] Cited from the edition of M. L. Klein, *The Fragment-Targums of the Pentateuch According to their Extant Sources*, 2 vols. (Biblical Institute: Rome, 1980).

[52] See *GM*. Gen. 32: 22–9 is represented in Oxford Bodleian Ms. Heb. b 4, fo. 18v; and Gen. 35: 9–15 in Leningrad, Saltykov-Schedrin, Ms Antonin Ebr. III B 542, fo. 2r. See also U. Glessmer, *Einleitung in die Targume zum Pentateuch*, Texte und Studien zum Antiken Judentum, 48 (Mohr: Tübingen, 1995), 108.

[53] See A. Sperber, *The Bible in Aramaic: III The Latter Prophets According to Targum Jonathan* (Brill: Leiden, 1962).

[54] On the relationship between Hebrew 'man' and 'prince' in the sense of angel in Bible and later literature, see now Fishbane, *Biblical Myth*, 75–6.

שר or Aramaic רב, he is a prince, one who himself possesses angelic characteristics. Targum Jonathan of Hosea 12: 4–5 makes use of the same interpretative strategy: just as the Pentateuchal Targumim had rendered שרית, 'you have striven', with reference to being prince and superiority, so Hosea 12: 4's note that Jacob שרה את אלהים, 'strove with God', was taken to mean that he 'gained superiority with, became a prince with, the angel', a statement repeated exactly at the beginning of the following verse.[55]

With the exception of TO, whose interpretation will shortly be analysed separately, these Targumim associate Jacob's struggle at the Jabbok with the angelic recitation of the heavenly service in a manner reminiscent of *b. Ḥull.* 91b–92a. Most strikingly, TN of Gen. 32: 25 named Jacob's opponent as Sariel, who further identified himself at Gen. 32: 27 as 'the chief of those who utter praise'. The appearance of the dawn marks the time for formal service to be offered to God, and the angel needs to be in heaven, not on earth, to fulfil his obligations as leader of the heavenly choir! The angel confronting Jacob according to PJ of Gen. 32: 25 is none other than Michael, the heavenly patron of Israel; but he is held fast by Jacob-Israel, and begs to be released to offer praise on the one day when his appointed time to sing the service has arrived. Again, we recall *b. Ḥull.* 91b, and the various opinions there expressed about how many times the angels utter praise. FTP and *CG* of Gen. 32: 27 display the angel as 'the chief of those who utter praise'; unnamed, this being reacts to the rising of 'the column of the dawn', being withheld from heavenly service until Jacob should release him. Even FTV of this verse, which does not record the angel's official position, notes his wish to return to heaven because 'the hour has arrived for the angels to utter praise'. All these Targumim show us a Jacob who is able to detain a celestial being from the performance of the heavenly service of God, and imply that Jacob, who becomes Israel, holds the precedence, the superiority, the princely status in respect of angels, when it is a question of the regular, formal, and unceasing praise of the Almighty. In other words, the heavenly service with its celestial singing to the

---

[55] For recent English translations of these Targumim with commentary, see B. Grossfeld, *The Targum Onqelos to Genesis*, The Aramaic Bible, 6 (Clark: Edinburgh, 1988); M. McNamara, *Targum Neofiti 1: Genesis*, The Aramaic Bible, 1A (Clark: Edinburgh, 1992), which includes translations of Fragment Targum and Geniza material; and M. Maher, *Targum Pseudo-Jonathan: Genesis*, The Aramaic Bible, 1b (Clark: Edinburgh, 1992).

Almighty is a central concern of all the Targumim of Gen. 32: 22–33, with the exception of TO and, as we shall see presently, a Targum fragment preserved in marginal glosses to TN of Gen. 32: 27.

The Targumim of Gen. 35: 9–15 present us with common features in a picture similar to that described for Gen. 32: 22–33. Thus, with the exception of TO and PJ, all the extant Targumim of Gen. 35: 9 (TN, its two marginal glosses, FTP, FTV, and *CG*) have in common a lengthy expansion offering proof from God's own actions that Jews are required to bless bride and bridegroom, to visit the sick, and to bless the mourners. This little homily does not concern Jacob's change of name, and plays no part in my present discussion.[56] All Targumim of this verse, however, and in all the following verses of this section of text, in translating the Hebrew text invariably replaced 'God' with 'the Lord' or 'the Memra of the Lord'. At Gen. 35: 11, Jacob-Israel receives a promise that kings would issue from him: TO, TN, and *CG* all specified these as 'kings who rule over the nations', PJ alone of the Targumim to this verse standing aside from such an interpretation. Those Targumim recall the concerns of *Jubilees*, which closely associated Jacob's reception of a new name with a divine promise of his universal rulership.[57] Finally, all extant Targumim of Gen. 35: 13 (TO, PJ, TN and its marginal and interlinear gloss, and *CG*) note that Glory of the Lord, or the Glory of the Lord's Shekhina, went up from Jacob-Israel, whereas the Bible states simply that 'God' went up from him.[58]

Each individual Targum, however, displays its own particular emphasis in expounding Jacob's change of name. As I have remarked, TO is very distinctive, particularly in its apparent attempts to dissociate Gen. 32: 22–33 from liturgical matters,

[56] Systematic analysis of the homily may be found in B. B. Levy, *Targum Neophyti 1. A Textual Study*, vol. 1 (Lanham: New York, 1986), 212–19.

[57] See *Jub.* 32: 16–19, and discussion above, pp. 133–6.

[58] The language of Glory and Shekhina 'going up from upon' an individual recalls the Targumim of Gen. 17: 22 and 18: 33 in respect of Abraham. The idea that the Fathers constitute the Merkabah as in *Gen. Rab.* 82: 5 may be in evidence here: see A. M. Goldberg, *Untersuchungen über die Vorstellung von der Schekhinah in der Frühen Rabbinischen Literatur* (Berlin, 1969), 239–40; D. Muñoz Leon, *Gloria de la Shekina en los Targumim del Pentateuco* (Consejo Superior de Investigaciones Cientificas Instituto 'Francisco Suárez': Madrid, 1977), 51, 53, 63; Fishbane, *Biblical Myth*, 247–9.

whether earthly or heavenly. PJ presents us with astonishing similarities both with material in the Second Temple Book of *Jubilees*
and with the late midrash *Pirqe de Rabbi Eliezer*. TN's naming
Sariel as the angel who confronted Jacob at the Jabbok will introduce us to a celestial being known from 1 Enoch and the Qumran
texts; while the fragment of a Targum preserved in its marginal
gloss to Gen. 32: 27 will recall Rabbinic discussions recorded in
Genesis Rabbah. In fine, the Targumim seem to have preserved a
vast range of interpretative material relating to Jacob's change of
name, which must now be pondered in some detail. In the translations of the Targumim offered hereafter, all Targumic variations
in respect of MT are printed in italics.

6.1 *Targum Pseudo-Jonathan of Gen. 32: 25–33; 35: 9–15*

PJ expanded Gen. 32: 25 with a wealth of circumstantial detail
unpresented in any other of the extant Targumim of this verse.
Thus we read:

And Jacob was left on his own *on the other side of the Jabbok*. And *an angel
in the likeness of* a man fought with him, *and said: Did you not promise* (lit:
*say) to tithe all that is yours? And behold, you have twelve sons and one
daughter, and you have not tithed them. At once he separated four first-born
sons of the four Matriarchs, and eight were left. Then he counted again from
Simeon, and Levi came up as the tenth. Michael answered and said: Master
of the universe, this is Your allotted portion! And on account of these things he
[Michael] was delayed below at the wadi* until *the column of* the dawn
came up.

Alone of the Targumim, PJ tells us exactly where Jacob was
when his name was changed: he was 'on the other side of the
Jabbok'. According to Gen. 32: 23–4, he had already brought
across the Jabbok his family and possessions; so the Hebrew
Bible's note that he was alone must mean that he was separated
from them. As we have seen, *b. Ḥull.* 91a and other texts explain
why Jacob was alone, and they, too, without pedantically explaining his exact location, assume that he is on the far side of the
Jabbok, outside the land of Israel. For PJ, this is a matter of some
significance. In commenting on Gen. 32: 23, this Targum specified that Jacob had brought his family and possessions across 'the
ford of Jabbok', מגזת יובקא, a phrase found only once elsewhere in
the whole of PJ. It occurs at Exod. 15: 16, in a Targumic addition
to the Hebrew of the Song of the Sea: the verse describes how
Israel should

cross *the wadis of the Arnon*, until *the time that these* people whom You purchased should cross *the ford of the Jabbok*.

The ford of the Jabbok was one of the recognized boundaries of the Land of Israel (Deut. 2: 37; 3: 16). By so referring to the Jabbok in Gen. 32: 25, PJ invites readers or hearers to associate Jacob's activities with the future triumphant Exodus from Egypt and acquisition of the Land described in Exod. 15: 16. In this, PJ appears to have an affinity with the LXX translators, who also took care to locate Jacob's struggle with the mysterious man outside the borders of the Land, to accord with their view of this episode as an event qualifying Jacob and his descendants for future possession of the Holy Land.[59] This brief note invites the reader to view the incident at the Jabbok as being as momentous in its way as the Exodus from Egypt.

The 'man' who, according to the Hebrew Bible, engaged with Jacob becomes in PJ 'an angel in the likeness of a man', an interpretation shared with TN, its marginal gloss, and *CG* of this verse. This expression occurs also at TN and PJ of Gen. 18:2, 22 describing the three mysterious men who visited Abraham: it is thus the property of the Palestinian Targum tradition, and its appearance in *CG* suggests that it may belong to an early stratum of it.[60] The same general tradition is also represented in *PRE* 37: 2, declaring that God sent an angel who appeared 'as if he were a man'. PJ eventually identifies this angel as Michael, and states unambiguously that he fought (אתכבש) with Jacob: this same verb is used by the Peshitta, but not by the other Targumim. It expresses physical combat of a sort described elsewhere in the midrashim.

Peculiar to PJ is the angel's reminder to Jacob of his vow, made earlier on his first visit to Bethel, to tithe his possessions (see Gen. 28: 22). Jacob had made the vow on condition that God should be with him on his journey, giving him food and clothing, and in the hope that *he should return to his father's house* (Gen. 28: 20–1). If all these things were granted, Jacob promised that the Lord should be his God; that the stone he had set up in Bethel should be 'the house of God'; and that he would give tithes. *Jubilees* 27: 27 recorded this vow almost without alteration. The Bible does not record whether

---

[59] See above, pp. 52–6.
[60] See M. Taradach, *Le Midrash. Introduction à la Littérature midrashique* (Labor et Fides: Geneva, 1991), 88–9; U. Glessmer, *Einleitung in die Targume zum Pentateuch*, 8–10, 105–19.

or when Jacob fulfilled it. Thus, when Scripture says that a man attacked Jacob, it needed little imagination on the ancient commentators' part to discover the cause of that attack in Jacob's apparent neglect of this vow to offer tithes. PJ would later explain in similar fashion an apparently unjustified angelic attack on Moses as arising from his failure to carry out religious duties, in this case the circumcision of one of his sons (PJ of Exod. 4: 24–6). Although *Jubilees* entirely omitted the story of Jacob's struggle with the angel, it provided a lengthy account, not present in the Bible, of Jacob's *return visit to his father's house*: the conditions for fulfilling his vow to tithe had thus been met, according to *Jubilees*; and Isaac consequently exhorted his son to carry out his vow (*Jub.* 31: 26–8), warning him that delay or failure to fulfil it would result in his being 'called to account in respect of it' (*Jub.* 31: 29). This is the very situation which PJ of Gen. 32: 25 presents.[61]

According to PJ, Jacob tithed his sons in such a way that Levi was separated as God's own portion. *Jub.* 32: 1–3 described Jacob tithing his property (about which PJ says nothing) and his sons, and recorded his method of counting the latter: he numbered his sons upwards from Benjamin the youngest, so that Levi fell to the Lord's lot, whereupon his father clothed him with the priestly vestments. *PRE* 37: 3, however, in similar vein to PJ, notes that Jacob 'separated the four first-born sons of the four Matriarchs, and eight were left'; but there the similarity between PJ and *PRE* ends. The angel, according to PJ, was Michael and was at loggerheads with Jacob, engaged in physical combat with him; *PRE* 37: 1 named the angel as Israel, who was sent to deliver Jacob and save him from the threat posed by Esau.[62] This, according to *PRE* 37: 2,

---

[61] See discussion of the *Jubilees* material above, pp. 130–1.

[62] Identification of the opposing angel as Michael is found also in *Yalqut Shim-'oni* Gen. 132, and may be related in some way to the equation of Esau's guardian angel with the evil Sammael in Tanhuma וישלח 8 and later sources, as suggested by Urbach, *The Sages*, i. 170; ii. 761. Smith, 'The Prayer of Joseph', 702, n. 13, remarks that the angelic designation Israel, which is sometimes represented in Greek and Latin sources as Istra(h)el, appears 'only in late Jewish magical materials': he cites *Sefer Razi'el* 4b, 41b, but does not refer to *PRE* 37: 3. He notes that Yisriel is the form encountered in earlier texts such as *Sefer Ha-Razim* and *Ḥarbe de Moshe*, and that in Greek 'Israel' appears as an angelic name only as one of the three *archai* in Justin's Book of Baruch, cited by Hippolytus, *Refutatio* V. 26. 2. This may have some connection with traditions surfacing in the *Prayer of Joseph*, discussed above, pp. 194–219; but it does not seem to impinge upon analysis of the Aramaic Targumim.

explains why Jacob did not want him to leave when the dawn arose. As far as *PRE* 37: 3 is concerned, the matter of the tithe did not arise until Jacob wished (רצה) to cross the Jabbok into the Land. This matter finds no place in PJ; but for *PRE* it is crucial, since the angel is friendly throughout, protecting Jacob against Esau's schemes, and gently reminding him that, if he intends to cross the Jabbok into the Land, he will need to pay his tithes. The angel of *PRE* does not violently attack Jacob over his failure to carry out an obligation.[63]

PRE included Jacob's property (מקנה) in the tithe. Of this, PJ says nothing; but *Jub.* 32: 2 was aware of it. Only after this did *PRE* speak of Jacob's sons as untithed: it did not give their number as twelve (contrast PJ); said nothing of Jacob's daughter (again, unlike PJ); and did not represent this tithing as Jacob's immediate reaction to angelic prompting. *PRE* simply noted Jacob's separation of the four matriarchal first-born, leaving eight sons; and this, in truth, is the only point at which PJ and *PRE* exactly agree. For even though both texts remark that Jacob began his counting of the tithe from Simeon so as to end with Levi, what is simple uncontested assertion in PJ emerges in *PRE* as part of a complex discussion entirely lacking in the Targum.

Indeed, close scrutiny of *PRE* 37: 3, PJ of Gen. 32: 25, and *Jub.* 32: 1–3 reveals three different versions of how precisely Jacob arrived at Levi as the tithed son. PJ says simply that Jacob counted from Simeon until he reached Levi; that is the end of the matter. *PRE*, however, says that he first counted from Simeon and arrived at Benjamin, who was yet unborn; so he then counted again from Simeon, and Levi emerged in this second computation as the holy tithe. While PJ made no allusion at all to Benjamin, *Jub.* 32: 3 did just this very thing, to say that Jacob knew that Rachel was pregnant with Benjamin, and therefore for the purposes of the tithe counted from this unborn Benjamin upwards, thus arriving at Levi as the tenth son. This tradition of Second Temple times was known to the compilers of *PRE*, who recorded R. Ishmael's judgement that Jacob had thereby counted his sons 'in an irregular manner'. Normally, said the Rabbi, items for tithing must be visible; but Jacob had counted the unborn Benjamin, and had so

---

[63] The fact that the angel is called Israel in *PRE* strongly underlines his role as Jacob's protector: see G. Friedlander, *Pirqê de Rabbi Eliezer (The Chapters of Rabbi Eliezer the Great)* (Hermon Press: New York, 1965), 282, n. 8; M. Pérez Fernández, *Los Capitulos de Rabbi Eliezer* (Institución San Jerónimo: Valencia, 1984), 260.

settled on Levi as the tithe-son. *PRE* 37: 3, in fact, recorded three approaches used by Jacob to determine the tithe-son. There is the approach on which R. Ishmael commented, involving a counting of sons upwards from the unborn Benjamin: this is the method represented also in *Jub.* 32: 1–3. Then there is the method of counting downwards from Simeon to Levi, which is represented also in PJ of Gen. 32: 25. Finally, a third method, peculiar to *PRE*, involved a counting downwards from Simeon to Benjamin, a process rejected by Jacob. The presence of yet a fourth system of computation in *Gen. Rab.* 70: 7 and *Tanhuma* דאר 14 strongly suggests that all the ancient documents which discuss this matter represent variant versions of an earlier general tradition which they have refined in their several ways and for their own purposes.[64] For PJ, the matter of the tithing is so addressed as to ensure that Jacob's change of name is directly linked with Levi's formal and straightforward selection for the priesthood; the presence of Michael on earth when he should have been in heaven; his announcing of the name Israel; and the correspondingly greater importance of these matters than Michael's presence above to chant the heavenly liturgy.

   Michael's presence in these events is central to *PRE* 37: 3 as well, but in a manner quite different from PJ's account of Michael as the one combating Jacob, reminding him of his religious obligations, and consequently being detained on earth. In complete contrast to this, *PRE* presents Michael as coming down from heaven and carrying off Levi to the supernal realms into the presence of the Lord. Admittedly, both *PRE* and PJ make Michael address God as Master of the universe and declare that Levi is His allotted portion; but PJ is clear that when this happens Michael is on earth, not in heaven as *PRE* would have it. In any event, the divine title Master of the universe is common Targumic property, and cannot be pressed to argue PJ's supposed dependence on *PRE* at this point. Nor, indeed, can the description of Levi as the Lord's allotted portion; for *PRE* 37: 3 not only adds to this description words not found in PJ, but immediately reports that God

stretched out His right hand and blessed him (Levi), so that the sons of Levi should minister before Him on earth like the angels of the service in heaven.

[64] Friedlander, *Pirqê de Rabbi Eliezer*, 283–4, notes in particular the similarities between material in *Jubilees* and *PRE*.

Nothing in PJ compares with this. Rather, one is forcefully reminded, not of the Targumim at all, but of *Jub.* 31: 14, where Isaac blessed Levi and his sons with a prayer that God should set them apart to minister in His sanctuary 'like the angels of the presence and the holy ones'.

Given all this, it seems highly improbable that PJ of Gen. 32: 25 should depend on *PRE* 37: 1–3. The radical differences between the texts far outweigh the few similarities; and if any doubt should remain, *Jubilees* settles the matter. The latter witnesses to a tradition existing already in the second century BCE, to the effect that Jacob was reminded by a third party of his obligation to fulfil the vow of tithing he had made at Bethel; that he accordingly tithed his property and children, including the unborn Benjamin in their number; that he counted his sons and thus arrived at Levi as the tithe-son; that Levi thus chosen became God's priest; and that Levi and his sons were blessed, again by a third party, with a formula indicating their correspondence to the angels serving God in heaven. PJ and *PRE* are best understood as individual variants of this general tradition, which in essence is older than both of these texts in their present forms.[65] It may be that this general tradition itself was originally not of one piece, and that the version preserved in *Jubilees* is yet another variant of an even more ancient non-biblical narrative. But this is to speculate.

What can reasonably be established, however, is that PJ's version of Gen. 32: 25 cannot be explained as a summary of materials found in *PRE*. It has its own, distinct lineage, and its own clear message: it was Michael who reminded Jacob of his vow to tithe, a vow which PJ understood as referring to Jacob's sons, not his property. Levi was the tithe-son, selected without difficulty or dithering by Jacob: his choice was at once ratified by Michael, Israel's heavenly patron, who acquainted the Master of the universe with the accomplished fact that Levi was His allotted portion. So significant was this business that Michael, the highest of all the chief angels, was detained on earth until it was accom-

---

[65] As noted by Friedlander, *Pirqê de Rabbi Eliezer*, 284, n. 10. D. M. Splansky, 'Targum Pseudo-Jonathan: Its Relationship to Other Targumim, Use of Midrashim and Date', unpublished Ph.D Thesis, Hebrew Union College: Cincinnati (1981) has argued that much of PJ's expansional material depends on *PRE*. His view is not supported by the evidence set out here, and can be questioned on other grounds also: see C. T. R. Hayward, 'The Date of Targum Pseudo-Jonathan: Some Comments', *JJS* 40 (1989), 7–30.

plished. For PJ, Levi's emergence as the Lord's portion had a higher priority than Michael's duties in the heavenly liturgy when the 'column of dawn came up', the proper time for the recitation by Israel on earth of the Shemà and the traditional blessings (*m. Ber.* 1: 1). Not only PJ, but also TN and *CG* of this verse make use of this expression, which represents a fairly literal translation into Aramaic of a common Mishnaic idiom indicating the time for the start of formal prayer in Temple, synagogue, and in the home of the devout individual Jew.

PJ presents Michael as engaged in combat with Jacob, a theme continued in the next verse (Gen. 32: 26). Where the Hebrew records ambiguously that 'he saw that he did not prevail against him', PJ explained that Michael 'saw that he had no authority to harm Jacob', words which recall PJ's version of Gen. 31: 7, where Jacob asserts that God had not given Laban authority to harm him, a point he had already made to Rachel in almost identical words, according to PJ of Gen. 29: 12. In other words, three times PJ states that one heavenly and another earthly character 'had no authority' to harm Jacob: this was evidently an important motif for the Targum, and it coheres with the approach of the LXX translators, whose concern with Laban's attempts to injure Jacob have been noted.[66] Jacob can be harmed neither by angels nor by men; PJ's interpretation of Gen. 32: 29 will underline this, insisting that Jacob was properly Israel, who had been prince with angels and men, and had prevailed. Sensing this, the angel asked to be dismissed:

And he said: Send me away, because *the column of* the dawn has come up; *and the hour for the angels of the height praising the Lord of the universe has arrived. And from the day that the world was created my time to praise has not arrived, but (only) this one time.* And he said: I am not going to send you away unless you bless me. (PJ of Gen. 32: 27)

The words 'the column of the dawn has come up' appear yet again, as they did in verse 25. All extant Targumim of this verse (PJ, TN, FTP, FTV, and *CG*), with the notable exception of TO, use them; thus they underscore and highlight the central role of the formal worship of God in heaven and on earth which these Targumim envisage as essential to proper interpretation of this

[66] See above, pp. 39–49. In this way, PJ further suggests that Jacob is in control of events throughout this episode, an idea present also in Josephus' account of events and in the *Prayer of Joseph*.

episode in Jacob's life. PJ is very clear on the matter, presenting the chief angel Michael as held fast on earth at the very time, the only time, when he should be praising God in heaven. The Targum thus represents one of the opinions set out in *b. Ḥull*. 91b, that angels praise God only once in the whole of time, thus suggesting that Michael's privilege and duty in this manner is at the disposal of Jacob who is Israel, one who has princely-angelic status with both angels and men, as PJ of Gen. 32: 29 makes clear:

> And he said: Your name shall no longer be uttered as 'Jacob', but 'Israel'; because you have *been prince/gained superiority* with *the angels of the Lord* and with men, and you have prevailed *over them.*

To emphasize this superiority of Jacob-Israel, PJ of Gen. 32: 30 tells us that Jacob-Israel then went on to bless the angel:

> And Jacob asked and said: Declare, now, your name. And he said: Why do you ask my name? And *Jacob* blessed him there.

The Hebrew had merely stated that 'he' blessed 'him' there. PJ resolved the ambiguity, giving a practical demonstration of Jacob-Israel's higher status. Once the name Israel has been announced, Jacob is revealed as a character who can bless even the highest of the celestial beings. The Targum emphasizes Israel's status further in the following verse (32: 31), noting that Jacob called the place where all this had happened Peni'el because he had seen *the angels of the Lord* (for MT's 'God') face to face. Just as Michael explained that Jacob-Israel had been a prince-angel with *the angels of the Lord*, so now Jacob realized that he had seen those angels, and remains unharmed. This multiplicity of angels, lacking in the Bible's account of Jacob's fight at the Jabbok, was suggested to PJ by the long and well-known association of Gen. 32: 22–33 in exegetical tradition with Gen. 28: 10–22, where Jacob's first visit to Bethel was recorded. On that first visit, he had seen angels; and PJ of Gen. 28: 12 indicates that they were 'angels of the height' who knew who Jacob was: he was Jacob the pious one, whose likeness is fixed on the Throne of Glory, and whom they had desired to see. Like *Gen. Rab.* 68: 12; 82: 2; *Num. Rab.* 4: 1; *Lam. Rab.* 2.1: §2; *b. Ḥull*. 91b, and other texts we have examined, PJ was aware that Jacob-Israel was already known to the angels, his proximity to God demonstrated by the presence of his likeness on the divine Throne. Of all the high angels, Michael as Israel's patron might be expected to know this best of all, and to be able to announce to Jacob that he was, indeed, Israel, a matter already known in heaven to those great angels Michael, Gabriel, Raphael, and Sariel, the form of whose names is comparable with that of Israel.

Jacob's second visit to Bethel, which will be considered shortly, involved another report of his change of name to Israel; and Hosea 12: 5 had explicitly associated Bethel with his struggle with an angel. Indeed, PJ of Gen 32: 32 went further in joining together Jacob's first visit to Bethel with the struggle at the Jabbok quite explicitly:

And the sun, *which for his sake had set before its time when he went out from Beer-Sheba*, shone for him *before its appointed time* when he passed by Penu'el. And he *began to walk, and he* was lame upon his thigh.[67]

Here, the miracle which accompanied his first visit to Bethel is completed in another miracle: both miracles involved prayer, inasmuch as Jacob's first visit to Bethel involved his recognition of Bethel as the site of Temple, the house of God, which according to PJ of Gen. 28: 17 is a place kosher for prayers; and here at the Jabbok the sunrise for him represented the column of the dawn, when angels and Israel should praise the Lord and utter prayer. The note that he 'began to walk' is an expansion of the Hebrew, and may simply represent PJ's attempt to tell us how he came to know that he was lame. But the Aramaic 'to walk', לטייל, may be intended as a play on words with PJ of Gen. 35: 14, where we shall learn about what Israel's sons are to do at the feast of Sukkoth, Aramaic בחגא דמטלייא. The similar-sounding expressions suggest an association of these events with the feast of Sukkoth which, explicit in *Jubilees*, will become important for Jacob's second visit to Bethel, fixed by the Targum at that very festival.[68]

During that second visit, God confirmed Jacob's name as Israel (Gen. 35: 10) and, designating Himself as 'El Shaddai, promised that from Israel would arise a nation, a congregation of nations,

---

[67] PJ clearly represents the Rabbinic tradition as found in *b. Ḥull.* 91b; *San.* 95b; *Gen. Rab.* 68: 10; but the association of Jacob's first visit to Bethel with his change of name is already attested by Philo's writings, as shown above, pp. 173–4.

[68] See further C. T. R. Hayward, 'Jacob's Second Visit to Bethel in Targum Pseudo-Jonathan', in P. R. Davies and R. T. White (eds.), *A Tribute to Geza Vermes: Essays on Jewish and Christian Literature and History* (Academic Press: Sheffield, 1990), 175–92.

and kings (Gen. 35: 11). PJ's version of that promise is quite precise:

And *the Lord* said to him: I am 'El Shaddai. Increase and be many. A *holy* people and an assembly of *prophets and priests* shall arise from your *sons whom you have fathered*; and *furthermore two* kings shall come forth from *you*.

PJ's language deliberately recalls the divine command issued to the 'house of Jacob' and the 'sons of Israel' (Exod. 19: 3) that they be 'a kingdom of priests and a holy nation' (Exod. 19: 6). The formal constitution of the people Israel is here rooted in God's dealings with Jacob-Israel at Bethel. PJ here clearly resembles *Jubilees*, with its demonstration that 'Israel' comes properly into the world as a holy people with duly appointed kingly and priestly dynasties on this occasion of Jacob's visit to Bethel, when his name becomes Israel. It will be recalled that *Jubilees* fixed this event at the feast of Sukkoth; PJ of Gen. 35: 14 likewise associated this episode with Sukkoth, in a manner discussed below. Unlike *Jubilees*, however, PJ included prophets in Israel's divinely given constitution: for this Targum, prophets are an integral part of Israel's formal structure of governance. Indeed, according to PJ of Exod. 33: 16 and Deut. 18: 14, Israel's possession of true prophets sets her apart from the other nations just as much as her priestly purity and holiness.[69]

PJ's ability to blend together ancient and perhaps more modern exegesis is well illustrated by the final note that two kings shall arise from Jacob-Israel. The original Hebrew spoke simply of kings in general; but PJ alone of the Targumim of this verse speaks of *two* kings, in the manner of the midrashim: for example, *Gen. Rab.* 82: 4 offers identification of these rulers, either Jeroboam ben Nebat and Jehu, or Saul and Ish-bosheth are proposed. The Targum's failure to identify the monarchs, however, suggests that perhaps the older treatment of this verse along the lines laid down by *Jubilees*, where the promise of universal rulership for Israel is set forth, was more congenial to the interpreter; indeed, King Messiah is introduced into PJ's explanation of Gen. 35: 21. The Targum thus keeps its exegetical options open here; and the two kings in mind may, therefore, conceivably be David and his messianic offspring.

---

[69] Detailed commentary on these passages may be found in ibid. 183–5.

Quite distinctive is PJ's version of Gen. 35: 14, which recorded Jacob-Israel's setting up at Bethel of a pillar upon which he poured a libation, anointing it:

And *he* raised up there a pillar in the place where he had spoken with him, a pillar of stone; and he poured upon it a libation *of wine and a libation of water. For thus are his sons destined to do on the Feast of Tabernacles*; and he poured upon it *olive* oil.

Although the Hebrew text of this verse spoke only of 'libation' in the singular, PJ joined TO, TN, *CG*, the Vulgate, and the Peshitta in a tradition of reading the Hebrew suggesting 'libations', perhaps taking the singular form as a collective noun. Unlike the other representatives of this reading, however, PJ explains the libations by referring them directly to the feast of Sukkoth with its twin ceremonies of wine and water libations, as conducted according to first Pharisee and then Rabbinic custom (*m. Sukkah* 4: 9). Here PJ is firmly aligned with the tradition established as early as the time of *Jubilees*, that Jacob's name was changed to Israel at the time of Sukkoth celebrations, whose ceremonies the Patriarch himself observed. The Targum here stands in stark contrast to the rest of the Rabbinic corpus, which pays hardly any attention to this verse.[70]

We may summarize PJ's approach to Jacob's change of name as an attempt to preserve very ancient understandings of the Scriptural verses involved in the light of the Targum's own concerns, which often reflect those of other Rabbinic sources. Thus the basic outline of the '*Jubilees* approach' is maintained: Jacob becomes Israel when the full complement of his sons is in existence, so that he can tithe one of them to be priest. The underlying influence of Exod. 19: 6, that Israel is to be a kingdom, priests, and a holy nation, makes itself felt in this Targum as much as in *Jubilees*. Israel comes into being at the feast of Sukkoth, which Jacob himself celebrates. To this interpretation of events, which in all essentials goes back to the second century BCE or earlier, PJ adds his own embellishments, and the general Targumic sense that the name Israel indicates superiority in terms of angelic status, such that the formal prayers and service of the Jewish people on earth take precedence over that of the highest angels in heaven.

---

[70] PJ's exegesis, however, offers some kind of Scriptural support for the custom of a twin libation of wine *and* water upon the altar at Sukkoth: while the Temple stood, the Sadducees seem to have held this custom in contempt, as *b. Sukk.* 48b attests, while the Pharisees maintained it.

6.2 *Targum Neofiti of Genesis 32: 25–33; 35: 9–15*

The precedence accorded to Israel's earthly prayer and worship of God is signalled by TN at once in its version of Gen. 32: 25, which identifies the angel fighting with Jacob at the Jabbok:

> And Jacob was left on his own; and *the angel Sariel, in the likeness of a man,* wrestled *and closed* with him until *the time that the column of* the dawn came up.

Sariel, both in English transliteration and in its original Semitic form, is an anagram of Israel: this Sariel, whom TN of Gen. 32: 27 will identify as 'the chief of those who utter praise', will effectively yield his position to Jacob now called Israel, whose praise will take the first place. The name Sariel is very rare in Targum and other Rabbinic texts, and is nowhere found in exegesis of this verse or related contexts, except in TN.[71] Indeed, even outside Rabbinic writings the name is not well known. We encounter it in the Qumran War Scroll along with the names of Michael, Raphael, and probably Gabriel (the text of 1QM 9: 14–16 is fragmentary, but the restoration of Gabriel's name is almost certain);[72] and it appears also at 1 Enoch 9: 1 in the Ethiopic manuscripts.[73] In this last instance, however, the corresponding Greek versions have Uriel, whose name as the fourth archangel is well known, frequently appearing in Rabbinic texts along with Michael, Gabriel, and Raphael.[74] Sariel appears to be an ancient name for an angel who

---

[71] So Grossfeld, *Targum Neofiti 1*, 225.

[72] Ibid. 226, notes the mention of Sariel in the War Scroll, where the name is preserved 'beyond all doubt', according to Y. Yadin, *The Scroll of the War of the Sons of Light Against the Sons of Darkness* (Oxford University Press: Oxford, 1962), 302–3.

[73] The textual evidence is assembled by G. W. E. Nickelsburg, *1 Enoch 1. A Commentary on the Book of 1 Enoch 1–36; 81–108* (Fortress Press: Minneapolis, 2001), 202, who further (p. 207) addresses the question of the number of archangels (including Sariel) in Jewish literature. He notes the appearance of the name Sariel again at 1 Enoch 20: 6 (see pp. 294, 296), and argues that it should also be read at 1 Enoch 27: 2 (pp. 317, 319), although the textual support for it in this last verse is not strong. Yadin, *The War*, 237–8, notes the absence of Sariel from a number of sources, including the Greek version of 1 Enoch 9: 6, which speak of four archangels. The name is attested, however, in Aramaic Enoch: see *4QEn^bar* (= 4Q202), col. 3, line 7; and L. T. Stuckenbruck, 'Revision of Aramaic-Greek and Greek-Aramaic Glossaries in *The Books of Enoch: Aramaic Fragments of Qumrân Cave 4* by J. T. Milik', *JJS* 41 (1990), 36.

[74] See Nickelsburg, *I Enoch 1*, 202, n. b; Yadin, *The War*, 238; J. Z. Smith, 'The Prayer of Joseph', 708.

either later yielded up his duties and privileges to Uriel; was later for some reason renamed Uriel; or for whom it was imagined that Uriel might be an appropriate extra designation.[75] It is not, there-fore, without significance that in the *Prayer of Joseph* the opponent of Jacob-Israel at the Jabbok is said to have been Uriel; like the *Prayer*, TN from the outset presented its account of Jacob's struggle as a battle with a high angelic authority.

The struggle with Sariel went on until the column of the dawn arose; the socket of Jacob's thigh was weakened; but the angel did not prevail, and begged Jacob

Send me away! For *the column of* the dawn *has arrived—it* has come up— *for there has arrived the time of the angels of the height to utter praise; and I am the chief of those who utter praise*. And he said: I will not send you away, except you bless me. (TN of Gen. 32: 27)

Like PJ, TN records the importance of the dawn's appearance, for this angel is in charge of the heavenly service. Given the stress on this point, TN's choice of the name Sariel (שריאל) may have been motivated by the Meturgeman's discernment within the name of an allusion to the verb שיר, 'sing', an allusion also noticeable in the name Israel itself.[76] It is with this in mind that TN offers its inter-pretation of Gen. 32: 29, where Sariel declares:

Your name shall no longer be *called* Jacob, but Israel; for you have *been prince with angels from before the Lord* and with men and you have prevailed *over them*.

Although almost identical with the other Palestinian Targumim of this verse, TN's very specific exegesis of the verses preceding the

---

[75] The differing names of the fourth archangel, and possible explanations for the variations in name, are discussed by Yadin, *The War*, 239–40, and Smith 'The Prayer of Joseph', 708–9. In the Similitudes of Enoch, 1 Enoch 40: 9; 54: 6; 71: 8, 9, 13, the fourth archangel is neither Sariel nor Uriel, but Phanuel, the Greek term used by Symmachus and 'the Samaritan' of Gen. 32: 31, 32 and Josephus *Ant*. I. 334 to represent the Hebrew place-name Peni'el/Penu'el. This angelic name has a direct link to the story of Jacob's change of name, and its significance as an alterna-tive name to Sariel in respect of TN of Gen. 32: 25 is explored by G. Vermes, 'The Archangel Sariel', in J. Neusner (ed.), *Christianity, Judaism, and Other Greco-Roman Cults*, Part III: *Studies for Morton Smith at Sixty*, SJLA 12 (Brill: Leiden, 1975), 159–76.

[76] See Vermes, 'The Archangel Sariel', 159–76, and cf. Smith, 'The Prayer of Joseph', 708. The Meturgeman ultimately responsible for TN *may* sense, like *Prayer of Joseph*, that Israel as God's first-born son (Exod. 4: 22) is a name carrying angelic connotations, specifically related to the singing of the heavenly liturgy.

definition of Israel has given to that name a definite colour. This is a Targum determined to point to worship, the singing of the service on earth and heaven, and Israel's rank in the liturgy. Other considerations appear not to apply; and TN of the rest of the section offers nothing in the way of interpretation to upset this perception. Likewise, TN's version of Gen. 35: 9–15 does not disturb this picture of Israel, and confines its Targumic expansion to verse 11 alone, where God promises to Israel that from him shall come a nation, an assembly of nations, and kings. In TN, this becomes:

And *the Lord* said to him: I am the God *of Heaven*. Be *strong* and increase. A people and a congregation *of an assembly of righteous* peoples shall arise from you, and kings *who exercise dominion over the peoples* shall go forth from *you*.

The language of TN repays special attention, since the phrase 'a congregation of an assembly of righteous peoples' is found also at TN of Gen. 17: 4, 5 (God's covenant with Abraham); 28: 3 (Isaac's blessing of Jacob before his departure for the first visit to Bethel; and 48: 4 (Jacob's recalling of blessings). All of these verses refer directly to God's covenant with the Patriarchs: the effect of this kind of language in TN of Gen. 35: 11, therefore, is to portray the episode of Jacob's second visit to Bethel as confirmation of covenant promises made earlier to Abraham, and now ratified in Jacob who is Israel. Kings exercising dominion shall arise; but this is left vague: will their authority be universal, for ever, or limited and partial? We are not told. In fine, for TN 'Israel' is the one who has superiority principally in matters liturgical, her worship on earth taking precedence over the heavenly liturgy conducted by Sariel, the chief of the ones who praise. And 'Israel' is the heir to covenant promises made to Abraham, an assembly of righteous ones whose praises God accepts before all others. If a certain timelessness pervades the exegesis, no doubt that is consonant with the everlasting praise of God from angels and men throughout the ages.

6.3 *Fragment Targum, Marginal Glosses of TN, and the Geniza Fragments*

The portions of Targum offered by FTP and FTV lack a wider setting, consisting as they do of interpretations of isolated verses either complete or in part. Both, however, preserved complete versions of Gen. 32: 27, which has a direct bearing on our topic. Here, they represented the unnamed angel as seeking to be dismissed because the column of the dawn had come up, the time when the angels utter praise. FTP (though not FTV) and *CG* described the angel as 'the chief of those who utter praise', in line with TN, though without naming him.[77] The survival of this verse, intact, in two Fragment Targumim indicates its importance for the Targumic tradition generally in respect of the name Israel, and confirms the sense that Israel's place in the heavenly and earthly liturgy forms the key aspect of Targumic thinking. *CG* of Gen. 32: 27 is very close in wording to FTP, and offers the same interpretation of the verse.

Gen. 32: 27 also gave rise to Targumic exegesis preserved in the margin of TN, which differs significantly from that described to date. This marginal gloss seems to represent the angel as informing Jacob that the time has come for the angels of the height 'to be sent', and that he is the 'chief of the ones who are sent'. This variant Targum may be related to R. Simon's question in *Gen. Rab.* 78: 1, whether the one sending or the one sent is greater: in any event, the notion of 'sending' arises directly out of the Scriptural verse, the angel presumably acknowledging that Jacob has power to 'send' him away so that he in turn may be 'sent' on his duties by God. The marginal gloss of TN of this verse, therefore, may stand in some kind of relationship to concerns addressed in the midrash; on the other hand, it may represent a particular Targumic interpretation of the Hebrew of the verse. In either respect, it represents a Jacob-Israel whose angelic qualities consist not so much in liturgical service, as in the execution of divine commissions.

CG's interpretation of Gen. 32: 27 (Oxford Bodleian Ms Hebrew b 4, folio 18 *verso*) has already been noted: Jacob has fought with the 'chief of those who utter praise', and this until the column of the dawn has arisen (*CG* of Gen. 32: 25). Liturgical concerns are once more evident in this Targum, whose interpretation of Gen. 32: 29 expresses the angelic status of Israel in no uncertain terms:

---

[77] Note the close similarity of these Targumim in this point of detail to a first-century CE source, Pseudo-Philo's *LAB* 18: 6, where the angel is described simply as 'the one who was responsible for the hymns', *qui stabat super hymnos*.

And he said: Your name shall not *from now on* be *called* Jacob, but rather Israel; because you have *been a prince with holy angels from before the Lord in the likeness of* men, and you have prevailed *over them.*

This Targum is unique in eliminating any notion that Jacob has prevailed over human beings. The Hebrew of the verse had spoken of his engagement with God and with men: as in the other Palestinian Targumim, 'God' was taken by *CG* to signify 'angels', but the phrase 'and with men' of the Hebrew text was evidently pressed into service to perform another function altogether. The Meturgeman seems to have understood the Hebrew 'and' here as *waw explicative*,[78] to yield the sense: 'that is to say, with men', thereby providing Scriptural justification for the view of the Palestinian Targumim and many midrashim, that the angel had been in human form. The effect of the exegesis is to relate Israel's status entirely to the celestial world, not only in respect of Israel's privilege as the first in rank to offer praise to God, but also as regards Israel's status compared with all other angelic beings.

The *CG* of Gen. 35: 10–15 (Ms Leningrad, Saltykov-Schedrin, Antonin Ebr. III B 542, folio 2 *verso*) offers an expansion of Gen. 35: 11 not unlike that offered by TN, with language evoking the covenant and its divine promises. For this fragment of Targum, it seems plain that Jacob's second visit to Bethel was understood as ratifying Jacob's name of Israel in terms of the fulfilment of divine promises made earlier, both to the Patriarch himself and to Abraham his forefather.

6.4 *Targum Onqelos*

The distinctive traits of TO's exegesis I have analysed in detail elsewhere, and they are set out here in summary form.[79] They are to be understood in light of the crucial observation that, in these portions of Scripture, TO is careful *as a general rule* to keep as close as possible to the Bible, even ensuring that the numbers of Aramaic words in each verse are more or less equivalent to the number of words in the Hebrew original. Any difference between

---

[78] For *waw explicative*, see E. Kautzsch (ed.), *Gesenius' Hebrew Grammar*, 2nd English edn., rev. A. E. Cowley (Clarendon Press: Oxford, 1910), §154a (b); and B. K. Waltke and M. O'Connor, *An Introduction to Biblical Hebrew Syntax* (Eisenbrauns: Winona Lake, 1990), 648–9.

[79] See C. T. R. Hayward, 'Targumic Perspectives on Jacob's Change of Name to Israel', *Journal for the Aramaic Bible* 3 (2001), 121–37.

TO and the Hebrew, however small, thus appears all the more striking. Again, *as a general rule*, in translation TO uses the same Aramaic vocabulary as the other Targumim, such that departures from this common vocabulary are noticeable.

These observations bring into prominence TO's version of Gen. 32: 24 and its statement that 'a man engaged', וֹיֵאָבֵק אִישׁ, with Jacob. Whereas all other Targumim of this verse discerned in the Hebrew some kind of violent struggle, TO translated using the verb וְאִשְׁתַּדַּל, which has the primary sense of 'insinuate oneself, win favour'. Grossfeld quotes Löwenstein as saying that the word refers to verbal strife, and is used to avoid anthropomorphism.[80] In light of this explanation, we should recall the verbal 'battle of wits' between Jacob and his opponent described in *Gen. Rab.* 78: 2, where Jacob is represented as having defeated the angel on the intellectual as well as on the physical plane.[81] It is possible, too, that the Targum attempted to minimize the element of physical conflict for reasons which will soon become clear: such an interpretative move is likely indicated by TO's version of Gen. 32: 25, which offers an ambiguous translation of the Hebrew. Where the Bible tells us that the socket of Jacob's thigh was sprained or dislocated, TO's וְזָע פְּתִי יַרְכֵּהּ may be taken to mean either 'and Jacob's hip-pan shook', or as 'and he (*sc.* the opponent) shook Jacob's hip-pan'.[82] It is possible to construe this injury as nothing very serious: TO at the end of this verse once again used the verb 'insinuate oneself' to describe the encounter of the two.

Returning to TO of Gen. 32: 24, we observe that the Hebrew Bible's reference to the *dawn*, which is of such moment for the other Targumim, has been replaced by the general word for *morning*, Aramaic צַפְרָא. TO follows the same procedure in Gen. 32: 26, where the opponent asks to be dismissed because the *morning*, not the *dawn* as in MT and the other Targumim, has now arisen. There is thus no suggestion that the time of day might be of any importance. Certainly, TO has no reference to the time of prayer;

---

[80] See Grossfeld, *The Targum Onqelos to Genesis*, 117.

[81] See above, pp. 263–6.

[82] Indeed, the Aramaic verb used may mean simply that the hip pan was 'moved': PJ used the same expression, and (it will be recalled) explicitly noted that the angel had not been given authority to harm Jacob: see above, p. 292, and M. Maher, *Targum Pseudo-Jonathan: Genesis. Translated, with Introduction and Notes*, The Aramaic Bible, 1b (Clark: Edinburgh, 1992), 114.

and the liturgical concern so prominent in the other Targumim appears to be entirely lacking.

The biblical explanation of the name Israel's meaning in Gen. 32: 29 also merits unusual treatment by TO in the translation

And he said: Your name shall no longer be said as Jacob, but Israel; because you *are a prince before the Lord* and with men, and you have prevailed.

Where all the other Targumim of this verse, and Targum Hosea 12: 4–5, used a verb to render the corresponding Hebrew verbal form שׂרית, 'you have engaged, struggled', TO put a noun followed by a personal pronoun to give רב את, 'you are a prince, chief'. Furthermore, the Bible's notion of a struggle 'with God' was taken by TO as a reference to Jacob's princely status 'before the Lord': again, this differs from all the other Targumim of this verse, which interpreted the Hebrew term אלהים as signifying angels. TO seeks to emphasize that Jacob-Israel is, and always has been, a 'prince', that is, a mighty angel, before the Lord, rather than a 'prince' with other angels. Here, perhaps, we perceive why TO was keen to play down the physical aspects of Jacob's struggle and injury: the reality was that he had always been an angelic prince before the Lord, and the episode at the Jabbok was principally designed to announce a fact which was already known. In this respect, TO may share some of the presuppositions lying behind the *Prayer of Joseph*, for whom Jacob's angelic status is a present, timeless reality. Again, the sentiment recalls the *Book of Jubilees*, for whom Israel shares the unique privileges of the two highest orders of angels not as the result of any struggle, but as of right. Yet this same Jacob-Israel is also a prince with men; and as such at least the possibility exists in TO's exegesis that he is a figure who draws the heavenly and earthly realms together.

It is only at Gen. 32: 30 that TO reveals the angelic nature of Jacob's opponent, and then in a manner consistent with what we have already learned of this Targum's objectives:

And Jacob called the name of the place Peni'el: Because I have seen *the angel of the Lord* face to face, and my soul has been saved.

Unlike the other extant Targumim of the verse (TN and PJ) which spoke of the angels from before the Lord (TN) and the angels of the Lord (PJ) to translate the original Hebrew 'God', TO envisaged a singular angel, thus identifying the 'man' spoken of earlier in the narrative. By not talking here of angels in the plural, TO effectively rules out the exegetical contact between this verse and Gen. 28: 12, which the other Targumim seem to have assumed. TO points to this particular angel engaged with Jacob-Israel in this particular place, again rather in the manner of the *Prayer of Joseph*. The effect, throughout TO's retelling of the biblical narrative, is to publicize Jacob's exceptional high status before the Lord and with men.

This last point is taken up by TO of Gen. 35: 11. While the Targum for the most part stays close to the Hebrew in its interpretation of Gen. 35: 9–15, it accords verse 11 special treatment:

And the Lord said to Him (Israel): I am 'El Shaddai. *Increase* and be many. A people and an *assembly of tribes* shall come from you; and kings *who rule over the peoples* shall come forth from *you*.

Here the 'prevailing' authority of Israel's kingly descendants over 'men' is indicated in Targumic expansion of the Hebrew as 'kings who rule over the peoples': a very similar phrase appears in TN and *CG* at this point. Israel is also an assembly of tribes for TO: none of the other extant Targumim of the verse (PJ, TN, *CG*) uses this language. TO also makes the Hebrew of God's command 'be fruitful and multiply' resemble his Aramaic translation of Gen. 1: 22, 28 (see also PJ and Peshitta at this point), so that the reader might the more easily pick up the possible allusion to God's command to Adam to fill the earth. Adam was to be God's vice-regent on the earth: at the very least, TO now hints that Israel is to be the same.

6.5 *Targum of Hosea 12: 4–6*

In a short section alluding to episodes in Jacob's life, the prophet Hosea spoke of the Patriarch using words and phrases which recall Gen. 32: 25–9. His attitude to Jacob is not entirely complimetary; but the Targum is careful to pursue its usual course of softening any criticism of the Fathers which the Bible might offer. At 12: 3 Hosea had alluded to the Lord's intention to enter into a lawsuit with Judah, so as to punish Jacob according to his ways and to repay him according to his deeds. Then (Hosea 12: 4) we read concerning Jacob:

In the womb he tripped up his brother by the heel (עקב את אחיו): and in his strength he strove/engaged with God (ובאונו שרה את אלהים).

Targum Jonathan's version of the version runs as follows:

O prophet! Say to them, Was it not stated of Jacob before he was born that he should be more than his brothers? And through his strength he *became prince/gained superiority* with *the angel*.

Here the Targum deftly sidestepped Hosea's original reference to Gen. 25: 6, which told how Jacob's hand at birth had grasped hold of his brother's heel, by taking the Hebrew 'in the womb' as an allusion to what had happened *before* the birth. This was described in Gen. 26: 23, when the Lord had told Rebekah that two nations were *in her womb*, of whom one would be stronger than the other: this last promise is represented in Targum Hosea 12: 4 with the word יסבי, which I have translated above as 'he should be more'. The word may signify numerical strength, recalling God's later command to Israel in TO and PJ of Gen. 35: 11 to increase; but it may also indicate a general thriving and growth. Thus the Hebrew verb עקב, 'trip by the heel', is given a good interpretation, first as referring to Jacob by play on words, and then as having an almost allegorical significance of outstripping his brother in respect of growth.

   Targum Jonathan understood the second half of the verse as referring to events at the Jabbok. Hosea's Hebrew recalled Gen. 32: 29, and the Targum followed suit. Jacob, through his strength, gained princely status with the angel, the Targum adopting a by-now familiar interpretation of the episode in general and of the Hebrew verb 'engage, strive' in particular. That his engagement was with an angel is an understanding shared at this point between Targum, Vulgate, and Aquila's version; and the following verse explained the engagement more precisely:

And he strove/engaged with an angel and prevailed. He wept and made supplication of him. At Bethel he found him, and there he shall speak with us.

In Targum Jonathan's version, this became:

And he *was prince/gained superiority with the* angel and prevailed. He wept and made supplication of him. At Bethel he *was revealed to* him, and there he shall speak with us.

Once more, the similarity of this exegesis to that displayed by the Targumim of Gen. 32: 29 is evident. It it also clear, however, that the name Israel itself occurs neither in the Hebrew nor the Targum of Hosea 12: 4–5, so it is all the more significant that the Targum very clearly directs its hearers and readers back to the books of Moses. The Targum of Hosea 12: 6 does this simply, by explaining who the one who shall 'speak with us' might be:

This refers to the Lord, the God of Hosts, *who was revealed to Abraham, Isaac, and Jacob, even as it is stated through Moses's agency:* The Lord is His memorial *to all generations.*

The Targum of Hosea, then, points us back to the Book of Genesis and, by implication, to the Targumic interpretation of those events. Hosea's words are not seen as adding to, or detracting from, the sense that Jacob gained princely-angelic status in his conflict with the angel, and that this status qualified him for the revelation to him of the divine Presence: the influence of Gen. 35: 9–15 and its Targumim, which at verse 13 spoke of the presence of the Glory of the Lord (TO) or the Glory of the Shekhina of the Lord (TN, PJ and *CG*) with Jacob at Bethel, is very strong.

7. SUMMARY

The Mishnah represents the oldest Rabbinic work to discuss the account of Jacob's change of name; and its interests are confined to the law of the 'sinew of the thigh'. The Tosefta, likewise, displays an interest in this commandment but, like the Mishnah, offers no direct explanation of the name 'Israel' which is so central to the biblical narrative describing the origin of the law. Both texts, however, insist by implication that 'Israel', namely the Patriarch and his descendants, is the title given to those who observe the halakhah as determined by the Rabbis. Debates there might be about the precise requirements of that halakhah, and about its exact relationship to incidents in the life of Israel the Patriarch; but the central assumption of these two texts, that 'Israel' is involved in the acceptance and observance of particular divine laws in particular ways, is never in doubt.

The Tosefta and the *Mekhilta de Rabbi Ishmael*, noting that Jacob retained his old name after he had been accorded the title Israel, put forward the suggestion that one of the names is to be regarded as essential, the other an addition, differences of opinion among the Rabbinic authorities as to the 'essential' name being set forth. The context of this discussion, however, is not debate about the 'sinew of the thigh', but analysis of Jeremiah's prophecy about the final redemption of Israel. The prophet's words might be taken to mean that the Exodus from Egypt will no longer be mentioned in formal prayer when God acts to deliver the Jews from 'the north country' at the end of days: if that is so, should not the name Jacob be abrogated in favour of the name Israel by analogy, since Israel is a name of victory granted after struggle and oppression? Both texts explain that both Exodus and the names Jacob and Israel will continue to feature in formal prayer in the days of deliverance; in this way, they indicate very clearly that the title Israel can be divorced neither from the liturgical forms regularly used by Jews, nor from the Jewish expectation of a future, definitive deliverance from oppression.

Deliverance from the capricious and sinister, even occult, might of Rome comes to the fore in *Genesis Rabbah*, whose interpretation of events at the Jabbok, which to some degree includes the concerns of the Mishnah, Tosefta, and *Mekhilta*, is prefaced by a remarkable homily featuring Israel in the guise of Jeshurun, who is 'like God'. Significantly in this respect, the resurrection of the dead is brought to the reader's attention: this, the most arresting of divine miracles, was performed in times past through the agency of Elijah, one of the 'praiseworthy and distinguished' Israelites who might be said to be 'like God'. Once introduced, this theme of final redemption and the resurrection of the dead runs through the rest of the exegesis, which from various angles examines questions of permanence and change. The midrash accepts without question that Jacob's opponent at the Jabbok was an angel, and it soon becomes apparent that the angel was Esau's guardian, Esau here representing Rome. No sooner is this established, however, than we are told that the angels, with the exception of Michael and Gabriel, have no permanent names, rather, they are returned each day to the River of Fire, and emerge with new personae to praise the Almighty. Jacob's opponent, who is Esau's guardian, cannot tell the Patriarch his name, for the simple reason that the name he bears while attacking Jacob will soon be altered. Thus Rome's celestial counterpart is revealed as ephemeral, mutable, and unstable—unlike Jacob, whose name Israel indicates his superior strength to such ephemeral angels, and whose likeness is permanently engraved on the Throne of God. Try what tricks he will, this angel cannot undermine Jacob. The change which takes place in the course of Jacob's becoming Israel as he defeats the power of Esau-Rome and realizes his status as one who is as close to God as it is possible to be is paralleled by the resurrection of the dead to eternal life, as they discard for ever impermanence and change.

Genesis Rabbah, however, is realistic in assessing the history of the Jewish people. Expounding Jacob's second visit to Bethel, the midrash accepts that the 'Israel' who will issue forth from the Patriarch will include sinners, who offer improper divine service tinged with idolatry, and unsatisfactory kings. Yet this somewhat bleak picture, reflecting the realities of the biblical narrative and its records of Israel's disobedience, is ultimately brought into line with what has been said about the meaning of the name Israel beforehand: this Israel's likeness is engraved on the Throne of Glory, and the midrash ends its discussion of the episode by reminding readers that the Fathers of this Israel constitute the Merkavah itself.

The matter of the 'sinew of the thigh' features in *b. Ḥullin* 91a also; but the Talmud soon shifts discussion to Jacob as a man of prayer, exemplified by his first visit to Bethel: this introduces the subject of angels, and Jacob's relationship with them. The Talmud presents them as jealous of Jacob's privileges and status, and proceeds to a lengthy demonstration of Israel's superiority over them. Israel takes precedence over the angels, we are told, in matters liturgical; and fewer prerequisites for pronouncing the Divine Name apply to her than to the angels. In short, by becoming Israel, Jacob was made a 'prince' over the angels, whose attitudes to Israel seem to be marked by jealousy and rivalry. The Talmudic discussion has nothing to say about the world to come, or the resurrection; but the name Israel itself is understood as indicating Jewish superiority in respect of angelic service of God, and as founding in Scriptural authority the position of the Head of the Diaspora and the Nasi of the Land of Israel. For in those two great constitutional offices the Talmud perceived the true meaning of Israel as one who has achieved superiority 'with men'.

Song Rabbah, we saw, presents a picture of an Israel reasonably satisfied with her present conditions in this world; these, however, obtain only because of Jacob's victory at the Jabbok, the dust of which ascended to the Throne of Glory. For this Midrash, it is a matter of amazement that the corrupt authority of Rome still stands!

The Aramaic Targumim display a complex interplay of ancient and more recent tradition; but all agree that 'Israel' is a name signifying superiority and angelic principality. With the exception of TO, all are concerned to emphasize Israel as holding liturgical primacy, with rights to sing the praises of God before any angelic creature; indeed, for many of the Targumim, the angel whom Jacob held fast on earth was none other than the heavenly choir-master himself. While different emphases are apparent in the several Targumim—TO, for instance, making plain Israel's eternal angelic status, *CG* insisting on his superiority to all angels, and PJ associating Israel's liturgical primacy with the Temple Service and the institution of the priesthood—all centre their exegesis on an Israel defined as one who shares vital qualities with the angels. The Targumim, indeed, express clearly what is present or implied in all the other Rabbinic texts I have examined, that in a particular manner 'Israel' is that people which links the earthly and the heavenly realms.

9
New Testament Engagements*

The writers of the New Testament offer few references or allusions, direct or indirect, to the story of Jacob's change of name as it is described in Gen. 32: 22–33; 35: 9–15; or Hosea 12: 3–6. This particular biblical episode seems to have held little interest for them, even though the sense that individual events in Jesus's life represented and recapitulated central experiences of the nation Israel is sometimes expressed.[1] Thus the Baptism of Christ and his Temptation in the wilderness are by some New Testament writers presented as analogous to Israel's Exodus from Egypt and sufferings in the desert;[2] and Christ is portrayed as the Patriarch Jacob-Israel with his twelve 'sons' at the head of an ideal nation of Israel over which the twelve Apostles are destined to exercise authority (see esp. Matt. 19: 28; Luke 22: 30).

Among individual writers, St Luke in particular expresses concern for the 'restoration of Israel' to political and religious integrity: see Acts 1: 6, where the disciples ask the risen Christ whether he intends now to restore the kingship to Israel; and Luke 2: 22–39, where the solemn Temple ceremonies of the purification of Christ's Mother after childbirth are described (Luke 2: 24 in accord with Lev. 12: 8), and the redemption of Jesus as firstborn son is recorded (Luke 2: 22–3 in accord with Exod. 13: 2,

---

* I am particularly indebted to the valuable comments, generous assistance, and encouragement of my Durham New Testament colleague Loren Stuckenbruck in the preparation of this chapter.

[1] New Testament uses of the title Israel are listed and discussed by G. Harvey, *The True Israel: Uses of the Names Jew, Hebrew and Israel in Ancient Jewish and Early Christian Literature* (Brill: Leiden, 1996), 225–50. His single mention of Gen. 32, along with Gen. 28, may be found at p. 247, where he suggests (correctly, in my view) that these chapters informed St John's presentation of Jesus's future disciple Nathanael as a true 'Israelite' (John 1: 47).

[2] See U. W. Mauser, *Christ in the Wilderness: The Wilderness Theme in the Second Gospel and Its Basis in the Biblical Tradition*, SBT 39 (SCM Press: London, 1963).

12). These ceremonies are witnessed by the just and pious elder Simeon, one of those who awaited the *consolation* of Israel (προσδεχόμενος παράκλησιν τοῦ Ἰσραήλ, Luke 2: 25), and by the prophetess Anna who prayed daily in the Temple, and who spoke of these events to all who were waiting for the *redemption* of Jerusalem (καὶ ἐλάλει περὶ αὐτοῦ πᾶσιν τοῖς προσδεχομένοις λύτρωσιν Ἰερουσαλήμ, Luke 2: 38; cf. 1: 68). According to this Gospel, Christ's final act is the blessing of his followers in the manner of the Priestly Blessing in the Temple, as he lifts up his hands pronouncing the formula of benediction and ascends to heaven (Luke 24: 50–1), thus bringing to a conclusion a narrative which began in the Temple (Luke 1: 5–8). This story of Christ Luke has apparently presented as a priestly service effecting what the Temple Service carried out, namely, the joining together of earth and heaven: note how at Christ's birth the 'multitude of the heavenly host' praised God with the formula 'glory to God on high, and on earth peace among men of (God's) good pleasure' (Luke 2: 14); and how at his triumphal entry into Jerusalem and its Temple the earthly 'multitude of the disciples' praised God with mighty voice in respect of the king, blessed in the Name of the Lord, uttering the formula, 'in heaven peace, and glory on high' (Luke 19: 38). Thus earth and heaven are conjoined in a single angelic and human worship. The well-known text from the Dead Sea Scrolls entitled Songs of the Sabbath Sacrifice (4Q400–407 *Shirot 'Olat Ha-Shabbat*) describes in great detail how one group of Jews at least in Second Temple times understood this conjoining of the earthly and heavenly realms in the service of the Almighty.

This, perhaps, is the most dramatic New Testament presentation of Christ's activities as related to a restoration of Israel, and it has been related here not only because the reader will doubtless hear within it echoes of matters discussed earlier, but also because other New Testament texts can be understood in terms of a programme set forth by 'the historical Jesus' for the restoration of Israel. E. P. Sanders is probably the best-known scholar writing in English to espouse this model of things: he views as historically certain, or virtually certain, Jesus's call of twelve disciples (representing twelve sons of Israel); his expectation of a new or renewed Temple; and his proclamation of an 'eschatological' kingdom. Sanders further argues that it is highly probable historically that the 'eschatological' kingdom of Israel would have within it twelve

tribes, leaders, and a functioning Temple.[3] When read in tandem
with Jewish discussions and expositions of the *meaning* of the *name*
Israel assembled here, Sanders's thesis makes a good deal of sense.
Nonetheless, my concern here is not so much with attempts to
determine what the 'historical Jesus' might have proclaimed, as
with the opinions of the New Testament writers themselves on the
name Israel; and whether Sanders's thesis is correct or not, it is
clear from St Luke alone that the restoration of Israel was a topic
which animated some of them. Their apparent lack of interest in
Jacob's acquisition of this name (Sanders has no references in his
index to any of the Hebrew Bible texts which have concerned us
here) is thus puzzling—until we recall two particular texts. The
first of these is the first chapter of St John's Gospel, which, as we
shall see presently, may not unreasonably be held to include a discussion of what 'Israel' means from a Christian perspective. The
second, while much more Jewish in tone, offers serious text-critical
problems: it is the famous description in Luke 22: 43–4 of the
angel's appearance at Christ's passion strengthening him in his
'agony'. We shall need to tackle these two passages quite separately.

1. THE FIRST CHAPTER OF ST JOHN'S GOSPEL

This famous chapter offers a number of statements recalling the
accounts of Jacob's struggle at the Jabbok and traditional Jewish
exegeses of the same. As the Gospel narrative progresses, it is
possible to discern the Evangelist's further engagement with
contemporary Jewish understandings of the name Israel. Here I
shall attempt to disclose some of the thought-processes which lie
beneath the Evangelist's claims, and to suggest ways in which his
work may represent a kind of debate in relation to the Judaism of
his day.

It is remarkable that the Gospel does not quote directly any
Scriptural verse or portion of verses from the texts examined in

---

[3] See E. P. Sanders, *Jesus and Judaism* (SCM Press: London, 1985). A summary
of his historical conclusions, graded I. certain or virtually certain; II. highly probable; III. probable; IV. possible; V. conceivable; and VI. incredible may be found on
pp. 326–7 of this book, and it is these results that are quoted here. For a more recent
study arguing in favour of the restorationist agenda of the historical Jesus, see N. T.
Wright, *Jesus and the Victory of God* (SPCK: London, 1996); and on the views of
the Third Evangelist in particular, see D. Ravens, *Luke and the Restoration of Israel*
(Sheffield Academic Press: Sheffield, 1995).

this monograph. It will be necessary, therefore, to show in the first instance that a case can be made for an argument supporting the Evangelist's interest in these biblical chapters. A beginning may be made with John 1: 18, which roundly asserts that no one has ever seen God, Θεὸν οὐδεὶς ἑώρακεν πώποτε. Any reader familiar with the Jewish Scriptures would be able to construe this assertion as flat contradiction of Jacob-Israel's words when he named the place of his fight with the angel Peni'el (Gen. 32: 31), saying, 'I have seen God face to face, and my life has been preserved'.[4] No other biblical character, not even Moses, claims to have seen God in precisely these terms. Such apparent contradiction between the words of Jacob-Israel and the Gospel, however, implies that these same words of Jacob-Israel were in the Evangelist's mind; and this perception is confirmed by John 5: 37, where Jesus informs the Jews that they have never heard the voice of God (here defined as Jesus's Father, 5: 36), nor, says he, 'have you seen his form', οὔτε εἶδος αὐτοῦ ἑωράκατε. The term εἶδος 'form', is found only here in the entire Gospel; and LXX used it just twice to speak directly of God, at Gen. 32: 31, 32, where they translated the place named by Jacob-Israel as Peni'el-Penu'el with Εἶδος θεοῦ, 'form of God'. It is unlikely that the Evangelist here has in mind Moses's words at Deut. 4: 12, 15, when he reminded Israel that at Horeb when God gave the Torah they saw no 'form': the Hebrew of this word, תמונה, is rendered by LXX as ὁμοίωμα, 'likeness', and is used absolutely, without direct reference to God. For the Evangelist, it would seem, the Patriarch Jacob-Israel is in mind. According to John, he saw neither God nor the form of God. Quite what this means we shall have to consider.

That the Evangelist had Jacob's struggle at the Jabbok in mind when he wrote the first chapter of the Gospel is supported by two further facts: the business of 'seeing' is repeatedly drawn to the reader's attention in this chapter, which contains the only occurrence of the word 'Israelite' in the Gospel (1: 47), along with two of the four occasions on which the title 'Israel' appears (1: 31, 49).[5] As far as 'seeing' is concerned, we may record no fewer than fifteen occasions in this single chapter where some kind of sight is spoken

[4] LXX follows the Hebrew closely: εἶδον γὰρ θεὸν πρόσωπον πρὸς πρόσωπον. See above, pp. 67–9.
[5] The remaining occasions are 3: 10, where Jesus refers to Nicodemus as a teacher of Israel, and 12: 13, where the crowds acclaim Jesus as the King of Israel.

of.[6] The single mention of Israelite further defines the one so designated, Nathanael, as 'truly' Israelite and 'without guile', which indicates that the Evangelist may be concerned to offer a particular definition of a 'real' Israelite: it is this same 'Israelite' Nathanael who will go on to identify Jesus as King of *Israel* (1: 49) in the course of a discussion with Jesus involving talk of 'seeing' (1: 48–51); by this means, we may infer, John the Baptist's responsibility for manifesting Jesus to 'Israel' (1: 31) is carried out *in nuce*, since he is displayed to the one who is truly Israelite 'without guile'. That the Evangelist intended to portray Jesus as in some sense analogous to Jacob is clear from John 1: 51, where Gen. 28: 10 is quoted with reference to Jesus as the one upon whom angels ascend and descend, as they did upon Jacob according to one particular reading of the Hebrew text of that verse.[7]

Prima facie, then, there is a case for believing that the biblical accounts of Jacob's change of name to Israel were a matter of concern for the Fourth Evangelist. The final form of the Gospel is commonly dated to around 90–5 CE, although some students are prepared to date it a decade earlier.[8] Whichever of these dates is accepted as the more likely, there is no doubt that among Jews interpretation of the name 'Israel' as having to do in some way or other with seeing God was one of a number of possible explanations of the name current by that time. In this regard, we need only consider the writings of Philo, with their reiterated declarations that Israel is 'one who sees God', and, very possibly, the *Prayer of Joseph* and its similar definition, arguments for whose

[6] See 1: 14, 18, 29a, 29b, 32, 33, 34, 36, 38, 39, 46, 47, 48, 50, 51. Cf. also 1: 31 and 1: 42.

[7] The Hebrew of Gen. 28: 12 informs us that, in Jacob's dream of the ladder at Bethel, the angels of God went up and down עליו, which may be construed as 'upon it', i.e. the ladder; or 'upon him' or 'on his account', i.e. with reference to Jacob. Such an understanding of the Hebrew seems to underlie John 1: 51, which otherwise has affinities with traditional Jewish exegesis extant in Targum and midrash: see E. G. Clarke, 'Jacob's Dream at Bethel', *Studies in Religion*, 4 (1974–5), 367–77; C. C. Rowland, 'John 1: 51: Jewish Apocalyptic and Targumic Tradition', *NTS* 30 (1984), 498–507; and J. L. Kugel, *In Potiphar's House: The Interpretive Life of Biblical Texts*, 2nd edn. (Harvard University Press: Cambridge, Mass., 1994), 112–20.

[8] For a convenient summary of views on the date of the Gospel, see R. Kysar, article 'John, the Gospel of', in *ABD*, iii. 918–19. See further R. E. Brown, *The Gospel According to John*, 2 vols., Anchor Bible (Doubleday: New York, 1966), vol. 1, for extended discussion of the tradition behind the Gospel (pp. xli–li) and further observations on its date (pp. lxxx–lxxxvi) and authorship (pp. lxxxvii–civ).

antiquity I have set forth above.[9] In any event, both the Hebrew
Bible and LXX make it plain that Jacob's change of name to Israel
had happened at a place called Peni'el-Penu'el, where Jacob-Israel
declared that he had seen God face to face. It is entirely possible,
therefore, that the Evangelist sought to engage with this common
definition of the name Israel. Furthermore, if the Evangelist were
a Jew, as many modern commentators now suggest,[10] then his willingness to treat of this matter needs to be set alongside the writings
of his contemporary Flavius Josephus, whose *Jewish Antiquities*
was published around 93–4 CE, since this writer presents us with an
analogous handling of the tradition about Israel's name, which
denies to Jacob what the Fourth Gospel ascribes to Jesus. As we
have seen, Josephus was keen (for reasons of his own) to eliminate
from his account of Jacob's struggle with the angel any sense that
the name Israel might mean 'one who sees God', and was equally
keen to redefine the significance of the place-name Peni'el-Penu'el
without referring to any claim on Jacob's part that he had seen
God.

Two further elements in this Gospel may betray the Evangelist's
interest in Jacob's change of name. The first of these is the key role
played by the feast of Sukkoth, the Temple Service for that feast,
and *Shemini 'Atseret* in the actions and discourses of Jesus set out
in John 7: 2–8: 50. No other New Testament writer makes mention
of these days and the customs associated with them. As we have
seen, the *Book of Jubilees* located the gift of the name Israel to
Jacob at Sukkoth, and regarded *Shemini 'Atseret* as a commemoration of the event. It was at this festival, *Jubilees* declares, that
Israel came fully into existence as a 'kingdom, priests, and holy
nation': the royal tribe of Judah, the priestly tribe of Levi, and the
nation of the twelve sons of Jacob purified from all uncleanness
was then constituted at Bethel, the whole story of its future being
committed to Jacob-Israel by the hands of an angel. *Jubilees*, it will
be recalled, has portrayed this moment as the point at which the
work begun by the Almighty in creation is perfected: now that

---

[9] See above, pp. 215–19.

[10] See J. Ashton, *Understanding the Fourth Gospel* (Clarendon Press: Oxford,
1991), 205–37. Even if he were not a Jew himself, he seems fully conversant with
Jewish exegesis of Scripture, a point well illustrated in recent Johannine scholarship by the discussion of John 1: 19–51 and its indebtedness to Jewish interpretation of Exod. 19 offered in F. J. Moloney, *The Gospel of John*, Sacra Pagina, 4
(Liturgical Press: Collegeville, 1998), 50–7.

Israel has come into the world, the Sabbath may be properly observed on earth as it is in heaven by the Angels of the Presence and the Angels of Sanctification.[11] Secondly, the Evangelist speaks of Jacob in relation to a well which flowed at Shechem, as he presents Jesus in dialogue with a Samaritan woman (John 4: 5–6), a conversation which leads the woman to ask Jesus if he is 'greater than Jacob our father'? (John 4: 12). All of these things suggest that the Evangelist was concerned to engage with the matter of Jacob-Israel, and to redefine it in the light of his Christian convictions.

Set in the light of the Jewish texts expounded here, certain aspects of the Gospel stand out. In the opening chapter, the Evangelist appears to engage with the notions of seeing, sight, and vision as directly connected in Jewish tradition with Israel and Israelites; yet with these things he involves no sense of struggle, fight, combat, or wrestling with supernatural or natural opponents. Expressed in other terms, we might say that John agreed with (for example) Philo, the traditions informing the *Prayer of Joseph*, and LXX that Israel is a title whose proper meaning is expressed with reference to seeing or vision. These writings, however, assert that Israel has to do with seeing God, whom, according to John 1: 18, no one has ever seen. Yet a moment's reflection allows us to recall that Philo, for whom the sense of Israel as 'one who sees God' is standard, was careful to point out that Israel's object of sight is not the essence of the deity as he is in Himself, but rather an aspect of God's being appropriate for human contemplation which has several names, one of which, significantly, is Logos. This Logos, according to Philo, might be called 'chief angel', and unites the kingly and creative attributes of the Lord.[12] Furthermore, the Aramaic Targumim without exception indicate that what Israel saw at the Jabbok was not God in His essence, but an angel (TO) or angels of the Lord (Palestinian Targumim). The Gospel, then, perhaps stands closer to Jewish models of thought than might at first appear; but these it utilizes for its own particular Christian purposes, to produce a line of thinking which may be articulated as follows:

(a) No one, not even the great Patriarch Jacob who became Israel, has ever seen God.

---

[11] See above, pp. 150–3.
[12] See above, pp. 163–4, 208.

(b) In truth, the name 'Israel' means 'one who sees God' as Gen. 32: 31 implies; but what the Patriarch saw was an angel or angels, as Jewish tradition has always averred.

(c) On one level, Jesus may be compared with Jacob (John 1: 51). The Hebrew Bible, read in one particular way, tells how angels ascended and descended on him at Bethel. This event has long been directly associated in traditional Jewish understanding with Jacob's reception of the name Israel, which was confirmed at Bethel.

(d) Nathanael is a true 'Israelite' who will see what the Patriarch saw: he will see angels. But he will see more than that: he will also see Jesus *in persona Israel* with the angels going up and coming down upon him. This Jesus may be analogous to Jacob; but he is, for the Evangelist, greater than Jacob, inasmuch as he, as well as the angels, becomes the object of sight to whom the vision of the true Israelite Nathanael will be directed. Such status the Patriarch Jacob himself never quite enjoyed, since this Jesus is the Logos (John 1: 1), that very reality with which, according to Philo, Jacob had wrestled in order to see God.

All this could be implied in what John is saying in the opening of his Gospel, and it carries with it the strong suggestion that Jesus's proper 'location', his home, as it were, is the heavenly realm where the angels dwell: Nathanael will 'see the heavens opened' as he discerns the angels ascending and descending upon Jesus. The heavenly origin and dwelling of Jesus are explicitly declared later in the Gospel, when he says that he has come down from heaven (John 6: 38, 41–2, 50, 51, 58): like the angels going up and coming down upon him, he has both come down from heaven and will also go up to heaven again (John 3: 13). This, the Evangelist hints, is hardly surprising, since Jesus is 'from above' and 'not of this world' (8: 23); he is the King of Israel recognized by the Israelite Nathanael (John 1: 49), who will declare to Pontius Pilate that his kingdom is 'not of this world' (John 18: 36).

According to some midrashim and Targumim, the image of Jacob is engraved upon the Throne of Glory: there is a sense in which he is 'not of this world', and the angels at Bethel went down to compare the image above with the living reality below.[13]

---

[13] See above, pp. 243–4, and n. 7 and the literature cited there and pp. 266–8. It is possible that the Evangelist has alluded to this tradition at 12: 41, where he states

According to Targum Onqelos of Gen. 32 and the *Prayer of Joseph*, Jacob-Israel always has been and is a 'prince with God', one who dwells in the heavenly realms. It is not necessary for the Evangelist to have known these texts, which in their present form are almost certainly later than his day. It is enough to note that the traditions which inform those texts were most likely known to him, because material provided by the *Book of Jubilees* offers sufficient evidence to show that the basic raw materials out of which the midrashic-Targumic traditions are constructed were current around 200 BCE. For *Jubilees*, Jacob, as we have seen, is 'written into' the creative actions of God, organically and structurally tied into the origins, order, and functioning of the cosmos. His earthly representative throughout time is the 'children of Israel', that sacral nation-state constituted within time along lines laid down by Exod. 19: 6, and coming into existence only when Jacob becomes Israel at the feasts of Sukkot and *Shemini 'Atseret*. Then, and only then according to *Jubilees*, is Sabbath celebrated on earth by 'Israel' along with the Angels of the Presence and the Angels of Sanctification. Then and only then, *Jubilees* indicates, is the creation of the cosmos complete. Jacob's becoming Israel is the final and supremely glorious act in God's creation of the cosmos, for this Jacob who becomes Israel is 'at home' both in heaven and on earth, linking the two realms particularly through weekly celebration of Sabbath with the highest angels as the 'day of the holy kingdom'.

Some of this thinking may clarify words of Jesus according to John. From the outset, the Evangelist presents Jesus as analogous to Jacob; like Jacob in Jewish tradition, Jesus belongs 'above', and he comes from above to the earth, to be 'manifested to Israel'. He unites the realms of heaven and earth, the presence of angels with him testifying to this. His contentious statement that his Father is working on the Sabbath up to the present, just as he is working—
ὁ πατήρ μου ἕως ἄρτι ἐργάζεται κἀγὼ ἐργάζομαι (John 5: 17)—might

that Isaiah saw 'his glory': the glory is almost certainly that of Christ perceived by the prophet during his inaugural vision in the Temple (Isa. 6), as pointed out by R. Schnackenburg, *The Gospel According to St. John*, 3 vols. (Crossroad: New York, 1990), ii. 416–17, who also refers to the Aramaic Targum of Isaiah at this point. Furthermore, there is some evidence to suggest that St John may have been aware of the teachings of those 'who descend to the Merkavah', for whom the presence of Israel's likeness on the Throne of Glory was a matter of sublime significance: see Ashton, *Understanding the Fourth Gospel*, 348–56.

be deliberately provocative: seen against statements of *Jubilees* we have examined, it could be taken to mean that Sabbath is not yet inaugurated, that God is still in process of creating the cosmos, awaiting the arrival of 'Israel' for its perfection and completion. It is well known that John presents the passion and crucifixion of Jesus as a revelation of divine glory (see 3: 14, where it is associated with Jesus's descent from and ascent to heaven; 8: 28; 12: 34), reaching its climax in Jesus's triumphant shout of τετέλεσται (John 19: 30), 'it is completed', echoing the report of creation's completion according to LXX Gen. 2: 1–2, 'and the heaven and the earth and all their cosmos were completed (συνετελέσθησαν); and God completed (συνετέλεσεν) his works which He had made'. It is precisely now, John might be saying, that Sabbath can be brought in, with Israel and angels celebrating the feast both in heaven and on earth.[14]

The place where heaven and earth meet is the Temple, the house of God, that Bethel where Jacob saw angels ascending and descending and the name Israel was ratified as his own. All the Aramaic Targumim of Gen. 28 understood Bethel to be the place of the Temple (Beth-el meaning literally 'house of God'). *Jubilees* in some manner preceded the Targumim in this by explicitly linking Jacob's change of name with Temple building and sanctuary provision. Certainly the Gospel has much to say of the Temple, which the Evangelist believes Jesus to be (see John 2: 19–22; 4: 24 comparing 1: 32; 14: 26; and 20: 22), since the true worshippers 'in spirit and in truth' will find Jesus to be the place where the Spirit remains, as well as the truth itself (14: 6–9). Thus for the Evangelist Jesus is 'greater than our father Jacob', who according to *Jubilees* planned to build a Temple at Bethel, but was dissuaded from doing so by an angel at the feast of Tabernacles. This feast, *the* feast, known both from *Jubilees* and Targum Pseudo-Jonathan of Gen. 35: 14 as the feast during which Jacob's name was ratified as Israel, is also the feast which John chooses for Jesus to reveal his true identity, as the 'I am' who existed before Abraham (8: 58).

[14] For the *Jubilees* material, see above, pp. 150–3. Commentators on John's Gospel regularly note John 20: 22, with its note that Jesus bestowed the Holy Spirit on his disciples when he 'breathed' (ἐνεφύσησεῖ) upon them, as marking the beginning of a new creation, since LXX Gen 2: 7 reports that God breathed ἐνεφύσησεν the breath of life into the first man: see Brown, *The Gospel According to John*, ii. 1037; Moloney, *The Gospel of John*, 535.

Insofar as any analogy between Jacob and Jesus remains after
this declaration at the feast of Tabernacles, the notion of Jesus as
Jacob-Israel is utterly transformed; and such transformation corresponds to John's 'trumping', as it were, the matter of 'seeing
God' with which 'Israel' is traditionally associated by his elevation
of belief as a supreme virtue. Thus the Johannine Jesus declares to
doubting Thomas: 'Blessed are they who have not seen, and yet
have believed' (John 20: 29), and the Gospel itself is explicitly
written 'so that you may believe' (20: 31). Even so, this 'seeing',
characteristic of Israel in the Jewish tradition, is itself the supreme
fruit of belief as far as John is concerned: Jesus tells Martha: 'If
you believe, you will see the Glory of God' (11: 40), and informs
his disciples that they both know and see the Father (that is, God),
since 'he who has seen me has seen the Father' (14: 9). Here we
have entered the world of John's Christology, which carries us far
beyond the Jewish texts we have studied. Yet it would seem, at the
same time, that it owes a good deal to them.

It is well known that this Gospel draws on many different
sources and ideas in constructing its theology, and it is quite
possible that Jewish texts examined here have played their part. I
do not claim that they alone can necessarily account for all the
complexities of his writing; but enough has been said to indicate
that further enquiries into the Evangelist's familiarity with
Jubilees and its understanding of Israel might prove fruitful. At the
very least, both writings have declared interests in the number
seven: the Sabbath, the seventh month, and the seven times seven
years which make up a jubilee in the case of the former; for the
latter, the seven signs (2: 1–11; 4: 43–54; 5: 1–15; 6: 1–15, 16–21; 9:
1–34; 11: 1–44), the seven 'I am' statements (4: 26; 6: 35, 48; 8: 12;
10: 7, 11; 14: 6), and the six stone water-jars whose purificatory
contents are transformed into a seventh draft of wine fit for the
celebration of God's betrothal to his people Israel (2: 1–11). In all
this, John has presented Jesus as a Jacob-Israel figure who 'is
greater than our father Jacob', breaking the parameters of the
tradition so far known, yet depending to some extent on Jewish
models, reinitiating that creation into which Jacob was written
from the beginning.

2. ST LUKE'S PASSION STORY

Compared with the three other accounts of Jesus's experiences in Gethsemane, Luke's version (Luke 22: 40–6) offers a number of peculiarities. Indeed, his whole narration of Jesus's passion differs, at times considerably, from those of Matthew and Mark; but perhaps the most striking episode, told only by Luke, concerns the appearing of an angel to Jesus. After celebrating with his disciples what is explicitly called a Pesaḥ meal (22: 15), he goes with them at night to Gethsemane, where he separates himself from his followers by a space 'about a stone's throw' (22: 41). This detail is peculiar to Luke: Jesus is presented as being some distance away from his disciples, on his own. He then prays, asking that 'this cup', that is, the coming sufferings, be taken from him, nonetheless petitioning that God's will be done rather than his own. At this point, some witnesses to the text of the Gospel have these words:

And an angel from heaven appeared to him, strengthening him; and being in agony he prayed more zealously. And his sweat was like gouts of blood descending to the ground.

This translation attempts to represent as literally as possible the original Greek, which reads:

ὤφθη δὲ αὐτῷ ἄγγελος ἀπ᾽ οὐρανοῦ ἐνισχύων αὐτόν καὶ γενόμεμος ἐν ἀγωνίᾳ ἐκτενέστερον προσηύχετο καὶ ἐγένετο ὁ ἱδρὼς αὐτοῦ ὡσεὶ θρόμβοι αἵματος καταβαίνοντες ἐπὶ τὴν γῆν.

These verses find no place in some of the most ancient witnesses to the text of the Gospel. Thus they are lacking in (apparently) papyrus 69 and certainly in papyrus 75, both of the third century CE; in codex Sinaiticus (first corrector), codex Alexandrinus, codex Vaticanus, and a number of other important witnesses, including the Fathers Clement, Origen, Athanasius, and Cyril. On the other hand, they are represented in codex Sinaiticus main text; codex Bezae, the Koridethi Gospels, and in the writings of Justin, Irenaeus, Hippolytus, and Jerome. A list of witnesses to both readings is given by Fitzmyer, who has exhaustively studied the textual problems involved, concluding that 'the decision to admit them into the text or to omit them is not easy; the matter is hotly debated among textual critics today'.[15] He himself judges the

---

[15] See J. A. Fitzmyer, *The Gospel According to Luke X–XXIV*, Anchor Bible, 28A (Doubleday: New York, 1985), ii. 1443. The most recent detailed and extensive

verses a secondary, though ancient, addition to the text, and omits
them, while noting that 'one cannot . . . be apodictic about the
matter'.[16] Others, however, are convinced that they form part of
the original Gospel text, a view maintained recently by Joel B.
Green. In terms of textual criticism pure and simple, the evidence
for and against their inclusion is finely balanced.[17]

Textual problems aside, however, the vocabulary and content of
these two disputed verses seem to recall fairly clearly LXX Gen.
32: 23–32. First we have the verb ἐνισχύω, found only here in the
entire Gospel tradition (but part of Lucan vocabulary, as Acts 9: 19
shows); then the term ἀγωνία, one of whose primary meanings is
'wrestling about, athletic exercise', occurring nowhere else in the
New Testament; and finally the mention of the angel, which had
become a standard feature of Greek presentations of Gen. 32: 23–
32 based on LXX, as Demetrius the Chronographer and Philo
demonstrate. It seems very probable, indeed, that Luke 22: 43 was
written with LXX Gen. 32: 23–32 in mind. In the cases of both
Jacob and Jesus, the activity takes place at night; and both characters are alone. Both Jacob and Jesus are involved in a wrestling
bout: LXX Gen. 32: 26 is explicit on this point and, as we have

studies of the verses have been undertaken by B. D. Ehrman and M. A. Plunkett,
'The Angel and the Agony: The Textual Problem of Luke 22: 43–44', *CBQ* 45
(1983), 401–16; J. B. Green, 'Jesus on the Mount of Olives (Luke 22. 39–46):
Tradition and Theology', *JSNT* 26 (1986), 29–48; and R. E. Brown, *The Death of
the Messiah: From Gethsemane to the Grave*, 2 vols., Anchor Bible Reference Library
(Doubleday: New York, 1994), i. 115–16 (bibliography), 179–90. None of these
treatments refers to LXX Gen. 32: 25 as having possibly influenced the author of
the disputed verses. Brown, *Death*, i. 186, notes the possible significance of LXX
Deut. 32: 43, but neither develops this insight nor relates it to Jacob's struggle.

[16] See Fitzmyer, *Luke X–XXIV*, 1443–4. On the case for omitting the verses, see
also B. M. Metzger, *A Textual Commentary on the Greek New Testament* (United
Bible Societies: London, 1971), 177; and Ehrman and Plunkett, 'The Angel and the
Agony'. All discussions of the verses agree that the Christological concerns of (1)
the tradents of the New Testament text and (2) of the early Fathers need to be
considered. These concerns, however, may point in opposite directions: while the
verses could be used by Catholics to counter Docetism in showing Christ as truly
human, they could also suggest to (say) Monarchian heretics a subordinationist
Christ who required angelic help, lacking his own sufficient power.

[17] See Joel B. Green, *The Gospel of Luke* (Eerdmans: Grand Rapids, Mich.,
1997), 776, and id., 'Jesus on the Mount of Olives'. The verses are accepted as
genuine, 'but with very considerable hesitation', by I. H. Marshall, *The Gospel of
Luke: A Commentary on the Greek Text*, The New International Greek Testament
Commentary (Paternoster Press: Exeter, 1978), 831–2, who gives a list of commentators for and against their inclusion in Luke's text.

seen, the reference to ἀγωνία in Luke 22: 44 can refer to a wrestling bout: certainly violent physical exercise is in the Evangelist's mind, since Jesus sweats mightily, like a wrestler or prize-fighter.[18] His sweat, it should be noted, does not consist of blood, as some commentators have maintained; but it is *compared* with gouts of blood: it is heavy, thick, and fetid, the product of a hard, sustained struggle.[19]

One important difference between the LXX account of Jacob's struggle and Luke 22: 43–4 only serves to emphasize the indebtedness of the latter to the former. As we have seen, the general impression given by LXX is that the supernatural being who encountered Jacob at the Jabbok wrestled *against* him as an opponent. Along with Marguerite Harl, I also noted, however, that the Greek of LXX Gen. 32: 25, which states that the being wrestled μετ᾽ αὐτοῦ, might be more naturally understood to mean that the 'angel' wrestled *in company with* Jacob, against some unspecified and unnamed foe. The original Hebrew of that verse might also be read in this way.[20] It would seem, then, that the author of Luke 22: 43–4 could properly have taken Gen. 32: 25 to mean that an 'angel' had fought alongside Jacob in the face of a common, unnamed enemy. In terms of Luke's account of the Passion, there can be little doubt what that common enemy might be: it is the power of evil, the forces of the devil represented by the darkness.[21] This Jesus makes plain a little later to those who hand him over to death, in yet another saying peculiar to Luke's Gospel: 'this is your hour, and the power of darkness' (Luke 22: 53). Luke alone,

---

[18] This point is noted, in my view correctly, by Joel Green, *The Gospel of Luke*, 780–1, but without reference to Jacob's wrestling at the Jabbok. The athletic aspects of 'agony' are discussed at length by Brown, *Death*, i. 189–90.

[19] See again Green, *The Gospel of Luke*, 780, n. 19. My analysis of the verses further supports his stance in this matter, against those who consider that Jesus might have 'sweated blood': see e.g. A. Plummer, *St. Luke*, International Critical Commentary, 2nd edn. (Clark: Edinburgh, 1922), 510–11, and Brown, *Death*, i. 184–5. Mention of the sweat and agony suggest to some commentators that the verses seek to portray Jesus as undergoing a martyr's death, possibly of the sort ascribed to Isaiah's 'suffering servant': see esp. Ehrman and Plunkett, 'The Angel and the Agony', 412–16.

[20] See above, p. 59, and M. Harl, *La Bible d'Alexandrie, 1: La Genèse*, 243, who suggests that LXX Hosea 12: 4–5 might best be understood in this way, with obvious consequences for interpretation of Gen. 32: 25.

[21] See R. E. Brown, *Death*, i. 188–9; Marshall, *Gospel of Luke*, 832; and Green, *The Gospel of Luke*, 781.

furthermore, records (23: 45) that at Christ's death the sun was darkened.[22]

The verb 'strengthen', ἐνισχύω, is of particular significance inasmuch as LXX use it at Gen. 32: 29 to offer their version of what the name Israel means: 'you have been strong/strengthened yourself (ἐνίσχυσας) with God, and with men you are powerful.' It will also be recalled that LXX, in their distinctive version of Deut. 32: 43, used this same verb to speak of angels strengthening themselves in God. According to Luke 22: 43, the angel strengthens Jesus, and is seen by him, just as Jacob according to LXX is somehow endowed with strength, and sees his supernatural companion, a companion otherwise in Jewish tradition explicitly designated as an angel.

If Jewish interpretation of Gen. 32: 23–32, particularly the kind of interpretation expressed in LXX of that section, lies behind Luke 22: 43–4, then we should understand those verses as presenting Jesus at Gethsemane in the person of Jacob at the Jabbok. It is night, and he is alone. He is faced with a mighty adversary, and against this foe an angel from heaven appears to him, giving him strength just as, on one reading of LXX, a supernatural being fought alongside Jacob in his wrestling bout against his adversary. Jesus, too, is in a wrestling bout with his foe: he prays, but the struggle is fierce and prolonged, his profuse sweat a witness to this. On this interpretation, what the angel grants to Jesus is not power to pray more earnestly, as many suppose, but power to fight. To put matters in other words, he is seen to be 'on the side of the angels'. The victory over his adversary, the powers of darkness, is assured: by having the angel strengthen (ἐνισχύων) Jesus, Luke alludes to Jacob's victory and the prize for that victory, the celebrated name Israel which signifies one who is strong, or strengthens himself (LXX Gen 32: 25, ἐνίσχυσας) with God and like the angels of God (LXX Deut. 32: 43) against the enemies of God. After the night has passed, Jacob met his brother and enemy Esau; that meeting, following the events of the previous night, passed off without incident, despite Jacob's fears of the preceding day. After the night in Gethsemane, Jesus goes to Calvary, meeting his death according to Luke with equanimity—saying to the thief: 'Today thou shalt be with me in paradise' (23: 43); expiring with the

---

[22] For the textual problems presented by this verse, some witnesses of which speak of an eclipse of the sun, see Brown, *Death*, ii. 1039–43.

words: 'Father, into thy hands I commend my spirit' (23: 46)—
defeating the powers of darkness and rising with the sun 'at early
dawn' (24: 1) to new life as Israel, the one who has been strong and
has strengthened himself with God.

Some such explanation of Luke 22: 43–4 in the light of Gen. 32:
23–32 does not seem far-fetched, given the evidence available; and,
if it is correct, it may help to account for, and even resolve, the
textual problem the verses present. For a start, the interpretation
advanced here suggests strongly that Luke wrote these verses.
Fitzmyer lists five arguments to the contrary, all but one of which
can be countered.[23] First, he invokes the rule *lectio brevior potior*;
but this is a general rule only, and against it can be invoked the
equally general rule *lectio difficilior potior* since, as we shall see
presently and as has often been observed, these verses would have
presented almost insurmountable difficulties to certain readers of
the Gospel, bringing about their excision from manuscripts. Second, Fitzmyer notes that the verses have no counterpart in the
parallel Synoptic accounts: this is hardly a strong argument, since
we encounter (for example) verses in Mark (e.g. 4: 26–9; 8: 22–6)
without parallel elsewhere which are nonetheless accepted as
genuine by radical critics. What Fitzmyer means precisely is that
these verses do not feature in other accounts of Christ's *passion*.
But this may signify very little: Luke is well known for introducing
throughout his Gospel material not found elsewhere. On the interpretation offered here, however, the *purport* of these verses is far
from unique, since all three Synoptic accounts of the passion present Christ as tackling the forces of darkness.[24] The idea that the
verses are contrary to 'the sober thrust' of Luke's passion story,
adding 'emotional details to what is otherwise a sober abridgment
of the Marcan text', makes up Fitzmyer's third argument, which
is not a little subjective and, given the interpretation outlined
above, improbable.[25] Christ is involved in a deadly serious combat

---

[23] See Fitzmyer, *Luke X–XXIV*, 1444.

[24] See Brown, *Death*, i. 291–3 for Luke 22: 53 and its reference to the power of
darkness, noting (pp. 292–3) that some of Luke's references to darkness 'overlap an
attitude found widely elsewhere in the NT (and at Qumran), where it is the domain
of sin and ignorance presided over by Satan, a domain opposed to Jesus, who is light
and whose followers must walk in light'.

[25] Fitzmyer's opinion is representative of a number of commentators who
emphasize the emotional elements in the verses, as witness Ehrman and Plunkett,
'The Angel and the Agony', 416; Green, 'Jesus on the Mount of Olives', 32–3.

like the ancestor of the Jewish people; and on the outcome of that combat a good deal depends for the future not only for the Jews, but for the whole world. That the verses are absent from the oldest manuscript of the Gospel extant is the fourth and only incontestable argument. The final argument, that the verses betray 'later parenetic or hortatory concerns', is again subjective, and possibly misconceived when the evidence presented here is taken into account; although the verses certainly could have been read by later generations of Christians as an exhortation to martyrdom.

If we accept that Luke could have written these verses, and that they present Jesus in the manner of Jacob fighting a powerful foe with supernatural help, becoming Israel, the one who is strong with God or who strengthens himself with God, as LXX have it, then it is easy to see how some people in the second and third centuries CE, reading these verses, might have sought to expunge them from the Christian record. Pre-eminent among these would be the blasphemous heretic Marcion, who detested the Hebrew Scriptures and the Jews: a man with a scholarly bent, he (none better) would have been able to recognize the Gospel's allusions and indebtedness to Gen. 32. Such a thing would no doubt have stuck in Marcion's gullet: he had taken Luke as 'his' Gospel, ruthlessly cutting out the stories of Christ's infancy because of their witness to the Jewishness of Jesus. If anything, Luke 22: 43–4 would have been even more unacceptably 'Jewish' from Marcion's point of view, and it is no surprise that 'his' Gospel of Luke does not have the verses. Marcion's anti-Judaism is notorious; and it is a sad fact that he was not alone in what might broadly be termed 'Christian circles' in his virulent hostility towards the Jewish tradition.[26] *Lectio difficilior potior*: from the point of view of such early Christians as were hostile to Judaism, these verses represented a massive affront to their sensibilities, an unwelcome 'difficulty'. How much more satisfactory for those disdainers of the Jews if Luke 22: 43–4 were simply to disappear.

For other early Christians, approaching the verses without Marcion's prejudices, another problem may have suggested itself. The text could be read as evidence for a 'low Christology', and in the hands of certain interpreters might have been construed as indicating that Jesus was a frail specimen of humanity who needed

[26] See M. Simon, *Verus Israel*, 69–82.

angelic help to accomplish his mission. Faced with the possibility of these verses being invoked to support the views of dynamic Monarchians, who held that Christ had been a mere man on whom the Holy Ghost had happened to descend, orthodox scribes may have felt that the quiet removal of the problem might be no bad thing.[27] Given that they could have engendered problems both for Marcion and for the orthodox, the case for the originality of the verses is correspondingly strengthened.

3. CONCLUDING REMARKS

The two Gospels according to Luke and John were composed more or less at the same time as Josephus was writing his *Jewish Antiquities*. As we have seen, that historian carefully re-presented the Bible's account of Jacob's becoming Israel, a name whose precise meaning he defined very narrowly and carefully with reference to a single episode in the past life of the Patriarch. At the same time, Josephus laid great stress on a glorious future promised to Jacob by a 'phantasm' who wrestled with him; but he rigorously excluded from his account any suggestion that 'Israel' has to do with seeing God, with blessing, or with dawn and daybreak. No doubt, as I argued earlier, Josephus was keenly sensible of possible criticisms that his Roman readership might make of the Jews on the basis of this story; but that did not prevent him from signalling obliquely to his countrymen an awareness of different Jewish ways of reading the Bible's account, and using that account to assure them that he, too, believed that the Jewish nation would never cease. That assertion of the continuing validity of the Jewish nation might also, in some measure, have been directed against the new group called Christians, some of whom may have been suggesting that the destruction of the Temple meant the end of the Jews as God's people. It is impossible to *demonstrate* that Josephus had Christians in mind when he wrote about Israel; but the Apostle Paul's assertion that God had not cast aside His people whom He foreknew was made specifically in his epistle to Christians in Rome (Rom. 11: 2), where Josephus was writing his *Antiquities*. Josephus, then, may have had in his sights not only Jews and

---

[27] For an account of the dynamic, or adoptionist, Monarchians, see J. N. D. Kelly, *Early Christian Doctrines*, 4th edn. (Black: London, 1968), 115–19.

Romans, but also Christians active in Rome, claiming that the Jews had ceased to be God's people, when he wrote about 'Israel' as he did.

The Christian writers discussed here oddly contrast with Josephus in adhering more openly and positively to Jewish tradition on the one hand, while reinterpreting it on the other in ways inconceivable to the historian. John, whom we examined first, is the more daring of the two writers. Accepting that Israel has something to do with seeing, a matter which Josephus suppressed, he goes on to rework Jewish traditions of the sort particularly found in *Jubilees*. Like *Jubilees*, John's engagement with the Israel 'theme' has no hint of struggle with opponents; it elaborates a picture of Jesus *qua* Israel establishing and incorporating the Temple and its worship linking heaven and earth, angels and men, this Jesus, one who is greater than the Jacob 'written into' creation according to *Jubilees*, being the 'finishing' point of that creation and bringing in the final, definitive Sabbath. One observes the highly selective nature of the Evangelist's use of Jewish traditions, not least its concentration on those interpretations of Genesis 32 which link that chapter to the Temple (via Genesis 28), the feast of Tabernacles, creation, and the keeping of Sabbath. *Jubilees*, however, had said little about Israel as one who sees God; the philosopher and exegete Philo had made most of that etymology, and it is unlikely that John the Evangelist was unaware of the fact. This same Philo had linked Israel as one who sees God with Logos, both being presented as boundary figures ensuring harmony between earth and heaven. It is more than interesting to note that John's first chapter introduces his readers not only to Logos, but also to 'Israel' and 'Israelite' now redefined in terms of Jesus Christ.

I have argued that Luke 22: 43–4 most probably constituted part of the original Gospel, and that it represents an attempt by the Evangelist to portray Jacob's nocturnal struggle at the Jabbok as a type of Jesus's fight in Gethsemane against the powers of darkness. Luke's treatment of Gen. 32 is much more conservative than John's, and involves the exploitation of an ambiguity in the Hebrew and its LXX counterpart which permits the reader to discern that Jacob's supernatural angelic companion came to his help against an unnamed foe. 'Israel' here has connotations of strength and victory over the powers of evil, and fits into one of the oldest Christian understandings of Jesus's death and resurrection as a

battle against and victory over the devil, with the help of God.[28]
To a fair degree, both John and Luke stand in some sort of
continuity with their Jewish predecessors as they apply Gen. 32 to
the life of Jesus; and it could reasonably be argued that the full
meaning of what they have to tell us cannot be adequately appreciated without knowledge of the Jewish tradition. As we shall now
learn, some of their Christian successors were to view things rather
differently.

---

[28] On the theme of Christ's defeat of the devil as a central element of early
Christian belief, see G. Aulén, *Christus Victor: An Historical Study of the Three
Main Types of the Idea of the Atonement* (SPCK: London, 1970), esp. 47–60; and
for the powerful hold which it exercised in early Patristic theology, see L. Munk,
The Devil's Mousetrap (Oxford University Press: Oxford, 1997), 3–23.

Some Patristic Approaches to the
Name Israel

There can be little doubt that the majority of the Greek and Latin
Fathers of the Church particularly favoured that interpretation
of the name Israel which took it as signifying a man, or a mind,
who sees God. There is equally little doubt that the widespread
Christian interest in and use of onomastica helped to spread and
reinforce this interpretation: these lists of Hebrew names and their
meanings were immensely popular, and their influence was far-
reaching. Yet the onomastica usually offered no philological
grounds for their explanations of the names included, but gave
clear and apparently unambiguous interpretations of the Hebrew
forms.[1] So widespread and influential was the view of Israel as 'a
man who sees God' that St Jerome, writing in the last decade of the
fourth century, felt moved to comment on the matter at some
length in his *Hebrew Questions on Genesis*:

Now in the *Book of Names*, the statement which explains Israel as meaning 'a man seeing God' or 'a mind seeing God', a cliché of almost every-
body's speech, seems to me to explain the word not so much accurately as
in a manner that is forced. For Israel in this verse [Jerome is commenting

---

[1] As noted above, pp. 156–7, it is possible that Philo used onomastica for his
explanations of Hebrew names: see Grabbe, *Etymology in Jewish Interpretation*,
102–3, 172–3. The influence of Philo on early Christians in the matter of etymologies of names was considerable, and to him was attributed authorship of a Book of
Names, the *Liber Nominum*: see Eusebius, *Hist. Ecc.* II. 18. 7. No longer extant, this
work apparently listed Hebrew names in Greek forms, supplying them with explanations. F. X. Wutz, *Onomastica Sacra: Untersuchungen zum Liber Interpretationis
Nominum Hebraicorum des hl. Hieronymus* (J. C. Hinrichs: Leipzig, 1914/15), 14–24,
showed that Philo is unlikely to have been the author of this work. Jerome translated it into Latin, his work being commonly known under the title *Liber de
Nominibus Hebraicis*. But the relationship of the lost work to Jerome's version is not
straightforward: see A. Kamesar, *Jerome, Greek Scholarship, and the Hebrew Bible:
A Study of the* Quaestiones Hebraicae in Genesim (Clarendon Press: Oxford,
1993), 103–7.

on Gen. 32: 29] is written with these letters: *iod, sin, res, aleph, lamed,* which means 'prince of God', or 'directed one of God', that is, εὐθύτατος θεοῦ. But 'a man seeing God' is written with these letters: 'man' is written with the three letters *aleph, iod, sin* (so that it is pronounced *is*); and 'seeing' with three, *res, aleph, he,* and is pronounced *raa.* Then *el* is written with two letters, *aleph* and *lamed,* and means 'God' or 'strong one'. So although those men are of powerful influence and eloquence, and the shadow of those who have understood Israel as 'man or mind seeing God' weighs down upon us, we are led rather by the authority of Scripture and of the angel or God who called him Israel, than by the authority of any secular eloquence.[2]

Jerome here seems determined to convince his readers that the written form of the word Israel has absolutely no connection with 'seeing God', even spelling the word letter by letter to prove his point. He is aware, too, of the hostility this observation will arouse among his co-religionists, some of whom were deeply suspicious of his association with Jews, his preference for the Hebrew text of Scripture over the Septuagint, and his implicit criticism of the authority and prestige of Origen, whose writings had in the first place helped to popularize and establish the definition of Israel as a man or mind seeing God (see, among many examples which could be cited, *De Prin.* 4.3; *Hom. in Num.* 11. 4. 7; 12.2; 16.7; 17.4; *Ep. ad Africanum* 10; and *Comm. in Ioann.* II. 31. 25, which preserves the largest fragment extant of the *Prayer of Joseph*).[3]

Jerome evidently regarded it as his duty to correct this misapprehension, and to give an interpretation of the name which is in full accord with Jewish tradition: Israel he took as 'prince of God' in the manner of the Targumim and midrashim, and as one

---

[2] Translation of Jerome's comment on Gen. 32: 28–9 in C. T. R. Hayward, *Jerome's* Hebrew Questions on Genesis: *Translated with an Introduction and Commentary* (Clarendon Press: Oxford, 1995), 70–1. For the date of *Hebrew Questions,* see the survey of scholarly opinion in ibid. 23–7: the work was certainly composed towards the end of the fourth century, probably in the 390s, although a date in the late 380s was favoured by early twentieth-century scholars.

[3] The list of Christian authorities who followed Origen in understanding Israel to mean a man or a mind seeing God is impressive: see the evidence assembled by Kamesar, *Jerome, Greek Scholarship and the Hebrew Bible,* 119–20, who also illustrates the lengths to which this etymology could be taken. To his list may be added Novatian, *De Trinitate* 19; Hippolytus *Frg.* 16 on Gen. 49: 7; *Contra Noetum* 5; and Clement, *Paid.* 1. 7 (*PG* 8, cols. 317–20): see further Harvey, *The True Israel,* 254–255.

'directed of God', a phrase which (as we shall see presently) is related to the title Jeshurun which plays such an important role in *Gen. Rab.* 77: 1. What Jerome does not say in this section of his *Hebrew Questions*, but which he reports later in his *Comm. In Esaiam* XII. 17 on Isaiah 44: 2, is that the sound of the word 'Israel' in pronunciation may signify 'a man seeing God'.[4] Even there, however, he is keen to point to another Hebrew sense of the name as 'the upright one of God', and is apparently less than happy with the explanation still current in Christian scholarly circles. The influence of the *onomastica* was still apparent, even though, by the time Jerome was composing his commentary on Isaiah (408–10), the influence of Origen had begun to wane.

While Origen's influence certainly accounted for much of the reverence in which Christians held the name Israel as 'a man seeing God', Origen himself was not the first Christian scholar to take up this definition which has its pre-Christian roots in the writings of Philo and, most probably, in older exegetical tradition known to him. And while Jerome clearly perceived an excessive emphasis on 'seeing' in explaining the name Israel as dependent on the sway and eloquence of powerful figures within the Church, other Christian writers of earlier times were equally aware of different senses of 'Israel'. Jerome himself implicitly acknowledged as much in a section immediately preceding the passage quoted above, referring to the interpretation of the name Israel by Josephus as one who 'stood against the angel', an interpretation which Jerome himself rejected, noting that 'after careful and wide research' he had been unable to find it in the Hebrew.[5] Yet this interpretation, as we shall see presently, was known to Justin Martyr and Novatian, and was therefore not unfamiliar to other Church Fathers in both east and west. And as we shall see, early Fathers by no means discarded the idea that Israel had something to do with strength and victory over hostile forces. Against the interpretation of the name Israel advanced by Josephus, Jerome summoned the aid of Aquila, Symmachus, and Theodotion, whose renderings will claim attention later: these, too, will not have been unknown to

---

[4] For the text, see R. Gryson, *Commentaires de Jérôme sur le Prophéte Isaïe; Livres XII–XV* (Herder: Freiburg, 1998), 1348–9: 'proprie enim iuxta Hebraeos et litterarum fidem Israhel "rectus Dei" dicitur, "vir" autem "videns Deum" non in elementis, sed in sono vocis est.'

[5] On this point, see Kamesar, *Jerome, Greek Scholarship and the Hebrew Bible*, 120–1.

Greek-speaking Christian scholars.[6] Interestingly, the explanation of Israel as 'one seeing God' was not taken up either by one of the earliest Christian writers known to us, Clement of Rome, to whose writing I now turn.

1. THE FIRST EPISTLE OF CLEMENT

Clement of Rome wrote his Epistle to the Corinthian Christians around the year 95–6 CE. He did not cite passages of Scripture which speak of Jacob's change of name, nor did he record a direct interpretation of the name Israel. What he offered, however, was a perception of Jacob-Israel as the blessed ancestor of a holy and priestly people offering pure worship to God, in a manner recalling earlier Jewish authorities such as *Jubilees* and Philo. Thoughts of Exod. 19: 5–6 seem never to be far from his mind. Central in Clement's message to his disputatious audience is a reminder that they are called to be pure and holy, a priestly people, a requirement which he links directly to Jacob-Israel's status before God. He insists that his hearers approach God

in holiness of soul, lifting up pure and undefiled hands unto Him, with love towards our gentle and compassionate Father who has made us an elect portion unto Himself. For thus it is written: When the Most High dispersed the sons of Adam, He fixed the boundaries of the nations according to the number of the angels of God. His people Jacob became the portion of the Lord, and Israel the measurement of His inheritance (LXX Deut. 32: 8–9). And in another place He saith: Behold, the Lord taketh for Himself a nation out of the midst of the nations, as a man taketh the firstfruits of His threshing floor; and the holy of holies shall come forth from that nation.[7]

Without question or explanation, Clement applied to the Christians at Corinth the status of 'the Lord's portion' and 'the measurement of His inheritance', gifts which Philo in particular had associated with the name Israel.[8] Since, Clement goes on to say, they are a portion of the Holy One, they should carry out everything that pertains to holiness with the ultimate aim of acquiring

---

[6] See below, pp. 349–51.

[7] So 1 Clem. 29. The Greek text and English translation of 1 Clement are here cited according to the edition of J. B. Lightfoot, *The Apostolic Fathers* (MacMillan: London, 1926).

[8] See above, pp. 163–4.

God's blessing (1 Clem. 30). Now it will be recalled that the acquisition of blessing had exercised Jacob himself when the name Israel was conferred on him (Gen. 32: 27, 30; cf. 35: 9), and Clement seems to understand that blessing in terms of the twelve tribes and the priests and Levites who minister to the Lord. This becomes plain in 1 Clem. 31, when he answers his rhetorical question what the 'ways of blessing' might be. Abraham, he declares, was blessed because he performed righteousness and truth through faith; and Isaac's faith consists in his having been led with confidence, and as knowing the future, to be 'a willing sacrifice'. In saying this, Clement appears to betray knowledge of contemporary Jewish interpretation of Gen. 22, according to which Isaac knew and accepted his sacrificial status before his father bound him upon the altar, a significant point given the Jewish character of the exegesis which will follow.[9] For Clement will go on to speak of Jacob, whose blessing involved his departure from his land because of his brother, his service with Laban, after which the twelve tribes of Israel were *given* to him. Then he explains these ways of blessing:

If any man will consider them one by one in sincerity, he shall understand the magnificence of the gifts that are *given* to him. For of Jacob are all the priests and Levites who minister unto the altar of God; and of him is the Lord Jesus as concerning the flesh; of him are kings and rulers and governors in the line of Judah; yea and the rest of his tribes are held in no small honour, seeing that God promised saying, Thy seed shall be as the stars of heaven. They all therefore were glorified and magnified, not through themselves or their own works, but through *His will*. And so we, having been called through *His will* in Christ Jesus, are not justified through ourselves or through our own wisdom or understanding or piety or works which we wrought in holiness of heart, but through faith, whereby the Almighty God justified all men that have been from the beginning; to whom be the glory for ever and ever. Amen. (1 Clem. 32)

---

[9] Clement's brief note about the sacrifice of Isaac recalls, first, the account of the event in Josephus, *Ant.* I. 228–36, according to which Abraham told Isaac, a mature man, what was to happen, Isaac accepting this with joy and 'rushing to the altar'. We may also recall Philo's remark in *De. Abr.* 172, that Abraham and Isaac went forward to the sacrifice with equal speed not so much of body as of mind, that is, intention. Similarly Pseudo-Philo's *LAB* 32: 2–3 presented Abraham as telling Isaac beforehand that he was to be the sacrifice, and Isaac's willing acceptance of the role of victim. These pre-Rabbinic texts show the essential antiquity of the Rabbinic understanding of the Akedah: see G. Vermes, 'Redemption and Genesis xxii', in *Scripture and Tradition in Judaism*, 2nd edn. (Brill: Leiden, 1973), 193–227; R. le Déaut, *La Nuit pascale* (Pontifical Biblical Institute: Rome, 1963), 131–208.

Two things in particular should be noted here. First, the picture of Jacob as the source of the twelve tribes, followed at once by mention of this Patriarch as the source of the priesthood, the Levites being specially named, is in no way characteristic of biblical narrative, but rather of Second Temple Jewish thinking. Observe here how, just as in the *Book of Jubilees*, Jacob is first the father of the twelve tribes, and then depicted as source of the priesthood and the house of Levi; only then are kings of the house of Judah mentioned. We may also compare Philo's remarks in *De Sob.* 62–7, depicting Jacob first as origin of the twelve tribes, and then of a royal house which is 'the sanctuary in reality, and alone inviolate'.[10]

Secondly, the repeated references in the passage cited above to *the will of God* are central to Clement's argument. The blessings conferred on Abraham, Isaac, and Jacob came about through that will; and it is through that same will that Christians enjoy their status. In what follows, Clement pursues the matter further: in the created order, he declares, God gave a pattern for human behaviour by adorning Himself with good works. Human beings, therefore, must conform themselves to God's will, by doing the works of righteousness (1 Clem. 33). More precisely, this means that we must 'submit ourselves to His will; let us mark the whole host of His angels, how they stand by and minister to His will' (1 Clem. 34). This last point is illustrated with a quotation of Daniel 7: 10 and Isaiah 6: 3, the angels of the heavenly Temple ministering in worship to the Almighty, chanting aloud and proclaiming His holiness. Clement in this way transports us from earth to heaven, preparing us, after a further exhortation to follow God's faultless will (1 Clem. 35), to look steadfastly to the heights of the heavens through Jesus Christ, the 'high priest of our oblations' (1 Clem. 36).

Thus Clement's exhortation to holiness and purity on the part of the elect, who are called Jacob-Israel in line with Deut. 32: 8–9, is couched in language of a strongly sacerdotal kind, deriving its force from a sense that Jacob himself is the origin of the priesthood, itself a blessing conferred by God, Jacob and his forefathers

---

[10] See above, pp. 126–8, 185–6, Harvey, *The True Israel*, 251, suggests that the Israel spoken of in 1 Clement has nothing to do with Jews, being so closely identified with Christians that any other reference is unthinkable. Matters are not quite so clear-cut, however: the sections quoted above present Jewish institutions in a positive light, and Clement's acceptance of post-biblical Jewish tradition suggests an approval of Jewish interpretation of Scripture on certain key issues.

having merited the blessing which belong to those who do God's will. The doing of God's will is, in Clement's view, both a matter of righteous action and a liturgical service, most perfectly offered by the highest angels in a heaven where now, for the Christians, the high priest is located, a high priest towards whom all their offerings should be directed. The implication is that Clement's addressees should be perfectly conformed to the angels in their submission to God's will, to deserve the blessings whose character he has so carefully described as granted to the Jewish Patriarchs. The similarities between Clement's understanding of Jacob-Israel the elect of the Lord in union with angelic worship, and non-biblical Jewish sources analysed elsewhere in this book, are hardly difficult to discern; and they suggest that Clement himself was most likely familiar with widely known non-biblical Jewish traditions about these matters. Certainly his epistle contains no trace of polemic against contemporary Jews; on the contrary, the reverence with which he treats the Jewish institutions for worship, and the authority he accords to them, are remarkable.

2. JUSTIN MARTYR'S *DIALOGUE WITH TRYPHO*

Justin, who lived from *c.*100–*c.*165 CE, was born near Shechem, and in his youth may have acquired some general knowledge of how contemporary Jews and Samaritans interpreted the Scriptures. His *Dialogue with Trypho*, composed around 160 CE, includes a discussion of the meaning of the name Israel which is of considerable interest, since it seems indebted to a number of different Jewish ideas, albeit translated into Justin's version of Christianity, while the Jewish substratum of his exegesis remains more or less visible throughout.[11] Nonetheless, Justin's thought is sometimes difficult to follow, since he is intent on arguing several cases at once, and his use of his Scriptural material is not always consistent.

His first appeal to the story of Jacob at the Jabbok may be found in *Dial.* 58, where he is intent on demonstrating that the terms 'God', 'angel', and 'Lord' are all designations of the one supreme Being who appeared to the Patriarchs. The story of Jacob plays a key role in this: according to Gen. 31: 11, Jacob experienced an 'angel of God', who apparently defined himself further at Gen. 31:

[11] The text of the *Dialogue* is cited from M. Marcovitch, *Iustini Martyris Dialogus cum Tryphone* (de Gruyter: Berlin, 1997): translations are mine.

13 as 'the God who appeared to you in the place of God'.[12] Then Justin moved to Gen. 32: 22–30, which he quoted at length as showing that Jacob who became Israel was strong with 'God', and gave to the place where he had wrestled with the 'man' the name 'Form of God'. And he had wrestled *with a man*: Justin quoted LXX Gen 32: 25 faithfully, saying nothing about an angel. Later, at *Dial.* 126.17, he again underscored the point that this 'man' who wrestled with, appeared to, and blessed Jacob was God. He concluded his case by citing the second biblical account of Jacob's reception of the name Israel, noting that according to Gen. 35: 6–10 it was 'God' who had appeared to Jacob. Thus, Justin concluded, 'He is called God, and God He is and shall be'. He understood, like many before him, that the 'man' who engaged with Jacob was a being who could be described later in the narrative as 'God'. Then again he noted that the same being is angel, and God, and Lord, appearing 'in the form of a man' to Abraham, just as he wrestled 'in the form of a man' with Jacob. Just so do the Aramaic Targumim of Gen. 32: 25 describe the appearance of the angel who wrestled with Jacob.

The name Israel itself Justin expounded in *Dial.* 125. He asked his interlocutors what might be the 'force' or 'power' (δύναμις) of the name Israel, and when they were silent, he gave his own explanation. The sense of 'force', 'might', and 'power' emerges clearly in this exposition:

There the name Israel signifies as follows: 'A man being victorious over power' (ἄνθρωπος νικῶν δύναμιν). For 'Isra' means 'a man conquering', and 'El' means 'power'. For what Christ would become when he had been made man was also foretold through the mystery of that wrestling which Jacob wrestled with the one who appeared, inasmuch as he was ministering to the Father's will to the end that he might be the first-born of all the creatures. For after he had become man (as I have said), the devil, that is, that power (δύναμις) which is called the serpent and Satan, approached him, tempting him and striving to make him prostrate himself by demanding that he worship him.

Several traditional Jewish motifs are intertwined here. Fairly clear is the influence of LXX Gen. 32: 29 and the underlying Hebrew text, expounding Israel as one who is 'powerful' or who 'prevails' with men and providing a general Scriptural support for Justin's exegesis. The 'Is' element in the atomized 'Isra'

---

[12] See also Justin, *Dialogue* 58: 6–8.

presumably represents Hebrew '*îš*, 'man', as St Jerome would later explain it; and Hebrew *'el* can certainly mean 'powerful one' or 'strong one', as well as 'God'. The remaining '-*ra*' element in 'Isra' might well represent some contracted form of a triliteral Hebrew stem beginning with a sibilant, to be explained either via Hebrew *śārāh*, 'exert onself, strive'; *śārar*, 'be a prince, get superiority'; or *šārar*, 'be hard, be firm'. All of these stems figured in earlier Jewish explanations of the name, and any one of them might lie behind Justin's etymology. Indeed, the etymology he gives is clearly related to Jewish prototypes, which he could easily have encountered in his early days in Shechem. But the overwhelming sense of the name Israel for Justin is that of one who conquers a power, a power in the supernatural realm, as we shall see.

Justin also regarded the events at the Jabbok as a prophetic 'mystery' pointing to the future: to this limited and general extent, he recalls the treatment of this passage by Josephus, a Jewish author who, like Justin, explained the name Israel in terms of resistance to a supernatural power. It is no more necessary to assume that Justin had read Josephus than it is to suggest that he had a detailed knowledge of Hebrew; for much of what he says about 'Israel' at this level he could have gleaned from the world of his boyhood. His Christian interpretation of the episode, however, led him to conclude that Jacob's struggle at the Jabbok mysteriously prefigured Christ's conflict with and victory over that 'power' called the devil (see Matt. 4: 1–11), who went away from the confrontation 'broken and convicted'. In this conflict, Justin declared, Christ ministered to his Father's will, to become 'the first-born of all creatures', words recalling Paul's epistle to the Colossians (1: 15). Reference to the 'first-born' is of some interest, given God's designation of Israel as His first-born son in Exod. 4: 22, and the role played by Israel as first-born in the writings of Philo, the *Prayer of Joseph*, and other post-biblical texts treated above; indeed, one particular aspect of these Jewish texts he may represent later on, as we shall see. But at this precise point Justin does not develop it, and one is left wondering whether the notion of 'first-born' was introduced into his exegesis because of some general *Christian* understanding of the name Israel which he felt it appropriate to include. Here we may note that, while Colossians chapter 1 does not speak directly of Christ engaged in conflict like Jacob at the Jabbok, Col. 2: 15 certainly envisages Christ triumphing over principalities and

powers by his death, his subsequent resurrection marking him out
as 'first-born from the dead' (Col. 1: 18).

This last point is possibly strengthened when *Dial*. 75 is brought
into the picture; for in that place Justin states that Christ himself
was called Israel. More will be said about the setting of this statement in a moment; but its presence serves only to complicate what
is already a difficult exegetical state of affairs. According to *Dial*.
125, the character who wrestled with Jacob and named him Israel
was 'God', 'angel', 'Lord'—we have seen that Justin holds them as
coterminous—in the form of a man. Applied 'through a mystery'
to Christ, consistent interpretation would suggest that Christ, prefigured by Jacob-Israel, had been in conflict with God. On the
surface, this would make little sense, and would contradict Justin's
explicit statement that Christ had been in battle with a power not
divine, but demonic, namely Satan himself. The only possible way
out of this morass is provided through LXX Gen. 32: 29, which
Justin himself quoted, if we may take the ambiguous Greek to
mean that Jacob (prefiguring Christ) had wrestled *with the help* of
God-angel-Lord *against* some unnamed power, now revealed by
Justin as Satan. While this does make sense within Justin's exegetical framework, he himself provides no clue that this meaning
might be the one he intends, unless such a thing be implied in what
follows in *Dial*. 125. For he goes on to declare that the Jabbok
incident also predicted Christ's passion (the angel's numbing of
Jacob's thigh he interpreted as a reference to Christ's agony and
passion on the cross); and this passion Justin would have understood from the New Testament writings as both initiated by God
(Acts 2: 23) and at the same time a combat against the devil (John
12: 31). Thinking of this kind may go some way to explain what
could be seen as a 'dual identity' of Jacob's companion at the
Jabbok as now an angel or God fighting *in company with him*, and
now the devil fighting with him as powerful adversary.

Whatever the solution to all this, Justin next announced that
Christ's name was Israel:

Now Israel was the name for him from above, which he named the blessed
Jacob by blessing him with his own name, and through this proclaiming
that all who flee through him to the Father are blessed Israel.

This strongly suggests that 'Israel' is a heavenly name. It is 'from
above', Greek ἄνωθεν, a term used by the fourth Gospel to describe
Christ's heavenly origin and status: see John 3: 31, describing him

as the one who comes from above (ἄνωθεν) and who is before all things; and compare Christ's statement in John 8: 23 that he is 'from above' (ἐκ τῶν ἄνω). At the same time, it is strongly reminiscent of Philo's statement about God's first-born, the heavenly Logos, in *De Conf. Ling.* 146: one of the names Philo ascribed to that Logos was 'Israel'. We may also recall the tenor of the *Prayer of Joseph*, that Israel is the heavenly designation of the one whose name among human beings is Jacob. Again, much of what Justin has to say appears to have strong affinities with Jewish sources; but it has also been given a very definite Christian 'twist', so as to make the term Israel now apply to those who flee to God (as Jacob had fled from his brother Esau, according to *Dial.* 125) through an Israel now identified as Christ.[13]

These observations throw some light on the earlier passage in *Dial.* 75 where Justin had identified Israel as Jesus. He noted that the Book of Exodus recorded that God's Name had not been made plain to Abraham and Jacob, but that it was announced to Moses. What follows is not, as might be expected, a discussion of Moses at the burning bush, but a reference to Exod. 23: 20. In that verse, God spoke to Moses about the angel who should go in front of the Israelites as they journeyed towards the Land of Israel; he is urged to pay attention to this angel because, God declares, 'My Name is in him'. This angel, who brought the Israelites into their territory, was none other than Jesus, according to Justin:

> For if you examine this carefully, you would also understand the fact that the name of that being who said to Moses 'for My Name is in him' was Jesus. For he was also called Israel, and he appointed this name for Jacob.

In this passage, the name Israel is clearly the name of an angelic being: although this understanding has been implicit in what Justin has said elsewhere, it is here made very plain. Again, Jewish antecedents for the angelic status of Jacob's adversary have already been noted, particularly in the writings of Philo and in the *Prayer of Joseph*; but Justin here states that Israel was the name of the angel who gave Jacob his new name Israel. This statement *may* represent the earliest witness to an opinion voiced in some later Jewish texts, that Jacob at the Jabbok was confronted by an angel called Israel: the eighth–ninth century CE work *Pirqe de Rabbi Eliezer* (*PRE* 37: 2) afforded one instance of this which was

---

[13] See further ibid. 11: 5; 123: 7; and Simon, *Verus Israel*, 171–3.

examined above, and J. Z. Smith's commentary on the *Prayer of Joseph* noted other occurrences of the same view in *Sefer Raziel* 4b, 41b, and other sources.[14] All of these are post-Talmudic in date. Given Justin's patent concern to promote a Christian interpretation of the incident at the Jabbok, it is necessary to keep an open mind whether he owed the identification of the angel as Israel to a Jewish tradition which, in any event, cannot be traced in Jewish sources written in Hebrew or Aramaic anywhere near contemporary with him. Indeed, the most likely source for Justin's thinking is Philo, who in *De Conf. Ling.* 146 had given Israel as a secondary title of the Logos. Justin's primary concern, however, is to show that Jacob was a prefiguration of Christ; that he received the name Israel from the heavenly Israel, who was Christ; that this constituted a blessing; and that those who wish to be similarly blessed must 'flee to the Father' through this Israel, who is Christ.

In fine, the Christian Apologist Justin seems to have reformulated a number of non-biblical Jewish traditions in his exposition of Jacob's struggle at the Jabbok. From Jewish sources earlier than or contemporary with his writing, he could have derived:

(1) the sense that name Israel has to do with victory: so LXX, Josephus, and Philo in particular;

(2) the notion that Jacob struggled with a supernatural power, and that this struggle portended future events: so Josephus especially;

(3) the widespread view that this adversary could be described, *inter alia*, as an angel: so Demetrius the Chronographer, Philo, Pseudo-Philo's *LAB*, and the *Prayer of Joseph*, whose basic contents were probably known in Justin's time;

(4) the tradition that 'Israel' was in reality the designation of a heavenly being: so Philo, and the *Prayer of Joseph*;

(5) and, just possibly, the opinion that Jacob's adversary represented a power opposed to the elect people of God, a power

---

[14] See above, pp. 288–9, and Smith, 'Prayer', 702, where he also notes that this angel can sometimes be called Israēl, a form found (for instance) in Akhmim papyrus of Greek 1 Enoch 10: 1, on which see Nickelsburg, *1 Enoch 1*, 216, who suggests that this name may be a corruption of some other name, Sariel or Uriel. The form Istrahel, however, is found also in Old Latin texts of Gen. 32: 29, where the name Israel is expounded: see the evidence collected in B. Fischer, *Vetus Latina Genesis* (Herder: Freiburg, 1951–4), on Gen. 32: 29, 33; and 34: 7, but not at Gen. 35: 10. See further below, n. 30.

like Esau-Rome and the demonic force animating such opposition.

By 'Jewish sources', I mean explications of Scripture that Justin may have encountered in his days at Shechem, coming to him by word of mouth and from various quarters. Included in those 'Jewish sources' might also be some written material: here I have in mind the writings of Philo, whose name figures prominently in the list set out above, and whose philosophy, with its claims about the Logos, was evidently of interest to Justin. What he may have received from Judaism, however, Justin was determined to mould into Christian form; and it is the Christian reading of the tradition that prevails in his *Dialogue*, however exegetically perplexing the results may sometimes appear. Thus both Jacob and the 'angel' can be used as prefigurations of Jesus Christ in one set of arguments, while in another the 'angel' or 'man' prefigures the demonic 'power', whom Jacob-Israel-Christ will defeat. Such problems seem not to have worried him; and the same Justin who set out to prove from Scripture that Jesus was God, angel, and Lord, was the Justin who in the last resort was prepared to suffer death for that conviction.

3. CLEMENT OF ALEXANDRIA'S *PAIDAGOGOS*

Clement (*c.*150–215 CE), leader of the Christian catechetical school in Alexandria, dealt with Jacob's change of name in his *Paidagogos* 1: 7. As the title of this work indicates, Clement was concerned with instructing his hearers and readers;[15] and in this section he asserted that the Christians' instructor is 'the holy God Jesus, the Logos, who is the guide of all humanity'. He offered proof of his assertion from Scripture, demonstrating that it is God Himself who is our tutor from Deut. 32: 10–12. He reinforced this by quoting Exod. 20: 2 and Gen. 17: 1–2, verses in which God addresses human beings directly in first person speech: this, Clement argued, was evidence that God Himself had announced clearly that He was the instructor par excellence. God had 'openly appeared' as Jacob's instructor during the latter's first visit to Bethel (Gen. 28: 15); and later He was said to have wrestled with the Patriarch. Clement quoted LXX Gen. 32: 25, with its mention of a 'man' who wrestled

---

[15] For the text, see *PG* 8, cols. 317–20. Cf. also *Paidagogos* 1: 9, *PG* 8, cols. 341–2. Translations are mine.

with Jacob: that man was the instructor, 'who led, and brought, and wrestled with, and anointed the athlete Jacob against an evil one'. His words are very similar to Philo's descriptions of Jacob's encounter with the Logos, who trained him in his athletic wrestling bout with the passions and led him to victory, a pattern of interpretation now familiar to us. One obvious difference separating Philo and Clement, however, lies in their identification of Jacob's adversary. For Philo it is the passions, while Clement spoke of an 'evil one'. In this detail, Clement recalls Justin's remarks examined in the previous section about the name Israel; but it will be observed that Clement, at this juncture, has said nothing at all about that name. Indeed, he was careful not to, because he himself would need to make use of the name later in a setting which he wished to keep apart from notions of struggle and of wrestling against evil and the devil.

Like Philo before him, Clement went on to identify the one who had wrestled with Jacob as the Logos. That Logos was the trainer, the instructor of human beings. When asked his name, he refused to divulge it, 'because he kept back the new name for the new people'. Here we have Clement's reason for not bringing into earlier discussion the name Israel: he was writing under the conviction that this name is the proper designation of the Christians, the 'new people' whom, as we shall see, the events at the Jabbok prefigured. Indeed, Clement asserted that when he wrestled with Jacob, the Logos had not been named, since the Lord God had not yet become man. However close he may stick generally to Philo's interpretations, Clement's words stand revealed as driven by Christian assumptions which, already in this early period, apparently need no explicit articulation. It would not suit his argument at this point to accept in its entirety Philo's famous report about the various names of the Logos set out in *De Conf. Ling.* 146, for in that passage the Logos is the most senior of the angels with many names. Clement was concerned to stress that Jacob had seen God *tout court*; he had called the place of his encounter 'Face of God' since he knew that he had seen God face to face, the 'Face of God' being the Logos by whom God is manifested and made known. It is almost as an afterthought that Clement now added that Jacob was also named Israel, 'because he saw God the Lord': this mention of the name he could not avoid, but his reluctance straightforwardly to present it as a gift or blessing granted to Jacob by his opponent is striking.

Evidently, then, Clement had been aware of Philo's interpretation of events at the Jabbok and of the name Israel, and much of this he reproduced, presenting the Logos as an instructor and athletic trainer to a Jacob engaged in a wrestling bout. Even his description of Jacob's adversary as an 'evil one', although owing something to Christian theology expressed already by Justin, is not so far from Philo's perception of the human passions as forces hostile to the contemplation of God. It is those aspects of Philo's exegesis which he does not repeat, however, which show how far Clement has travelled from the opinions of his Jewish mentor. Where Philo had spoken of Jacob's victory in his wrestling crowned with a change of name, a change which also involved him in a change of character from Jacob the 'practiser' to Israel 'the one who sees God', Clement was silent. Clement's Logos was unnamed when Jacob met him at the Jabbok: Philo's had many names, and these included the name Israel. What Jacob perceived, said Clement, was indeed God in his yet-unnamed Logos by whom He is manifested to human beings; but his Christian readers would understand that the 'new name' Israel was kept back for a 'new people', and was properly applicable to Jesus, the Logos incarnate as the instructor and tutor to lead the world to God.

4. TERTULLIAN

Tertullian lived from *c*.160 to *c*.225 CE, and desired a martyr's death which would proclaim his fidelity to Christ and ensure his place in heaven. He displayed great hostility to the Jews of his day, insisting that God's covenant with them had been a temporary affair; for the most part, he continued to refer to them as Israel.[16] On the other hand, the element of struggle and victory inherent in the biblical explanation of the name Israel according to the LXX and Old Latin versions appealed to him, since it appeared to accord biblical authority to the early Christian desire to embrace martyrdom as the highest goal of the Christian vocation. Writing in *Adv. Marc.* IV. 39, he quoted Christ's command to his followers (Luke 21: 12–14) not to be anxious about what they should say before hostile tribunals.[17] Like Balaam, to whom God gave a message he

[16] See Simon, *Verus Israel*, 77–8, 119–21.

[17] *PL* 2, col. 456. Tertullian's understanding of Israel as 'one who prevails with God' is ultimately drawn from LXX Gen. 32: 29 through an Old Latin source; and he stands as one of a small band of Fathers to stay to close to this biblical explanation of the name, which is represented also in Origen's writings and, possibly, in those of Epiphanius: see Kamesar, *Jerome, Greek Scholarship, and the Hebrew Bible*, 119.

had never thought of, and like Moses, who was slow of speech, they would be prompted by God in a manner irresistible, just as Isaiah had predicted that 'one shall say, I am the Lord's and call himself by the name of Jacob; and another shall surname himself by the name of Israel' (Isaiah 44: 5). Such simple and public confession was, for Tertullian, the mark of the martyr, the 'one who prevails with God'; and that is exactly what the name Israel means. Tertullian offered no further explanation, although we may gloss his words by noting that the martyr, as far as Tertullian was concerned, surely prevails with God's help.

In *De Carne Christi* 3, Tertullian cited Jacob's struggle with the angel along with other biblical passages to show that angels could take human flesh, and even wrestle with human beings; but of the name Israel he said nothing.[18] It may be that he found the Scriptural note that Jacob had seen God face to face problematic, for he never alluded to Israel as signifying 'one who sees God'. Indeed, in *Adv. Prax.* 14 he quoted Gen. 32: 30 to illustrate the teachings of the modalist monarchians, heretics who seem to have argued that the Scriptural verses telling how Moses spoke with God face to face, and how Jacob saw God face to face, somehow proved that the invisible Father and the visible Son were identical persons, since both operated 'face to face' with human beings.[19] Tertullian strenuously opposed this exegesis, while perhaps leaving to us traces of the exegesis which the monarchians themselves had adopted. Tertullian apparently wished to steer clear of any suggestion that the name Israel involved seeing God face to face: for him, it was principally a lofty title worthy of the martyr.

5. ORIGEN

For many early Christians, Origen (*c*.185–*c*.254 CE), Clement's successor as head of the school at Alexandria, possessed an authority second only to the apostolic writings which they had received by tradition; as St Jerome was to remark, his endorsement of the explanation of Israel as 'a man, or a mind, seeing God' had far-reaching effects. This state of affairs may not be unconnected with the fact that Origen evidently knew a certain amount of Hebrew, which he had acquired in his attempts to revise the text

[18] *PL* 2, col. 757.
[19] *PL* 2, col. 172.

of LXX.[20] Like Clement, he owed a debt to Philo in the matter, as in his *Hom. in Num.* 16, where he defined Jacob as representing struggle against powers and forces and rulers of this world, while Israel signified 'one who sees God' through purity of belief and thought. Jacob-Israel thus represents two worlds, Origen declared: as Jacob, he battled in this world, of which Egypt is a symbol. He went down into Egypt with his sons, a matter which would attract Origen's attention in his other writings. But as Israel, he sees God; that is, he sees the world to come and its bliss.[21]

Philo's teachings are once again reflected in Origen's *Hom. in Exod.* 11, where he understood the name Jacob to refer to the one who struggles in order to become Israel,[22] and again in his *Comm. in Cant., Prologue* 3. This whole passage portrayed Abraham as symbolizing moral philosophy and obedience, and Isaac natural philosophy: Jacob became Israel 'because of his seeing God'.[23] The whole explication strongly recalls Philo's words about the Patriarchs in *De Mut. Nom.* 11. Interestingly, Origen went on to expound the name Israel, not with reference to Gen. 32: 22–33, but in relation to Gen. 28: 10ff., the account of Jacob's first visit to Bethel. Jacob was called Israel because he saw the heavenly hosts and the house of God and the way of the angels and the ladder reaching from earth to heaven: such interpretation of Israel in light of the Bethel episode is again characteristic of Philo, and recalls the detailed exegesis set out in *De Som.* I. 129–31.

Jacob and his offspring, the Israelites, went down into Egypt. Origen accorded to this event a high position in the history of salvation. In *De Prin.* IV. 1. 24 he wrote that the 'going down' of the 'holy fathers' into Egypt was granted to the world by divine providence, its purpose being the enlightenment of others and of the human race.[24] To them alone, he insisted, was granted communion with God; for their race alone is said to see God, this being the interpretation of the name Israel.

[20] For an assessment of Origen's knowledge of Judaica, see especially N. R. M. de Lange, *Origen and the Jews* (Cambridge University Press: Cambridge, 1976); and Kamesar, *Jerome, Greek Scholarship, and the Hebrew Bible*, 4–29, 98–103.

[21] See his *In Numeros Homilia* 16, *PG* 12 (333), col. 699; the whole work is of interest in view of his contrast between the darkness and obscurity of Balaam's prophecies and the light and vision represented by Israel.

[22] See *In Exodum Homilia* 11, *PG* 12 (170), col. 378.

[23] See *In Canticum Canticorum Prologus, PG* 13 (32–3), col. 76.

[24] See *PG* 11 (187), col. 395.

6. NOVATIAN

The presbyter Novatian (died *c*.257–8 CE) was Origen's contemporary, and apparently assumed his readers' knowledge of several of the interpretations surveyed above. He discussed Gen. 32: 22–33 in his *De Trin*. 19, like Justin noting that the angel of God spoken of at Gen. 31: 11–13 was to be indentified with God and, more specifically, with God the Son who is angel, God, and also man. This last point Novatian demonstrated from Gen. 32: 24ff. Jacob had wrestled with a man, but called the place where the fight took place 'vision of God'; hence Novatian calculated that Jacob's opponent had prefigured Christ, who is both God and man.[25]

So much is familiar from Justin and other earlier Fathers. Yet in what follows Novatian introduced a new theme. Jacob, he observed, had wrestled with the 'man' who prefigured Christ, and proved strong enough to hold him fast, thus foreshadowing the struggle that would arise between Christ and the sons of Jacob. In the Gospel accounts of Christ's passion, Novatian declared, Jacob's people stand revealed as more powerful than Christ, gaining 'the victory of their iniquity'; then, because of their 'crime', they hesitated in the path of faith and salvation, a hesitation foreshadowed in Jacob's limping after his wrestling bout.[26] Novatian maintained that they are still stronger than Christ, yet stand in need of his mercy and his blessing. All this obviously depends on an interpretation of Israel as one who is strong, struggles, prevails, and is victorious; and Novatian's particular use of it seems dictated by a need to explain why Judaism has survived at all in the face of Christian fulfilment of it, reflecting perhaps some specific contretemps with Judaism which had involved him personally.

Jacob was named Israel; and Novatian continued by observing that, if Israel was the man who sees God, then the Lord was showing that the one who wrestled with Jacob was not only man, but also God. Jacob did indeed see God as he wrestled, even though he

---

[25] Passages from Novatian are cited in the translation provided in A. Roberts and J. Donaldson (eds.), *The Ante-Nicene Fathers*, vol. 5 (Eerdmans: Grand Rapids, Mich., repr. 1978), 611–44.

[26] The Jews' attitude to Jesus was described as a 'crime' by Origen, *Contra Celsum* IV. 22, and became common in Christian writings after his time: see Simon, *Verus Israel*, 68.

was holding fast 'the man' in his struggle; yet again, however, Novatian returned to the struggle as prefiguring the conflict between Christ and the sons of Jacob who, although they had the strength, were inferior because they had been shown to be guilty. In these words, there is no mistaking Novatian's evaluation of contemporary Jews, and he concluded his remarks by reiterating his contention that Jacob's wrestling with a man who was also God was in reality a type fulfilled in Christ, proving the latter to be both God and man. If the etymology of Israel as 'one who sees God' has any significance in this exposition, it is directed only towards this end: the man whom Jacob saw was God, and Jacob's victory over him, seemingly effective even in Novatian's day, was not the end of the story.

Clement of Rome, Justin, Tertullian, and Novatian are among the exceptions, as it were, which prove Jerome's rule that most Christian teachers up to his time had followed Origen, and understood the title Israel in terms of a man or a mind seeing God. The 'exceptions' explored here are of interest, inasmuch as they betray some lingering association with Jewish exegesis surveyed in earlier chapters; may in passing attest to its antiquity and currency in their own day; and may, too, reflect some general Christian awareness of it as a living reality which required their attention. It should, however, be emphasized that the majority of these writers had already concluded that Israel was a title properly belonging to the Christian Church, and wrote accordingly: any search or investigation on their part for the *meaning* of the name Israel was undertaken with that belief in mind and sometimes, as we have seen, with hostile intent towards Jews. St Jerome alone of early Christian writers seems to have made a concerted effort to undertake research into the meaning of the name; and it will be evident that he took some care over this matter.

7. ST JEROME

Jerome was born sometime in the 340s, and died in 420 CE. In his *Hebrew Questions on Genesis*, commenting on Gen. 32: 28–9, he presented a sustained and detailed examination of what the name Israel might mean, a section of which has already been quoted at the beginning of this chapter. After translating the Hebrew text of the relevant verses, he remarked at once that the explanation of the name given by Josephus in his *Jewish Antiquities*, to the effect

Jacob was called Israel 'because he stood against the angel', could
not be substantiated on the basis of the Hebrew. Jerome stated that
he had undertaken wide research before coming to this conclusion.
Some of that research probably features in what he goes on to say;
and in dismissing Josephus he was presumably motivated by what
he had come to understand as the meaning of the Hebrew verb
שׂרית, which he transliterated as *sarith* and interpreted as meaning
'prince'. Indeed, Jerome set Josephus aside by asking rhetorically
why he should have to seek for the conjectures of individuals, when
the Bible itself gave the meaning of the name?

At this point he again quoted Gen. 32: 29, and proceeded to list
three Greek renderings of the Hebrew clause כי שׂרית עם אלהים,
'because you have striven with God'. The first is that of Aquila, a
Jew responsible for translating anew the Hebrew Bible into Greek
(around the year 125 CE), in a manner generally described as 'very
literal'.[27] He took the words to mean 'because you have ruled with
God', discerning in the Hebrew explanation of Israel the stem
śārar, 'rule, be a prince'. As we have seen, this interpretation
coheres with that offered by the Aramaic Targumim, *b. Ḥull.* 92a,
and other Rabbinic sources referred to earlier: its appearance in
Aquila's version supports its claim to be an old, traditional interpretation linking Israel to the world of the great angelic princes. A
little later, Jerome would declare that Jacob's opponent had
declared him to be a prince because he had wrestled with one who
was either God or an angel, different people interpreting the word
God in this verse in different ways. Since that was so, how much
more would he be able to fight with men, that is, with Esau, whom
he should not fear? Again, we note the broad similarity between
this exposition of the name and those sections of *Gen. Rab.* 77–8
where Jacob's encounter with the angel (Esau's guardian) is viewed
both as training for his future struggle with Esau-Rome, and as a
sure indication that he will ultimately prevail.[28]

---

[27] See, however, the careful study of the nature of Aquila's translation technique
and its purpose outlined by L. L. Grabbe, 'Aquila's Translation and Rabbinic
Exegesis', *JJS* 33 (1982), 527–36. For Aquila's date and background, see Tov,
Textual Criticism, 146, and L. J. Greenspoon, article 'Aquila's Version', *ABD*, i.
320–1.

[28] See above, pp. 255–9. The possible influence of Rabbinic traditions on Jerome
as he explicates the translations of Aquila and Symmachus is (rightly, in my view)
suggested by Kamesar, *Jerome, Greek Scholarship, and the Hebrew Bible*, 121–2, not
least because, like *b. Ḥull.* 92a, *Gen. Rab.* 78: 3, and TO Gen. 32: 29, he makes use

While the meaning of Aquila's Greek translation of the Hebrew is straightforward, the second Greek rendering which Jerome cited is highly problematic: he merely quoted it, without further comment. It is the version of Symmachus, who translated the key Hebrew word for 'you have striven' with the Greek ἦρξω, the second person singular aorist middle of ἄρχω, meaning 'you have begun'. Jerome himself, however, may well have understood Symmachus to mean much the same as Aquila, who had translated the Hebrew with ἦρξας, another active form of ἄρχω, a verb which can also (as in Aquila's translation here) bear the sense of 'to rule'. Quite what Symmachus meant is open to debate; and it is even possible that the fragment of Symmachus at our disposal is corrupt.[29] The meaning 'you began, you have begun', however, is very likely what Symmachus intended, as Alison Salvesen indicates in her study of this translator; she further suggests that he perceived in the Hebrew text of Gen. 32:29 the root שׁרי, an Aramaic stem which can have the sense of 'begin'.[30] Indeed, his Greek can mean 'to begin a religious act', in relation to God; perhaps Symmachus had in mind an understanding of Israel of the sort displayed by *Jubilees*, where the emergence of this title heralds the inauguration of a fully developed religious system on earth.[31] In any event, the third Greek translation which Jerome quoted, that of Theodotion, is the same as LXX Gen. 32: 29, and need not detain us further.

of a noun, 'prince', rather than a verbal form 'you have been a prince, gained superiority' in his exposition of Gen. 32: 29, even though Aquila, Symmachus, and Theodotion had all been faithful to the Hebrew and used verbal forms. Note also his criticism of Butterweck, *Jakobs Ringkampf*, 185–6, and Miller, *Mysterious Encounters*, 215, both of whom seem to have misunderstood Jerome's remarks at this juncture.

[29] See further Kamesar, *Jerome, Greek Scholarship, and the Hebrew Bible*, 122.

[30] See Salvesen, *Symmachus in the Pentateuch*, 49–50, and 283–97 for the identity and dates of this translator. Her mention of the Aramaic stem שׁרי may shed some light on another matter, for the ithpael form of this root, אשׁתרי, may have been used by the marginal gloss of TN of Gen. 32: 25 to describe Jacob's struggle with the angel: see Díez Macho's suggestion in his edition of *Neophyti 1 Génesis*, 217. I observed above (n. 14) that some sources name Jacob's angelic opponent as Istraēl: perhaps this form was derived from the Aramaic words under consideration here, or through another Aramaic form also noted by Salvesen, namely אשׁתרר, 'be strong', used by the Syriac translator at Peshitta of Gen. 32: 29 to translate Hebrew 'you have striven'. The name Istraēl would thus be a suitable designation for an opponent of Jacob.

[31] See above, pp. 130–3.

In the course of explaining that Israel means 'prince of God', it will be recalled, Jerome provided an alternative explanation of the name as ἐυθύτατος θεοῦ, 'most direct, upright one of God', which he explained more fully in his *Comm in Os.* 3 on Hosea 12: 4(3) as being related to the Hebrew word יָשָׁר, 'upright, honest'. As Kamesar has shown, Aquila's influence on Jerome may be clearly detected here, and not least in his use of the adjective in the superlative degree to express what 'Israel' means. For the Greek word 'most direct, most upright' which Jerome cites is used only by Aquila among Greek translators of the Bible, and then to represent the title Jeshurun.[32] This rare word Jerome himself explained as 'most upright' and 'right, upright', noting also LXX's translation of it as 'most beloved', in his *Comm. in Is.* XII. 17 on Isaiah 44: 2; and this observation of Jerome's is striking, given the central role accorded by *Gen. Rab.* 77: 1 to the title Jeshurun in introducing a most complex series of insights into the implications of Jacob's being designated Israel. In this matter again, he may owe as much to contemporary Rabbinic theological thinking absorbed from his Hebrew teachers as he did to Aquila and Symmachus, whose versions he had diligently studied before choosing appropriate foreign equivalents for the Hebrew originals.

Jerome alone among early Christian exegetes had sufficient knowledge of Hebrew to realize the exegetical possibilities inherent in the Hebrew form of the term Israel. In his Vulgate translation of the Bible, however, he was careful to preserve some links with the LXX familiar to his Christian readership, although he could not resist including some of the insights he had gained from his Hebrew studies. Thus in the Vulgate version of Gen. 32: 28(29), Jacob's opponent explains that he will be called Israel 'because if you have been strong against God, how much the more will you prevail against men!' His wider researches, however, remained available to Christian scholars in the west; for many, indeed, they provided for years to come the only access available to the *Hebraica veritas* which Jerome himself had come to value so dearly.

---

[32] For all this, see further Kamesar, *Jerome, Greek Scholarship, and the Hebrew Bible*, 123–5.

Conclusion

Towards the end of the Psalter, the Psalmist speaks of the nation named after their ancestor Israel as a people near to God (Psalm 148: 14); and the Almighty Himself declared, with reference to the priests, that He would sanctify those who draw near to Him (Lev. 10: 3). Although the Hebrew Bible very rarely speaks of Israel directly and explicitly in terms of her status as 'near to God' (the Psalm verse is most unusual in this respect, and commentators often have difficulty in finding any other similar verses to compare with it), for the ancient exegetes Israel's nearness to God, and thus by implication her priestly status, seem to have provided the starting-point for investigations which led the interpreters to consider in great depth what might be the character of this nation and its ancestor suggested by the biblical accounts of the name Israel and its appearance in the historical record. The Bible insists that none may remotely be compared to the Holy One (Isaiah 40: 18, 25; 46: 5); yet this Holy One is the Holy One of Israel (Isaiah 10: 20), the people who are near to Him. The exegetes set themselves the task of further explicating this, each in ways appropriate to contemporary needs and concerns.

The angelic qualities revealed by the exegetes as inherent in the name Israel should come as no surprise; for beings nearest to the divine are precisely those 'ministers of flame and fire' which the prophets and seers of the Hebrew Bible had so often described (cf. Psalm 104: 4). Among the texts examined here, perhaps *Jubilees* and the *Prayer of Joseph* most clearly set forth the implications of Israel's angelic connections. The former does not doubt the necessary qualifications on Israel's part for the continuation of those connections: they consist of holiness expressed through a particular understanding of purity; a legitimate priesthood appointed by God, duly instructed in the ways of worship revealed to the Fathers in ages past; and a royal house ordering civil life in accord with the divine will revealed in the Law. Such, *Jubilees* would have it, was the substance of God's command to Moses, that Israel be a kingdom, priests, and a holy nation (Exod. 19: 6). Israel is at home in two worlds, and must operate in both: the *Prayer of Joseph*, though little is preserved of it, makes this point as forcibly as *Jubilees*. Unlike the *Prayer*, however, *Jubilees* is clear that the priestly service of Israel on earth corresponds to the priestly service of the highest orders of angels in heaven; that the order and stability of creation is linked to this union of heavenly and earthly service of God; and that one day in the future Israel will be the centre of a renewed universe whose stability will be forever guaranteed by God, resident on Zion in His everlasting sanctuary.

That Philo's thoughts on the subject of Israel should reflect the thinking of *Jubilees* in certain respects is one of the most interesting results of this survey. Best known for his explanation of the name Israel as 'one who sees God', Philo's interest in Israel's status as a boundary figure involved in both earthly and heavenly realms is not far removed in its general understanding from the central argument of *Jubilees*, that Israel is that earthly polity to whom the Almighty has entrusted His service on earth, so that harmony (a word dear to Philo's understanding of Israel) might be maintained between the various constituent parts of the created order in general and the human creature in particular. The subduing of the earthly passions, which Philo insists is necessary for those who wish to 'see God' and thus become 'Israel', is itself only possible with that training and instruction which divine reason itself provides. Neither *Jubilees, the Prayer*, nor Philo regarded the process whereby Jacob became Israel as anything but arduous; even *Jubilees*, which omitted the biblical account of Jacob's struggle at the Jabbok, envisaged the emergence of Israel as the product of a protracted, demanding, and difficult period of preparation in Jacob's life, involving setbacks and opposition, and even now under threat from the powers of evil (see *Jubilees* 10: 7–9 for the continuing threat posed by Mastema and the forces of evil to the people of Israel).

That Israel's nearness to God should be associated with struggle is a central message of the biblical accounts of Jacob's change of name. The LXX version of this is instructive on several counts, and foreshadows many of the discussions which later exegetes would take up and develop. This is so whether or not those who translated the Hebrew accounts of Jacob's change of name to Israel did so with the conscious *intention* of producing narratives of the sort I have surveyed here. What is significant is that their translation (whatever intentions may have lain behind it)—as a 'stand-alone' representation of what the Hebrew Bible available to them signified—can be read as a particular account of what 'Israel' means. Their account, as we now have it, resulted in the emphasizing of certain aspects of the narrative; one of these is the matter of seeing, of vision, of divine oversight, which is indicated by a particular choice of vocabulary and is impressed upon the reader by the variety of ways in which it is expressed. I noted the importance of *epiphany* in this version as a means of expounding what Israel might mean; this word, massively significant for the Greek-speaking world but very rarely used by the LXX translators, in their version is associated with angels of God, whose presence in and effect upon the narrative I have taken care to note. The translation which those Greek-speaking Jews produced made no attempt to conceal the fact that the name Israel was conferred on Jacob after a wrestling bout, a physical combat in which he had been strong, or had strengthened himself with God, thereby equipping himself with the qualifications necessary for what was yet to come in his life.

If Philo 'interiorized' this combat which Jacob had endured to acquire the title Israel, Rabbinic authorities found the element of struggle involved a constant inspiration in their dealing with a non-Jewish world which could sometimes display great hostility towards Judaism. We have seen how midrash *Genesis Rabbah* in particular elaborated a many-coloured picture of Israel being trained in many different ways by God to face the most terrifying of enemies, secure in the knowledge that Israel is a name representing permanence in the midst of the bewildering changes of earthly dominions, and even of the angelic hosts. So near, so close, is Israel to God that the likeness engraved on the Throne of Glory itself is none other than that of the Patriarch Jacob who became Israel, this nearness to God guaranteeing the permanence which characterizes the title Israel in distinction from transient angelic and terrestrial potentates. At the same time, this midrash allows us to see quite clearly how such nearness to God on Israel's part cannot be separated from Israel's eagerness to order her life according to the halakhah; for central to the midrashic discussion is the commandment forbidding consumption of 'the sinew of the thigh' (Gen. 32: 33), a commandment which derives from, and in some sense constitutes a memorial of, the struggle of Jacob-Israel at the ford of the Jabbok.

Some centuries before the redaction of *Genesis Rabbah*, the earliest extant Rabbinic compilations preserved in the Mishnah and the Tosefta had singled out from the story of Jacob's reception of the name Israel the law of the 'sinew of the thigh' as a matter of the highest importance. The Qumran document 4Q158 indicates that serious debate about the precise application of this commandment had already begun in Second Temple times; even so, the authors of *Jubilees* and the *Prayer of Joseph*, Ben Sira, Philo, and Pseudo-Philo pay little attention to it. For some Qumran Jews and the Rabbis, however, the commandment of the 'sinew of the thigh' is central; and the discussions of it in the Mishnah, Tosefta, and other Rabbinic texts surveyed here should leave us in no doubt that conformity to halakhic principles as determined by the Rabbinic authorities is a fundamental aspect of Israel's character as it was understood by the Rabbis, and this conformity to the halakhah is what ultimately underlies Israel's status as permanent, eternally significant in the sight of the Almighty. Whatever angelic qualities, of whatever kind, may adhere to Israel—and the Rabbinic texts we have examined make no attempt to conceal those qualities—Israel's agreement in her earthly existence with halakhic authority (which, by definition, is not in heaven: see R. Joshua's rejoinder to R. Eliezer b. Hyrcanus recorded in *b. Baba Metzia* 59b) is constitutive of her status as near to God. The privileges attendant on the right observance of this commandment can hardly be overestimated, since it constantly calls to the Jewish mind, as day succeeds day and year succeeds year, what the Patriarch Jacob-Israel endured, and how he triumphed over adversity in this world.

The theme of angelic jealousy towards Jacob-Israel has surfaced in a number of the documents examined here, most especially in the Babylonian Talmud tractate *Ḥullin*, the Aramaic Targumim, and the *Prayer of Joseph*, all of which are careful to indicate Israel's superiority to the angels in the sight of God. A powerful interest in Israel's liturgy is evident both in the Talmud and the Targumim, as well as in some midrashic sources I have noted: the formal service of the synagogue is understood as being offered along with the heavenly service of the angels, yet nonetheless taking precedence over it in several respects. As in the case of the 'sinew of the thigh', so in the case of the formal worship of God, the actions of Israel on earth, carried out in conformity with halakhic principles laid down by Rabbinic authority, bring Israel to a nearness to God which the highest angels might envy. In some of the documents examined here this nearness is expressed in terms of Israel as God's unique son, His first-born, who *ipso facto* merits special blessings. Israel's first-born status, indeed, is divinely announced, without qualification, at Exod. 4: 22, and this biblical datum strongly influenced many of the later attempts to define Israel's character.

Thus we find the witnesses to the text of Hebrew Ben Sira speaking now of Israel as first-born; now as blessed; now as Jeshurun, a rare, biblical, honorific title which the LXX translators had understood as indicating Israel's position as God's beloved, unique, and thus first-born son. Centuries after Ben Sira's time, the title Jeshurun was to reappear in *Genesis Rabbah* as signifying the best and noblest in Israel, who are there said to be 'like God'. *Jubilees* expressed matters more obliquely; but this document perceived Israel as 'written into' God's creation of the universe from the very first, while Philo was to address the matter of Israel as first-born son of God directly. So also the *Prayer of Joseph* concerned itself with this matter; and I have argued here that this mysterious document had as one of its principal objectives the explication of how it was that the Bible could present Israel as God's first-born son, and at the same time as son of Isaac and Rebekah.

Of all the Jewish documents considered here, the attempt of Josephus to expound the title Israel appears the most idiosyncratic. I have suggested that the historian's very short account of events at the Jabbok are patient of a number of different interpretations, depending on whether the reader is a Jew, a non-Jew with some knowledge of the Bible (most likely LXX), or a non-Jew with no knowledge of Judaism. In restructuring the Bible's account of how Jacob became Israel, Josephus acts quite drastically; the resulting narrative as it left his pen is utterly distinctive, and may possibly be understood on one level as directed towards his Roman patrons, seeking to allay their fears that Jews are inveterate fighters, intent on anti-Roman military activity. Yet Josephus predicts a great future for Israel, which he understood as a title describing a people that would never be brought to an end, and which could never fully be overcome by others. It is just possible that he was aware of the Christians, who had taken to themselves the name Israel, claiming that all the privileges of that title had been transferred from the Jews to themselves.

The New Testament contains little that directly engages with Jacob's change of name to Israel; but what little there is commands attention. I have argued here that the first chapter of Saint John's Gospel may with profit be read in the light of contemporary discussions of what the name Israel might mean, and who might be properly entitled to make use of it. The Evangelist seems aware of an explanation of Israel as 'one who sees God', and of associations of the name Israel specifically with angels and the heavenly world. Although it is impossible to be certain, some engagement on the Evangelist's part with Jewish traditions on these points is not inconceivable. In the case of the third Evangelist, however, I have argued that a well-known crux in his account of the Passion can very likely be resolved, if we are prepared to admit his use of the LXX version of Jacob's struggle at the Jabbok. If this be the case, then Saint Luke sought to present the sufferings of Jesus in the light of Jacob's wrestling bout, a fight from which the Patriarch emerged victorious with a new name, Israel. For the Evangelist, the triumphant resurrection of Jesus from the dead would then display the full significance of the title Israel granted to Jacob at the beginning of Israel's history. It might also be that the Evangelist was concerned, in some manner, to justify Christian use of the name Israel, and sought to do so by interpreting Jesus's agony in Gethsemane as the antitype of Jacob's struggle at the Jabbok.

The final chapter on the Church Fathers is deliberately selective, and is concerned to illustrate a matter that is sometimes neglected. Although much Patristic writing, following Philo, accepts that Israel means something to do with 'seeing God', and applies this vision of the divine to the Christian Church, there remains within the Patristic tradition an awareness of other senses that the name might bear. It is not invariable, either, that the Church Fathers always used the term in anti-Jewish polemic. The Epistle of Clement of Rome repays attention here, as do the writings of Origen, who seems to have been in direct contact with Jews on this matter. I have no opportunity here to take these matters further; but it is known that in the period before the first Council of Nicea (325 CE) relations between Christians and Jews in some places were cordial, even friendly; and the positive appreciation of the name Israel in some of the Patristic documents may reflect such contacts between the two religions. We end with Saint Jerome: he bequeathed his learning to a Western Church which, with a few notable exceptions, soon came to lack scholars willing to learn Hebrew and to take Jewish traditions seriously. Jerome was certainly capable of attacks on Jews—he was rather given to attacking people, even his closest friends and allies—and on his own admission, his Jewish teachers had been generous to him. At the same time, Jerome preserved for the Christian West important Jewish traditional material, including his observations on the meaning of the name Israel which could, in the course of time, lead his co-religionists to a better-informed understanding of the nature of that Israel in which they claimed an inheritance.

Bibliography

ABEGG, M. Jr., FLINT, P., and ULRICH, E., *The Dead Sea Scrolls Bible: The Oldest Known Bible Translated for the First Time into English* (Harper-Collins: New York, 1999).

ALTER, R., *The World of Biblical Literature* (SPCK: London, 1992).

ANDERSON, A. A., *New Century Bible Psalms*, 2 vols. (Oliphants: London, 1972).

ASHTON, J., *Understanding the Fourth Gospel* (Clarendon Press: Oxford, 1991).

AULÉN, G., *Christus Victor: An Historical Study of the Three Main Types of the Idea of the Atonement* (SPCK: London, 1970).

BACHER, W., *Die Agada der Tannaiten*, 2 vols. (Strassbourg, 1890).

BARR, J., *The Concept of Biblical Theology* (SCM: London, 1999).

BARTHES, R., 'La Lutte avec l'ange: analyse textuelle de Genèse 32.23–33', in R. Barthes, F. Bovon, *et al.* (eds.), *Analyse Structurale et exégèse biblique* (Delachaux et Niestlé: Neuchâtel, 1971), 27–40.

—— *The Semiotic Challenge* (Hill & Wang: New York, 1988).

BARTON, J., *Reading the Old Testament: Method in Biblical Study*, 2nd edn. (Darton, Longman, & Todd: London, 1996).

BERGER, K., *Das Buch der Jubiläen: Jüdische Schriften aus hellenistisch-römischer Zeit*, Band II, Lieferung 3 (Mohn: Gütersloh, 1981).

BERNSTEIN, M., 'Contours of Genesis Interpretation at Qumran: Contents, Contexts and Nomenclature', in J. Kugel (ed.), *Studies in Ancient Midrash* (Harvard University Press: Cambridge, Mass., 2001), 57–85.

BIRNBAUM, E., *The Place of Judaism in Philo's Thought: Israel, Jews, Proselytes*, Brown Judaic Studies 290. Studia Philonica Monographs, 2 (Scholars Press: Atlanta, 1996).

BOGAERT, P.-M., 'Les Trois Rédactions conservés et la forme originale de l'envoi du Cantique de Moïse (Dt 32, 43)', in F. Lohfink (ed.), *Das Deuteronomium: Entstehung, Gestalt, und Botschaft* (University Press: Louvain, 1985), 329–40.

BORGEN, P., *Bread from Heaven* (Brill: Leiden, 1965).

—— *Philo of Alexandria—An Exegete for His Time* (Brill: Leiden, 1997).

BRETTLER, M. Z., *The Creation of History in Ancient Israel* (Routledge: London, 1998).

BRIGGS, C. A., and BRIGGS, E. G., *The Book of Psalms*, 2 vols. (Clark: Edinburgh, 1906).

BROOKE, G. J., *Exegesis at Qumran: 4QFlorilegium in its Jewish Context*, JSOT Supp. Series 29 (JSOT Press: Sheffield, 1985).

—— 'Reworked Pentateuch^a or Reworked Pentateuch A?', *DSD* 8 (2001), 219–41.

BROWN, C. A., *No Longer Be Silent: First Century Jewish Portraits of Biblical Women* (John Knox Press: Louisville, Ky., 1992).

BROWN, R. E., *The Gospel According to John*, 2 vols., Anchor Bible (Doubleday: New York, 1966).

—— *The Death of the Messiah: From Gethsemane to the Grave*, 2 vols., Anchor Bible Reference Library (Doubleday: New York, 1994).

BUTTERWECK, A., *Jakobs Ringkampf am Jabbok. Gen. 32, 4ff in der Jüdischen Tradition bis zum Frühmittelalter*, Judentum und Umwelt 3 (Peter Lang: Frankfurt-am-Main, 1981).

CAQUOT, A., 'Grandeur et pureté du sacerdoce: Remarques sur le Testament de Qahat (4Q542)', in Z. Zevit, S. Gitin, and M. Sokoloff (eds.), *Solving Riddles and Untying Knots: Biblical, Epigraphic and Semitic Studies in Honor of Jonas C. Greenfield* (Eisenbrauns: Winona Lake, 1995), 39–44.

CHARLES, R. H., *The Book of Jubilees* (Black: London, 1902).

CHILDS, B. S., *Introduction to the Old Testament as Scripture* (SCM: London, 1979).

CLARKE, E. G., 'Jacob's Dream at Bethel', *Studies in Religion*, 4 (1974–5), 367–77.

CLINTON, K., 'The Sanctuary of Demeter and Kore at Eleusis', in N. Marinatos and R. Hägg (eds.), *Greek Sanctuaries: New Approaches* (Routledge: London, 1993), 110–24.

COHEN, G. D., 'Esau as Symbol in Early Medieval Thought', in A. Altmann (ed.), *Jewish Medieval and Renaissance Studies* (Harvard University Press: Cambridge, Mass., 1967), 19–48.

DAUMAS, F. and MIGUEL, P., *De Vita Contemplativa, Les Oeuvres de Philon d'Alexandrie* 29, ed. R. Arnaldez, C. Mondésert, and J. Pouilloux (Cerf: Paris, 1963).

DELLING, G., 'The "One Who Sees God" in Philo', in F. E. Greenspahn, E. Hilgert, and B. L. Mack (eds.), *Nourished with Peace: Studies in Hellenistic Judaism in Memory of Samuel Sandmel* (Scholars Press: Chico, 1984), 27–41.

DE LANGE, N. R. M., *Origen and the Jews* (Cambridge University Press: Cambridge, 1976).

DEMBITZ, L. N., Article 'Shemini 'Atseret', *JE*, xi. 270.

DI LELLA, A. A., Article 'Wisdom of Ben-Sira', *ABD*, vi. 931–45.

DOGNIEZ, C. and HARL, M., *La Bible d'Alexandrie, 5: Le Deutéronome* (Cerf: Paris, 1992).

DORIVAL, G., *La Bible d'Alexandrie, 4: Les Nombres* (Cerf: Paris, 1994).

EHRMAN, B. D. and PLUNKETT, M. A., 'The Angel and the Agony: The Textual Problem of Luke 22: 43–44', *CBQ* 45 (1983), 401–16.

EISSFELDT, O., *The Old Testament: An Introduction*, trans. P. R. Ackroyd (Blackwell: Oxford, 1966).

ENDRES, J. C., *Biblical Interpretation in the Book of Jubilees*, *CBQ* Monograph Series 18 (Catholic Biblical Association of America: Washington, DC, 1987).

FALK, D., *Daily, Sabbath and Festival Prayers in the Dead Sea Scrolls* (Brill: Leiden, 1998).

FELDMAN, L. H., 'Josephus's Portrait of Jacob', *JQR* 79 (1988–9), 101–51.

——Article 'Josephus', *ABD*, iii. 981–98.

——*Jew and Gentile in the Ancient World: Attitudes and Interactions from Alexander to Justinian* (Princeton University Press: Princeton, 1993).

FISHBANE, M., *Biblical Myth and Rabbinic Mythmaking* (Oxford University Press: Oxford, 2003).

FITZMYER, J. A., *The Gospel According to Luke X–XXIV*, Anchor Bible, 28A (Doubleday: New York, 1985).

FLUSSER, D., 'Sanktus und Gloria', in O. Betz, M. Hengel, and P. Schmidt, (eds.), *Abraham Unser Vater: Festschrift für Otto Michel zum 60. Geburtstag* (Brill: Leiden, 1963), 129–52.

FOHRER, G., *Introduction to the Old Testament*, trans. D. Green (SPCK: London, 1970).

FRIEDLANDER, G., *Pirqê de Rabbi Eliezer (The Chapters of Rabbi Eliezer the Great)* (Hermon Press: New York, 1965).

GAMBERONI, J., Article 'מקוֹם *māqôm*', *TDOT*, viii. 532–44.

GARCÍA MARTÍNEZ, F., and TIGCHELAAR, E. J. C., *The Dead Sea Scrolls Study Edition* 2 vols. (Brill: Leiden, 1997, 1998).

GLESSMER, U., *Einleitung in die Targume zum Pentateuch*, Texte und Studien zum Antiken Judentum, 48 (Mohr: Tübingen, 1995).

GOLDBERG, A. M., *Untersuchungen über die Vorstellung von der Schekhinah in der frühen Rabbinischen Literatur*, Studia Judaica, 5 (de Gruyter: Berlin, 1969).

GOODENOUGH, E. R., *By Light, Light: The Mystic Gospel of Hellenistic Judaism* (Yale University Press: New Haven, 1935).

——*The Politics of Philo Judaeus: Practice and Theory* (Yale University Press: New Haven, 1938).

GOULET, R., *La Philosophie de Moïse. Essai de reconstitution d'un commentaire préphilonien du Pentateuque* (J. Vrin: Paris, 1987).

GRABBE, L. L., *Etymology in Early Jewish Interpretation: The Hebrew Names in Philo*, Brown Judaic Studies, 115 (Scholars Press: Atlanta, 1988).

——'Aquila's Translation and Rabbinic Exegesis', *JJS* 33 (1982), 527–36.

GRAY, J., *I and II Kings: A Commentary* (SCM Press: London, 1964).

GREEN, J. B., 'Jesus on the Mount of Olives (Luke 22: 39–46): Tradition and Theology', *JSNT* 26 (1986), 29–48.

—— *The Gospel of Luke* (Eerdmans: Grand Rapids, Mich., 1997).

GREENSPOON, L. J., Article 'Aquila's Version', *ABD*, i. 320–1.

GROSSFELD, B., *The Targum Onqelos to Genesis*, The Aramaic Bible, 6 (Clark: Edinburgh, 1988).

—— *Targum Neofiti 1: An Exegetical Commentary to Genesis* (Sepher-Hermon Press: New York, 2000).

GUNKEL, H., *Genesis*, trans. M. E. Biddle (Mercer University Press: Macon, Ga., 1997).

GUTBROD, W., Article 'Ἰουδαῖος, Ἰσραήλ, Ἑβραῖος in Greek Hellenistic Literature', *TDNT*, iii. 369–75.

HANSON, J., 'Demetrius the Chronographer', in J. H. Charlesworth (ed.), *The Old Testament Pseudepigrapha*, vol. 2 (Darton, Longman & Todd: London, 1985), 843–54.

HARL, M., *La Bible d'Alexandrie, 1: La Genèse* (Cerf: Paris, 1986).

—— G. DORIVAL, and O. MUNNICH *La Bible Grecque des Septante. Du Judaïsme Hellénistique au Christianisme ancien* (Cerf: Paris, 1988).

HARLÉ, P. and PRALON, D., *La Bible d'Alexandrie, 3: Le Lévitique* (Cerf: Paris, 1988).

HARRIS, H. A., *Greek Athletics and the Jews* (University of Wales Press: Cardiff, 1976).

HARVEY, G., *The True Israel: Uses of the Names Jew, Hebrew, and Israel in Ancient Jewish and Early Christian Literature* (Brill: Leiden, 1996).

HASPECKER, J., *Gottesfurcht bei Jesus Sirach. Ihre religiöse Struktur und ihre Literarische und doktrinäre Bedeutung*, Analecta Biblica, 30 (Pontifical Biblical Institute: Rome, 1967).

HAYES, C. E., *Gentile Impurities and Jewish Identities* (Oxford University Press: Oxford, 2002).

HAYWARD, C. T. R., 'Jacob's Second Visit to Bethel in Targum Pseudo-Jonathan', in P. R. Davies and R. T. White (eds.), *A Tribute to Geza Vermes: Essays on Jewish and Christian Literature and History*, *JSOT* Supp. Series 100 (Academic Press: Sheffield, 1990), 175–92.

—— *Jerome's* Hebrew Questions on Genesis: *Translated with an Introduction and Commentary* (Clarendon Press: Oxford, 1995).

—— *The Jewish Temple: A Non-biblical Sourcebook* (Routledge: London, 1996).

—— 'Balaam's Prophecies as Interpreted by Philo and the Aramaic Targums of the Pentateuch', in P. J. Harland and C.T.R. Hayward (eds.), *New Heaven and New Earth: Essays in Honour of Anthony Gelston* (Brill: Leiden, 1999), 19–36.

—— 'Targumic Perspectives on Jacob's Change of Name to Israel', *JAB* 3 (2001), 121–37.

——'The Sanctification of Time in the Second Temple Period: Case Studies in the Septuagint and Jubilees', in S. C. Barton (ed.), *Holiness Past and Present* (Clark: London, 2003), 141–67.

HENGEL, M., *Judaism and Hellenism*, trans. J. Bowden, 2 vols. (SCM: London, 1974).

HUNZINGER, H., 'Babylon als Deckname für Rom und die Datierung des I. Petrusbriefes', in H. Reventlow (ed.), *Gottes Wort und Gottes Land: Festschrift für H.-W. Hertzberg* (Vandenhoeck & Ruprecht: Göttingen, 1965), 67–77.

JACOBSON, H., *A Commentary on Pseudo-Philo's* Liber Antiquitatum Biblicarum, 2 vols. (Brill: Leiden, 1996).

JAPHET, S., *I and II Chronicles* (SCM Press: London, 1993).

JAUBERT, A., *La Notion d' alliance dans le Judaïsme aux abords de l'ère chrétienne* (Seuil: Paris, 1963).

KAMESAR, A., *Jerome, Greek Scholarship, and the Hebrew Bible: A Study of the* Quaestiones Hebraicae in Genesim (Clarendon Press: Oxford, 1993).

KELLY, J. N. D., *Early Christian Doctrines*, 4th edn. (Black: London, 1968).

KIPPENBERG, H. G., *Garizim und Synagoge* (de Gruyter: Berlin, 1971).

KNIGHT, D. A., Article 'Tradition History', *ABD*, vi. 633–8.

KOGUT, S., 'Midrashic Derivations Regarding the Transformation of the Names Jacob and Israel According to Traditional Jewish Exegesis: Semantic And Syntactic Aspects', in M. Cogan, B. L. Eichler and J. H. Tigay (eds.), *Tehillah le-Moshe: Biblical and Judaic Studies in Honor of Moshe Greenberg* (Eisenbrauns: Winona Lake, 1997), 219*–233* [in Hebrew].

KRAUSS, S., *Griechische und lateinische Lehnwörter im Talmud, Midrasch und Targum*, 2 vols. (repr. Olms: Hildesheim, 1965).

KUGEL, J., 'Levi's Elevation to the Priesthood in Second Temple Writings', *HTR* 86 (1993), 1–64.

——*In Potiphar's House: The Interpretive Life of Biblical Texts*, 2nd edn. (Harvard University Press: Cambridge, Mass., 1994).

——'4Q369 "Prayer of Enosh" and Ancient Biblical Interpretation', *DSD* 5 (1998), 119–48.

——*Traditions of the Bible: A Guide to the Bible As It Was At the Start of the Common Era* (Harvard University Press: Cambridge, Mass., 1998).

KUGLER, R. A., *From Patriarch to Priest: The Levi-Priestly Tradition from* Aramaic Levi *to* Testament of Levi, SBL Early Judaism and its Literature 9 (Scholars Press: Atlanta, 1996).

KUHN, K. G., Article 'Ἰσραήλ, Ἰουδαῖος, Ἑβραῖος in Jewish Literature after the OT', *TDNT*, iii. 359–69.

KYSAR, R., Article 'John, the Gospel of', *ABD*, iii. 912–31.

LANE FOX, R., *Pagans and Christians in the Mediterranean World from the Second Century AD to the Conversion of Constantine* (Penguin Books: Harmondsworth, 1986).

LAQUEUR, R., *Der jüdische Historiker Flavius Josephus* (Munchow: Giessen, 1920).

LARCHER, C., *Le Livre de la Sagesse ou La Sagesse de Salomon*, Études Bibliques N.S. 1–3 (Gabalda: Paris, 1983–5).

LE BOULLUEC, A. and SANDEVOIR, P., *La Bible d'Alexandrie, 2: L'Exode* (Cerf: Paris, 1989).

LE DÉAUT, R., *La Nuit pascale* (Pontifical Biblical Institute: Rome, 1963).

—— *Targum du Pentateuque, 1: Genèse* (Cerf: Paris, 1978).

—— *Targum du Pentateuque, 4: Deutéronome* (Cerf: Paris, 1980).

LEVENSON, J. D., *The Death and Resurrection of the Beloved Son* (Yale University Press: New Haven, 1993).

LEVISON, J. R., *The Spirit in First Century Judaism* (Brill: Leiden, 1997).

LEVY, B. B., *Targum Neophyti 1: A Textual Study*, vol. 1 (Lanham: New York, 1986).

LIEBERMAN, S., *Tosefta Ki-Fshuta: A Comprehensive Commentary on the Tosefta. Order Zera 'im Part 1* (Jewish Theological Seminary Of America: New York, 1955) [in Hebrew].

—— *The Tosefta according to Codex Vienna: the Order of Zera 'im* (Jewish Theological Seminary of America: New York, 1955).

LOEWE, R., 'Gentiles As Seen By Jews after CE 70', in W. Horbury, W. D. Davies, and J. Sturdy (eds.), *The Cambridge History of Judaism*, Vol. 3, *The Early Roman Period* (Cambridge University Press: Cambridge, 1999), 250–66.

LUND, S. and FOSTER, J., *Variant Versions of Targumic Traditions Within Codex Neofiti 1*, SBL Aramaic Studies 2 (Scholars Press: Missoula, 1977).

LUST, J., EYNIKEL, E., and HAUSPIE, K., *A Greek-English Lexicon of the Septuagint*, 2 parts (Deutsche Bibelgesellschaft: Stuttgart, 1992, 1996).

MACINTOSH, A. A., *Hosea*, International Critical Commentary (Clark: Edinburgh, 1997).

McNAMARA, M., *The New Testament and the Palestinian Targum to the Pentateuch*, Analecta Biblica, 27 (Pontifical Biblical Institute: Rome, 1966).

—— *Targum Neofiti 1: Genesis*, The Aramaic Bible 1A (Clark: Edinburgh, 1992).

MAHER, M., *Targum Pseudo-Jonathan: Genesis, The Aramaic Bible*, vol 1b (Clark: Edinburgh, 1992).

MAIER, J., *Die Qumran-Essener: Die Texte vom Toten Meer. Band II Die Texte der Höhle 4* (Reinhardt: München, 1995).

MANN, J., *The Bible As Read and Preached in the Old Synagogue*, 3 vols., with Prolegomenon by Ben Zion Wacholder (Ktav: New York, 1971).

MARBÖCK, J., 'Das Gebet um Rettung Zions Sir 36, 1–22 (G: 33, 1–13a: 36, 16b–22) im Zusammenhang der Geschichtsschau ben Siras', in J. B. Baur and J. Marböck (eds.), *Memoria Jerusalem. Freundesgabe Franz Sauer zum 70. Geburtstag* (Akademische Druck-u. Verlagsanstalt: Graz, 1977), 93–116.

MARSHALL, I. H., *The Gospel of Luke: A Commentary on the Greek Text*, The New International Greek Testament Commentary (Paternoster Press: Exeter, 1978).

MARTIN-ACHARD, R., 'Un Exégète devant Genèse 32: 23–33', in R. Barthes, F. Bovon, *et al.* (eds.), *Analyse structurale et exégèse biblique* (Delachaux et Niestlé: Neuchâtel, 1971), 41–62.

MAUSER, U. W., *Christ in the Wilderness: The Wilderness Theme in the Second Gospel and Its Basis in Biblical Tradition*, SBT 39 (SCM Press: London, 1963).

METZGER, B. M., *A Textual Commentary on the Greek New Testament* (United Bible Societies: London, 1971).

MEYER, G., *Index Philoneus* (de Gruyter: Berlin, 1974).

MIDDENDORP, T., *Die Stellung Jesus ben Siras zwischen Judentum und Hellenismus* (Brill: Leiden, 1973).

MILGROM, J., *The JPS Torah Commentary: Numbers* (Jewish Publication Society: Philadelphia/New York, 1990).

MILLER, W. T., *Mysterious Encounters at Mamre and Jabbok*, Brown Judaic Studies, 50 (Scholars Press: Chico, 1984).

MOBERLY, R. W. L., *The Bible, Theology, and Faith: A Study of Abraham and Jesus* (Cambridge University Press: Cambridge, 2000).

MOLONEY, F. J., *The Gospel of John*, Sacra Pagina, 4 (Liturgical Press: Collegeville, 1998).

MONTGOMERY, J. A. and GEHMAN, H. G., *The Books of Kings* (Clark: Edinburgh, 1951).

MULDER, M. J., Article 'שׁרוּן *y^e šurûn*', *TDOT*, vi. 472–7.

MUNK, L., *The Devil's Mousetrap* (Oxford University Press: Oxford, 1997).

MUÑOZ LEON, D., *Gloria de la Shekina en los Targumim del Pentateuco* (Consejo Superior de Investigaciones Científicas Instituto 'Francisco Suárez': Madrid, 1977).

NEUSNER, J., *Genesis Rabbah: The Judaic Commentary to the Book of Genesis. A New American Translation*, 3 vols. (Scholars Press: Atlanta, 1985).

——*Judaism in the Matrix of Christianity* (Fortress Press: Philadelphia, 1986).

NICKELSBURG, G. W. E., *Jewish Literature Between the Bible and the Mishnah* (SCM: London, 1981).

——'The Bible Written and Expanded', in M. E. Stone (ed.), *Jewish Writings of the Second Temple Period*, *CRINT* Section 2 (Van Gorcum: Assen, 1984), 89–156.

——*1 Enoch 1: A Commentary on the Book of 1 Enoch Chapters 1–36; 81–108* (Fortress Press: Minneapolis, 2001).

NITZAN, B., *Qumran Prayer and Religious Poetry* (Brill: Leiden, 1994).

OGNIBENI, B., *La Seconda Parte del* Sefer 'Oklah We'oklah (Instituti de Filología del CSIC: Madrid–Fribourg, 1995).

OLOFSSON, S., *God is My Rock: A Study of Translation Technique and Theological Exegesis in the Septuagint*, Coniectanea Biblica OT Series, 31 (Almqvist and Wiksell International: Stockholm, 1990).

PLUMMER, A., *St. Luke*, International Critical Commentary, 2nd edn. (Clark: Edinburgh, 1922).

POTIN, J., *La Fête Juive de la Pentecôte*, 2 vols., Lectio Divina, 65 (Cerf: Paris, 1971).

RAJAK, T., *Josephus: The Historian and his Society* (Duckworth: London, 1983).

RAST, W. E., *Tradition History and the Old Testament* (Fortress Press: Philadelphia, 1972).

RICKENBACKER, O., *Weisheitsperikopen bei Ben Sira*, Orbis Biblicus et Orientalis, 1 (Vandenhoeck & Ruprecht: Göttingen, 1973).

RÖNSCH, H., *Das Buch der Jubiläen oder die Kleine Genesis* (Fues's Verlag: Leipzig, 1874).

ROSENBAUM, M. and SILBERMANN, A. M., *Pentateuch with Targum Onkelos, Haphtaroth and Rashi's Commentary* (Hebrew Publishing Co.: New York, 1946).

ROWLAND, C. C., 'John 1: 51: Jewish Apocalyptic and Targumic Tradition', *NTS* 30 (1984), 498–507.

SALVESEN, A., *Symmachus in the Pentateuch* (Victoria Press: Manchester, 1991).

SAMELY, A., *Rabbinic Interpretation of Scripture in the Mishnah* (Oxford University Press: Oxford, 2002).

SANDERS, E.P., *Jesus and Judaism* (SCM: London, 1985).

SANDERS, J. T., *Ben Sira and Demotic Wisdom*, SBL Monograph Series, 28 (Scholars Press: Chico, 1983).

SCHÄFER, P., *Rivalität zwischen Engeln und Menschen. Untersuchungen zur Rabbinischen Engelvorstellung*, Studia Judaica, 8 (de Gruyter: Berlin, 1975).

——*Der verborgene und offenbare Gott* (Mohr: Tübingen, 1991).

SCHAPER, J., 'The Unicorn in the Messianic Imagery of the Greek Bible', *JTS* n.s. 45 (1994), 117–36.

——*Eschatology in the Greek Psalter*, WUNT 2. Reihe 76 (Mohr: Tübingen, 1995).

SCHIFFMAN, L. H. and SWARTZ, M. D., *Hebrew and Aramaic Incantation Texts from the Cairo Geniza: Selected Texts from Taylor-Schechter Box K1* (Sheffield Academic Press: Sheffield, 1992).

SCHÜRER, E., *The History of the Jewish People in the Age of Jesus Christ*, 3 vols. in 4, revised and ed. G. Vermes, F. Millar, M. Goodman, *et al.* (Clark: Edinburgh, 1973–87).

SCHWARZ, E., *Identität durch Abrenzung. Abgrenzungsprozesse in Israel im 2. vorchristlichen Jahrhundert und ihre traditionsgeschichtlichen Voraussetzungen, zugleich ein Beitrag zur Erforschung des Jubiläenbuches* (Europäische Hochschulschriften. Theologie: Frankfurt-am-Main, 1991).

SCHWARZ, J., 'Jubilees, Bethel, and the Temple of Jacob', *HUCA* 56 (1985), 63–86.

SEGAL, J. B., *The Hebrew Passover from the Earliest Times to A.D. 70* (Oxford University Press: Oxford, 1963).

SEGAL, M., '4QReworked Pentateuch or 4QPentateuch?' in L. H. Schiffman, E. Tov, and J. C. VanderKam (eds.), *The Dead Sea Scrolls: Fifty Years after their Discovery 1947–1997. Proceedings of the Jerusalem Congress July 20–25, 1997* (Israel Exploration Society and Shrine of the Book: Jerusalem, 2000), 391–9.

SEGAL, M. Z., *Sefer Ben Sira Ha-Shalem* (Bialik: Jerusalem, 1958) [in Hebrew].

SHEMESH, A. and WERMAN, C., 'Halakhah at Qumran: Genre and Authority', *DSD* 10 (2003), 104–29.

SIMON, M., *Versus Israel: A Study of the Relations Between Christians and Jews in the Roman Empire* AD 135–425, trans. H. McKeating (The Littman Library of Jewish Civilization: London, 1996).

SKEHAN, P. W., 'A Fragment of the "Song of Moses" (Deut. 32) from Qumran', *BASOR* 136 (1954), 12–15.

——'Qumran Manuscripts and Textual Criticism', *VTSupp.* 4 Congress Volume Strasbourg (Brill: Leiden, 1957), 148–60.

——'Structures in Poems on Wisdom: Proverbs 8 and Sirach 24', *CBQ* 41 (1979), 365–79.

SKEHAN, P. W. and DI LELLA, A. A., *The Wisdom of Ben Sira*, Anchor Bible 39 (Doubleday: New York, 1987).

SMALLWOOD, E. M., *Philonis Alexandrini Legatio ad Gaium* 2nd edn. (Brill: Leiden, 1970).

SMELIK, W. F., *The Targum of Judges* (Brill: Leiden, 1995).

SMITH, J. Z., 'The Prayer of Joseph', in J. H. Charlesworth (ed.), *The Old Testament Pseudepigrapha*, vol. 2 (Darton, Longman & Todd: London, 1985), 699–714.

SPLANSKY, D. M., 'Targum Pseudo-Jonathan: Its Relationship to Other Targumim, Use of Midrashim and Date', unpublished Ph.D thesis, Hebrew Union College: Cincinnati (1981).

STEIN, E., 'Zur apokryphen Schrift "Gebet Josephs" ', *MGWJ* 81 (1937), 280–6.

STRACK, H. L. and STEMBERGER, G., *Einleitung in Talmud und Midrasch*, 7th edn. (Beck: München, 1982).

STUCKENBRUCK, L. T., 'Revision of Aramaic-Greek and Greek-Aramaic Glossaries in *The Books of Enoch: Aramaic Fragments of Qumrân Cave 4* by J. T. Milik', *JJS* 41 (1990), 13–48.

——*Angel Veneration and Christology*, WUNT 2, Reihe 70 (Mohr: Tübingen, 1995).

SWARTZ, M. D., *Scholastic Magic: Ritual and Revelation in Early Jewish Mysticism* (Princeton University Press: Princeton, 1996).

TARADACH, M., *Le Midrash. Introduction à la Littérature midrashique* (Labor et Fides: Geneva, 1991).

TCHERIKOVER, V., *Hellenistic Civilization and the Jews* (Atheneum Books: New York, 1974).

THOMPSON, A. L., *Responsibility for Evil in the Theodicy of IV Ezra*, SBL Dissertation Series, 29 (Scholars Press: Missoula, 1977).

TIGAY, J. H., *The JPS Torah Commentary: Deuteronomy* (The Jewish Publication Society: Philadelphia, 1996).

TOV, E., *Textual Criticism of the Hebrew Bible* (Fortress Press: Minneapolis/Van Gorcum: Assen, 1992).

——'4QReworked Pentateuch: A Synopsis of Its Contents', *RQ* 16/64 (1995), 647–53.

URBACH, E. E., *The Sages: Their Concepts and Beliefs*, trans. I. Abrahams 2 vols. (Magnes Press: Jerusalem, 1979).

VANDERKAM, J., 'The Putative Author of the Book of Jubilees' *JSS* 26 (1981), 209–17.

——Article 'Jubilees', *ABD*, iii. 1030–2.

——'Genesis 1 in Jubilees 2', *DSD* 1 (1994), 300–21.

——*Calendars in the Dead Sea Scrolls* (Routledge: London, 1998).

VAN GOUDOEVER, J., *Fêtes et Calendriers Bibliques*, Théologie Historique, 7, 3rd edn. (Beauchesne: Paris, 1967).

VAN SETERS, J., *Prologue to History: The Yahwist as Historian in Genesis* (Westminster/John Knox Press: Louisville, 1992).

VATTIONI, F., *Ecclesiastico. Testo ebraico con apparato critico e versioni Graeca, latina e siriaca* (Seminario Semitistica: Naples, 1968).

VERMES, G., 'Bible and Midrash: Early Old Testament Exegesis', in P. R. Ackroyd and C. F. Evans (eds.), *The Cambridge History of the Bible*, vol. 1 (Cambridge University Press: Cambridge, 1970).

——*Scripture and Tradition in Judaism*, 2nd edn. (Brill: Leiden, 1973).

——'The Archangel Sariel', in J. Neusner (ed.), *Christianity, Judaism, and Other Greco-Roman Cults, Part III: Studies for Morton Smith at Sixty*, Studies in Judaism in Late Antiquity, 12 (Brill: Leiden, 1975), 159–76.

——*The Complete Dead Sea Scrolls in English* (Penguin Press: Harmondsworth, 1997).

VON RAD, G., *Genesis: A Commentary*, trans. J. H. Marks (SCM: London, 1970).

WALTON, K. A., *Thou Traveller Unknown: The Presence and the Absence of God in the Jacob Narrative* (Paternoster: London, 2003).

WEISER, A., *The Psalms* (SCM: London, 1979).

WENHAM, G., *Genesis 16–50*, Word Biblical Commentary 2 (Word Books: Dallas, 1994).

WERMAN, C., 'Jubilees 30: Building a Paradigm for the Ban on Intermarriage', *HTR* 90 (1997), 1–22.

WESTERMANN, C., *Genesis 12–36*, trans. J. J. Scullion (SPCK: London, 1986).

WEVERS, J. W., *Notes on the Greek Text of Genesis* (Scholars Press: Atlanta, Ga., 1993).

WILLIAMSON, H. G. M., *Ezra, Nehemiah*, Word Biblical Commentary 16 (Word Books: Waco, 1985).

WINTERMUTE, O. S., 'Jubilees', in J. H. Charlesworth (ed.), *The Old Testament Pseudepigrapha*, vol. 2 (Darton, Longman & Todd: London, 1985), 35–142.

WOLFF, H. W., *A Commentary on the Book of the Prophet Hosea*, Hermeneia, trans. G. Stansell (Fortress Press: Philadelphia, 1974).

WOLFSON, H. A., *Philo: Foundations of Religious Philosophy in Judaism, Christianity, and Islam*, 2 vols. (Harvard University Press: Cambridge, Mass., 1948).

WRIGHT, B. G., *No Small Difference: Sirach's Relationship to its Hebrew Parent Text*, SCS 26 (Scholars Press: Atlanta, 1989).

WRIGHT, N. T., *Jesus and the Victory of God* (SPCK: London, 1996).

WUTZ, F. X., *Onomastica Sacra: Untersuchungen zum Liber Interpretationis Nominum Hebraicorum des hl. Hieronymus* (J. C. Hinrichs: Leipzig, 1914–15).

YADIN, Y., *The Scroll of the War of the Sons of Light Against the Sons of Darkness* (Oxford University Press: Oxford, 1962).

——*The Temple Scroll*, 3 vols. (Israel Exploration Society: Jerusalem, 1977–83).

ZEITLIN, S., 'The Origin of the Term Edom for Rome and the Christian Church', *JQR* 60 (1969), 262–3.

ZOBEL, H.-J., Article 'ישראל, *yiśrā'ēl*', *TDOT*, vi. 399–412.

ZUNZ, L., *Die gottesdienstlichen Vorträge der Juden historisch entwickelt*, 2nd edn. (Frankfurt-am-Main, 1892).

Index

**TARGUM
PSEUDO-JONATHAN**

**APOCRYPHA &
PSEUDEPIGRAPHA**

Maher, M.   274 n.41, 284 n.55, 302
 n.82
Mann, J.   256 n.24
Marböck, J.   95 n.11
Marcus, R.   181
Martin-Achard, R.   23
Marshall, I.H.   322 n.17
Mauser, U.W.   310 n.2
McNamara   130 n.24, 284 n.55
Metzger, B.M.   322 n.16
Middendorp   91
Miguel, P.   188 n.53
Milgrom, J.   140 n.32
Miller, W.T.   38 n.1, 58 n.33, 61 n.37,
 62 n.38, 66 n.48, 350 n.28
Moberly, R.W.L   26 n.11
Moloney, F.J.   315 n.10, 319 n.14
Montgomery, J.A.   141 n.35
Mulder, M.J.   99 n.18, 102 n.23, 103
 n.24
Munk, L.   329 n.28
Munnich, O   38 n.1, 43 n.11
Muñoz Leon, D.   285 n.58
Muraoka, T.   74 n.59

Neusner, J.   248 n.13, 252 n.18
Nickelsburg, G.W.E.   112 n.1–2, 208
 n.22, 297 n.73, 297 n.74, 341 n.14
Nitzan, B.   34 n.36, 100. n.21

O'Connor, M.   301 n.78
Ognibeni, B.   29 n.16
Olofsson, S.   86 n.81

Pérez Fernández, M.   289 n.63
Plummer, A.   323 n.19
Plunkett, M.A.   322 n.15, 322 n.16, 323
 n.19, 325 n.25
Potin, J.   117 n.8, 130 n.24
Pralon, D.   149–50

Rabin, Ch.   119 n.15
von Rad, G.   25 n.8
Rajak, T.   220 n.1
Rast, W. E.   23 n.5
Ravens, D.   312 n.3
Rickenbacker, O.   95 n.11
Rönsch, H   140 n.32
Rowland, C.C.   314 n.7

Salvesen, A.   225 n.11, 350, 350 n.30
Samely, A.   24
Sanders, E.P.   311, 312 n.3
Sanders, J.T.   91
Sandevoir, P.   40 n.3, 70 n.52, 81 n.73,
 179 n.37, 185 n.50, 255 n.23
Schäfer, P.   207 n.21, 242 n.3, 260 n.29,
 262 n.31, 262 n.32, 263 n.33, 266
 n.35, 267 n.36, 269 n.40, 275 n.42,
 276 n.43
Schaper, J.   103
Schiffman, L.H.   146 n.41, 257 n. 27
Schnackenburg, R.   318 n.13
Schürer, E.   38 n.1, 112 n.1, 188 n.53,
 194 n.1, 195 n.2, 220, 221 n.4, 279
 n.48
Schwarz, J.   132 n.28
Segal, M.Z.   30 n.23, 32 n.25, 93, 96
 n.13, 97–8, 107 n.31, 108 n.33, 149
 n.52
van Seters, J.   22 n.3
Shemesh, A.   246 n.10
Simon, M.   325 n.25, 340 n.13, 344
 n.16, 347 n.26
Skehan, P.W.   65 n.45, 94 n.9–10, 96
 n.13, 99, 99 n.17, 105, 106 n.30,
 106–7, 202 n.15, 234 n.17
Smallwood, E.M.   157 n.2
Smelik, W.F.   43 n.11
Smith, J.Z.   194, 195, 199 n.10, 210,
 288 n.62, 341, 298 n.76, 341 n.14
Sperber, A.   283 n.53
Splansky, D.M.   291 n.65
Stein, E.   194
Strack, H.L.   252 n.18, 279 n.47, 279
 n.48
Stemberger, G.   252 n.18, 279 n.47,
 279 n.48
Strugnell, J.   111 n.37
Stuckenbruck, L.   208 n.22, 297
 n.73
Swartz, M.   257 n.27, 258 n.28

Taradach, M.   287 n.60
Tcherikover, V   57 n.31, 92 n.6
Thompson, A.L.   202 n.15
Tigay, J.H.   65 n.46, 84 n.79, 104
 n.28
Tigchelaar, E.J.C.   100 n.21